Contending ideologies in South Africa

THOMAS KARIS

Contending ideologies in South Africa

edited by
James Leatt, Theo Kneifel and Klaus Nürnburger

David Philip   Cape Town & Johannesburg

Wm B Eerdmans   Grand Rapids

First published 1986 in Southern Africa by David Philip, Publisher (Pty) Ltd, 217 Werdmuller Centre, Claremont 7700, South Africa

Published 1986 in the United States of America by Wm. B. Eerdmans Publishing Co., 255 Jefferson Ave. S E, Grand Rapids, Michigan 49503

ISBN 0-86486-038-2 (David Philip, Southern Africa and Australia)
ISBN 0-8028-0182-X (Wm. B. Eerdmans, the rest of the world)

Library of Congress Cataloging-in-Publication Data

Main entry under title:
    Contending ideologies in South Africa.

    Bibliography: p.
    Includes index.
    1. South Africa—Politics and government—1978—
2. Capitalism—South Africa.   3. Socialism—South Africa.
4. Communism—South Africa.   I. Leatt, James.
II. Kneifel, Theo.   III. Nürnberger, Klaus, 1933—
JQ1911.C.67   1986   320.5'0968   86-531
ISBN 0-8028-0182-X

Printed and bound by Creda Press (Pty) Ltd, Solan Road, Cape Town, South Africa

Contents

Acknowledgements

A large number of people have contributed time, energy and expertise in varying measures to this book, all of which we acknowledge with thanks. Firstly, to the South African Council of Churches, which initiated the project and funded the commission, and especially to Wolfram Kistner, Director of its Justice and Reconciliation Division, for his hospitality, encouragement and painstaking work as rapporteur. Secondly, to my co-editors who have given unstintingly of their considerable knowledge to this project. Thirdly, to our publishers, and especially to David Philip and Russell Martin, for their encouragement and faith in the project, and to Caroline Bundy without whose editorial skill this book would have been immeasurably impoverished.

I should like to thank the other core members of the commission for their serious grappling with the issues addressed in this book: C. J. Alant, Norman Bromberger, Willie Cilliers, John Cumpsty, G. de Fleuriot, John de Gruchy, Raphael de Kadt, Jimmy Palos, Tom Manthata, Buti Tlhagale and Abraham Viljoen; as well as D. Mateman, J. Sebidi, J. Wolfaart and A. Pop.

Johan Degenaar, Hermann Giliomee, Charles Simkins, Charles Villa-Vicencio, and André du Toit made invaluable critical contributions to the commission and to the editors at various stages. Glenda Kruss provided research support for Part Two, as did Ian Sakinofsky and Colin Bundy for the bibliography. Caroline Bundy has done a skilful job on the index. Shaan Ellinghouse and Debbie Stubbs typed and retyped versions of the chapters with characteristic patience and accuracy.

Indebted as we are to all these people, the editors accept responsibility for the final shape the book has taken.

Preface

The late 1970s and early 1980s were turbulent times in South Africa. Violence in black urban areas, the banning of black consciousness organisations, deaths in detention, growing black labour militancy, and mass removals of blacks, all contributed to this state of unrest. American and European governments exerted moral and economic pressures on South Africa, and overseas multinationals adopted codes of employment practice for their South African subsidiaries. The South African government sought to respond to the crises by introducing changes in its labour, economic, and constitutional policies, in its foreign relations with the frontline states and its allies in the West.

Events on South Africa's borders were no less dramatic. After a protracted struggle, Angola and Mozambique gained their independence from Portugal, and South Africans saw the advent of Afro-Marxist states on their borders. The bushwar in Rhodesia finally ended with Robert Mugabe winning a landslide victory at the polls and with the birth of Zimbabwe as a socialist state. For some South Africans these newly independent states were an apocalyptic sign of an impending communist victory in the region. For others they were a sign of hope for political liberation and economic equity in South Africa.

This troubled environment heightened the ideological conflict in South Africa, and formed the immediate context for this book. Inspired by a similar venture of the Lutheran World Federation on an international scale, the National Conference of the South African Council of Churches commissioned a study of conflicting ideologies in South Africa and the possible theological responses. A national study commission was set up. It was to report its findings in a way which would inform church leaders and concerned lay people. A diverse group of people from different denominations, language groups, and races were invited to serve in an honorary capacity on the commission. The commission met quite frequently, usually for two or three days at a time, over an extended period.

Approaching the task

The commission faced three immediate problems when it met. Given the diverse backgrounds of the members of the group, considerable time had to be spent on establishing lines of communication with each other, seeking to understand the context of each member and clarifying concepts and goals.

Secondly, it had to agree on an approach to ideologies. After discussion we finally concluded that it would not be possible to agree on a single normative theoretical or even ideological framework with which to identify and describe conflicting ideologies in South Africa. And even if we had arrived at a consensus of opinion, we could not be sure that our projected audience would necessarily accept it.

There are fundamentally different, even contradictory, ways of approaching ideology. Confusion abounds, not only concerning the contents of the differing and antagonistic ideologies themselves, but also concerning the concept of ideology itself. One of the ironies of our times is that the term 'ideology' has itself become ideologised. Three basic perceptions of ideology can be distinguished, a critical, a positive, and a neutral one. From a critical perspective, ideology is bias, oversimplification, emotionalism — an expression of prejudice by a section of the public. More precisely, it is the legitimation of particular group interests. The positive perspective sees ideology as a socio-political charter, a vehicle for propaganda, designed to win converts to a particular political programme. The neutral stance strives for a non-evaluative approach to ideology, claiming that all systems of thought are ideological by definition. This in turn raises the question of where ideology stops and social scientific inquiry begins.

The confusion surrounding the term is compounded in our deeply divided society. Each party claims to have the truth: 'I have a social philosophy; you have political opinions; he has an ideology.' Many would argue that it is futile to use the term 'ideology' at all in such a situation. Some would say, therefore, that analysis of South African society must move 'beyond ideology' to encompass more illuminating social-scientific categories such as economy, class, race, power-sharing, or democracy. But even the detractors of ideology would agree that these terms take on quite divergent meanings when used by an African socialist, an Afrikaner nationalist, or an English liberal.

The commission took the view, therefore, that people live by what the social philosopher Georges Sorel has called 'social myths', sets of ideas which infuse meaning into the lives of people, lift them above their captivity in the ordinary, inspire powerful visions of the future, and infuse them with the capacity to realise their visions. In the eyes of some, for example, 'African socialism' is impractical; others may regard 'free enterprise' as utopian. But whether they are irrational and impractical or not, people live by these myths. Ideologies are as much a part of social reality in South Africa as Soweto or the Drakensberg. Why some prefer to live by a capitalist, others by a socialist, some by a nationalist, and others by a liberal myth, is quite another question. It can only be answered with reference to their position in the social system and the traditions into which they have been socialised.

A specific ideology has, as Peter Berger has shown, its own 'clue concepts', key explanatory categories which are used with a specific meaning within the ideology in question, and conjure up a set of specific responses that are functional to that ideology. Within a western capitalist framework, for example, terms like free enterprise, modernisation, economic growth and productivity, are clue concepts. Socialist thought, again, employs such clue concepts as alienation, exploitation, dependency, neo-colonialism, and liberation.

For this reason we adopted what may be called a 'soft phenomenological' approach. It seemed to make sense to describe ideologies in their *own terms*, as a first step to grasping their irresistible appeal for some, and the heated opposition they evoke in others. This implied that we had to bracket, so to speak, our own judgments on specific ideologies and to deal with them descriptively — recognising that the very act of describing something already intrudes on what is being described. Complete objectivity is impossible.

Another difficulty with the descriptive approach is that it tends to erase the nuances and divergencies within a movement such as black consciousness or Afrikaner nationalism. Furthermore, to describe an ideology in its own terms can easily create the impression of a propaganda exercise for the ideology in question. We decided, therefore, to introduce a critical perspective into our discussion by outlining, wherever possible, the way a particular ideology, such as black consciousness, is perceived from other ideological perspectives, such as liberalism or Afrikaner nationalism. In other words, what we present is the beginning of a dialogue or confrontation between such ideologies, in which they begin to relativise each other.

The third difficulty the commission faced was how to approach the task of arriving at a theological critique of ideology as a concept, and how to apply the critique to the specific ideologies in question. There is no single Roman Catholic or Protestant approach to ideology, let alone to capitalism, African socialism, or Afrikaner nationalism. Some would even argue that christian theology itself, because it reflects thought and action in a particular socio-cultural context, is by definition ideological.

Differences of theological opinion became painfully apparent within the commission and accompanied it throughout its work. [Eventually we decided that the only practical way to deal with this issue within the space and time at our disposal was to present the reader with two contrasting theological perspectives in our final chapter] Since the majority of people in South Africa profess allegiance to the christian faith in one form or another, these two perspectives may serve as models for helping them to deal with their relationship between faith and ideology.

The procedure of the commission

The commission spent a lot of time gathering material on the various ideologies. Knowledgeable persons were frequently called in to give information or undertake specific tasks. The initial drafts were written by individuals or small groups, circulated to all members, read and discussed intensively in plenary, and then redrafted. All deliberations were carefully minuted and taken into consideration. In most cases the documents were redrafted two or three times, often by more than one person. The basic material is, therefore, the outcome of a team effort by many people of divergent backgrounds developed over a couple of years. In the last stages of preparation, however, the editors were allowed a great deal of latitude, and are responsible for the final shape and content of the book.

The unique contribution of this book

As editors we are enthusiastic about this book. Not because we think the final word has been said on the subject! On the contrary, it is meant to be open-ended, incomplete, and open to challenge. If an individual scholar had written such a book it would, without doubt, have been more consistent and coherent. But it may have been the poorer. What we have lost in internal consistency and academic rigour is compensated for, in our view, by the feeling that, [if so diverse a group of South Africans as ourselves could find each other in the process of grappling with so controversial a topic as ideology, there is hope that others who read the book may come to understand the partial perspectives which drive South Africans to contend for a place in the sun in our deeply divided and unequal society.]

Ideologies cannot be grasped by detached theorising. For one thing, they are embodied in the structures and struggles of society. For another, their real power emerges when people meet and challenge each other's convictions. This book is both the outcome of and a call to 'confrontational study'. Dare we hope that its use will lead to a more just order in South Africa? #

Part one
CAPITALISM AND SOUTH AFRICA

Whereas much of the debate in South Africa has focused on race and race relations, we take the view that the way the capitalist economy has developed historically has fundamentally influenced race relations and political developments, and has materially affected the interests of various groups in South Africa. Part One, therefore, concentrates on capitalism and capitalist development in the West in an attempt to clarify concepts and describe the various stages through which it has gone, before introducing some of the standard critiques which it has evoked. Thereafter, the growth of the capitalist economy in South Africa is described, due attention being paid to historical and contemporary issues. Finally, we attempt an overview of critiques of South African capitalist development, ranging from free-market to radical Marxist perspectives.

Those familiar with the literature on South Africa's capitalist development will know the analysis has been controversial, and is still in its formative stages. Our contribution will no doubt also evoke controversy. It is meant to place our description of contending ideologies in South Africa in context, but we acknowledge its tentative nature.

1 Capitalism: an introductory history and assessment

Origin and stages of capitalism

As an ideology capitalism upholds private ownership of the means of production, the necessity of material incentives for maximum output, free enterprise, free competition on the basis of the market mechanism (the balance between supply and demand), the sovereignty of the consumer, and a minimum of state intervention.

Capitalism appeared fairly late on the stage of economic history. A brief historical survey of economic systems would have to begin with *subsistence economy*. In this system each family produces what it consumes by gathering, hunting, rearing livestock and tilling the ground. There is no specialisation, division of labour, building up of stocks, or trade on any appreciable scale. Almost complete economic equality obtains, but on a very low level.

Nearly all the great ancient civilisations developed on the basis of a change from subsistence agriculture to an economy based on *slavery*. Slaves are people who are owned and utilised like animals to provide labour. While slavery was cruel, for a long time it was thought to be unavoidable if higher levels of civilisation were to be achieved.

The third stage we need to consider is *feudalism*. In this system, society is divided into the aristocracy — mainly landlords, who own large tracts of lands — and the common people, mainly peasants and, later, craftsmen. The peasants work the land of the landlords, from whom they receive protection and justice, and in return owe allegiance and a share of their produce. Each person has an inherited position in society, with certain rights and obligations.

Pre-industrial or merchant capitalism emerged towards the end of the Middle Ages, with the growth of the wool industry, particularly in England. Those who produced more than they consumed invested the surpluses in the development of trade routes, ships, warehouses and, later, machines and factories. New continents were discovered and their riches exploited. Trade began to expand considerably. The inflow of precious metals, especially from the mines in Mexico, Peru and Bolivia, caused a

severe price inflation lasting for many decades. Landlords suffered because their rents did not keep pace with living-costs; labourers suffered
because wages also fell behind rapidly. Those who did gain considerably
were the merchants and manufacturers, who sensibly invested their
profits. Gradually they developed into an economically powerful and
politically influential 'middle class'.

Political rulers came to realise that their own strength depended on
the prosperity of the capitalists, and they sought to create conditions
favourable to economic development. Internal duties were abolished to
allow domestic free trade; tariffs imposed to protect local manufacturers
and merchants from foreign competition (a system called *mercantilism*);
harbours and means of transport were provided; internal stability and
external security developed. In the process capital rapidly accumulated
in the hands of the middle class. The latter invested their gains, and thus
the wealth created by the employment of wage labourers was not consumed but transformed into greater productive capacity. The economy
as a whole grew steadily.

In the eighteenth century a series of important inventions opened the
way to more efficient modes of production. Because the necessary capital had accumulated, these inventions could be introduced on a large
scale. This led to the industrial revolution, occurring first in England,
later in other European countries. The shift in emphasis from trade to
industry marks the beginning of *early industrial capitalism*. The manufacturing process moved from rural households to urban factories. Craftsmen could not compete with the output of machines and were reduced
to becoming wage labourers. They were joined by impoverished peasants.
Great masses of people moved into the cities, where they lived in slum
conditions and worked long hours for pitiful wages. There was a tremen-
dous population explosion, which added to the general misery. The factories and commercial undertakings were in the hands of a small capitalist class, the bourgeoisie, whose economic power and political influence
rose steadily.

The French Revolution and the Napoleonic Wars swept away the last
remnants of the feudal system and crushed the power of the aristocracy.
The capitalists acquired as a result a free hand to develop their full potential. Liberal economists pleaded for the dismantling of state intervention in economic affairs and for the free play of the market mechanism, enabling the balance between supply and demand to find its own
level. Economic development made national states more powerful, and
they looked after their interests on the international scene: trade routes
were protected, colonies established, and world-wide empires were at
length built up. Colonies were exploited in varying degrees to the ad-

vantage of the colonising nations. As well as being commercially advantageous, the colonies provided outlets for the surplus populations from the home country.

The accumulation of resources, the demands of the new methods of production, and the concomitant optimistic and progressive world-view, led to a strong upsurge in the fields of science and technology. It seemed to many as if human progress was boundless, and the working people wanted a share in the fruits of that progress. The ideas of equality and democracy, and the necessity for social services gained ground. The Marxist critique of capitalism was elaborated theoretically, and captured the imagination of many people. Emigration, social unrest, the formation of powerful trade unions which could negotiate with employers from a position of strength, and a series of revolutions, were socially transforming and ameliorating factors for the underprivileged in Europe. The combination of a capitalist system with a strong strain of socialist principles and practices produced what we term the western democratic order.

Twentieth century capitalism emerged as a result of profound structural changes. Two world wars weakened the leading European countries: their empires declined and finally collapsed. The colonial peoples gained their independence and acquired more political power. Two giant countries, Russia and China, have undergone communist revolutions, absorbed a number of smaller countries into their orbit and progressively challenged the western sphere of influence in the Third World. The great depression of the 1930s rocked the whole capitalist system to its very foundations. World War Two broke the leadership of western Europe. The USA emerged as the unchallenged economic and military superpower of the West, Europe and Japan becoming the largest of its many satellites. With the rapid advance of the USSR as the second superpower, the world was divided into the economic interest spheres of two giant power blocs, each with its own affiliates. More recently, the potential of China as another superpower has become apparent.

Many Third World countries opted for some form of socialism. Moderate socialism was introduced in a number of European countries. In others, social institutions such as trade unions, free education, medical schemes, unemployment and old-age insurance, developed more fully. The state entered the sphere of economic activity and became the largest national investor of capital, in competition with private enterprise. The state also developed a cumbersome bureaucratic machinery to supervise and regulate economic life.

In the private sector there were fundamental changes as well. Smaller firms amalgamated to form huge multinational corporations, which have extended their control of productive capacity far beyond the capitalist world. Although Third World countries are politically independent, their economies are to a large extent manipulated in the metropolitan centres of the world. The idea that a large number of entrepreneurs should compete with each other in a free market is a thing of the past. Modern mechanised production and distribution methods call for huge organis-ations. Small firms cannot compete. So the market is dominated by mon-opolies (with a single entity in control) or by oligopolies (with a few in control). Consumption is largely determined by shrewd salesmanship and aggressive advertising. Capital ownership is spread to thousands of shareholders, who have little say in the running of the firm. A self-perpetuating hierarchy of paid managers wields all decision-making power. Investment is no longer a matter of private savings; the big firms regularly withhold part of the profits for planned investment. Scientific research and technological innovation are no longer left to the ingenuity of individuals but have become institutionalised by the state and by large corporations.

What started on the basis of the daring initiative of gifted individuals has become a self-perpetuating, institutionalised process of considerable power. In this and other respects, present-day capitalism bears little re-semblance to early capitalism. There are indications that the most ad-vanced industrial countries are now moving into what can be called *late or mature capitalism*. This is characterised by automation, electronic control, nuclear power and the concentration of economic and pro-ductive capacity in a few global centres, which are beyond competition from peripheral areas. We are witnessing an accelerating exploitation of the earth's limited resources and the pollution of the environment; the development, stockpiling, and proliferation of exceedingly destructive weapons; and an increasing gap between the poor countries, undergoing a population explosion, and the rich countries, undergoing an industrial explosion. Some experts predict a global catastrophe within half a cen-tury if these trends continue unabated. Others believe that the system is flexible enough to meet the new demands.

The convictions of liberal capitalism

The basic world-view

The emergence of capitalism has to be understood within the context of the cultural development of western Europe from the eighteenth to the twentieth century. Through the Renaissance the delights of Greek and Roman culture, centred in the potential of man, were rediscovered, and Humanism assumed this heritage. Responsibility and freedom of the individual over the authority of church and state was emphasised by the Reformation. Its Calvinistic wing produced the ethic of hard work and frugality, and its doctrine of predestination seemed to imply that secular success was a sign of grace. A powerful world-view arose from the blend of Renaissance thought, the acceptance of responsibility for one's own destiny, and progress through human achievement.

During the Enlightenment a highly critical spirit developed among thinkers in Europe. The authority of inherited doctrines, traditions and institutions (the 'dead hand of the past') was rejected. Everything supernatural — revelations, superstitions, miracles — came under radical questioning. Nature became the sole criterion of reality as well as the only ethical guideline. Two schools of thought combined in a number of variations. The first maintained that we find a mirror of reality in our reason. To understand we simply have to make use of our capacity to think (*rationalism*). The other school trusted only what could be demonstrated by means of the human senses (*empiricism*). The merger of these approaches produced modern science and its handmaiden, technology.

The idea of individual freedom developed concurrently. Equality of dignity, responsibility and opportunity became powerful watchwords. Each individual, it came to be believed, has the right and the obligation to develop his own potential. The collective, the state, the church or other institutions, should not interfere. The state should be responsible only for order and security. Work dedicated to the glory of God was replaced by the free pursuit of self-interest. Man, it was believed, is essentially good and could develop to perfection, if released from the fetters of traditions, regulations, and institutions. If each person tried to achieve the best for himself, society as a whole would benefit too. Self-realisation and the pursuit of self-interest became not a vice but a virtue. The desire of man for individual happiness was taken to be natural and worthy of fostering. The whole realm of nature was at the disposal of man to attain his goals. For this, man needed education. Education did not mean bland acceptance of pre-formulated doctrines but developing powers of reason and observation.

Man became more convinced that nature is engaged in a process of development towards higher forms, and that man is perfectible through his own achievement. This belief resulted in an enormous zeal for scientific and technological advance, a drive to eradicate human suffering and humiliation, an urge to go 'forward and upward', to produce 'bigger and better', and also to bring the 'light of civilisation' into the 'dark corners' of the universe.

In combination these convictions carried enormous consequences.

The rapid accumulation of wealth and economic power in the hands of capitalists was but one. What also came about was a series of revolutions to establish representative democracy, the incredible achievements of science and technology, the industrial revolution and the emergence of modern urban civilisation, the colonisation of almost the entire world by the European countries, and the decline of religion and its substitution by material fortune as a prime value (*materialism*). Man was taken to be the master of his own destiny and of reality as a whole.

These developments perfectly matched the interests of the new commercial and industrial middle class. Their pursuit of private profit, their risk-taking initiative, their shrewdness in a situation of fierce competition, their spirit of achievement and progress, and the growth of their economic power as a class, were sanctioned by the new philosophy and ethic, and developed freely without interference from state or church. Economic liberalism as a doctrine (*laissez-faire*) and the so-called free-enterprise system derived from these developments.

Laissez-faire was given its classical formulation in Adam Smith's famous work, *The Wealth of Nations* (1776), and was further developed by J. S. Mill, Bentham, Cobden, Bright and others. Smith attacked the mercantilist system of his time because of the way the state acquired power through regulating the economy in its own favour by protections, monopolies and restrictions, especially those concerning foreign trade. The state, argued Smith, should maintain order in society but keep its hands off the economy. Every person naturally avoids pain and seeks pleasure and is the best judge of his own happiness. He will make use of his gifts and resources to his best possible advantage. If everybody does likewise, society as a whole will reap the benefit.

Fundamental assumptions

The free-enterprise system is based on the principle of *laissez-faire*. Let us summarise some of its fundamental assumptions. The first is the private ownership of the means of production. Each individual has the right and the obligation to look after himself, take his own economic decisions for better or for worse, work hard, and make use of all his resources to his best advantage. All resources, whether in the form of land, labour, or capital, are to be privately owned and controlled. The reward a person receives will be roughly proportionate to the productivity of his resources, that is, to the skill with which he can make the most out of what he has at his disposal.

The second fundamental assumption is the sovereignty of the consumer. People use their income to satisfy their needs and desires. Thus producers will only supply goods and services for which there is a demand on the free market. The more successful a producer is in finding gaps in the market and satisfying consumers, the more money he will make. The quantity and quality of the product, therefore, are determined by the needs and wishes of those who want to make use of it.

The third assumption is that of free competition. Producers have to compete with each other in a free market. A producer who is able to offer more in terms of quantity and quality for less money than his counterpart will have an advantage. Fierce competition leads to maximum effort to outwit and outdo all others. In the process people will think imaginatively and work efficiently, developing better techniques and products. If not, they will simply drop out. The same principle applies in the labour market. Higher qualifications and more efficient work are rewarded with higher salaries, because they lead to higher productivity.

The fourth assumption deals with the mechanism of the free play of the market. This means that in a situation of free competition the price of anything and everything is determined by the relative strength of supply and demand. If more potatoes are produced than consumers are prepared to buy for a given price, they have to be offered for less. Soon farmers will switch to other crops for which there is a better market, or else face bankruptcy. But if consumers want more potatoes than producers have at hand, the price will go up and the increase will induce farmers to plant more. The same is true for various skills on the labour market. If there are more architects than can be employed in the current building programme of a nation, some will find themselves out of work and will switch to other occupations. High qualifications are well paid because they are generally scarce, while unskilled labour is 'cheap labour' because there is an over-supply. The market mechanism encourages people to better their qualifications and fill the gaps in the higher ranks, thus easing the situation at lower levels.

In every sphere the market mechanism is believed to ensure that the right quantities and qualities are supplied at the right price and that everybody is rewarded according to the relative contribution he is able to make towards satisfying the needs of society. Of course all this presupposes that the state does not interfere, and that amongst producers, consumers or distributors, amongst employers, workers or landowners, nobody has the power to dictate the price or the volume of goods and services of a particular kind, through holding a monopoly. The state should ensure free competition.

The achievements of capitalism

It is clear that at present most of the assumptions enumerated above no longer exist in a totally pure form in modern capitalist societies. But the basic convictions are still upheld in western society. Beyond doubt they have helped to achieve a rapid development of science and technology, extremely efficient methods of production and distribution, forms of organisation, management techniques and allocation of resources, and the large-scale accumulation of productive capital. They have also provided a great motivation to do one's very best, to improve one's capabilities, to make use of one's potential and time, to take rational decisions, to be goal-orientated, to eliminate corruption and favouritism (at least where it is economically harmful), and so on. The incredible growth in technological capability and productive capacity which is found in modern industrialised countries and is without parallel in world history, can be at least partly ascribed to these beliefs, values and norms, as embodied in legislation and social organisation. Even socialist countries need to adopt some of these values in the interests of progress and to achieve higher standards of living.

The economic advantage of the free-enterprise system to some people is evident. What, however, are the human advantages? The most common response to that question is to emphasise the importance of the freedom of the individual. Related to personal freedom is the satisfaction to be obtained from achieving goals for oneself. These achievements can also affect future generations and lead to an ongoing sense of creativity and discovery.

Capitalists argue that greed or self-aggrandisement is preferable as a motive to fear or group coercion, that a degree of material inequality is better than forced equality. Great store is set on the need to be self-reliant, to compete in the task of overcoming the challenges of nature and society, and to provide for one's own future security. Achievement is measured not so much in material terms as by the opinion of one's peers. To be accepted for what one has achieved is better than to be accepted in spite of what one is. Out of this sense of individuality and struggle comes a strong self-image in relation to that which confronts one, and a desire to transcend it.

In corporate achievement lies the additional sense of being part of a team of individuals come together for a purpose in competition with others.

Critique of capitalism

Capitalism has led to enormous achievements. Karl Marx, the radical critic of capitalism, was among the first to point this out. But capitalism is beset with inherent problems and undesirable side-effects, which cannot be overlooked, even by its most ardent supporters.

The myth of economic freedom. Is capitalism as free as it claims to be? Production and distribution are today largely controlled by giant corporations under the management not of capital-owners (shareholders) but of paid executives. Moreover, the capitalist economy is not run so much by private entrepreneurs with personal initiative, who work hard, take risks, and compete with each other on a free market, as by a number of collectives with oligopolistic power. Instead of *laissez-faire* there is strong state intervention and state participation in the economy. The slogans of economic liberalism seem to function as an ideological mask concealing the stark realities of inequality and power concentration.

Capitalism must grow or collapse. In the capitalist system more is produced than is consumed. The surplus is invested in additional productive capacity, which produces even more goods. Obviously this is possible only if the whole system keeps growing.

New needs and desires must be created artificially to induce the public to consume the additional products that are marketed.

Products are made in such a way that they do not last too long. In this 'planned obsolescence' new models and fashions replace obsolete ones in a rapid sequence.

Industrialised countries are forced to turn to the Third World to find raw materials, markets for their surpluses, and investment possibilities for their surplus capital. Inevitably they start to control the economy of such countries in their own interest. Lenin maintained that this process is the root of imperialism. Today Third World countries are politically independent but they are, to a large extent, economically dependent on the developed industrial nations (*neo-colonialism*).

A vast proportion of the surplus productive capacity is channelled into arms production. The arms race is believed by some critics to be an economic necessity of the system.

Despite what has already been said, overproduction cannot be avoided. Profits dwindle, firms cut down on their investments, industrial plants become idle, workers are retrenched, and economic recession occurs. Investors become active only when profit-making is once again in sight, that is, when demand outstrips production. The result is that the economy constantly oscillates between boom and recession (the 'business cycle'), which causes much disruption and hardship.

Wastage. It is wasteful if desires are created artificially and products are forced on unwitting consumers. It is wasteful if products are purposely made in such a way that they end up in the rubbish-bin as soon as possible. It is wasteful if manufacturing capacities run idle and healthy workers are unemployed during a recession.

Consumer demand is irrational. In the capitalist system everything depends upon consumer demand. But this is subject to irrational factors such as fashions, moods, social tensions and weather conditions. Some argue that, in an age where man is able to control his destiny through science and technology, it does not make sense to leave the economy to be manipulated by chance factors.

Public needs are neglected. Because private satisfactions have priority over public needs there are too many luxury items and too few public services. The state is seen as an unwelcome intruder, which extorts moneys for public purposes through taxation. To retain its popularity in a democratic system the state is inclined to limit its expenditure to the minimum and favour those who can push their case hardest.

The rich determine production. In capitalist countries a small elite commands the greatest buying-power. This means that luxury and prestige items are produced out of proportion to the actual needs of the majority. Since the rich are the reference group for the poor, they set standards which the poor try to attain. The latter buy cars and TV sets which they cannot afford. Their expectations are always higher than their income, even if income levels rise. This dissatisfaction can only be contained through constant increments in salaries. The standard of living in industrialised countries is constantly pushed up and has already reached unrealistic levels, threatening the ecological balance of the planet itself.

The income gap is growing. While the poor have nothing but their labour to sell, capital, power, education, prestige, privilege, self-esteem and initiative accumulate in the hands of the rich. There are vicious circles of poverty and golden spirals of plenty. These are inherent in the working of the capitalist system. They cause envy, hatred, social tensions and political instability. In modern times workers have organised themselves into trade unions and political parties, which are able to negotiate from a position of strength. Higher wages and social securities (medical aid, pension schemes, free education, unemployment insurance) have been secured as a result. But these are socialist, not capitalist, inventions. Of course, capitalism is an open system which allows such adjustment to take shape.

The powerless are the victims. Groups who are not organised are often the victims of the power struggles of organised groups. In South Africa they are those sections of the black workforce which are not able to organise effectively; on the international scene they are the peoples of the Third World, who sell their raw materials to the industrialised countries cheaply while having to import expensive industrial products.

There is too much power in the hands of a few. Capitalism has led to enormous concentrations of economic power in the hands of a small elite. By 1980 about 300 large multinational corporations controlled three-quarters of the world's manufacturing assets. If these firms should decide to slacken their investments, millions of people would lose their jobs. Such interest groups form power blocs, which may threaten rather than serve society. Economic strength is political power; governments cannot afford to overlook those who wield economic power. Indeed, it is alleged that political crises are sometimes artificially created to stimulate the economy through increased arms production. Industrialised countries often interfere directly or indirectly in the internal affairs of Third World countries to protect or enhance their economic interests.

Capitalism has brought about the centre–periphery structure of the world economy. The world is today divided up between metropolitan centres, where the industrial economy grows rapidly and the population remains fairly constant, and poverty-stricken periphery regions, where the population grows rapidly while the economy is stagnant. Both processes may lead mankind as a whole into catastrophe within a century because industrial growth depletes scarce resources and pollutes the environment, and food production cannot keep pace with population growth much longer.

The achievement norm is socially harmful. Capitalism offers strong incentives for people to utilise fully their energy and potential. This is its greatest advantage but the obverse holds true too. The gifted and privileged are rewarded in addition to their gifts, the handicapped are punished in addition to their handicaps. Both suffer from social and economic insecurity. The successful have anxiety symptoms. The unsuccessful develop inferiority feelings, grudges, lethargy and fatalism. Social securities foster the attitude that society owes recipients a living, that they do not have to pull their weight. Where there are no social securities, anxiety and fear of losing income and status dictate people's actions.

Mass unemployment is unavoidable. Unemployment insurance can alleviate physical hardships for families affected by unemployment, but it cannot eradicate detrimental psychological and social effects.

A capitalist response to the critique

Those who are convinced of the merits of capitalism will counter this critique with arguments such as the following:

While freedom in capitalist countries is not perfect, it surpasses that of any other system. The same is true for competition. Egalitarian systems tend to curtail individual freedom, thus fettering originality and creativity. They hinder the development of the full potential of the talented and the hardworking. An egalitarian system taxes the diligent and efficient, while it subsidises the lazy and inefficient. Ultimately it is society that suffers.

While it is true that the rhythm of boom and recession is painful, the long-term trend is upward. No system has proved itself to have the potential for overcoming poverty and creating large-scale prosperity for such great numbers of people as the capitalist system found in many countries today.

Inefficient bureaucracy and faulty allocation of resources in a planned economy make socialism more wasteful than capitalism.

In socialism, particularly the Marxist–Leninist variety, the concentration of power in the hands of a few is far greater than in capitalist countries. The question is not who owns the capital but who is in effective control. In the West, capitalists compete with each other, and their powers are further limited by trade unions, consumer organisations and anti-monopolistic legislation. Economic power is not in the same hands as political power. Politicians are subject to democratic procedures, and the poor have a chance of influencing economic policy to their advantage. There is also an independent judiciary. In Marxist–Leninist countries, all power — economic, political, social, military, ideological — is concentrated in a small party elite and can be manipulated at will.

Soviet imperialism is no less pernicious and no more altruistic than capitalist imperialism. The tangible economic advantages of the latter outweigh the advantages offered by Soviet imperialism.

Much of the critique levelled against capitalism is, in fact, a critique of technological advance and industrialisation, which socialist countries cannot avoid if they want to attain high standards of living.

2 The growth of a capitalist economy in South Africa

Economic and political ideologies form the main concern of this book. But ideologies never operate in a vacuum. They reflect or conceal, legitimate or challenge, existing social structures. The purpose of this chapter is to offer a rough outline of the historical evolution of the South African economy. Such a survey is of necessity sketchy, tentative and controversial. Nevertheless, it should suffice to give a first impression of the transformations that have taken place in the subcontinent in recent history, forming the background of ongoing changes taking place at present.

During the last decade the theory has been postulated that the capitalist system is the root cause of pervasive forms of discrimination and oppression in South African social life. Since there is likely to be a good deal of future debate about the most desirable economic system for this country, it is worth making the assertion that the economic growth of modern South Africa has taken place within a capitalist framework. To do so is to complicate the task ahead, because it requires a judgment about whether certain features of the South African economy result from characteristically capitalist interests being pursued in a particular setting, or whether they represent impositions on and restrictions of normal capitalist institutions and behaviour. To put it rather more bluntly — if one is to discuss capitalist growth in South Africa, one is forced to make judgments about the links between capitalism and 'racialism' (to use a rather imprecise shorthand), and there are aspects of this relationship that are not easy to unravel.

If we use the attributes of a capitalist society that were established in the previous chapter, we can assume that the South African economy is largely a capitalist one. The qualification follows from the fact that there are areas in the country (the reserves, homelands, black states) in which natural resources, particularly land, are not in full private ownership and cannot be freely bought and sold. Within these areas, too, domestic labour may be as important as wage labour. And the existence of these areas is closely related to important features of the South African economy — migratory labour, controls of geographical mobility, regional inequality, and so on. Moreover, there is a great deal of state intervention in the economy, and it can be argued that restrictions based on race are incompatible with the liberal presuppositions of the capitalist system, and detrimental to its objectives. Still, there does not seem to be a problem about calling the overall economy capitalist. Many critics maintain that racial fragmentation can be compared with a structure of class domination typical of the early stages of capitalist development.

In important ways modern South Africa is a very different society from what it was 150 years ago. It is far from easy to summarise in a short chapter the highlights of change during this period. Different ideological standpoints carry with them different historical perspectives. Much new work is being done on the social and economic history of South Africa at present, and it is not easy to absorb or assess it all. At the same time there are huge uninvestigated areas in South African social and economic history, which render an account of social transformations rather speculative in places. Nevertheless, we can go some way towards providing a framework for understanding the development of modern South Africa.

Political framework

In most of our discussion we shall concentrate on socio-economic changes, but it is worth remembering that there is another set of issues which has had great importance in South African history. Briefly, these events may be classified as political: they relate to the drawing of state boundaries, the relations between conquerors and conquered, the distribution of power within states, and the implementation of racial policies.

Especially during the nineteenth century, 'change' largely involved wars and conquests, the annexation of territory and the partial dispossession of indigenous peoples, the large-scale movement of peoples both within the subcontinent and from abroad as immigrants, the destruction and creation of states and the eventual forging of a single major state in the area under white control. Some 150 years ago, say in 1828, there was no entity known as the Republic of South Africa, nor the Union of South Africa, nor was it conceived of as 'South Africa'.

At the beginning of the nineteenth century much of the subcontinent was settled by fairly small-scale societies of Bantu-speaking Africans. It is customary to divide them in terms of language and culture into the Sotho–Tswana grouping of chiefdoms (on the highveld, stretching westwards to the Kalahari), the Nguni peoples (down the east coast and its hinterland), the Venda (in the northern Transvaal), and the Tsonga (along the coast from northern Zululand into Mozambique). In the early years of the century there erupted a series of interconnected wars and conflicts which resulted in massive population dispersals (known as the *difaqane* by the Sotho and as the *mfecane* by the Nguni). This period of troubles profoundly affected the pattern of settlement in African areas and resulted, among other things, in the emergence of several larger-scale political groupings (or states). The most famous of these was the Zulu kingdom, which established hegemony over most of present-day Natal. Moshoeshoe consolidated his kingdom composed both of Sotho speakers and of many other disparate refugee elements, and the Swazi kingdom also emerged in this period. Offshoots of the northern Nguni established the Shangaan state over the Tsonga, the Ndebele (or Matabele) state first in the Transvaal and then in what is today Zimbabwe, and Nguni areas of dominance as far north as present-day Zambia, Malawi and Tanzania.

Meanwhile major political developments were taking place which led to the establishment of white-controlled states in parts of southern Africa. Some 4 000 English-speaking settlers arrived in the eastern Cape, while Dutch-speaking migrants from the Cape penetrated into both the highveld and Natal areas in the aftermath of the *mfecane* and founded the South African Republic in the Transvaal and the Republics of the Orange Free State and Natalia (or the Colony of Natal as it became after British annexation). Relations between these Boer states and British power (centred on the Cape) were problematic, and it was only by the 1860s that their independence was guaranteed — though this did not prevent the temporary annexation of the South African Republic by Britain in the late 1870s.

By the 1860s and 1870s southern Africa was composed of a number of relatively consolidated African kingdoms (with a number of smaller chiefdoms), and the white-controlled republics and colonies. In the latter part of the nineteenth century the African states lost their independence and were incorporated in one way or another into the white polities. Most of the southern Nguni (those living in the areas now known as Ciskei and Transkei) were absorbed into the Cape; the greater part of the Zulu kingdom was annexed to Natal; Basutoland, Bechuanaland, and Swaziland became protectorates under the British Empire; the Pedi, the Venda, and some of the Tswana areas fell under the jurisdiction of the South African Republic. In this process African societies suffered a substantial loss of land, to which they formerly had access, though the process of political incorporation did not leave them entirely dispossessed.

After a bloody and destructive war in 1899–1902, the two Boer republics likewise lost their independence to Britain and were annexed as colonies. By the end of the decade the four colonies had been politically merged and in 1910, by an Act of the British Parliament, the Union of South Africa was created.

The growth and development of a capitalist economy

From the 1820s new forms of trade and production began to transform social and economic life throughout the subcontinent. These economic activities represented the impact on South Africa of the growing international capitalist system. During the nineteenth century South Africa became firmly linked to this system through the production and export of wool, diamonds, and gold. The impact of international capitalism was not, however, uniform over time or space: some parts of the area were affected more than others (especially the mining centres of Kimberley and Johannesburg). The degree and pace of change intensified considerably after the 1870s, as the mineral discoveries ushered in a new era. These changes, however, did not take place independently of the political forces and events we have already considered, nor can political events in turn be understood without reference to these fundamental economic changes. Thus, the Anglo–Boer War can be seen not only to have paved the way for the creation of the Union of South Africa but also to have forged a single market with co-ordinated transport arrangements, in which internal tariff barriers were abolished — thereby facilitating the growth of a vigorous capitalist economy. At the same time it is not possible to account for the Anglo–Boer War without some reference to the development of capitalist gold-mining on the Reef. In fact, it was the discovery of diamonds and gold that thrust British control, which was originally concerned with the protection of the Cape sea-route, into the interior.

When the rule of the Dutch East India Company ended at the Cape in the late eighteenth century, the local economy maintained very weak links with the world system. Such links as existed (and of course they had been the original reason for white settlement) had developed as a result of the 'world market' coming to the Cape in the form of passing ships. At least this was largely true on the demand side (there was, though, some export of wheat and wine to Europe and the Dutch colonies in the East). On the supply side, the outside world provided some manufactured commodities for a narrow market largely based in Cape Town and for the wheat and wine farming area in its vicinity. It also supplied slaves, mainly from other parts of Africa and from Madagascar, who were vital for the economy of the region. When we consider the internal constitution of the Dutch colony, we can distinguish at least three components: the economy of the western Cape centred on Cape Town; the pastoral economy of the Dutch trekboers, which extended north and east from Cape Town; and the African economies of the high-veld and south-eastern coastal belt.

The Dutch East India Company, one of the great trading companies in the period of mercantilism, provided the economic and political framework at the Cape until 1795. It was licensed by the Dutch government to monopolise trade (and, in this case, exercise political jurisdiction and sovereignty) over a vast area. In eighteenth-century Europe even though capitalists had begun for some time to organise production, employing workers for wages, independent artisans and small farmers or peasants still produced most of what was required. The Cape itself represented in some ways such an economy, although the colonial context introduced certain distinctive features. In the agricultural areas of the western Cape, farmers owned the land privately or leased it from the Company, and employed labour to work it — both whites and free blacks for wages, as well as slaves. This practice suggests a move towards more fully capitalist relations on the land (as compared with small family farming). Labour and production were specialised, so that most production took place for exchange and not subsistence. However, markets were heavily circumscribed by mercantilist controls such as state monopolies and licensing.

In the interior of the Cape, trekboers had established a largely pastoral economy during the eighteenth century. Naturally their economic activities and organisation bore certain similarities to those nearer the port, but there were differences as well. In general there was less division of labour and less market exchange; families farming on extensive pastoral farms with Khoisan dependents produced for the most part their own subsistence requirements, although they needed to purchase some commodities, such as gunpowder and coffee, from Cape Town. Their technology was simpler than that of their metropolitan colleagues, but of the same kind. Their transport was based on the horse and the oxwagon, and they used firearms for hunting and warfare. The basis of their material existence was provided by wild game and the fat-tailed Cape sheep, which were well adapted to the relatively dry areas of the Karoo. In better-watered areas, they also raised cattle, which they bartered from the Khoikhoi.

In the process of expansion, the land of the interior passed into what was effectively private ownership. An informal system of loan-farms developed, whereby large tracts of land were privately appropriated in return for an annual payment to the Company. In practice these farms could be bequeathed, alienated and subdivided even though the law did not permit such transactions. Controlling natural resources on this scale, the farmers required additional labour to that provided by their own families, and they owned some slaves (though not as many as the wine and wheat farmers) and employed and 'apprenticed' Khoikhoi, who often lost their stock and their independent access to land and water in the process. The Khoikhoi economy seems to have collapsed as a result of the monopolisation of land and water by white settlers. In summary, the economy of the interior was largely a subsistence economy, with certain important links to the Cape Town market and with ownership and employment patterns characteristic of an early colonial form of capitalism.

It is not simple to describe the main characteristics of the African economies of southern Africa. Like that of the trekboers, these African economies were substantially based on stock-raising, with the emphasis on cattle rather than sheep. However, the people were also hunters, and cultivators of sorghum and a range of vegetables. Their technology involved the use of metal implements (iron and copper), and the Sotho in particular had a well-developed tradition of craftsmanship in the making of metalware, wood-carvings and clay pots. Hoes rather than ploughs were used. In some areas oxen were used for riding and as pack animals. Maize was beginning to be adopted as a crop. Within this framework of subsistence production there were, however, trading links, involving the exchange of ivory and other commodities obtained by hunting and craft manufacture. It is important to remember that, in addition to European settlement at the Cape, further European settlements and sources of market supply and demand existed: the Portuguese settlements on the coast of Mozambique, of which Delagoa Bay was the most important, and those in Angola. There is evidence of trading activities over long distances. Trade of this kind (which fell under the control of the chiefs and tended to increase chiefly wealth and power) probably had some influence on the genesis of the *mfecane*.

What distinguishes this economy from that of the trekboers is the lack of private ownership of land and natural resources, as well as the absence of the institution of wage labour. (There was probably a parallel in some African communities to the serf-like status of the Khoikhoi on trekboer farms, that is, people who became attached to tribal groups with an inferior status.) Pastures were essentially held and utilised by the community as a whole, and even cultivated plots were subject to allocation by the political heads of these small-scale communities, and were not fully allotted to individuals or families. This does not mean that production was communal: cattle was owned and fields were cultivated by individual families in their own interest.

In the course of the nineteenth century, the British occupation of the Cape led to a quickening of economic tempo and to the expansion of the market economy. British settlers came to the western Cape and to the eastern Cape frontier. Cape Town and existing rural towns grew in size, and new towns and villages like Port Elizabeth and Grahamstown developed. Market links with Europe based on maritime transport were strengthened; more adequate systems of local government and road communications were established. Internal trading and banking networks were created, and experimentation began in agriculture — the most successful venture being the introduction of merino sheep. From the 1830s the spread of merino flocks in the Cape midlands and the north-eastern Cape provided enlarged incomes for farmers and encouraged the spread of a market-directed economy. Wool was produced for the overseas market of England, where a demand existed for this raw material in the factories of the expanding woollen-textile industries. Nevertheless, the scale and tempo of economic change were small by comparison with what was then taking place in Australia. There the production and export of wool provided the basis for a substantial inflow of white immigrants, the investment of overseas capital, and a much more sustained development of commerce. Nonetheless, a foundation was being laid in South Africa for the economic developments to come.

What set South Africa unambiguously on its modern course was the discovery of diamonds and gold in the 1870s and 1880s. This ushered in a period aptly described as the 'mineral revolution'. Southern Africa began to realise the potential for producing commodities which the expanding economies of Europe, America and elsewhere required. Since these natural resources were located in the interior, the economic growth to which they gave rise had an impact on existing local economies, which were less advanced technologically and organisationally and in which capitalist patterns of ownership and 'relations of production' were less pronounced. The sluggishness of the economy gave way to rapid expansion. By the end of the century a network of railways had been constructed; white immigrants flowed in, bringing with them capital, technical know-how and skills; urban markets developed; and the commercial and financial networks moved from the coastal areas to Kimberley and Johannesburg. As the scale of mining activities grew, large numbers of men, both black and white, were employed as wage workers — there were already 100 000 in the Witwatersrand by 1890, and 325 000 (of whom 285 000 were Africans) by 1912. Within this framework a host of market opportunities arose, in transport, agriculture and small-scale manufacturing.

In explaining the economic growth that took place at the time as well as the patterns it was to assume in subsequent periods, we need to emphasise that its roots lay in the linking of the South African economy to the most developed capitalist economies of the world. A substantial proportion of the required technology, skills, labour, entrepreneurship and capital was imported into South Africa from abroad, without which it is impossible to imagine that economic growth could have taken place on the scale and at the speed that it did. (It soon became clear, for instance, that gold-mining on the Witwatersrand would involve deep-level operations and processes of chemical extraction, demanding a scale of capital investment possible only with the technical and financial resources of advanced European capitalism.) Changes in African and trekboer economies did not, therefore, proceed in an evolutionary fashion but involved the violent irruption of a far more sophisticated and large-scale economy into the local sphere. It became possible, however, to maintain economic growth through bypassing these economies to some degree rather than by mobilising and transforming them.

In comparison, when the Japanese economy began its rapid growth in roughly the same period, a fundamental reorganisation of Japanese agriculture was undertaken, which affected the peasants of the countryside as producers. As a result, the surplus for industrial and infrastructural investment was squeezed from the now more productive indigenous economy. The contrasting South African pattern, to which there are parallels in other colonial and South American economies, bore consequences which are still with us. In particular, the spread of the capitalist system and the advanced technology which it necessitated was more limited in impact than it would have been had the history of South Africa been closer to that of Japan or Europe.

The twentieth century has witnessed a continued process of economic growth, and a structural transformation of other economic sectors after the initial take-off by the mining sector. In particular, the process was marked by the commercialisation of white agriculture and the establishment of the manufacturing sector. In general terms, we can say that in the present century mining and agriculture have declined in relative significance as secondary industry has expanded. However, this trend does not imply retrogression in these two primary sectors: in fact, both experienced expansion of scale and output as well as considerable technical change and progress.

The increased urban market to which the mining revolution gave rise stimulated the local production of food and raw materials, although imports of food from abroad were heavily relied on in the early days. Notwithstanding the overall trend of expansion in the agricultural sector, the 1920s and 1930s brought serious problems, partly because of the impact of the world depression. In response, government undertook to subsidise agriculture, and to organise and control the system of distribution and marketing of agricultural products: it is from the 1930s that we can trace the emergence of a series of control boards which today dominate agricultural marketing. White agriculture has experienced something like a revolution since the Second World War as a consequence of tariff protection, the sustained economic growth which the overall economy experienced from the mid-1930s to the early 1970s, and state support for the agricultural sector. Even though the number of white farmers on the land has diminished, the average size of farm and the total area under cultivation and irrigation have increased. In addition the post-war period has seen the application of modern technology — the replacement of animal power by petrol-driven vehicles and the extended use of fertilisers, pest controls and a range of similar chemical agents.

The substantial growth of the manufacturing sector coincides roughly in time with the transformation of agriculture, but can perhaps be thought of as pre-dating it by a decade. The mining boom of the 1930s (which followed the increase in the price of gold once South Africa left the gold standard in 1933) provided a framework of rising incomes, which stimulated the development of manufacturing. Moreover, government policies encouraged manufacturing by means of tariff protection and by direct participation (the clearest example of which is the establishment of ISCOR as a steel producer). Not surprisingly, manufacturing was largely concentrated initially in the production of consumer goods, including the processing of food and agricultural products. Canning, beverages, clothing, footwear and leather products, even motor car assembly, were all leaders in early industrialisation. The isolation of South Africa from overseas supplies during the Second World War gave an additional impetus to the development of local manufacturing, and this process continued after the war. Increasingly sophisticated branches of production were introduced, including chemicals, electrical goods and, within the metal and engineering fields, some capital goods.

The rapid growth during the 1960s saw the construction industry expand to cater for the needs of business enterprise in cities and to house a new class of relatively affluent suburban whites. As in other industrial societies, there was a more than proportionate expansion of the tertiary sector, providing services to business (transport, banking and finance, insurance, etc.) and to private consumers (travel and tourism, entertainment, education and other community-provided services).

As this sketch has indicated, South Africa developed the core of its economy on the model of the major overseas capitalist economies. Perhaps the major difference is that the capital-goods manufacturing sector is less developed in South Africa. Linked with this, the new technologies that are employed in South Africa are not self-generated but are imported from abroad — typical of what is called 'peripheral capitalism'.

The incorporation of less advanced economies into the emerging capitalist economy

We now need to consider how the expanding capitalist core of the South African economy affected those small-scale economies which, before the mineral revolution, had covered a substantial part of the interior of South Africa. When describing these economies, we attempted to characterise the extensive pastoralism of white farmers and the largely pastoral economies operated by Africans. While in both cases technology was simple, production was fundamentally for subsistence, and market links were not well developed, we distinguished between them on the grounds of their land-tenure systems and their systems of labour organisation. If we had to affix labels to them we might choose to refer to the white pastoral economy of the interior as early capitalist with some quasi-feudal features, and the African economies as tribal or pre-capitalist. Between these economies and the expanding capitalist core a complicated pattern of linkages, mutual interdependence, and dominant–subordinate relationships emerged. In the process the precapitalist and quasi-feudal systems were transformed, the latter more clearly than the former, although the overall system that has been produced as a result maintains dual characteristics.

By the early twentieth century the white pastoral economy was in a critical condition and continued to be so for at least three decades. The crisis was speeded by the impact of markets and new commercial opportunities, but there were various intrinsic reasons involved: the closing of the frontier as trekboer expansion reached the boundaries of the state; destructive methods of land-use which did not conserve the natural pastures; increasing population density due to natural reproduction; the process of subdividing farms according to the provisions of Roman-Dutch Law. Extrinsic forces aiding the crisis included: the commercial pressures and opportunities which promoted progressive farmers to reduce the unproductive use of their land by white *bywoners* and other dependents; uncertainties created by fluctuations in market prices; and problems created for credit-dependent farmers by natural disasters (disease and drought). There were also the devastating effects on white farms of the Anglo–Boer War and, later, the great depression.

The outcome of these pressures was the creation of a substantial class of 'poor whites' on the land, numbering 200 000 to 300 000 in the 1930s. Increasingly the poor whites tended to move out of rural areas into the growing towns where they were not well equipped with either education or occupational skills, or prepared for the competition with relatively cheap African and coloured labour. It is in this context that we must understand the expansion (though not the genesis) of the system of protection of white labour (of which job reservation is the clearest example) and the elaboration in the 1930s of the economic programme of Afrikaner nationalism. In the years of urbanisation and widespread economic distress among the white poor, Afrikaner nationalism received a new impetus. The Afrikaners used all the means at their disposal — the franchise and the bureaucracy — to try to diminish the relatively disadvantaged position they held in relation to the English. The growing nationalism of this class was fuelled by newly urbanised elements which had been ejected from the countryside. The results of economic growth and of the eventual political triumph of Afrikaner nationalism have been: the complete incorporation of white agriculture in the capitalist economy; the increased participation of Afrikaners in the ownership and control of substantial parts of the non-agricultural sectors; and the creation of a class of relatively affluent Afrikaner wage-earners at semi-skilled, skilled, and supervisory levels.

By contrast, the indigenous African societies have had a very different experience in relation to the modern sector.

In the sudden expansion of economic activities at the time of the mineral revolution, market opportunities arose for anyone with enterprise, some access to resources, and the necessary motivation. As we have seen, the development of mining involved a radical break with the type and tempo of economic activities in the interior. Prior to the last quarter of the nineteenth century, there was no developed system of transport, little commercial agriculture, and few of the services required for booming mining-towns. These conditions, given the substantial incomes being created in mining, led to considerable rewards for those ready to become suppliers.

It is now clear that a great number of Africans responded to these new market opportunities in various roles. By so doing they accelerated or even set in motion changes in their traditional economy and society.

Africans went out to work as wage labourers in enterprises owned and controlled by whites. They went to the mines, they worked on farms, they were employed in the construction of railways and roads. In most cases they worked initially for wages on a temporary basis, for instance during harvest time, but on the mines it was customary to return home after a longer period of absence (6 to 18 months). However, there were those who had already become detached from their tribal economies and entered full-time wage employment. Employment provided them with the opportunities of earning money incomes, which they needed to pay taxes and wanted to spend on a range of consumer and producer commodities that the market economy could provide (firearms, livestock, blankets, cooking utensils, wagons and ploughs). One must also emphasise that in the early stages many Africans chose not to work for wages. To take an interesting example, Indian indentured labourers were brought to Natal from the 1860s and 1870s because it proved impossible to induce sufficient Zulu to leave the land and provide for the labour requirements of the developing sugar industry. The employment of Mozambican workers on the gold mines similarly illustrates the shortage of local supply.

What is less well-known is that in the first two or three decades of this period there was a significant development of agricultural production by Africans for the market. These producers were situated both within tribal economies and beyond (around mission stations and on land which they either had bought freehold or were renting from white owners, in particular from large land-holding companies both in Natal and the Transvaal). Fundamental to this development was the introduction of the ox-drawn iron plough, which made possible the cultivation of increasing areas of land in response to the increased demand for food. It is impossible to provide here the fine detail which would build up a convincing picture of the emergence of small-scale African peasant producers, but a few illustrations will suffice to suggest the outlines of the picture. As early as the 1830s the Basotho were trading grain with Griqua and trekboers in the Orange River area. In the 1870s when the Kimberley mines were opened quantities of food were exported from Basutoland to this market. By 1872, 100 000 muids (84 kg each) of grain and 2 000 bales of wool a year were exported abroad and commodities were imported via a network of 30 trading stores. The Rand also received food from Basutoland in the 1880s.

There is similar evidence of increasing agricultural production in Ciskei and Transkei. At one stage, Bundy notes, the prosperity of Queenstown depended more on the enterprise of African peasant producers than on that of the local white settlers.

In the Transkei, the four magisterial districts of Fingoland had been among the foremost areas of African response and prosperity during the 1870s and 1880s. Travellers, magistrates and missionaries penned encomiums upon the hard-headed, hard-working Mfengu peasantry, who had subscribed thousands of pounds to the building of schools and roads, raising much of the money through their transport-riding and sales of wool, grains and vegetables. Another area singled out for particular mention was Emigrant Tembuland (Xalanga and St Mark's districts), where similar reports of industry and progress were the rule rather than the exception in the 20 years before 1890. The prosperity enjoyed by the substantial peasants in these districts was in some respects more firmly based than that of their counterparts in the Ciskei. The Transkei was far less penetrated by white settlers, so better land and more land was available; the region was better watered and the population density lower.

As these factors would suggest the 1890s saw continued instances of enterprise and economic reward in Fingoland and Emigrant Tembuland. African peasants still disposed of surplus grain and wool; there was 'an enormously increased trade' in the Territories, wrote the Chief Magistrate after the good harvests of 1892. African farmers near the Mbashe river experimented with coffee; in Emigrant Tembuland thousands of fruit trees were planted in a cash venture; in Xalanga 4 000 bags of wheat were threshed by machinery and 'the prize wheats of the last show were pronounced by competent judges to have been equal to the best grown in the colony'. In the same district, 125 houses valued at from £20 to £600 were built by African farmers and the Cala and Indwe markets were supplied with the vegetables they grew.

In Natal, where much land had been subsumed by land companies, many Africans farmed land as tenants, and from such sources there was a similar expansion of market production. As already mentioned in connection with the Mfengu, transport riding was a lucrative undertaking for any who could put together an ox span and acquire a wagon.

Fascinating details have come to light about African enterprise in the early days of Johannesburg. Zulu men moved into the field of urban transport as rickshaw operators, and others organised laundry businesses, hiring water-rights on rivers from white farmers, and arranging the collection and distribution of the laundry. As we move into the twentieth century, this initial set of market responses changed and was narrowed down. As the response of wage labour came to dominate other forms of labour, the role of Africans as independent agricultural producers for market, as traders and transport operators declined. Africans became in the main a wage-labour force, though a substantial number retained some access to land. The African economies changed in important ways but this transformation fell short of the full-scale substitution of a capitalist system for the traditional one.

The decline of African market enterprise on an independent basis is a complex process. The pervasive effects of exclusionist pressures against blacks by the white-controlled state must not be underestimated. The crisis that affected agriculture in white-owned areas in the first three decades of the twentieth century has certain parallels for blacks. A substantial part of the later success of white agriculture has resulted from massive inputs of resources and organisation by the state. These were not available on anything like the same scale to African agriculture — which, moreover, was less well-served with transport links to markets than most white farming areas.

In addition, whites have used their political power since Union to limit access by Africans to the land. The Land Acts of 1913 and 1936 legislated against those Africans who held land under capitalist forms of tenure outside the areas declared as reserves. At another level, as job opportunities and wages increased, as the population grew, and African demands for the products of the market economy expanded, wage labour became more attractive than agricultural production in crowded reserves on overstocked and eroded lands.

Two further points need to be considered. Firstly, although the expanding core of the economy exercised a consistent demand for African wage labour, that labour was admitted on disadvantaged terms. On the one hand, limits were set to African occupational mobility by statutory and conventional job reservation; on the other, restrictions were placed on the free access of black labour to the labour market by influx control. Thus, the labour markets contained elements of what one might call a forced-labour system. Secondly, it has been argued that one reason why the state did not push through the capitalist transformation of the African areas — with the free sale of land, the emergence of a class of black capitalist farmers owning the land, and the establishment of a wholly committed workforce with nothing to sell but their labour power and employed permanently in towns or on farms — was that it suited the white-controlled economy to maintain the vestiges of a subsistence economy. By these means part of the costs of subsistence and reproduction could be borne and social control exercised over the new class of industrial workers.

Of course, much more needs to be said about the role of Africans in the South African economy. There are a series of restrictions which have been imposed on African traders and businessmen in urban areas. They have been confined to the African townships, where incomes are lower and the potential for expansion smaller, and they have been limited in the number and size of businesses which they have been allowed to operate. Skilled white immigration, capital-intensive technology, growing scale of operations, credit dependence and managerial sophistication, all seem to have tilted the competitive odds against African entrepreneurs. Moreover, if we are to understand their current role in economic activity we need to note how educational and health services have been allocated in a way which has favoured whites — so that the competitive position of blacks has been weakened. The cumulative effect of legal discriminations, the inferior provision of training and social services, and a degree of unfamiliarity with the modern exchange economy, have limited the emergence of a group of successful African urban businessmen. It is fairly clear that if the social and political system had not possessed discriminatory features, a far larger group of prosperous black capitalists would have emerged, but it may well be that they would still have formed a relatively small percentage of the overall black population.

To obtain a rounded picture, some mention must be made of the coloured people and the Indians. In brief, the roles they play in the modern capitalist economy represent a fuller incorporation into the modern economy than do those of Africans. In particular, they have had legal access to land, although especially in the last three decades this right has been circumscribed by the Group Areas Act. In the western Cape, where most of the coloured population is resident, job reservation in favour of whites has been partial and a class of coloured skilled workers is well entrenched. Similarly, a class of traders, agriculturalists, and small manufacturers has developed among the Indians. Their operations have been hampered by various segregatory devices, but these have not prevented their expansion. A full explanation of their relative success would probably require us to say something about the economic culture that they brought with them, their experience of an exchange economy, and their release from traditional cultural bonds. It is interesting to note that enterprising Africans usually emerged not from the core but from the fringes of traditional communities.

We have suggested that prior to the colonial period Africans were deeply involved in a precapitalist and preliterate economy and culture, and undoubtedly there have been forces of cultural conservatism at work as well as forces of adaptation and innovation in African responses to the market economy.

It is difficult, however, to assess the relative importance of all these factors. The *bywoners* on white farms were also disadvantaged, but structural opportunities made it possible for them to catch up with other whites. One could argue that the Land Act and similar curtailments of opportunities for Africans have led to the stagnation of their economic potentials. In addition, one has to consider the probability that much of the 'backwardness' of Africans was in fact a form of resistance to political, economic, and cultural imperialism. Had there been a non-dominating relationship with the white culture, their adaptation to the new economic opportunities may have been much faster.

Our discussion has tended to emphasise the capitalist nature of the economic forces at work in changing South African society in the last 150 years. This emphasis should not weigh too heavily. A good deal of economic change has been effected by the introduction of new technologies and forms of social and economic organisation which they impose. Had industrialisation and economic growth in South Africa taken place under a socialist regime, a good deal of the story might have been unchanged. In all probability wage-employment would have been introduced in factories and mines and on farms, people would have congre-

gated in large urban areas, and the scale of social life (with all its consequences for family structure, occupational differentiation, and political
relations between people) would have increased in the way with which
we are familiar. We are not suggesting for a moment that there would
not have been some important differences in such a society: what we
wish to stress are the similarities. One way of summarising the pattern
of differential incorporation of various groups into the South African
economy is to look at the distribution of income and wealth that has
resulted from the process of economic growth. Since, as we have seen,
whites in general have been more favourably incorporated than others,
it is the interracial distribution that concerns us here. In very rough
terms, over a considerable period of time up to 1970 the African share
of national income has averaged around 20 per cent whereas they have
formed slightly under 70 per cent of the population. If we include
coloureds and Asians the percentage rises to around 30 per cent. Some
estimates suggest that in the 1970s this percentage had shifted in favour
of blacks and reached something like 35 per cent by 1975, with the
prospect of this shifting trend continuing. We have argued that the explanation of this marked degree of inequality is to be found in a complex
set of factors and is not the simple product of either African tradition-
alism on the one hand or white discrimination on the other.

The transformation of African societies effected by capitalism

It seems plausible to argue that there is a set of institutional arrangements which suit capitalist development; and that if capitalist growth
does take place it will tend over time to transform social institutions
and arrangements in directions which suit it. Land and labour will tend
to become commodities, which can be bought and sold or hired in markets. This tendency ought eventually to have some undermining effect
on the authority and power of chiefs and similar rulers of small-scale
states who historically derive power from their rights of allocating land
(and, perhaps, some part of labour-time). Smaller political units will
tend to be aggregated into larger 'national' units, in which there is more
extensive geographical mobility of producers, producers' equipment, and
money, goods and services. Within this larger competitive arena, 'market
forces' will lead to a concentration of land and productive assets in the
hands of capitalist employers, and the emergence of a class of 'prolet-
arians' who work for the employers (possibly after more directly coercive
forces have been applied at an earlier stage).

Although capitalist transformation has taken place in South Africa,
the extent of its reach has not been total. In much of the homeland
countryside, land cannot be bought or rented (at least not legally) for

money. Chiefs with 'tribal councils' rule (in some senses of the word) and some command genuine respect; they are not all recent creations. Significant numbers of African families are not 'severed from the land' in the full sense, even though the breadwinners are urban industrial workers. Important sections of the law under which they live have substantial continuity with 'traditional' legal provisions. Despite capitalism being the predominant productive system, fully capitalist relationships — especially those that define people purely as wage earners — do not exist across the entire face of the country.

At this stage one can argue that the apparently 'traditional' social and economic relations have in fact been changed in content, and serve to integrate Africans in a subordinate fashion into the capitalist economy. On the political level at least, one can see how the institution of chiefship often has the effect of exercising conservative social control in the countryside, probably limiting both small-scale capitalist development and political dissent.

If one asks how these non-capitalist institutions and relationships have come to be retained, one moves into controversial territory — the more so if one considers as well the development of certain coercive and discriminatory features of the social order, which are not necessarily linked to the preservation of 'tribal' institutions, but which involve restrictions on market freedoms of residence, movement, competition, withholding labour, and so on. The evidence suggests a very complex process of determination. Stanley Greenberg is correct to argue that the class interests of commercial farmers and mining capitalists led them to elaborate and extend the racial order in pursuit of control over labour and, as time went by, over land farmed by labour tenants and 'squatters'. It is not obvious that mine-owners saw immediately the benefits of migrant, semi-proletarianised labour, or that they engineered it; but over time they came to rely on it.

However, even within this framework, one can see the constraining power of the white working class in preventing a free flow of capital, and thus increasing the probability of black labour costs being restrained by management. Greenberg shows how, beyond this, the systematic danger of undercutting led different groups of white workers to adopt alternative protectionist strategies (whether or not they were formally racialist), which restrained black advance and access. Although such policies must be understood within the context of capitalist labour markets, it seems to be stretching things to regard these restraints on job entry (including entry to towns) as expressive of 'capitalist class interests', although the point can be argued.

It seems obvious that at the military, political, and demographic levels the pressures of settler colonialism and its leverage on imperial resources were not strong enough to bring about a complete conquest of African society, and appropriation of land and natural resources.

Given these relative strengths and respective controls over resources, there was for some considerable time a degree of mutually beneficial interaction between capitalist and non-capitalist economies. Mpondo households, whose herds were decimated by rinderpest in 1897, found ways of rebuilding herds by sending sons to the mines in return for cattle advances (*joyini inkomo*). In the last decades of the nineteenth century, the Chopi of southern Mozambique found entering into wage labour in the capitalist sector in South Africa a way of escaping oppression and interference in their productive forces by the Gaza state. In earlier decades, educated christianised Africans, among others, had found wage labour a complementary form of economic activity with peasant farming, since it provided the cash resources for the investments in wagons, iron ploughs, trained ox-teams, axes and other requirements for new styles of rural life and agricultural activity.

Arguably, within a context of considerable technological and cultural disjunction in which modern mining capitalism burst upon the interior of South Africa without long 'organic' development of the preconditions for local involvement, it was possible and in fact easier for the new mode to bypass to some extent the indigenous communities, and recruit skills, enterprise, even unskilled labour abroad. Thus, Indians were indentured when Zulu were not forthcoming for work in sugar. What would have been the long-term consequences of Chinese permanence? Possibly very favourable, but their presence in the short-run facilitated black withdrawal and white bypassing. And of course there were white immigrants; and blacks from 'abroad' were crucial for the mines.

It could be argued that the degree of neglect of the 'homelands' is not permanent and reflects the natural uneven geographical pattern of development in a capitalist economy. In South Africa this is reinforced by the skewing effect on resource-allocation resulting from monopoly of political power.

Finally, we must stress that the policies of territorial segregation were, in addition to everything else, a political device conceived by elements in the colonial settler state who looked apprehensively to the future and were concerned about the long-run consequences of geographical 'integration'.

We have so far argued that capitalist class interest and economic factors have, at certain stages, supported seeming irregularities such as incomplete capitalist transformation and job limitation. In addition, there is today a much reduced capitalist stake in the racial order. Greenberg summarises it: 'By what will seem like a tortuous process, each of the class actors comes to depend less on the racial order and state racial apparatus.'

Why has South Africa a capitalist system?

Granted that, with some qualifications, South Africa is a capitalist country, it is worthwhile to consider why it has not evolved into a socialist state. By socialism we might distinguish between Soviet-type economies in which (ignoring ideological niceties) capitalism has been abolished, and advanced capitalist economies in which social democracy has made more or less substantial inroads, creating mixed economies.

Capitalism became established in South Africa through linkage to the economies of the major capitalist powers and their initiation of, and participation in, economic growth here, via foreign investment, colonial settlement, and trade. Capitalism has continued because, we propose, it has never been seriously challenged by socialism, though there have been socialist influences and movements at work. The socialist challenge has thus far been neither successful nor really serious because the conditions which favour transitions to Soviet-type or welfare-state-type systems have not existed in South Africa.

From the mid-seventeenth century, the proto-South African economy was to be transformed by the intervention of precisely those nations from Europe which were in the forefront of the development of early capitalism. Features of this early-capitalist world were transplanted to the region – for instance, mercantilist state regulation of economic life, slavery (which was characteristic of the colonies in north America, parts of Latin America, the Caribbean, and the East Indies), and serf-type dependent labour (to which there were parallels in eastern Europe and Latin America). As the capitalist economy expanded in the nineteenth and twentieth centuries these features were abolished or replaced by arrangements more characteristic of advanced capitalism. We know that the transformation to classic capitalism was never complete and that important deviations from that model were entrenched. New types of controlled-labour arrangements were constructed (compounds, passes and influx control, limitations on collective bargaining); fully capitalist relations of production were never established in the African reserves. African land-ownership, entrepreneurship, and vertical labour mobility in the geographical areas of maximum development were denied or restricted.

There have been working-class movements and political groups with varying socialist programmes, but they have not thus far constituted a serious challenge. The working class in South Africa has been a divided one — divided not only on racial lines but also in various other ways (ethnically, by degree of involvement in the 'modern' sector, and ideologically). This, however, is not to deny that industrial conflict has been at times intense. In the early twentieth century white workers were involved in major strike activity: in 1897, 1907, 1913–14 and 1922. Among the issues involved were threatened wage-reductions, recognition of unions in collective bargaining, and the protection of white workers against replacement by African (or Chinese) workers. But in 1913–14 and 1922 the repressive action of the state widened the issues: Davenport says of the 1913–14 episode that 'syndicalist leaders tried to turn the strike into an attack on capitalism itself'. Military force was required in both 1913–14 and 1922 to put down the strikes/insurrections.

The fact remains that white workers had political power. In the aftermath of 1922 the South African Labour Party shared power with Hertzog's National Party in the Pact Government of 1924-9. There were also Labour representatives in the 1929-33 cabinet and the war cabinets of 1939-43 and 1943-48. After the 1958 election the Labour Party finally disappeared as a separate entity. Under the Pact Government the Labour Party achieved the major objective of an institutionalised collective-bargaining system, securing official recognition for white trade unions within the capitalist system. It further supported, and was partly responsible for inventing, the Hertzog programme of political segregation; and was also responsible for (or supported) the Apprenticeship Act, the Wage Act, and the 'civilised labour policy', in terms of which apprenticeship conditions, wage levels, and government recruitment practices were so organised as to protect white workers in conditions of unemployment and competition for jobs. After the demise of the Pact Government, the sustained growth of the economy from the 1930s onwards saw the increased affluence of this group and their rise to supervisory, skilled, and middle-class positions within the capitalist system.

Secondly, we need to refer to black political and trade-union organisations, and their relation to socialism. In the 1920s the Industrial and Commercial Workers' Union of Africa (ICU) grew to a membership of 100 000, but by 1931 was more or less a spent force. According to Bonner, the objectives of the leadership were 'a fundamental redistribution of economic and social power', but they were less clear as to how this was to be achieved. Surprisingly, their membership was heavily rural, consisting of labour tenants under threat of eviction. After the expulsion of communists from their ranks they made even less headway in urban areas, and did not even attempt to create a factory-based organisation. Bonner concludes: ' I do not . . . think of the ICU as a failure so much as a movement appropriate to a time characterised by rural impoverishment without major industrialisation.'

Within the African National Congress, socialists (or communists) have at various stages wielded influence, the more so as industrialisation proceeded and a stabilised black proletariat emerged. But it is important to note that their presence has given rise to ideological conflict. In the late 1920s there was a reaction against the radicalism of Gumede (this was the period of the Communist Party's 'Native Republic' policy) and Congress suffered a decline. Similarly, in the 1950s the eventual breakaway of the PAC was bound up with both the multiracialism and the mild socialism of the ANC, expressed in the 1956 Freedom Charter.

Finally, we need to ask why working-class and socialist movements have not been stronger or more effective in challenging the capitalist system in South Africa. White labour, on the one hand, has been able to entrench itself so firmly in a position of privilege through political means that a socialist solution including blacks would threaten its interests. On the other hand, the swing towards radical forms of socialism by black groups opposing the system, has been met by escalating repression from the white state. The latter has had sufficient political and economic power so far to counter all attempts at fundamental change. We should remember that social change requires more than programmes and intellectual prescriptions; it calls for social groups to be organised in pursuit of programmes which they perceive as furthering their interests, and it requires that such groups shall be stronger than those opposing them. And, whether these conditions are met or not will usually depend on deep-seated structural conditions and not only on will, leadership and vision.

3 Ideological critiques of South African capitalism

The South African economic system has come under fire from at least three ideological perspectives: the liberal free-market school of thought; various radical or revisionist approaches; and black, anti-racist opinion, which may lean either to the liberal or to the radical school, but at the same time draws on traditional African values. While economists may take issue with these critiques, it is important for our purposes that we should understand what they are. In what follows the critiques will be articulated in the terms typically adopted by each of these perspectives.

A liberal free-market critique of South African capitalism

For radicals the problem of South Africa lies in the fact that it is capitalist in the first place. All other problems arise from this. In contrast, the liberal free-market school argues that the problem lies in the fact that South Africa is not sufficiently capitalist. We can distinguish four levels of this liberal free-market critique.

Historical factors

Capitalist production was imposed on a pre-capitalist society (black and white). It initially bypassed the local population to a considerable extent (for example through white and Indian immigration), and only sluggishly integrated the local population into its mechanisms as its labour requirements grew. While white, and to a certain extent Indian and coloured, labour and agriculture have in the meantime been integrated into the system, large sections of the black population are still caught up in a relatively unproductive subsistence economy. This cannot feed the growing number of blacks and makes them dependent on selling their unskilled labour on a migratory basis. Such lack of integration is the cause of poverty in the non-capitalist sector, and of a poorer overall performance of the economy as a whole.

State intervention for ideological reasons

The fact that blacks have thus far not been fully integrated into the capitalist system is due to government intervention in the economy for ideological reasons. The official policies of tribal homelands, influx control, restrictions on geographical and social mobility, group areas, neglect of black education and training, job reservation, and restrictions on black entrepreneurship, have prevented blacks from developing their full potential within the capitalist system.

State controls which distort the economy

Among the state controls that distort the economy are a broad spectrum of price controls, labour regulations, import controls and geographical manipulation of industrial expansion.

State participation in the economy

Huge state corporations such as South African Transport Services, ISCOR, ARMSCOR, ESCOM, should ideally be in private hands and subject to competition in a free market.

All these factors are believed to impede the growth of an economy which has enormous potential but is plagued with social and political obstructions. While earlier research tended to assume that South Africa is one of the world leaders in economic growth, latest indications are that her performance in this respect is, in fact, quite dismal, particularly since 1970. Several reasons are offered:

(a) Productivity of white and black labour is low by international comparison. This is partly due to severe bottlenecks in the area of higher skills and at managerial levels, partly due to the insufficient development of the potential of the lower-income groups. Management tends to be overburdened, while the privileged employee enjoys standards of income, social benefits and leisure which only advanced industrial countries can really afford. Lower down, particularly among blacks, there is insufficient training, a low level of incentives, restricted mobility and lack of identification with the firm and with the system as a whole. Competition in the labour market is restricted, and townward-migrating blacks are prevented from becoming integrated into the system and internalising its norms.

(b) Geographical segregation is extremely costly, owing to unnecessary transport, administration of the control of movement, duplication of facilities, and obstruction of a rational resource-allocation by market forces.

(c) South Africa is still a small-scale market. The growth of its economy seems to depend on a widening export market. South Africa could become a market of close on 30 million people if purchasing power were not concentrated on an elite which demands the production and import of relative luxuries, while the basic needs of the majority are not satisfied. By channelling production into the export market to offset luxury imports, capacities are withdrawn from the internal market. The obvious solution is to raise the purchasing power of the black majority relative to that of the white elite so that its needs can be translated into an effective market demand, which would in turn rapidly stimulate production.

Closely connected with the preceding consideration is the apparent inability of the South African economy to cope with the problem of rising unemployment and underemployment. That the levels of under- and un-employment are unacceptably high and likely to rise rapidly in the future can hardly be doubted. That the problem may soon get out of hand is a distinct possibility. Once again, reasons for rising unemployment and underemployment are not difficult to find.

(a) Part of the problem is the exponential growth of the population. We can expect that the population of greater South Africa will have risen tenfold within one century from roughly 5 million in 1900 to close on 50 million in the year 2000. A stabilisation of the population can only be expected when living standards and social securities rise to adequate levels.

(b) Subsistence agriculture has long ceased to absorb the unemployed, even on the basis of underemployment. In fact the pressure on the land is so great that it may seriously affect the chances of increased agricultural production.

(c) Population pressure has been increased considerably by government policies to abolish the squatter system on white agricultural land, and the free search for work where it can be found. The practice of resettling all blacks not immediately required as labour for the smooth running of the white economy, in already overcrowded black areas, compounds the problem.

(d) Influx control, the lack of training, and increasing restiveness among black employees, lie behind the tendency to reduce the black workforce on farms, on mines, in industry and commerce, even in the services, and to replace (particularly unskilled) labour with mechanised, capital-intensive methods of production.

The overall problem, it is argued, lies in the fact that blacks are not considered part of the system. Black labour is an essentially foreign, hired factor of production, which employers want to reduce where possible. Until recently it was counted merely on the cost side, not as a potential market which needs to be developed by increased employment and purchasing power, let alone as part of the population which needs to be led to a higher quality of life. In fact, when its purely instrumental function is in doubt, black labour becomes a nuisance and is repatriated to the reserves.

The liberal free-market school normally deems huge discrepancies in income as unavoidable in the early stages of capitalist development, and instead regards it as a healthy incentive, believing that the gap closes as the system matures. But this presupposes non-interference on ideological grounds. Given massive restrictions on black advancement, liberals often express their apprehension about the likelihood of increasing social unrest and revolutionary ferment, a concomitant rise in the level of repression, a subsequent erosion of the rule of law and of human rights, increasing drains on human and financial resources by defence and security needs, and the economic effects of the country's pariah status in the international scene, including possible boycotts and flight of capital from the country. For all these reasons liberals attack the racial arrangements of the South African system, but not necessarily its capitalist presuppositions.

There is some awareness in liberal circles that free enterprise may be foreign to traditional cultural values of blacks. Employers complain about the lack of dependability, punctuality, efficiency and productivity of black labour. Scholars often stress that entrepreneurship in South Africa has to be derived exclusively from the relatively small white section of the population, because blacks have developed little initiative. These negative factors are then blamed on the cultural values of blacks which are said to be foreign to an enterprising or industrial spirit. Removal of restrictions on African business, it is hoped, will go some way to changing this.

More sympathetic observers stress the merits of African value systems: blacks believe in harmony within the community, not in competition and conflict; in equilibrium in nature and society, not in rapacious performance, growth and progress that lead to ecological destruction and social disruption; in communalist solidarity, not in individualist profiteering; in orientation towards people, not in orientation towards things. However, these moral assets render blacks uncompetitive in the modern rat-race. Realism demands, so it is believed, that they be abandoned in favour of the values of free enterprise.

Others believe that blacks respond more favourably to economic incentives than is generally conceded, in spite of their cultural background. Their lack of competitiveness is a result of their relative deprivation in terms of upbringing, nutritional standards, education and training, medical services, entrepreneurial and professional opportunities, and horizontal and vertical mobility. In short, it is not the culture which impedes but discrimination — a lack of freedom and equal opportunity in the economic, political, and social systems.

Finally, we draw attention to the controversy about the relation between the capitalist mode of production and institutionalised racism. One influential body of opinion maintains that the capitalist system will increasingly remove the constraints of racial policies by the sheer necessities of economic expansion. Others are convinced that racial segregation and the capitalist mode of production are not mutually contradictory, but interact with each other in an evolving process of mutual adaptation. The radical view is adamant that racial discrimination is only the particular form which the exploitation of the proletariat takes under South African circumstances. This brings us to the radical critique of South African capitalism.

A radical critique of South African capitalism

Radical opinion holds that the South African economy is an integral but dependent part of the world capitalist system, an offshoot of the metropolitan centres in the USA, Europe, and Japan. As South African investments yield substantial dividends and as the country is a supplier of minerals important to the metropolitan centres (not least for their military pursuits), international capitalism protects and supports the system in spite of rhetorical protests against racism and violations of human rights.

Seen in this light South Africa is a prominent example of peripheral capitalism such as is found in other semi-industrialised Third World countries (e.g. Brazil, Mexico, South Korea and Malaysia). Among the characteristics of peripheral capitalism are:

(a) Dependence on foreign capital. While South Africa has considerable levels of local capital formation and its own multinational corporations, it is heavily dependent on foreign investments.

(b) Dependence on the export of a few primary products to offset the import of indispensable capital goods (particularly machinery, weapons, electronic gadgets). In the case of South Africa the primary products include gold, uranium, diamonds, coal and agricultural products.

(c) A lack of capital goods, which necessitates importing such goods from the metropolitan centres.

(d) An elite market for luxury consumer goods, to which both local production and imports are primarily geared; on the other hand, there is large-scale impoverishment of the majority of the population, whose basic needs are not catered for, because their purchasing power is insufficient to translate need into market demand.

(e) The tendency of the elite to form a sophisticated and capital-intensive enclave economy serving itself. As this elite becomes independent of black labour, blacks are increasingly marginalised and abandoned to 'independent' homelands. This feature does not preclude the incorporation of Indian, coloured and certain urban blacks into the elite. Brazil — which also juxtaposes affluent urban areas and drastically impoverished rural zones — has been characterised as a 'Sweden superimposed on an Indonesia'; a similar description might apply to South Africa.

The centre-periphery structure of the world capitalist system is mirrored by the social and geographical discrepancies within the country. Economic power converges on a single overruling geographical centre, the Pretoria-Witwatersrand-Vereeniging complex, and smaller sub-centres. This statistical fact has been the target of government decentralisation policies for more than two decades. The same is true for the imbalance between white urban and rural areas. The gravity of geographical imbalances only becomes apparent, however, when one includes the black peripheral areas (variously called reserves, Bantustans, homelands, black states) in the picture. Their contribution to the gross domestic product of greater South Africa has hovered around 2-3 per cent for decades while almost half of the country's black population technically resides there. Population density has increased from roughly 25 persons per square kilometre in the 1920s, and 29 in the 1950s, to over 46 in the 1970s. Agricultural production of subsistence needs has correspondingly dropped from about 45 per cent (food only) in the 1920s to roughly 40 per cent in the 1950s and less than 20 per cent in the 1970s. It is no secret that these areas are hopelessly dependent on the incomes of migrant labourers and state grants to the black homelands. It has often been pointed out that while the black peripheral areas supply the white centres with their most important productive asset, labour, they have to bear most of the social costs of maintaining and reproducing this workforce — a cost which under normal circumstances would have to be borne by the centre economy. The migrant-labour system thus boils down to a subsidisation of the rich centre by the poor periphery.

Closely related factors to be considered are the discrepancies in income, educational facilities, medical services, and professional opportunities between the various race groups. South Africa is believed to be near the top of the world's inequality league. According to estimate, the top 20 per cent of the population received 75 per cent of the income in the country in 1980, while the lowest 20 per cent received only 2 per cent. The share of the different groups did not substantially change during the half century between 1920 and 1970. On a per capita basis, the disparity between white and African incomes was reckoned at 15 : 1 in 1970. There are doubts whether real black incomes per capita rose decisively at all between 1946 and 1970. While black wages rose relative to those of whites during the early 1970s, it is not clear whether the relative position of the black population as a whole has improved since then or not. To a certain extent the tendency of research to concentrate on the discrepancy between race groups is misleading. The figure for white incomes includes a few millionaires, and the figure for black incomes does not include proceeds from black subsistence farming but does take into account the population in the reserves. Furthermore there are substantial discrepancies within the groups, for example between rural and urban blacks. The overall picture, however, is one of a marked class structure, which largely follows racial lines. This does not exclude class divisions within the groups. Nor does it exclude the formation of black offshoots of the white power centre, the administrative personnel of the 'black states', who receive substantial privileges in return for their collaboration.

Revisionists have little time for the alleged benefits of economic growth in South Africa under capitalist auspices. They maintain:

Growth leads to poverty among blacks, either in absolute or in relative terms. Those who are convinced that capital accumulation depends primarily on labour exploitation argue that the richer the centre becomes, the poorer the periphery must be. Those who concede that capitalist growth may lead to an overall increase in material wealth, from which even the poor may reap some benefit, maintain that the relative share of the poor is likely to decrease, at least for those blacks marginalised completely by the system.

Growth depends on forced labour; the intricate system of labour control gives telling evidence of this.

Growth strengthens white supremacy by making the sophisticated machinery of administrative controls, state security and military build-up financially possible.

Growth is increasingly capital-intensive and does not benefit the masses of unskilled work-seekers.

It is no surprise then that while liberals favour substantial overseas investments in South Africa as a vehicle of change, radicals discourage it, claiming that it will only entrench white dominance. This does not mean that disinvestment would not lead to increased suffering among blacks, on whose shoulders the economic burden of such a boycott would undoubtedly fall. But radicals feel that this suffering must be faced by those who would benefit from the overthrow of the system and its replacement by a more equitable dispensation on socialist lines.

A black critique: black labour and white capitalism

Capitalism and apartheid

Over the past few years there has been a definite shift in the analysis of South African society. Many observers no longer explain the policy of apartheid in terms of racial or cultural factors but in terms of economic interests. A good example is the recent Manifesto of the Azanian People which was issued when the National Forum was founded in 1983:

Our struggle for national liberation is directed against the system of racial capitalism which holds the people of Azania in bondage for the benefit of the small minority of white capitalists and their allies, the white workers and the reactionary sections of the black middle class. The struggle against apartheid is no more than the point of departure for our liberation efforts. Apartheid will be eradicated with the system of racial capitalism.

The black working class inspired by revolutionary consciousness is the driving force of our struggle. They alone can end the system as it stands today as they alone have nothing at all to lose. They have a world to gain in a democratic, anti-racist and socialist Azania. . . .

In this view inequality and injustice in South Africa are to be understood not in terms of racial belonging, cultural identity, or ethnicity. The dominant factor in the South African society is class division. According to this analysis the fact that the dominating group happens to be white and the exploited group black is the essence of the problem.

However, there is another view that is also represented in black critiques of South African capitalism. Proponents of this view hold that by relegating racial and ethnic factors to the background one tends to ignore the different forces at work in the making of South African capitalism. Cultural and racial factors have also played their part. It has been the policy of the white government to promote a social structure that will guarantee the continuing dominance of whites as a class. Racial solidarity among whites and their preparedness to accept into their political system only those of their own kind have contributed, and continue to contribute, towards the consolidation of an economically secure group. Even the new constitutional dispensation which incorporates coloureds and Indians is but an extension of this policy: co-operation of minority groups to secure white dominance.

The myth of interdependence

That the continued growth of South African capitalism will eventually lead to the disappearance of racial policies is a myth which needs to be exposed. Behind such thinking lies the argument that the desire to maximise production will lead to a fair participation within the market economy. But this view overlooks the fact that the economic system is shaped by political factors. Since the government caters for the interests of a racially distinct group it will ensure the maximisation of profits while at the same time implementing its policy of separatism. It is bound, therefore, to deny black people the chance of participating in the white political system on any terms other than white self-interest.

The collusion between the Nationalist government and the dominant white minority has been an essential element in the growth of the South African capitalist system. The National Party has been reinstated in power because it guarantees a life-style according to which whites will continue to own most of the wealth and at the same time secure protection from competition by blacks. Even the poorer white workers are protected by legislation. Black people, on the other hand, have little that can protect them from a situation of exploitability — even black trade union rights are strictly controlled.

Myth of unity: black and white workers

It is sometimes held that there is a close affinity between black and white workers, that the two groups have more in common than white workers have with white capitalists. The origin of this myth lies in the fact that both black and white workers are in varying degrees exploited by capitalists. It is further enhanced by the view that capitalists are colour-blind so long as they can obtain profits.

But it must be said that, firstly, white workers are in a position of privilege to which black workers can hardly be deemed to belong. They possess the right to vote; they assure the party of support, while the party in turn guarantees them privileges and protection from black workers. Denial to black workers of training for skilled work or of forming trade unions, and the holding of wages at a minimum for decades, clearly establish a strong bias in favour of white workers.

White workers have a high income in comparison with black workers. This is made possible by the fact that black labour provides large returns, and white workers enjoy the benefits. At no stage in the history of the South African industrial society have white workers demonstrated their unity with black workers. On the contrary, black workers have posed a threat to white workers, hence the latter's firm vote for the party that protects them from black competition.

Ethnonationalism and capitalism

Ethnonationalism is a fairly recent phenomenon in South African history. This has emerged as a result of the continuous search by the dominant group for ways and means of maintaining its position of economic privilege. The shift to ethnonationalism has in no way affected the ideology of racial discrimination, which still holds sway in South Africa, for the division between those who own the means of production and those who provide cheap labour coincides with the racial divide. Nor has the creation of ethnic 'nations' affected the social structure of South Africa. The move to ethnonationalism can be understood simply as a new way of reinforcing the capitalist mode of production. Within the context of South African history, ethnic structures are assumed to derive from tribal bonds which were traditionally constituted by a network of kinship ties. These bonds are strengthened, it is claimed, by possession of a common language, common cultural traits and religious beliefs. In modern industrial South Africa, tribal structures are in fact a legacy of precolonial communities. As large numbers of black people from different cultural backgrounds converge in the towns and cities and a new mode of existence develops in the industrial civilisation, traditional world-views have of necessity been eroded.

While no one would dispute the existence of ethnic bonds this does not justify the government's using ethnicity as a basis for homeland policy. The division of black people along ethnic lines is an imposition by the white government, the agent of class domination. It is a calculated attempt to divide the blacks, and prevent a single united class of oppressed people from developing. The existence of ethnic bonds, especially amongst urban black workers, is a fiction of the mind.

Of course one cannot deny that black urban dwellers have historical links with past traditional societies. In today's industrial societies cultural traits do not adequately explain the nature of the solidarity that obtains among black workers. Yet the existence of apparent cultural links, the presence of traditional chiefs who link remaining ethnic groups to their past, the togetherness that has characterised such groups in the face of new obstacles, have enabled the Nationalist government to propound an ideology of ethnonationalism. The real intention is simply to exclude blacks from white political institutions as well as from the white-controlled economy, save as a labour reservoir on the borders of white industrial cities.

The homelands policy grants to black workers (and their dependents) citizenship rights in the homelands, thereby depriving them of rights within white industrial society, except for those they enjoy in trade unions. In short they are granted 'industrial citizenship' through South Africa's new Labour Relations Act of 1981 but continue to be denied political citizenship in South Africa.

The emergence of black capitalists

Some black people have accepted ethnic nations. Their justification has been that this is their only means of obtaining a platform for political expression. However, by accepting a homeland status, or homeland 'independence', these black people have accepted the dominant 'ideology of ethnonationalism'. It means that they have come to accept the capitalist mode of production, which aims exclusively at exploiting black labour. Those who accept such a position are in collusion with capitalism, which aims to maximise profits and minimise wages. The capitalistic aspirations of blacks are used in this way to explain black surrender to the ideologies of the dominant white group. Such surrender pays high dividends. It grants those blacks who conform, ownership of means of production. However, such ownership of property does not take place within so-called white industrial society but within the newly created ethnic states. And so, on one side the antagonists in the conflict are gradually changing: where once whites dominated and exploited blacks, now more and more their role is being assumed by the newly created black owners of property.

In order to enhance their credibility the emergent black capitalists must sell the ideology of their white counterparts. While the ideology of racial discrimination remains repugnant, the ideology of ethnonationalism is perceived as a leverage for blacks. Thus blacks themselves revive the myth of tribal identities, cultural bonds, tribal lands and common ancestral traditions, at the expense of the rights of black people to South African soil and to political power-sharing in South Africa itself. The reincarnation of tribal myths is simply an attempt to revive a golden past that never was. The realities of industrial civilisation are qualitatively different from the precolonial African world. Advocating ethnic nationalism merely serves to retard the struggle of black workers. This is the crux of the matter. The industrial endeavour has cut across ancient tribal ties. The solution to black exploitation lies, not in re-establishing old kinship ties or reviving common cultural traits, but in trying to establish an equitable distribution of benefits that accrue from black labour. Tribalism is only a stage in the development of a people within the South African industrial society — a stage that has long been superseded. For this reason black capitalists are a danger to the entire black working class. The creation of homelands has opened new avenues for them; the present structure is to their advantage. While the market of the white industrial society is completely white-controlled, the homeland market offers black owners of property a system of free enterprise.

The essence of black identity

The concerns of black township dwellers are expressed in a new cultural form: one of utter dependence on the dictates of a capitalist system. The black community's meaning derives, not from tribal traditions, but from the bitter struggle born of class division. The township culture is marked not by its ethnic distinctiveness, but by economic exploitation and resultant poverty, by political domination of white over black, and resultant powerlessness. Any tribal unities or bonds developing within the framework of township life are essentially forms of self-assertiveness, in response to the alienation of industrial society.

The essence of black solidarity is, therefore, not ethnic identity, but common aspirations, embodying the values and demands of human dignity, political self-expression, an equitable distribution of wealth and the right to the ownership of property. In these aspirations black workers have transcended the matrix of ethnocentricity, much publicised by the dominant white class.

Black workers in urban areas are united by their common experience of economic exploitation. There is no doubt that there exists a growing awareness of the potential power that workers can exercise *vis-à-vis* the capitalist system and the Nationalist government. Collective organisation of black workers is, however, frustrated by government laws. What is needed is an intensification of the programme to conscientise workers. It presents a fresh challenge for black workers: they must reduce their dependency status by exerting pressure on the Nationalist regime, which is responsible for the smooth functioning of the capitalist system. There is no doubt that labour is going to prove the future battlefield between the classes.

Part two
RACE, POWER AND IDEOLOGY IN SOUTH AFRICA

Part Two describes what we consider to be the current and dominant ideologies in South Africa: liberalism, Afrikaner nationalism, African nationalism, black consciousness, and emerging black ethnically based nationalisms. Each chapter documents historical developments, generative ideas, and critiques of the particular ideology under discussion.

Because the literature on South Africa has tended to concentrate on race relations and ethnicity, there are many articles and books on the ideologies we describe in Part Two, each more comprehensive than our chapters. But in a book of this kind we believe it is important to include a brief description of these ideological perspectives, and the critiques they have generated.

4 Liberalism in South Africa

Few will argue with the editors of *Outlook on a Century* that there has long been 'another tradition, a non-apartheid dimension' in South African history, one that may be called the liberal tradition. This tradition is not easy to describe because of its elusive and somewhat non-dogmatic character, and because it encompasses complex elements that include, for example, capitalism and constitutional democracy, the merits of which even liberals hotly dispute. But historically it is the tradition which has expressed an 'individual ethic' as opposed to the 'corporate ethic' of Afrikaner nationalism, and has sought to uphold individual liberty against the alternatives of socialism and ethnic or racial nationalism.

The liberalism as expounded in this chapter is characterised by a degree of pragmatism; a willingness to allow experience (history) to correct its position. That this applies only within the basic tenets of liberalism, however, can be illustrated by the liberal opposition to Alfred Hoernlé's 1939 proposal that the liberal perspective be enlarged to include the recognition and respect of groups, and Edgar Brookes's disclaimer in respect to similar proposals made by SPRO-CAS Political Commission of 1973. This unwillingness to modify liberalism in the context of the plural nature of South African society imparts to liberalism in South Africa an ideological character.

Whereas liberalism has often been cast as the Cinderella of South African politics, this chapter will show that developments in Afrikaner nationalism and black politics can only be rightly understood as responses to the liberal tradition in South Africa. As Alan Paton, one of South Africa's greatest liberals, has said:

I hold in contempt those young white radicals who sneer at liberals and liberalism. Who were their mentors? If it had not been for the Jabavus, Marquards, Hoernlés, they would have been in darkness until now. One cannot measure past labours in terms of present demands. One expects black power to sneer at white liberals. After all, white power has done it for generations. But if black power meets white power in headlong confrontation, and there are no black liberals and white liberals around, then God help South Africa. Liberalism is more than politics. It is humanity, tolerance and love of justice. South Africa has no future without them, least of all white South Africa.

But in order to understand these developments and liberalism itself, we must examine briefly the origins and development of liberalism in Europe in its classical and modern forms.

European roots

Throughout most of history man has been submerged in his group. Some would say that the unique achievement of the West has been the emancipation of the individual from the bonds of custom, law and authority. While liberalism can be regarded as having roots extending back to the Hebrew prophets, Greek philosophers, and the Sermon on the Mount, the organic solidarity characteristic of western society until the end of the Middle Ages did not provide the soil in which the seeds of liberalism could germinate. The emancipation of man as an individual was accelerated by the collapse of the hierarchical structure of Medieval Europe under the twin impacts of the Protestant Reformation and the revolutions which shook England and France in the seventeenth and eighteenth centuries. Indeed, classical liberalism is the product of these great collisions with religious intolerance and despotic kingship.

The economic foundations of liberalism were laid in the eighteenth and nineteenth centuries, and articulated most clearly in Adam Smith's doctrine of the sovereignty of the market and the 'natural harmony' of self-interest. Liberal economics argued for the free enterprise of individuals in an exchange economy, based on the division of labour, which would enhance the welfare of the whole society. Entrepreneurs and capitalists are 'servants of the consumer'. The market is 'a democracy in which every penny gives the right to vote'. Liberal economics upheld the right of private property and charged governments with its protection. It presupposed a view of man as a rational economic animal engaged in maximising gains (wages, profits, interest) and minimising costs. This position is articulated in the American Constitution and the French Declaration of the Rights of Man and of the Citizen, both outstanding liberal testaments.

The political principle of classical liberalism is based on an undeviating insistence on limiting the power of government: the government is best that governs least (Jefferson). Institutional devices for limiting power included the distribution of power between functionally separate agencies — the legislature, the executive, and the judiciary. In England this took the form of constitutional democracy: a monarch, an hereditary

chamber, and an elected chamber sharing power. This model, the Westminster system, was ultimately followed in South Africa in a modified
form.

The achievements of classical liberalism were spectacular. Feudal
patterns disappeared, representative government was established, and
individual human rights — freedom of worship, speech, the press, and
assembly — became hallmarks of modern democracy. A growing middle
class expanded the means of production and vastly increased the wealth
of society. By the turn of the twentieth century, however, the market
economy came under severe criticism. Free enterprise concentrated
enormous wealth in relatively few hands; the masses failed to benefit
sufficiently from the 'trickle effects' of capitalism, as had been anticipated by the theory; economic depressions raised serious problems; the
device of incorporation concentrated great power in the hands of the
capitalists or their managers, reminiscent of seventeenth-century des-
pots; and the near-atrophy of government created a power vacuum which
private enterprise readily filled.

Modern liberalism is a triumph of experience over dogma. Liberals
sought to correct the failures of the classical experiment by proposing a
more positive role for government in planning and control. They encouraged the formation of power centres outside business and government, and worked for the more just distribution of rewards by two
strategies: the organisation of workers and consumers, with power to
bargain collectively with employers and producers; and the evolution of
the welfare state, with its range of social services 'from the cradle to the
grave', paid for by a system of differential taxation.

Liberal convictions

It is misleading to speak of the liberal tradition in South Africa as the
preserve of English-speaking whites, for it includes Afrikaners and blacks
as well. While opinions may differ as to the best economic and political
expressions of the liberal spirit, South African liberals share with others
certain convictions, among them the beliefs that:

All men share a common humanity; differences between men are
secondary.

Man is viewed optimistically; as naturally good, capable of and responsible for shaping his own destiny.

Each individual has the same dignity and should be granted the same
basic human rights without regard to race, culture, sex, or creed. This
precludes discrimination.

There should be freedom of thought and conscience, speech and the
press, movement and association, freedom from arbitrary arrest and

undue interference in personal life.

Each person should receive the benefits of education and equal opportunity in all spheres.

By man's efforts, society will progress towards greater social justice, economic prosperity and political stability, and will minimise suffering. This progress ought to be achieved by evolutionary rather than revolutionary means.

In politics the power of reason and compassion should prevail over irrational attitudes and violent practices.

The individual is of supreme importance and his legitimate interests should not be overridden by the community. Individual initiative rather than reliance on the community is emphasised. The role of the state is to nurture this individualism.

Individual freedom should be linked with the emancipation of disadvantaged groups in society, and with independence for the nation-state.

Within the state there should be a division of power between the legislature and the executive, with an independent judiciary to check abuse of power as far as possible.

Arbitrary and authoritarian government can best be prevented by a multi-party democracy, in which every adult should ultimately have a voice and a vote, either in a unitary or in a federal state. But majority rule is no guarantee of liberty. The Rule of Law is necessary to protect both the individual and minorities, and can be safeguarded by a rigid constitution which includes a Bill of Rights and an independent judiciary.

Liberalism and democracy

Liberals in South Africa regard the 'Cape liberal tradition' as the historical political embodiment of their principles. By the late nineteenth century this tradition can be discerned as an entity: a society with a parliamentary system modelled on Britain; the Rule of Law based on an independent judiciary; an 'uncorrupt public service'; freedom of speech and conscience; and a free press. Identified with the tradition are names such as De Villiers, Solomon, Sauer, Merriman, Rose Innes, and Hofmeyr (Onze Jan).

Liberals in South Africa have been largely preoccupied with race relations. They acknowledge that the essential breach in the 'Cape liberal tradition' was made when liberals succeeded in getting their non-racial franchise entrenched in the South Africa Act of 1909 but at the same time conceded that whites only should sit in Parliament. From 1910 a succession of laws prevented Africans from retaining freedom of movement, acquiring fixed property where they wished, obtaining certain types of work, and joining forces to protect their rights as workers. The bulk of this legislation was passed prior to 1948, when the National Party came to power. Liberals see racial legislation after 1948 as a continuation of the divisive process begun much earlier.

The struggle between liberals and what they perceive as a growing body of illiberal legislation has given rise to liberal parliamentary and extra-parliamentary associations. The Liberal and Progressive parties (and some of their offshoots) have championed the liberal cause. As we shall see, the African National Congress and Indian and coloured people have also espoused the liberal spirit. The Institute of Race Relations, the National Union of South African Students (NUSAS), the Civil Rights League, and the Defence and Aid Fund, are all carriers of liberalism, as was the Torch Commando, established when the franchise of the coloured people was threatened, and the Black Sash, which arose in protest against their ultimate disfranchisement. Other supporters of the principles of the liberal tradition include the English press, English-speaking churches, some Afrikaans churchmen, English universities and certain Afrikaans academics, members of the bar and side-bar, businessmen and industrialists. These proponents of the liberal approach are not merely negative in their stand against apartheid; they argue that liberalism is a viable alternative in our greatly divided society.

Liberals in Parliament

In white party political terms South Africa has never had a liberal government or a liberal prime minister. The closest it came to liberal leadership during the thirties and forties was when Jan Hofmeyr was either deputy or acting prime minister in the United Party (UP) cabinet. Efforts to persuade Hofmeyr to leave the United Party to form a liberal party failed and were finally dashed when the National Party ousted the United Party in 1948, the year of Hofmeyr's premature death.

During the fifties a new breed of young politicians came to the fore within the United Party to strengthen the liberal wing of the party, which in turn came into conflict with UP politicians on the right. Finally, in 1959 thirteen liberal UP members resigned to form the Progressive Party (PP) under Jan Steytler.

The PP was born in turbulent times and had considerable promise, having won the support of the UP's major financial backer Harry Oppenheimer, Smuts's former Minister of Justice, Harry Lawrence, and the English-language press. However in the 1961 election all but one of the Progressive Party seats were lost. Only Helen Suzman was left to represent liberal values in Parliament. In the 1966 election the Progressives did not fare much better although they did win a respectable share of the popular vote. The Party was in crisis in 1968 when the Prohibition of

Political Interference Act was passed prohibiting racially mixed political parties. It made the momentous decision not to disband but to continue to fight within the arena of white politics.

During the seventies the Progressives, under the leadership of Colin Eglin, gained six additional seats in Parliament. A merger with reformists in the United Party swelled the number of MPs to thirteen. Ultimately the party changed its name to the Progressive Federal Party (PFP). By 1977, the PFP had twenty-four seats. At the next election, under the new leadership of Van Zyl Slabbert, the PFP had twenty-seven seats and increased its share of the popular vote to 19 per cent — a quarter of a million whites voted essentially for a power sharing policy.

The Liberal Party

Formed in 1953, the Liberal Party's first leader was Margaret Ballinger, 'Native Representative' in Parliament. The party was committed to a non-racial franchise on a common voters' roll and to the abolition of the colour bar in all areas of South African society. The Liberal Party never won a white seat in Parliament although it had the support of the four white Native Representatives in Parliament.

During its existence it was plagued by internal dissension and failure at the polls. One of its most prominent members, Patrick Duncan, believed that its founders were 'without an adequate appreciation of the part that political power plays in politics'. It was rejected by the white electorate, came into conflict with the Congress of Democrats over the Freedom Charter, and it refused to endorse the Defiance and Resistance campaigns. As a multiracial party it could do no other than disband in the face of the Political Interference Act of 1968.

Liberalism and capitalism

Historically the economic system of free enterprise (capitalism) was enthusiastically advocated by classical European liberals. Even when that system underwent modifications, liberals did not jettison the principle of a free market for an omnicompetent state. They remained convinced that private ownership of property guarantees individual freedom, and that a market economy leads to greater prosperity for all. In the liberal world-view, freedom of thought, free enterprise, and man's capacity for progress toward the good society, are intimately linked and balanced.

Historically and theoretically the relationship between liberalism and capitalism in South Africa is complex and controversial. Some liberals draw a distinction between those whose principles are rooted in economic theory and those who are mainly concerned with human rights. Hilda Kuper, for example, argued that liberalism in South Africa has been concerned primarily with fighting racialism in a humanist spirit, that liberal policies have tended towards the welfare state, and denies that it was committed to liberal economic theory. Critics of liberalism argue that there is little evidence of a fundamental uneasiness on the part of liberals towards capitalism, and accuse liberals of failing to address the fundamental issue of the relationship between race, state, and capitalism in South Africa.

Liberals have generally tended to take the capitalist system for granted and have devoted their energies on the economic front to critiques of capitalist praxis. Indeed, they have often expressed the hope that the force of economic circumstances will ultimately bring down the apartheid edifice. While there seems to be no logical reason why racial discrimination should disappear within a free enterprise system, it is strongly argued that apartheid is inimical to economic growth, and that legal and customary apartheid inhibits the growth of the economy.

Established principles within their tradition have enabled liberals to criticise capitalist praxis. They have upheld the rights of workers and consumers to bargain collectively, irrespective of race. They have also advocated the granting of social services, since there are gross inequalities in the distribution of such services among different races in South Africa. Liberals have long protested against the dependence of the economy on migratory labour, drawing attention to the economic and human costs of this system.

In the early stages of South Africa's industrial revolution, the achievements of English-speaking white liberals were considerable. They were in the vanguard of industrialisation, urbanisation, and the development of capitalism. But liberal achievements were also controversial. Afrikaner nationalists, for example, soon equated 'Englishness' with those things which most threatened their identity — imperialism, capitalism, and egalitarian liberalism.

Liberalism and the Afrikaner

The obvious commonalty which welded Afrikaners into a self-conscious community hinges on a 'corporate ethic', which is in stark contrast to the 'individual ethic' of liberals. Historically liberals have given scant attention to group identity. They tended to look down on the Afrikaners' efforts to establish and maintain their language and culture, and adopted an attitude of benign superiority towards all who did not share English ideals. Even Olive Schreiner wrote of the day when no 'boer' would speak 'the *taal*, save as a curiosity; only a great English-speaking South African people' would emerge. In fact, if African nationalism can be seen as a response to Afrikaner nationalism, Afrikaner nationalism can be seen as a response to the ideology of English superiority.

Liberals see the implementation of apartheid policy as a sustained attack on their tradition. The controversy springs in part from the different ethics of liberals and Afrikaner nationalists, but also from a semantic misunderstanding. In the late nineteenth century the Dutch and Afrikaans word *liberaal* referred to 'latitudinarians' within the Anglican communion who tolerated free thought on dogmatic truth and ecclesiastical organisation. This movement spread to Holland, where Dutch Reformed ministers were exposed to *liberale*. This is the context in which *liberaal* was translated into English as 'liberal'. Liberalism was thus equated with a form of unbelief, a denial of orthodox (that is, Calvinist, according to the Council of Dort) christian belief. The controversy between *liberale* and orthodoxy within the Dutch Reformed Church may have given the liberal tradition, as understood in this chapter, a negative meaning among Afrikaners to this day. Liberals, of course, come from many religious persuasions, and some have none. But they would reject the imputation that liberalism represents an unbridled permissiveness and lack of principle. On the contrary, their conflict with Afrikaner nationalism is seen by them as a clash of ideologies, the outcome of which will determine the future of South Africa.

Liberalism and black politics

The Cape liberal tradition exercised a profound influence on black politics for decades, well into the twentieth century. In the vanguard of black politics were the new elites, educated in church mission schools, and often trained in Europe and the United States. They espoused christian values such as the brotherhood of man based on the fatherhood of God; they recognised the economic interdependence of the races in this country; they witnessed the successes of civil rights movements such as the National Association for the Advancement of Coloured People in the United States; and shared the aspirations of those who desired western values and advantages for Africa.

Until 1912 African nationalism lacked a national organisational base. That year saw the formation of the South African Native National Congress (later renamed the African National Congress), largely as a response to the Union of 1910 and the increasing flow of discriminatory legislation that issued from the new parliament. Its leader was Rev. John Dube, who thus began a long tradition of involvement on the part of church leaders in the Congress.

Until the 1950s the efforts of the African National Congress, the South African Indian Congress and the South African Coloured People's Organisation towards social change were based largely on liberal principles. Even the Freedom Charter of 1955 reaffirmed fundamental liberal goals, though its economic policy did contain new elements — the deliberate redistribution of wealth and land, and state responsibility for key industries.

Within the ANC there had always been a commitment to the use of legal, non-violent means for change. But in the period after World War Two when protest was curtailed, there was an ideological shift away from this eminently liberal approach. The Congress Youth League and later the Pan-Africanist Congress were to concern themselves with disciplined organisation for extra-constitutional change, and the need to work for psychological emancipation and black self-confidence. However, after Sharpeville (1960) the ANC and the PAC were declared illegal organisations and went underground.

African nationalism lives on in the Black Consciousness Movement, which emerged in the late 1960s, and also influenced or gave birth to such organisations as the South African Students' Organisation (SASO), the Black People's Convention (BPC), Black Community Programmes (BCP), and the Interdenominational African Ministers' Association of South Africa, all of which excepting the last were declared 'unlawful' organisations in October 1977.

Since its inception black consciousness has mounted a sustained attack on (white) liberalism. This was dramatically illustrated in the breakaway of SASO from the multiracial student organisation, NUSAS, in 1970. In essence the argument against white liberalism is that in a non-racial, non-exploitative, egalitarian society black consciousness would be irrelevant. But in South Africa racism is institutionalised, and the economy exploits blacks, so that in the face of strong white racism (including that of liberals) there must be solidarity among blacks. They reject the liberal view that what is required to oppose apartheid is the formation of non-racial groups. White liberal efforts to alleviate black oppression, it is said, are counterproductive; in fact they sugar the bitter pill of apartheid and obscure the real fact of black–white polarisation which exists in South Africa. Efforts to form non-racial alignments in effect divert black energies from the prime task of 'politicisation of blacks by blacks'. On the economic front black consciousness has opted for 'black communalism', akin to African socialism in Tanzania. The ultimate goal is to break down capitalism in South Africa by instituting state control of the economy but without abolishing all private ownership of property.

Liberalism and the church

The church struggle

Historically, European liberalism may be traced on the one hand to Voltaire and Rousseau. This tradition saw Christianity as a divisive influence in the state, and was generally antagonistic to organised religion. Indeed, Rousseau was the 'father' of a civil religion, the dogmas of which were to be fixed by the sovereign in order to sanctify society's laws. On the other hand, there is the English liberal tradition, which extends back to John Locke — one not incompatible with religious belief, but in the vanguard of Enlightenment humanism, and championing Deism, with its emphasis on the primacy of reason over revelation, and its conception of a God aloof from human affairs.

It is not difficult to understand how European liberalism came to be associated in South Africa with anti-religious humanism, liberal biblical criticism, and rational theology — especially in the context of the Enlightenment philosophy, with its conception of man as the controller of his own destiny, and its utopian ideals of tolerance, justice, and material welfare.

In fact, both the Anglican and Dutch Reformed Churches in South Africa were rocked in the 1860s by doctrinal controversies which had their roots in Europe. The Anglican crisis was precipitated by Bishop Colenso, who introduced biblical criticism to the sub-continent, championed social justice for blacks, outlined an 'enlightened' missionary policy, and was the centre of a heated controversy concerning the 'establishment' of the Anglican Church in South Africa. The crisis in the Dutch Reformed Churches concerned the equivalent issues of Erastianism and 'liberal' theology. The Cape Church imposed a test of orthodoxy on ministers imported from Europe, and in several heresy trials, orthodoxy won the day in church courts, only to receive reversals in civil courts. Liberalism came to be associated in this way with the odium of heresy and secular interference in doctrinal matters. As Hinchliff shows, a by-product of the controversies which shook the Anglican and Dutch Reformed Churches was the suggestion about 1870 of a union between these churches in the colony — one which came to nothing, although it is interesting to conjecture what effect this could have had on subsequent South African history. The long-standing tensions and differences of perspective between 'English-speaking' churches and the Dutch Reformed Church in South Africa were shown to be irreconcilable after Cottesloe and the Message to the People of South Africa in the 1960s.

Colonial missionary policy

The influence of Christianity in Africa is today a controversial issue. In some eyes missionaries were agents of imperialism, even racism. It was common in the nineteenth century for missionaries, administrators, and philanthropists in England — home of a vast empire of 500 million, spanning a large part of the globe — to view their culture as the pinnacle of man's achievements. Wilberforce, for example, when speaking of the colonies ascribed their acquisition to 'our religious and moral superiority'. Robert Moffat after twenty years among the Tswana could not bring himself to believe they had any real religious apprehension. Such attitudes reflected a universal pride in Anglo–Saxon culture, which elevated the European to the top of the evolutionary ladder.

Some would argue that this sense of superiority on the part of the English was not racial, although there is convincing evidence to the contrary. Such feelings of superiority were no doubt reinforced by the fact that when the English came to South Africa racial stereotypes already existed, and racial domination by whites was already established.

The missionary was a child of the time and imbibed the superior and paternalistic attitudes of his culture. Western civilisation seemed so demonstrably superior in its technology, industry, literacy, political institutions, and weapons. In addition the missionary saw himself as a messenger of truth, and found it difficult to distinguish between cultural imperialism and the proclamation of the gospel.

The upper classes of Europe felt themselves called to govern and to spread 'civilisation', and this is reflected in the attitudes of the European-based missionary societies and their policies abroad. The colonial church was paternalistic, showed deference to civil authority, and used its influence to advance the cause of the colonial government.

But English-speaking churches in South Africa never quite forgot their prophetic role, especially in the cause of the disadvantaged. This was true of the Scottish missions and the London Missionary Society. The LMS, through men like Van der Kemp, Philip, and Livingstone, reflected the European nonconformist tradition in its struggle for the rights of indigenous people, and earned the opprobrium of the Afrikaner as liberal clerics. Anglicans like Colenso, and Methodists in the eastern Cape and Transvaal, also sought to combine evangelisation with a prophetic role in society.

Even the sharpest critics of the colonial church would not wish to underrate the labours of the missionary in education, medicine, and evangelism. The record speaks for itself. But from a black perspective missionaries 'consciously or unconsciously sought to Europeanise us before they would Christianise us. They have consequently jeopardised the entire Christian enterprise since . . . they have tended to make us feel somewhat uneasy and guilty about what we could not alter . . . — *our Africanness*' (Bishop Tutu). Institutions such as Lovedale and Zonnebloem created syllabi with the express intention of making the scholar a replica of his English or Scottish counterpart. In effect, however, this educational policy appears to have had little detrimental long-term effect, save that syllabi still tend to be western in orientation — a legacy which even theological seminaries have only recently begun to correct.

Perhaps the most serious legacy of the Europeanising tendency has been the spectacular rise of independent churches, which can partly be explained by the ethnocentrism of the early missionaries. Using the customary distinction between Ethiopian and Zionist independent churches, we can regard the former as a response to the political and ecclesiastical frustration experienced by blacks. The historical churches generally showed a reluctance to ordain and give leadership to blacks, because representation was often weighted in the favour of whites despite majority black membership. The rise of Zionism, on the other hand, can be seen as a response to missionary determination to stamp out African culture, especially important aspects of that culture such as polygamy and the ancestor cult. The failure to provide scope for the emergence of a truly indigenous Christianity is evidence of the paternalism of the church, whatever one may feel about whether the independent churches hold any such promise themselves.

A future for liberalism in South Africa?

To label liberalism an ideology is an affront to liberals, for whom individual liberty is a fundamental category, and an affront as well to christians, who believe the church can have no part in ideology. But is liberalism an ideology? Black consciousness would argue that it is because it belongs to the wider ideology of oppressive white racism. Radicals argue that both liberalism and apartheid, because they are ideologies of interest groups, have common features, the most important of which is their support of a capitalism resting on the exploitation of black labour. Moreover, liberals purport to fight for the freedom of individuals, but having achieved a measure of freedom they become conservative supporters of the status quo. Liberal failure to give due weight to class and ethnicity, understood in terms of Marxist sociology, is further evidence for radicals of its ideological character. Afrikaner nationalism views liberalism as naive, because it fails to take account of the complex, ethnically plural character of South African society, and as ideological, because of its attitude of superiority towards anything which is not English.

Ironically, avowed opponents of liberalism do not wish to see the positive fruits of the liberal tradition perish. They would wish to ensure that its traditions of tolerance, inclusion, individual freedoms, and protection of minorities, are incorporated into a future South Africa.

The real bone of contention is liberalism's insistence that the individual is the basic unit of social analysis; its refusal to give proper weight to the interests and aspirations of groups in a multiracial, pluralistic society. For liberals have long held that the tradition of individual liberty does not have to be cut according to the multiracial and culturally diverse cloth of South Africa.

There is evidence from within the tradition that liberalism is undergoing change. John Rawls's *A Theory of Justice* is an important recent attempt at a reconstruction of general theory, but it ought to be read in conjunction with Vernon van Dyk's attempt to apply it to groups.

An early liberal attempt in South Africa toward a recognition of groups was Alfred Hoernlé's work, *South African Native Policy and the Liberal Spirit* (1939), although it was repudiated by fellow liberals. Recently there have been attempts to take up Hoernlé's challenge. Notable among these are the SPRO-CAS Report of the Political Commission, and works by David Welsh, Johannes Degenaar, and others. We may expect further contributions in this vein from within the broad liberal tradition in the search for political alternatives in South Africa.

An unconcluding theological post-script

We are aware that some of South Africa's greatest sons and daughters — black and white, English and Afrikaans — have been christian *and* liberal. It may seem invidious to some therefore to raise questions about the relationship between Christianity and liberalism. But if our history is anything to go by the matter is far from simple, since christians have found elements within the liberal tradition untenable just as many liberals have found Christianity untenable.

Even if we are able to avoid the debate about whether Christianity can ever be involved with ideology as such, do we not still have to evaluate the theory and praxis of liberalism theologically? The heart of liberalism is the assumption that the individual is the basic unit of society, whose liberty is his greatest endowment. In the interests of a relevant theology for southern Africa it is important for the church to make a critical evaluation of certain basic assumptions of the liberal mind. While we can do no more than offer a schematic treatment in the space available, we believe the liberal assumptions most urgently requiring attention are its atomistic model of society, and its view of man's essence as freedom, with its consequent progressive view of history.

(a) Is the liberal model of society as a market place in which each individual competes equally, without regard to race, colour, language, or creed, really appropriate for a society characterised by extreme pluralism? A plural society is marked by the existence, side by side, of groups which are distinguished by relatively fixed qualities (for example, race and language), or fundamentally important beliefs and attitudes (for example, religion and nationalism), or by factors largely shaped by economics (for example, wealth, power and prestige). The quest for justice in a plural society must surely involve an ongoing search for more equitable balances of power between groups whose legitimate aspirations are in competition and sometimes in conflict one with another. While traditional liberal-democratic devices for ensuring the protection of minorities may go some way towards securing justice for groups, one suspects that they are nevertheless based on an unreconstructed atomistic model of society. The dilemma of secular and religious liberals in South Africa is that they believe it is hazardous to modify this model of society by according the right of self-determination to groups without appearing to endorse apartheid.

For christians the dilemma is also theological. How can we balance the unity of all men in Christ while at the same time recognising the real diversity of groups and cultures? Is it possible to give a political face to such diversity without appearing to condone apartheid?

(b) The view that man is radically free does not reflect very well the christian estimate of man. That tradition affirms the transcendence of God and the secularity of the world. Man realises his destiny by entering into a covenant with God in fulfilment of his purposes — a covenant which may be both individual and corporate. Man's freedom is circumscribed by that covenanted relationship with God in Christ. He is free to obey or disobey, to be responsible or apathetic, but he is not radically free.

By according dignity to the culturally diverse groups of South African society we will not, however, arrive automatically at a just society. This leads to our second theological difficulty with the liberal estimate of man. To speak of man's essence as dignity is to affirm that history has a destiny which man can realise, without denying the moral ambiguities of history symbolised in the Hebrew–Christian tradition as the fallenness of man. To say, as liberals do, that man is able to respond to appeals of reason, imagination, and social feeling is only one side of the picture. The other is the recognition that men do sin; that individuals and groups are prone to the sins of pride and lust for power, from which tyranny and injustice stem. A christian social ethic cannot afford to divorce *imago dei* and fallenness in its quest for justice in a pluralistic society, though it may want to give a more dynamic interpretation to fallenness than tradition has usually done. Must it not strive to balance the rights of individuals against those of the whole, the rights of one group against the interests of other groups, if it is to approximate a society in which power is shared?

5 Afrikaner nationalism as ideology

Afrikaner nationalism is a product of South Africa's complex history, and the force which mobilised the resources of 'Afrikanerdom' to fight the perceived challenges of British imperialism and a black majority in South Africa. It is the ideology of the Nationalist regime which has ruled South Africa for nearly forty years. For as long as this regime remains in power, therefore, the racial policies and ideological cast of Afrikaner nationalism will be the focus of the patterns of conflict and change in the entire southern African region.

It has become fashionable to speak of the 'rise and crisis of Afrikanerdom', the implication being that, at least since the 1970s, the regime has no longer been wedded to Afrikaner nationalism in its traditional form, that it has undergone significant 'reformist' changes and shed its extremist right wing. Others argue that the words may have changed but for all practical purposes the tune is the same — white domination over the black majority. As a phenomenon, Afrikaner nationalism has generated a vast amount of scholarly literature, and evokes emotionally charged public debate in South Africa and abroad. Overseas criticism and internal strife continue to escalate even as gradualist reformist policies are being implemented.

There have been many attempts to explain Afrikaner nationalism. These attempts can be grouped into four basic perspectives, which focus on the religious quality of Afrikaner nationalism; the analogy of the national security state; race and class; and ethnic mobilisation. Few would argue that any one of these perspectives is sufficient in itself to explain Afrikaner nationalism, though some would appear to have greater explanatory power than others. The following analysis of the different perspectives draws heavily on the work of Heribert Adam.

B. J. Vorster, prime minister of South Africa from 1966 to 1978, captured the *religious quality of Afrikaner nationalism* when he stated in 1977: 'Yes, I believe profoundly . . . that we [Afrikaners] have been appointed by Providence to play a role here [in South Africa], and that we have the human material to play that role.' As an explanation of

Afrikaner nationalism this perspective argues that a primitive or neo-Calvinist theology, developed in the harsh conditions of frontier existence, helped Afrikaners to shape an Old Testament vision of their role as a 'chosen people' with a 'manifest destiny' on the tip of the African continent. Jan Loubser, for example, speaks of the 'fundamentalist faith system' which helped Afrikaners to cope with their 'existential anxiety', caused by a large threatening black indigenous population and the fear of being swamped by British 'anglicisation' policies. W. A. de Klerk's popular book *The Puritans in Africa* argues that 'the key to the Afrikaner is Calvinism'. Other writers, notably T. Dunbar Moodie in *The Rise of Afrikanerdom*, believe that the driving force of Afrikanerdom was a 'theologised nationalism' or 'civil religion' which held that God had 'called' the Afrikaner as an 'elect' *volk* (nation) with a distinctive language, culture and history, to be His agent in southern Africa.

Some critical literature on Afrikaner nationalism adopts *the analogy of the national security state*, drawn from fascist Germany or more recently from regimes in Latin America, to explain the South African system. For example, the Seidmans in *South Africa and U. S. Multinational Corporations* argue typically: 'Over time, the white settlers in South Africa, particularly the more wealthy and powerful Afrikaner elements, succeeded in welding the majority of whites behind a powerful political movement built around the chauvinist ideology of white supremacy and centred in the Nationalist Party.' Through the use of state capitalism, 'the resulting system constituted fascism of a classic type'. In this perspective recent reformist measures of the South African regime are seen as 'the politics of survival of a powerful minority which has successfully co-opted non-Afrikaner whites, coloureds, and Asians'.

Institutionalised racism pervades South Africa's history and policies. The roots of segregation based on race go back a long way. But it was the legislative blitzkrieg that followed the National Party's accession to power in 1948 that entrenched apartheid — Afrikaner nationalism's policy of separation based on race.

Many commentators and critics make race the key category for explaining the rise to power of Afrikaner nationalism. Martin Legassick and Duncan Innes provide a classic Marxist explanation of racism in South Africa:

From its inception [apartheid] has operated simultaneously as an expression of the domination of capital in South Africa and as an expression concerned to reproduce (in changing forms) separate 'racial' and 'cultural' identities. Its real effects, as institutionalised through state policy, are to perpetrate oppression, uneven development, and exploitation inherent in capitalist relationships: its ideological functions are to present these realities as forms of 'racial' or 'cultural' conflict . . . 'solved' by varying modes of separation.

Non-Marxists have frequently drawn attention to the institutionalised racism which pervades South African history and policy, and which has given rise to inequalities in life chances and opportunities for those who are not white. The rigid system of stratification based on race that has always characterised South African society was given additional impetus with the structural entrenchment of racial segregation after 1948. Inherited biological distinctions based, in South Africa's case, on race, have given rise to different theories of racial antagonism to explain the ascendancy of the white group, and particularly Afrikanerdom.

The theories range from colour as constituting an independent cause, to racism as a device for breaking up working-class unity in the interests of capitalist expansion. Ascribing superior or inferior status to a group on the basis of such biological factors as race or gender has, of course, been a feature of social reality everywhere. The problem with explanations based on race is why race has the potency it does in societies like South Africa. Racialism as a category does not explain the caste-like qualities of classical apartheid.

Heribert Adam and Hermann Giliomee prefer *ethnic mobilisation* as 'the key for an appropriate understanding of contemporary white South African politics'. Ethnic mobilisation is seen as a process whereby the interests of a particular group are welded into a common cause, in terms of which its adherents can be mobilised to sacrifice, to act together, to believe in a better future. All this is in the name of a 'common bond (language, religion, race, ancestry, sex). . . . Groups mobilised in this fashion represent powerful collective actors, as the history of nationalism has proved everywhere.' Given the volatile political and economic history of the Afrikaner, ethnicity has been the engine of group mobilisation, and Afrikaner nationalism the name of the group's ideology.

Readers should draw their own conclusions about the explanatory power of these perspectives. The main focus of this chapter is to chart the rise of Afrikaner nationalism as the dominant ideology in South Africa, its content and mobilising appeal as a cause and as a consequence of Afrikaner ascendancy. Attention will also be given to the shift in the 1970s from the classical ideology of 'grand apartheid' to strategies of power politics usually expressed in the phrase 'reformist politics'. Critiques of Afrikaner nationalism from other ideological perspectives will conclude the chapter.

The rise of Afrikanerdom: an historical overview

The ideology and policies of Afrikaner nationalism are better understood viewed in historical perspective. For example, while Afrikaner nationalism did not invent ethnicity and racism in South Africa, it has gone further than the ideology of any other ruling group in making them ordering principles for a policy which distributes power, wealth, and privilege unequally on the basis of race and ethnicity. But this in turn is a product of the Afrikaner group's self-image, first as an embattled minority and later as the ruling group.

Settlement and the frontier

The Europeans who settled in the Cape after 1652 came from several countries. Dutch was their official language, Protestant Christianity their religion. They were white cultural chauvinists, like settler groups in other parts of the New World, and considered the indigenous people of the Cape to be 'heathens' and 'barbarians'. The burghers, ancestors of present-day Afrikaners, occupied the top rungs of a social hierarchy with Khoikhoi and slaves at the bottom. Virtually all the rich and privileged were white landowners or tenant farmers who did no manual labour themselves. 'Every man is a burgher by rank and a farmer by occupation', remarked an early nineteenth century traveller.

The white colonists who came to the Cape after 1652 considered themselves superior to indigenous people on grounds of their Christianity and civilisation. The doyen of Afrikaner nationalist historians, F. A. van Jaarsveld, asks:

Where then did the current conceptions of white superiority and resistance to equalization and blood admixture arise? . . . We know that from the beginning of the settlement 'Christian' and 'heathen' were distinguished from one another. During the second half of the eighteenth century there was an increasing tendency for the use of these terms synonymously with 'white' and 'coloured'. . . . In 1830 we read of *'Christen en beschaafde Natien'* (Christian and civilised peoples, that is, white) as opposed to *'Heidensche Volken zoo als de Hottentotten, de Kaffirs, enz.'* (heathen peoples such as Hottentots, Kaffirs, etc). 'Civilised' and 'uncivilised' thus became terms associated with whites and coloureds respectively.

The settler mentality, according to Van Jaarsveld, was a product of various factors: 'Physical detachment from their mother country, isolation in the interior, social and economic factors, influences such as the Calvinist heritage and the Old Testament went into the moulding of the Afrikaner.'

Evidence for this moulding can be discerned as early as 1803. Governor Janssens, for example, said of whites on the eastern frontier, 'they call themselves people and Christians, and the Kaffirs and Hottentots heathens'. In the same year Landdrost Alberti of Uitenhage noted that colonists could not be persuaded that the Khoikhoi should be given equal protection in law because they were heathen and therefore not truly human. Indeed, the Great Trek of the 1830s was precipitated largely by the issues of *gelykstelling* and the emancipation of slaves. *Gelykstelling* (equalisation) of Khoikhoi before the law in terms of Ordinance 50 of 1828 was listed by Anna Steenkamp as a cause of the Great Trek because it was 'in conflict with the laws of God and with natural distinctions of origin and belief'. To these issues must be added the growing insecurity of white colonists as Khoikhoi and Xhosa raids on their cattle escalated. Law and order was breaking down. But the 'main objection of the new [British] dispensation was the equalisation of coloured people with white' (Karel Trichardt). This conception of a group identity separate from and superior to non-whites was to be entrenched by the Voor-trekker settlements in the constitutions of the Free State and Transvaal. In these republics racial and ethnic cleavages were emphasised by the colonists' conception of themselves in Old Testament terms as 'chosen ones' who, like the people of Israel, were forbidden to mix with Canaan-ites (sons of Ham).

The rise of Afrikaner nationalist consciousness

In the eighteenth century colonists lost their sense of identity with the Netherlands and became a 'fragment culture'. By this we mean a culture in which consensus is heightened by gradual disengagement from Europe, and by participation in conflicts not experienced in Europe, such as the frontier conflicts with the indigenous black population. By the same token the Afrikaner 'fragment culture' was not significantly influenced by such historical processes as the Enlightenment which the Afrikaners' European counterparts were experiencing. Afrikaners devel-oped a national identity as a substitute for the European identity they were losing. 'The process of becoming indigenous or Africanised found expression in the term "Afrikaner", by which the colonists came to call themselves' (Giliomee). This term was first used, somewhat am-biguously, about 1707.

The shaping of a distinct Afrikaans-speaking group was not purely the result of interaction with blacks. Equally important was the impact of British rule. The British attempt to anglicise local political and social institutions met opposition in a growing Afrikaner identity, and hastened the process of national consciousness already evident in a distinctive spoken language, a common religious faith, and a shared historical past. 'Whereas slavery and settlement stimulated a racial consciousness, the Afrikaner clash with British imperialism brought the concept of a distinct white political entity to the fore' (Giliomee).

A major figure in the development of a national consciousness was

S. J. du Toit. He was a prime mover in the first Afrikaans language movement; author of the first Afrikaner nationalist version of South African history; founder of the Afrikaner *Bond*, the first political movement; protagonist of a neo-Calvinist interpretation of South African history and politics; and close ally of Paul Kruger. Du Toit defined the Afrikaner exclusively as someone of Dutch or Huguenot descent who spoke neither Dutch nor English but Afrikaans. By contrast J. H. Hofmeyr, co-founder of the Afrikaner *Bond*, defined the Afrikaner inclusively: descent did not matter, nor did language, and the term referred to anyone settled in the subcontinent and willing to work for the common good. Hofmeyr's view prevailed in the constitution of the Afrikaner *Bond*, which embarked on a policy of cooperation between English- and Afrikaans-speaking whites, though blacks were excluded from its membership.

At the turn of this century, the Anglo–Boer War and resistance to Lord Milner's aggressive policy of anglicisation further strengthened Afrikaner nationalism and gave sharper focus to the idea of 'Africa for the Afrikaner'. Suffering had now added a new dimension to Afrikaner nationalism.

The Anglo–Boer War resulted in bitter differences between the Afrikaners and the English. But these were to become muted with the advent of the Union of South Africa as part of the British Commonwealth, the rapid urbanisation of Afrikaners in the early twentieth century, and the political rule of the South African Party and later the United Party. In fact, General Smuts and General Botha adopted a deliberate strategy of compromise to deal with the potentially explosive language issue. Afrikaner nationalists like Hertzog and Malan, however, rejected this. They believed this compromise was at the expense of Afrikaner cultural identity, and opted for a policy of separatism until such time as Afrikaner political and economic power equalled that of the English. The Afrikaans language was to be used as a mobilising force to overcome the psychological alienation and economic disadvantage felt by Afrikaners — an outward and visible sign of their identity.

By the late 1930s Malan's Purified National Party had succeeded in rallying most younger Afrikaner intellectuals to its cause. Through the *Broederbond* a distinctive Afrikaner ideology, identity and sense of history emerged, with the notion of an exclusive *volk* that could be roused to self-upliftment. Symbolic of the power of Afrikaner nationalism was the *ossewatrek* of 1938 which demarcated the Afrikaner domain from the Cape to Transvaal as ox wagons retraced the history of the Great Trek, and climaxed in a *volksbyeenkoms* held at the Voortrekker Monument in Pretoria in 1939.

The Afrikaner cultural and business elite embarked on a strategy of ethnic mobilisation to improve the economic position of the Afrikaner. *Volkskapitalisme* was the name of the economic policy pursued in order to rescue 300 000 poor whites in a *reddingsdaad* and 'mobilise the *volk* to conquer the capitalist system' and 'transform it so that it fits our ethnic nature'. In addition Afrikaner workers had begun to organise themselves in trade unions to promote their interests against the (largely English) owners of capital.

The *Broederbond* spread the doctrine of Christian Nationalism. It adapted Dutch theologian Abraham Kuyper's doctrine of 'sovereignty in one's own sphere', and held that each nation had a separate identity accorded by divine will. This doctrine was translated into a policy of Christian National education, which greatly influenced Afrikaner educational institutions.

In 1948 the National Party won exclusive political power in South Africa. This victory was testimony to the unity of Afrikaners, although the party was critically dependent on a few parliamentary seats held by Hertzog's followers. One commentator summed up the essence of the victory thus: 'Apart from "putting the Kaffir in his place", 1948 also meant to the Afrikaners — particularly the professionals, educators and civil servants — "getting *our* country back" or "feeling at home once again in *our* country".' *Volkseenheid* (unity of the people) and *volksverbondenheid* (self-realisation through service of the people) had won the day.

The apparatus of apartheid

The National Party did not invent racial segregation in 1948. The roots of segregation in fact reach deep into the soil of South African history. But after 1948 as Afrikaner nationalism was consolidated, a vast apparatus of laws, regulations, and bureaucracies was created to reinforce Afrikaner ethnic unity and promote Afrikaner interests. Apartheid was racist in that it acted against miscegenation through the Mixed Marriages Act (1949) and the Immorality Act (1950). The Population Registration Act (1950), the Reservation of Separate Amenities Act (1953) and the Group Areas Act (1950) were passed to ensure the separation of races in the 'common area' of South Africa. Later, coloureds were removed from the voters' roll so as to prevent a coalition of coloured and English-speaking white voters.

Afrikaner nationalists do not generally subscribe to the view of the United States Supreme Court that 'separate means unequal'. Granting that separation can lead to inequities in the allocation of resources, Afrikaner nationalists do not believe that ethnically or racially separated schools and group areas are unjust. They project their own desire for separation and ethnic identity onto others and regard these policies as a logical extension of their own history and experience.

The homelands policy represents Afrikaner nationalism's attempt to ensure 'self-determination for *all* the peoples' of South Africa. It is presented as a way of giving self-government to black (African) 'nations', in order that each population group can eventually make its own choice regarding its political future. Ten homelands (or self-governing black states) have thus far been designated. Of these, four are independent: Transkei, Bophuthatswana, Venda and Ciskei. Four are 'self-governing': Lebowa, Gazankulu, Qwaqwa and KwaZulu. Two are still in the formative process: Kangwane and KwaNdebele. Among the most intractable conflicts arising from the 'homelands' policy are those that concern the economic viability of the homelands and those surrounding citizenship, for on 'independence' citizens of a 'homeland' have lost their South African citizenship.

South Africa's political system excludes blacks from any significant role in the central political process. Parliament was, until 1985, composed of whites elected by whites. The President's Council, formed in 1980, was charged with developing a new constitution. But the Council excluded blacks, and its Asian and coloured members were nominated, not elected. Subsequently a new constitution for the Republic was passed by Parliament in 1983. It gives coloureds and Indians a form of parliamentary representation, but still excludes Africans.

Africans were not always excluded from the franchise. Before 1910 the Cape Colony had a qualified franchise for coloured males and some Africans. In 1936 Africans were removed from the common voters' roll and placed on a separate roll, entitling them to elect seven white representatives to Parliament. In 1956 coloured males were placed on a separate roll and entitled to elect four white representatives. But in the 1960s they, too, were removed from the roll, and the elimination of all blacks from the central political process was completed. To defuse black discontent various types of councils were created, such as the Urban Bantu Councils for Africans, and the Coloured Persons' Representative Council (CRC). But they have failed to satisfy those they were created to serve. Effectively, Africans have no political representation, save in the 'homelands'. African freedom of movement has from the nineteenth century been restricted, and is now controlled by means of the Black Abolition of Passes and Coordination of Documents Act (1952), which requires African men and women to possess a 'reference book'. This Act, as well as the Black Urban Areas Consolidation Act (1945) and Black Labour Act (1964) (all variously amended), has effectively controlled the movement of blacks in and out of 'white cities'.

Two key laws, the Internal Security Act and the Terrorism Act (variously amended), as well as the Sabotage Act (1962), enable the South African government to silence almost anyone whom it considers a threat by means of detention without trial or by banning.

Afrikaner economic advance

A complex relationship exists between the ethnic mobilisation of a group, access to political power, and the economic fortunes of that group. Giliomee sums up the process this way: 'By 1974 the Afrikaners had risen from a poor, underdeveloped population group to a prosperous bourgeoisie.'

In the period 1910–24 Afrikaners mobilised economic resources — a publishing house, Nasionale Pers, was founded to print the first nationalist newspaper, *Die Burger*. Two insurance companies, Santam and Sanlam, were formed, as well as the KWV cooperative, and AVBOB — a burial society. In labour terms Afrikaners constituted the majority of the strikers in the gold miners' strike of 1922.

Giliomee highlights important developments in the period 1924–48. Afrikaners experienced rapid urbanisation. Depression and drought in the 1930s adversely affected the fortunes of Afrikaner workers and farmers. The Afrikaner cultural and business elite rallied to address the 'poor white' (mainly Afrikaners) problem, and to rescue 300 000 whites from the plight of poverty. By 1939 Afrikaner organisations were using the tool of *volkskapitalisme* to 'mobilise the *volk* to conquer the capitalist system and to transform it so that it fits our ethnic nature' (C. J. du Plessis). Trade unions were formed to enhance the Afrikaner workers' bargaining position against English capital. During the 1940s mobilisation focused on access to political power. The National Party succeeded in the 1943 elections in projecting itself as the sole representative of Afrikaner nationalist interests — a policy which gave it success at the polls in 1948.

The post-1948 period saw a dramatic improvement in Afrikaner economic status. They dominated skilled positions and the civil service. State funds were used to improve agriculture. Public and parastatal corporations were used to promote Afrikaner economic progress. A period of state capitalism ensued with a dramatic growth in the public sector's share of the economy. A number of Afrikaans businesses and associations were created to compete in the market place. A new breed of Afrikaner entrepreneur played a key role in the Afrikaner economic advance, such as Andreas Wassenaar (Sanlam), Jan Marais (Trust Bank), and Anton Rupert (Rembrandt).

Afrikaner economic advance has been achieved by a combination of ethnic mobilisation, accession to political power, and the use of the state to intervene on behalf of white and, particularly, Afrikaner interests. Today the state's role in the economy is very great and its policies have benefited private-sector interest groups such as businessmen, farmers, and white-collar workers. 'The state has been a major support of the Afrikaners' advance to prosperity' (Giliomee).

The achievements of *volkskapitalisme* have recently been critically interpreted from a neo-Marxist stance in Dan O'Meara's controversial *Volkskapitalisme: Class, capital and ideology in the development of Afrikaner nationalism, 1934–1948*. He argues that Afrikaner nationalism in the period 1934–48 was utilised for class interests in that Afrikaner capital was mobilised by the petty-bourgeois Afrikaner *Broederbond*. The *Broederbond*'s Afrikaner nationalism, therefore, had an economic basis, and, by extension, the Afrikaner capitalist class is dominant in Nationalist politics to this day. This thesis, it can be argued, tends to conflate Afrikaner political and economic concerns, tends even to be reductionist by explaining Afrikaner nationalism primarily in economic terms. But it does have the merit of highlighting the economic interests of Afrikaner nationalism — a fact often omitted in analysis.

Afrikaner nationalism has achieved unequalled power in South Africa. Later we shall examine some recent shifts in emphasis as it seeks to re-define its core, non-negotiable position in the face of mounting internal and external opposition. But first, what are the essential ingredients of the ideology?

Ingredients of the ideology

Any attempt to describe the essential ingredients of Afrikaner national-ism presents certain difficulties. Firstly, primary sources remain largely hidden, and what has been written on Afrikaner nationalism is from the bias of liberal, radical or Afrikaner nationalist perspectives. Secondly, there are and always have been tensions amongst Afrikaner nationalists themselves. To speak of the ingredients of Afrikaner nationalism is to infer that it is a static monolith. It is not. But if there is no essence there are family traits which can be identified, just as it is possible to describe the hallmarks of, say, liberalism in South Africa.

Johannes Degenaar's analysis of Afrikaner nationalism is pertinent:

Afrikaners are white South Africans whose mother tongue is Afrikaans. Nationalism is a belief system which gives priority to a people's striving towards self-determi-nation, the highest political loyalty of the citizen being due to the nation (nation state); ideology is a group's belief system which functions . . . [as a reflection of] the interests of that group.

To describe the main ingredients of an ideological system in process, such as Afrikaner nationalism, is a complex task. One needs to be aware of the historical, socio-economic and political events which form its context. This we have sought to do in our overview. The influential intellectual sources need to be identified, of which at least three have been pinpointed: pietism or the reformed evangelicalism of such formative religious leaders as the Murrays; the neo-Calvinism of Kuyper in the Netherlands; and the political philosophy of Fichtean nationalism in Germany. An analysis of these sources lies outside the scope of this book: the interested reader will find references in the bibliography.

One needs to be aware that no ideology can survive without its institutional 'carriers' such as the *Broederbond*, Christian National education, and the National Party itself. One also needs to be aware that an ideology such as Afrikaner nationalism undergoes shifts and even fundamental changes in response to the fluctuating fortunes of Afrikanerdom. Our task here is to identify and understand the themes which have been central to Afrikaner nationalism over time. According to Degenaar, these have been: self-determination, *volk*, race, structure and power. When attempting to understand these themes it should be borne in mind that each has undergone changes.

Self-determination

Nationalism can be understood as the idea that a group or a people have a right to strive for or to maintain a position of independence in relation to other groups or peoples. The positive aspects of self-determination in this sense locate political authority in the people, inspire them to liberate themselves from subjugation, give individuals a feeling of belonging, and overcome sectional interests. Evidence of Afrikaner nationalism as self-determination can be drawn from the earliest times to the present. The formative period was the nineteenth century.

Van Jaarsveld identifies the main features of self-determination during this period as a feeling of injustice and offended dignity; attachment to *volk* and fatherland; the urge towards self-preservation; a sense of having been called to a divine mission; and a love for the past of the *volk* which entails the use of history to cultivate nationalist sentiments. The period of industrial development and British rule did little to dampen this spirit. Indeed, embattled Afrikaner nationalism thrived on the conflicts that ensued. By the 1930s Afrikaner culture had become profoundly politicised and the National Party's victory at the polls in 1948 was a reflection of the potency of self-determination.

Volk

A *volk* may be defined as a distinctive group of people with a common life-style, language, religion and experience. *Volk* nationalism is an expression of self-determination for such a group. Usually it is believed that the state as a political organisation should be based on a culturally homogeneous group in a common land. *Volk* nationalism tends therefore to be exclusive.

Again it is possible to find examples in each phase of Afrikaner nationalism when the idea of *volk* nationalism is a driving force. Indeed, the history of Afrikaners provides a rich breeding ground for symbols of *volk* nationalism: Slagtersnek, the Great Trek, Blood River — symbols which in turn picture Afrikaners as the 'Israel of Africa', the Great Trek as the 'exodus to the Promised Land', the struggle against blacks on the frontiers and against British imperialism as 'sacred history' replete with victories, defeats, concentration camps, and martyrs.

The phenomenon of *kultuurpolitiek* (political culture) also exemplifies *volk* nationalism. Witness the *Ossewabrandwag* and the *Broederbond*, two cultural movements concerned to mobilise *volkseenheid* (the solidarity of the people) and to legitimate Afrikaner nationalism. Of course, the emergence of Afrikaans as a formal language itself greatly heightened *volk* consciousness.

Race

Race is a biological concept referring to genetic characteristics; it is also a social psychological term relating to genetically derived group consciousness, often manifesting itself in exclusivity, discrimination and prejudice.

Race has been an important ingredient in Afrikaner nationalism, especially as regards the fear of domination, absorption, or annihilation — for reasons that are not difficult to understand. The early settlers were white; the frontier experience was, among other important factors, a clash of races and cultures. Cultural, ethnic and religious differences have tended in South Africa to coincide with social, political and economic distinctions *and* have tended to be perceived in the popular mind in racial terms for the obvious reason that race is 'the most visible and easily conceptualized index of group differentiation' (Schlemmer).

The Afrikaners who regarded their identity as God-given believed that identity was threatened by mixing with indigenous people and by the imposition of alien policies, such as equalisation. In the early part of this century General De Wet put it succinctly: 'Providence had drawn the line between black and white and we must make that clear to the Natives, and not instil into their minds false ideas of equality.'

The National Party's first official statement defined the link between Afrikaner nationalism and race this way: 'In our attitude towards the

Natives the fundamental principle is the supremacy of the European population in a spirit of Christian trusteeship utterly rejecting every attempt to mix the races. The Party further aims at providing the Native with the opportunity to develop according to his natural talents and aptitudes.' The legal apparatus of apartheid since 1948 is a direct result of the views expressed in this statement, views which took shape in the historical development of Afrikaner nationalism itself. As Cronje, one of the architects of apartheid, said in 1945: 'The more radically racial segregation is carried through, the better it will be; and the more consistently we apply the policy of apartheid, the more efficient our purity of blood and our unadulterated European racial survival will be guaranteed.'

Race has played an important role in Afrikaner nationalist thinking and policy. In recent times a shift can be discerned from Afrikaner *volk* nationalism to white nationalism. According to Giliomee, for example, the Afrikaner has come to see himself as part of the white group and 'this *white* identity is reinforced by the privileged position the Afrikaner shares with other whites.' He concludes, to 'entrench this position, the support of other whites is needed, so that there is a shift from ethnic identification (as Afrikaner) to racial identification.'

Structure and power

How did Afrikaner nationalists succeed in mobilising people in terms of self-determination, *volk* and race? To answer this question we need to look at the organisational structure and power base of Afrikaner nationalism.

By structure we mean the bureaucratisation of Afrikaner culture and the development of organisational structures instituted by the Afrikaner elite to mobilise Afrikaners for Afrikaner nationalism. By power we mean the ability to act and direct behaviour towards Afrikaner nationalist goals. And, as Degenaar says, 'the crucial years are the thirties and forties and the crucial organisations are the Afrikaner *Broederbond* and the National Party.'

No ideology can survive or succeed in its objectives without institutions which give it plausibility, and Afrikaner nationalism is no exception. From its foundation in 1914 the National Party provided an organisational base for Afrikaner political aspirations and succeeded in politicising Afrikaner culture. Verwoerd referred to it as 'a nation on the move', being no ordinary political party.

The Afrikaner *Broederbond* was a secret society founded in 1919. It built an immense network of formal and informal influence at all levels of Afrikaner society. According to O'Meara, 'for much of its existence the *Bond* [has] dominated the institutional, ideological and financial life of Afrikaner nationalism'.

Outside of these two primary carriers of Afrikaner nationalism an elaborate organisational substructure was created to serve the interests of Afrikaner nationalism. On the cultural level the *Broederbond* established the FAK (*Federasie van Afrikaanse Kultuurverenigings*) in 1929, and by 1937 there were nearly 300 cultural bodies, church councils, youth and student groups, and scientific, education and charitable associations affiliated to it. This process has grown significantly since then.

On the economic level an impressive list of Afrikaans organisations were created, such as the *Afrikaanse Handelsinstituut*. A wide range of commercial enterprises were established to compete against English equivalents in insurance, banking, mining (*Federale Mynbou*) and finance, as well as workers' associations, staff associations and trade unions. Press and student organisations, as well as research institutes, were also created. Van Zyl Slabbert argues, in fact, that this process of bureaucratisation of Afrikaner life, which coincided with industrialisation and urbanisation, prepared the groundwork for Afrikaner unity. In those bureaucracies elite groups could 'interpret the events that the majority of Afrikaners were experiencing' and take collective action where necessary. The end result of this process was the National Party victory in 1948. 'Malan, in a sense, was a symbol of a collective ethos that had been bureaucratised.' The 1948 victory gave Afrikaner nationalism political power to consolidate the process whereby, first, Afrikaner and, later, white privilege and domination were perpetuated.

On one level the story of Afrikaner nationalism is remarkable for its success in mobilising the potent forces of self-determination, *volk*, race, and structures to gain power in a relatively short period. Since 1948 Afrikaner nationalism has succeeded in remaining in power despite strife and some fragmentation within its ranks, and despite white and black opposition and almost universal international opprobrium.

In a later part of this chapter we shall examine the debate about whether Afrikaner nationalism as expressed in the ruling National Party reformist policies of the 1970s denotes a significant shift in ideology. But first we must address the religious quality of Afrikaner nationalism, an aspect to which Degenaar gives only passing attention.

The religious quality of Afrikaner nationalism

Even the casual observer is impressed by the centrality of the church in Afrikaner history and culture — specifically the *Nederduitse Gereformeerde*, the *Gereformeerde*, and *Hervormde* churches. Indeed, one of the most hotly debated aspects of Afrikaner nationalism is its relationship to Calvinism and the degree to which a neo-Calvinist theology has given religious legitimation to Afrikaner nationalism. What is termed the 'Calvinist paradigm' has been used by many to interpret Afrikaner nationalism; among recent popular versions are W. A. de Klerk's *Puritans in Africa*, and James Michener's epic novel *The Covenant*.

The essential features of the 'Calvinist paradigm' have recently been outlined by André du Toit in the following way. The founding fathers of Afrikanerdom brought to the Cape the basic tenets of seventeenth-century Calvinism. In the harsh frontier situation the isolated *trekboers* lived by a 'primitive Calvinism', and in the nineteenth century this provided the rationale for the central event of Afrikaner history — the Great Trek. According to its teaching the *Voortrekkers* and Republican Afrikaners saw themselves as a chosen and covenanted people, like Israel in the Old Testament. This belief enabled Afrikaners to presume a divine mandate to keep the heathen people in their subservient position as 'hewers of wood and drawers of water', and in the twentieth century gave rise to and justified the unequal and racist character of modern Afrikaner-dominated South Africa.

Co-author of the seminal book on the early history of Afrikaner political thought, Du Toit has recently described the Calvinist paradigm as a myth. He claims that 'there is simply no contemporary evidence for the presence among early Afrikaners of a set of popular beliefs that might be recognised as primitive Calvinism or of any ideology of a chosen people with a national mission' in the records of the nineteenth century.

Even granting Du Toit's persuasive critique, there is no doubt that twentieth-century Afrikaner nationalism, like other nationalisms, reclaims past history for its own purposes, and reinterprets the pre-nationalist period for its own ends. F. A. van Jaarsveld's essay, 'The Ideas of the Afrikaner on His Calling and Mission' (1961), may be seriously flawed as history, as Du Toit has argued, but he does use the Calvinist paradigm powerfully in the service of Afrikaner nationalism. In his essay Van Jaarsveld writes: 'For the Afrikaners the parallel with the chosen of the Lord grew into a form of mysticism, by their suffering in fulfilling God's calling they would be purified.' This religious and political myth formed the basis for such Afrikaner nationalist beliefs:

that blacks are destined to perpetual servitude;

that miscegenation and *gelykstelling* (equalisation) are wrong;

that British colonial philanthropy towards blacks was misguided and dangerous;

that the Great Trek was the instrument which 'in God's hand . . . would *civilise* the non-whites and assist in their conversion to Christianity'.

It is this myth-making quality of Afrikaner nationalist ideology which has made it so powerful and dynamic a force in South African life, as well as giving it an enigmatic quality in today's world. Though even ardent Afrikaner nationalists would not overtly use the Calvinist paradigm today as a legitimation for their beliefs, echoes of it can still be heard at political and cultural rallies. Its historical veracity may be in question, but its potency is not.

From ideology to power politics

The liberalisation of Afrikaner nationalism?

We come now to the most controversial aspect of this topic. Some observers believe that the 1970s heralded a significant shift in Afrikaner nationalism. They argue that it is now misleading to speak of the Afrikaner as an embattled colonist inside his laager keeping an increasingly hostile world at bay, and containing — by repression and co-optation — the aspirations of the black majority. There has been a shift from the religious-political ideology of the manifest destiny of the Afrikaner to a more pragmatic, secular ideology of white survival which has necessitated making concessions to non-Afrikaner whites, to coloureds and to Asians, and even to urban blacks.

According to this view, the key to understanding the National Party lies in the strategies it has developed for maintaining political power. (These strategies are no longer justified in terms of the ideology of manifest destiny.) The doctrine of apartheid in the 1950s was racist, but the doctrine of separate development which emerged in the 1960s marks a shift from racism to self-determination based on ethnicity. By the 1970s there was a discernible trend towards the efficient management of power. The entrenched National Party was the vehicle for political change on its own terms. In foreign affairs it went from defence to attack and emerged as a regional superpower — witness the Nkomati Accord with Mozambique, support for Unita in Angola, unilateral actions in Namibia/South West Africa, and its dominance in trade and geo-politics with respect to the frontline states, including Zimbabwe.

Internal affairs since the 1970s have been dominated by National Party initiatives — an ambiguous victory for its new tricameral parliament which gives a measure of political say to coloureds and Asians, its granting of industrial citizenship and trade union rights to South Africa's black workers, and the granting of leasehold rights to urban blacks.

Since the mid-seventies a new economically inspired conception of what is in the best interests of whites has also begun to take its place alongside separate development. Giliomee sees this as partly due to changes in the structure of the economy. Up to 1940 agriculture and mining contributed more to the national income than commerce and industry together. By 1975 the position had changed markedly, and necessitated greater labour mobility and the creation of stable black urban communities. Given the demographic pressures of a growing and largely youthful black population, housing, education, and job creation became more pressing.

A new imperative for the generation of faster economic growth began to emerge as a priority. Whereas economics had previously been subservient to political ideology, or had at least to be harnessed for its own ends, now a new conception of the state founded on the ideology of free enterprise which encouraged growth and required 'non-discrimination against the black "insiders" in the urban heartland' gained currency. A carefully managed, but limited, policy of de-regulation of the economy, and a greater degree of privatisation were enunciated. Milton Friedman expressed this succinctly when he visited South Africa in the mid-seventies: 'Free market capitalist policies are the only way to a free and reasonably peaceful South Africa.' This view was taken up in the English and Afrikaans press and in business circles — evoking the journalistic response, 'Go for growth and apartheid falls away.'

There is evidence that a new breed of Afrikaner politicians, bureaucrats and academics is emerging, who have begun to influence policy. They believe that there is a close connection between capitalist growth and political freedom — or at least that 'grand apartheid' and capitalist growth are incompatible. In this context racial separation and discrimination are no longer plausible. The apparatus of apartheid must be dismantled piecemeal — including even such pillars of apartheid as the prohibition of mixed marriages, influx control, and the non-permanency of blacks in white urban areas.

The perspective we have been exploring is based on the assumption that the old-style ideology of divine mission and exclusivism is being replaced by a more pragmatic, secular style of survival politics. This ideology necessitates a strategy of political accommodation of non-Afrikaner whites, coloureds and Asians. It involves a new understanding of political economy. If the required economic growth is to be achieved, economic forces must no longer be made subservient to politics. Cornerstones of 'grand apartheid' have to go. World opprobrium expressed in the form of sanctions, arms embargoes, disinvestment, or constructive engagement cannot be ignored and will not be removed as long as South Africa practises racial discrimination. Black aspirations can no longer be swept under the carpet. The external and internal pressures building up against the regime cannot be confronted by force and military might, they have to be met politically.

The modernisation of racial domination?

Other observers take a different view. They point to the fact that at least since Soweto 1976 South Africa has been in a state of siege. Black townships have been in continual turmoil; South Africa has been engaged in a low-level border war; urban sabotage and guerrilla incursions have persisted despite the state's powerful counter-insurgency measures; literally hundreds of people — mainly black — have died resisting the regime.

In this view Afrikaner nationalism is not a spent force. The National Party, even more entrenched with the passage of the new constitution, can still depend on

a well-disciplined ethnic power base through its close alliance with Afrikaans churches, the Afrikaans press, a wide range of Afrikaans cultural, academic, student, professional and business organisations and societies, the *Broederbond*, etc. It has at its disposal a huge government bureaucracy; it is backed up by a loyal military, police and security force; and it is in league with organised commerce. What is there to counter this imposing organisational strength with its considerable resources? (André du Toit)

By its very nature, the changes which can be expected through National Party initiatives will be limited. It cannot distance itself too far from its voter support. It is constrained by the degree to which, if not the ideology of Afrikaner nationalism, at least modifications of its policy permit change. These modifications will be made in response to internal and external pressures. They will lead to more negotiations with those outside the white group, even to a new form of 'indirect rule' through recently established urban black representational bodies at national and local levels. But they will not go so far as to share power through representational democracy for all in a unitary state. Afrikaner nationalism may have changed, but by its very nature it cannot contemplate so radical a departure from its basic objective of ensuring white survival by all the means at its disposal, at least not in the short-to-medium term.

According to this view, we are witnessing the modernisation of racial domination. This means the forging of what might be called a common 'whitism' — an ideology-in-the-making which aims to preserve white economic privilege and political dominance. In terms of race relations, Afrikaner nationalist ideology has moved over time from *baasskap* (in which other races are believed to be inherently inferior), to guardianship (allowance is made for blacks to 'come to maturity'), to separate development (which concedes to blacks 'separate but equal' areas, facilities, and opportunities) to the modernisation of racial domination (whereby state power and technocratic control ensure white survival on an African continent whose landscape is strewn with examples of the failure of African majority rule in political and economic terms). Non-Afrikaner whites, coloureds, and Asians have been caught up in this process. It is even conceivable that some urban blacks will be co-opted in the process.

Whither Afrikaner nationalism?

Which view of Afrikaner nationalism is correct? The liberalisation of Afrikaner nationalism, or the modernisation of white domination? Not surprisingly, the answer depends on where you stand. If you are white, and committed to a process of gradual reform, either view could be right. If you are black your answer could be that the rhetoric of Afrikaner nationalism may have changed but the daily experience of the realities of ongoing repression have not. Certainly, recent research by Schlemmer indicates that the index of black anger, frustration and impatience is growing. What even the staunchest critics will concede is that Afrikaner nationalism has undergone changes. But, to use the oft-quoted cliché, they are too little, too diffident, and too late — the bottom line remains one of white survival.

In a booklet published by the National Party's federal information service (1985), the party concedes that its policies are flawed:

The homelands policy cannot be a sole solution to the race problem. Attempts to force urban blacks to accept citizenship of the homelands have failed — urban blacks must be able to influence policy where they live.

Black leaders with significant followings have refused to participate in the constitutional debate and the government's reformist initiatives because of their mistrust of government intentions.

Efforts at expelling blacks from white urban areas have failed.

Verwoerdian grand apartheid has failed because the homelands can at best accommodate no more that 40 per cent of the black African population, international recognition has been denied to the homelands and has hampered their development, and internal opposition to government policy has escalated dramatically.

Issues which have to be tackled, the booklet continues, include the question of black citizenship rights in South Africa, the problem that elected leaders, such as black urban councillors and coloured and Asian representatives in the tricameral parliament, do not have wide support. Large numbers have not participated in these elections, and recognised leaders have not made themselves available for election.

The booklet makes it clear that these issues must be addressed through ongoing discussions with a wide range of black leaders. But it also makes clear that for the party there are non-negotiables. The 'group nature' of South African society remains a point of departure for a future political dispensation. Segregated schools and residential areas will remain. A new dispensation must guarantee white, coloured and Indian existence and security in their own right, and have their approval as well as that of blacks. It must be drawn up in consultation with all groups and ensure peace and good order, safeguard western norms and satisfy the security needs of all.

Clearly the reformist path chosen by the National Party has cost it dearly, in terms of fragmenting its unity. Disaffected members have joined the breakaway *Herstigte Nasionale Party* (HNP), or the Conservative Party (CP). On the labour front staunch nationalists have accused the National Party of sacrificing their interests. Alienated nationalists have joined newly founded cultural organisations to defend Afrikaner identity and culture. Civil servants have questioned policy changes, and farmers have shown an unusual degree of protest and autonomy over government policies.

With regard to the role of religion, David Bosch has observed: 'From the outside . . . *Afrikanerdom* is, at the moment (1985), fragmented and in disarray, but the *Dutch Reformed Church* is still solidly united and impregnable, despite its exclusion from the World Alliance of Reformed Churches, and dissenting voices from within.' And the DRC has yet to declare itself on reformist initiatives. Paradoxically, as Charles Villa-Vicencio has shown, there is at the same time evidence of a process of secularisation and privatisation of religion in Afrikaner circles. He gives as evidence the contrast between the government-appointed Steyn Commission of Inquiry into the Mass Media (1981) and the Eloff Commission of Inquiry into the South African Council of Churches (1983). 'Readily discernible in the Steyn Commission's report is a patriotic theology — conserving, legitimating and moderate. . . . By contrast [just two years after] the language of the Eloff Commission is more qualified. The marked difference between this report and that of the Steyn Commission is that there is no explicit support in it for any kind of "political" theology, whether . . . "for the state" or "against the state".' If Villa-Vicencio is correct, Afrikaner nationalism has changed in another important sense — it is no longer as dependent on religion for its legitimation, and may even be loosening its ties with the Dutch Reformed Church. In turn the Dutch Reformed Church appears to be lagging behind the National Party on questions such as mixed marriages and other reformist measures.

It is simply not possible to give a definitive verdict on whether

Afrikaner nationalism in its classical form is being replaced by or transmuted into something else. It is also not beyond the bounds of possibility that P. W. Botha may yet confound his critics and startle his supporters. By an excess of statesmanship which transcends sectional interests he could unban the ANC and the PAC, allow political exiles to return and free Nelson Mandela, to prepare the way for a period of negotiation and bargaining about a viable political solution. That such a scenario is even conceivable points to the enigmatic quality of Afrikaner nationalism. If it should happen it would reflect a totally new era in South Africa's long and troubled political history — the recognition that the time has gone when even the entrenched Afrikaner nationalist can produce unilateral solutions — the massively supported African nationalist is an integral part of those solutions. Some, however, fear an alternative scenario. This would entail a right-wing backlash against National Party 'reformist measures'. If right-wing reaction were to grow significantly, reform measures, which are already difficult to implement without losing the centre, could be jeopardised.

Critiques of Afrikaner nationalism

There are certain elements which are common to the critiques liberals, black nationalists, and radicals offer of Afrikaner nationalism in its classical form. Typically, all would argue that because of its history, ideological commitment, and secure power base, Afrikaner nationalism defines the current political problem and future dispensation for all people in South Africa in terms of a template of its own devising. This template is superimposed upon South African society, and is non-negotiable. Other groups or classes may be consulted but not treated as partners in a negotiated future dispensation.

From a critical perspective, the non-negotiables of Afrikaner nationalism, at least for the foreseeable future, appear to include the following:

(a) All racial or ethnic groups are assured the right to self-determination within the framework of separate development and ultimate white control; but the framework itself is not in question.

(b) *Volkseenheid* has been the key to the Afrikaners' access to political and economic power and provides the key to maintaining that power. One can predict that nothing will be done to initiate any changes which would result in a large-scale *volkskeuring*. Such a split would result in pitting Cape against Transvaal, and dividing the Afrikaner press, and student, teacher, business and cultural movements in two. For this reason *verligtes* will temper reforms, and *verkramptes* will tolerate reforms, so long as a degree of *volkseenheid* is preserved and significant *volkskeuring* prevented. (The breakaway of the Conservative Party, however, raises the question as to whether *volkseenheid* can be maintained.)

(c) Even *verligtes* argue that ethnic groups, not individuals, form the basis for a constitutional future, because any alternative arrangement will lead to majority rule; that change should be determined in the final analysis by Afrikanerdom; that division of power (as in the homelands) rather than power sharing in a common society should be the basis for any future dispensation.

(d) Direct and indirect government involvement in the private sector can be diminished only if the state continues to assume the role of planning and managing the economy, and the private sector is made to perform certain state functions, such as policing influx control, and providing housing and tertiary education.

(e) Even if all racially discriminatory legislation were to be removed, the government would still see the 'communist threat' as a major justification for retaining a strong military establishment and much of the legislation restricting civil liberties in South Africa, because Afrikaner nationalism perceives its task as managing conflict on two fronts: the internal pressures for a new constitutional dispensation which would give blacks some form of representation in the political process; and limiting the external threat of communist expansionism.

Liberal attacks on Afrikaner nationalism are fundamentally fourfold. They criticise the use of ethnicity as an organising principle in politics; diminution of civil liberties, including freedom of speech, association and worship, a free press and open universities; socialistic interference in the free market system, both in terms of nationalised industries such as SASOL, ISCOR and SATS and the myriad apartheid laws and regulations which impede free-market processes; its inherent ideological nature which makes it virtually impossible to modify dogma in the light of pragmatic needs and experience, at enormous financial and social cost to the country.

Black nationalism is critical of the balkanisation of South Africa through the homelands policy, which is seen as a divide-and-rule strategy; the elevation of ethnic identity to a basic category for political analysis and policy making; the racism inherent in apartheid; the refusal to grant blacks full participation in the political and economic life of the country; the use of extensive security legislation and enforcement to crush black political organisations and control trade union activity; the unholy alliance of Afrikaner nationalism and capital; the myriad laws and regulations controlling virtually every aspect of black people's lives in South Africa; and the inequalities consequent upon apartheid policy in the allocation of wealth, power, and prestige. Whatever change may have occurred in Afrikaner nationalism, the five main pillars of its policy which directly affect blacks have remained unchanged. They are land apportionment, race and ethnic classification, denial of South African citizenship by means of the homelands policy, influx control, and group areas legislation. Change which does not address these issues is merely cosmetic.

The *radical* critique of Afrikaner nationalism challenges the validity of both the liberal perception of race and the Afrikaner nationalist perception of ethnicity as keys to understanding South Africa. Legassick, for example, contends that the doctrines and practices of apartheid have been determined by the needs of capitalism. Dan O'Meara is critical of attempts to understand Afrikaner nationalism in terms of the mobilisation of ethnic forces. He argues that ethnicity and nationalism, if these terms are to be used at all, merely reflect class forces which happen to be in alliance, and ought to be subsumed under the proper category of analysis, which is class.

6 African nationalism in South Africa

Black political organisations have a long history in South Africa. One of the first, *Imbumba Yama Afrika* (Union of Africans), was formed in 1882. Mahatma Gandhi founded the Natal Indian Congress in 1894. The African People's Organisation was founded in 1902 — the forerunner of many coloured political organisations.

Although Africans in South Africa founded and operated nationalist movements and engaged in political protest on a country-wide scale earlier than Africans elsewhere on the continent, their share in the formal political process has actually decreased over time. Profound social and political reasons no doubt account for the fact that Africans in South Africa, who constitute approximately 80 per cent of the population and contribute 70 per cent of the labour, have not succeeded in forcing significant change. In fact, though at one time they shared a non-racial franchise in the Cape with whites, Africans have had even their limited political rights removed, in spite of their concerted efforts to persuade the dominant white electorate to expand these.

The roots of African nationalism can be traced to the early nineteenth century — to the impact of christian missions and schools; the development in the Cape of a liberal non-racial constitution; and later the exposure of an African elite to international currents, especially the American civil rights struggle and the Pan-Africanist movement. By the late nineteenth century there were signs of organised rejection by Africans of white domination: they began to organise themselves collectively to represent their interests in church and state. *Imbumba Yama Afrika*, for example, was intended to cut across denominational lines and represent African interests in Transkei. J. T. Jabavu founded and edited the first African newspaper, *Imvo Zabantsundu*, in 1884, the same year in which Rev. Nehemiah Tile broke away from the Methodist Church to form the Independent Tembu National Church. In 1892 Rev. Mangena Mokone established the Ethiopian Church in Pretoria with the slogan 'Africa for the Africans'.

Thus, before the turn of the century, the lines were already being drawn, based on a difference in strategy, between Africans prepared to work with whites for a new political dispensation as expressed in the slogan 'equal rights for every civilized man south of the Zambezi' (a strategy represented by Jabavu); and Africanists (represented by the Ethiopians), who challenged white power through African unity. This difference, as we shall see, was responsible for the later breakaway from the ANC of the PAC in 1959, when the latter rejected ANC accommodation with non-Africans and took up a wholly Africanist position.

This chapter will seek to describe the history and philosophy of African nationalism primarily through a documentary overview of the most important policy statements from 1912 to 1960. Events after 1960, when the ANC and PAC were outlawed, will then be summarised, before an assessment is made of the ideological divisions within African nationalism.

From petition to challenge: 1912–1939

There were over 12 000 Africans on the common voters' roll in the Cape Colony in the last quarter of the nineteenth century. The Cape's non-racial, qualified franchise was allied to the right to own land outside the 'native reserves'. For African leaders, therefore, the Cape system represented a workable alternative to the policy of segregation practised in Natal and the boer Republics of the Transvaal and the Orange Free State.

Already in the late nineteenth century, when gold and diamonds were discovered and South Africa was experiencing its industrial revolution, African leaders recognised that all races were caught up in the process of urbanisation and migration from the land, and that they were economically interdependent.

In the aftermath of the Anglo–Boer War black political organisations began to spring up as it became evident that Britain was not going to insist on the extension of the Cape franchise policy to other regions. The first national body, the South African Native Convention (SANC), met in Bloemfontein in 1909. Its resolutions were, in essence, a plea for the extension of the Cape tradition, and were addressed to the all-white National Convention which was preparing a new constitution for a unified South Africa. The SANC resolved:

that all persons within the Union shall be entitled to full and equal rights and privileges subject only to the conditions and limitations established by law and applicable alike to all citizens, without distinction of class, colour, or creed.

The SANC failed to influence white South Africa. A delegation to London also failed. The draft constitution became law and the Union was established in 1910.

Two years later the South African Native National Congress was founded, and in 1923 was renamed the African National Congress (ANC). From its inception it opposed any threatened loss of African franchise and land rights as posed by the formation of the Union and the passage of the Natives Land Act of 1913. Its position on franchise was spelled out in the SANC resolution of 1909. Its attitude to the 1913 Land Act was to petition the Crown against the principle of territorial segregation and its consequences — the allocation of roughly 14 per cent of the land surface of the Union to Africans.

After years of unsuccessful petitioning Congress concluded that the Land Act was designed to 'throw Africans backward, to isolate them when they were . . . the common inheritors with the white race of the land of the Union of South Africa'.

Its concern about franchise and land led the ANC in 1923 to adopt the following 'Bill of Rights'.

ANC 'Bill of Rights' 1923

1. That the Bantu inhabitants of the Union have, as human beings, the indisputable right to a place of abode in this land of their fathers.

2. That all Africans have, as the sons of this soil, the God-given right to unrestricted ownership of land in this, the land of their birth.

3. That the Bantu, as well as their coloured brethren, have, as British subjects, the inalienable right to the enjoyment of those British principles of the 'liberty of the subject, justice and equality of all classes in the eyes of the law' that have made Great Britain one of the greatest world powers.

4. That the Bantu have, as subjects of his Majesty King George, the legal and moral right to claim the application or extension to them of Cecil Rhodes' famous formula of 'equal rights for all civilized men south of the Zambezi', as well as the democratic principles of equality of treatment and equality of citizenship in the land, irrespective of race, class, creed or origin.

5. That the peoples of African descent have, as an integral and inseparable element in the population of the great Dominion of South Africa, and as undisputed contributors to the growth and development of the country, the constitutional right of an equal share in the management and direction of the affairs of this land of their permanent abode, and to direct representation by members of their own race in all the legislative bodies of the land, otherwise, there can be 'no taxation without representation'.

The twenties and thirties were dominated by Prime Minister Hertzog's attempt to solve 'the native problem' by legislative means. Two statutes were involved. The first was the Native Trust and Land Act, which allocated marginally more land to the already overcrowded reserves. The second was the Representation of Natives in Parliament Act, which abolished the Cape common roll and introduced separate representation of Africans by whites in the House of Assembly and the Senate, and established an advisory body on 'native affairs' — the Natives' Representative Council (NRC).

The ANC vigorously opposed these bills, and by 1935 the groundswell of opposition led to the founding of a new body, the All-African Convention (AAC), led by Professor D. D. T. Jabavu and Dr A. B. Xuma. The AAC opposed the Hertzog bills, but it also attacked British colonial policy in sub-Saharan Africa. It argued that racial and land segregation led to 'two nations within one state'. It also argued that Britain was faced with a situation analogous to its own Victorian past. Since the races in the Union were 'inextricably interwoven' the franchise would have to be broadened to incorporate groups other than white only. Africans were prepared to accept some form of qualified franchise at this stage, but they insisted on political enfranchisement in a common South Africa.

The AAC, which encompassed the ANC and many other organisations and all races, nearly eclipsed the ANC during this period. Marxist influence was evident, and its policy was more militant than that of the ANC. Indeed by the thirties support for the ANC had fallen, and it was in organisational and ideological turmoil.

From challenge to protest: 1940s

At the outbreak of World War Two the ANC was at a low ebb. Two factors led to the resurgence of the ANC in the forties: the appointment of Dr A. B. Xuma as president-general of Congress from 1940 to 1949 and the publication of the Atlantic Charter signed by Roosevelt and Churchill in 1941, which was utilised by Congress to formulate its own policy.

Dr Xuma set about rebuilding the organisational base of the ANC and developed its policy in a series of speeches which challenged the whole range of South African policies affecting Africans. The mood of Congress changed as its base broadened and its policy crystallised. Delegations, resolutions and deferential petitions to the Crown were replaced by more assertive challenges, including a determination that Africans would bear responsibility for the reform of society. Full citizenship and equal opportunity were Xuma's themes, but he followed them through with specific demands, such as the abolition of the Department of Native Affairs. African affairs should not be separately administered, education for all South Africans should, for example, be controlled by a single department.

African Claims: 1943

The detailed policy of the ANC was published in 1943 in a document entitled *African Claims*. It was the product of long and serious reflection by a committee set up by Xuma and composed of many of South Africa's leading Africans. It took into account that African troops had fought with distinction in both world wars.

The first part of *African Claims*, 'The Atlantic Charter from the standpoint of Africans within the Union of South Africa', analysed the eight points of the Charter and applied them to blacks in South Africa. The second part was called, 'Bill of Rights: full citizenship rights and demands'. It said, 'We, the African people of the Union of South Africa, urgently demand the granting of full citizenship rights such as are enjoyed by all Europeans in South Africa.' These included rights of franchise, justice before the courts, freedom of residence and movement, freedom from arbitrary arrest, demands for rights to ownership of land, job opportunity, free compulsory education, and access to social welfare.

African Claims called for 'one man one vote' linked to separate representation in Parliament and local authorities. (This implied separate voters' rolls and a racial allocation of seats — an aspect of ANC policy modified in 1946 to 'one man one vote' on a common voters' roll.) It recommended that the Natives' Representative Council be given legislative and executive powers to address the specific task of governing the reserves. It demanded recognition for African trade unions, abolition of the colour bar in industry, abolition of pass laws, and freehold tenure.

The document was sent in draft to Prime Minister Smuts, who had increased his United Party majority in Parliament in 1943. Smuts was asked to reassess policy in the light of *African Claims*. His refusal marked a turning-point in the ANC, which was itself experiencing pressures from the newly founded and militant Congress Youth League. The gap between the ANC and Parliament widened even further when the Smuts government was ousted by Malan's National Party in the 1948 general election.

Racial segregation in South Africa was further entrenched through a spate of legislation passed in the wake of the National Party's victory. The scene was set for more militant confrontation by the ANC, pushed as it was by its own Youth League and the events of the day.

Congress Youth League

The inspiration for the inauguration in 1944 of the ANC Youth League (which subsequently led to the breakaway of the PAC) came from the charismatic leader, Anton M. Lembede. He expressed the growing dismay of younger members at the ANC's 'collaboration with the oppressors'. It was he who gave voice to an Africanist philosophy within the ANC, as an analysis of his speeches from this time shows.

Lembede's formulation of Africanism predates its ideological emergence in the rest of Africa. It derives from an eclectic range of sources. He identified the following basic assumptions of Africanism:

(a) Philosophically Africanism rejected a materialist view of man as an 'economic animal', as well as the Nazi view of man as a 'beast of prey'. Instead it adopted a holistic view of man as body, mind, and spirit. 'History is a record of humanity's strivings for complete self-realisation.'

(b) Darwin's 'law of variation' offered a scientific basis for Africanism. Each nation has its 'own peculiar character and make-up', each 'its own divine mission'.

(c) Paul Kruger's aphorism, 'one who wants to create the future must not forget the past', provided an historical basis for Africanism. Africans must recall 'the glorious achievements of our great heroes of the past, Shaka, Moshoeshoe, Hintsa. . . .'

(d) The economic basis of Africanism was socialism. 'The fundamental structure of Bantu society is socialistic.' The task of Africanism was to 'develop this socialism by the infusion of new and modern socialistic ideas'.

(e) Africanism was democratic. In 'Bantu society, the work of a man was not assessed by wealth. . . . In our Councils or *Khotlas* any citizen could take part in discussions.'

(f) Finally, there was the ethical basis. In the past fear of ancestors provided ethical sanctions. In the present time the immortality of ancestors is still upheld but the 'ethical system' had to be 'based on Christian Morals since there is nothing better'.

In an article of 1946, 'Policy of the Congress Youth League', Lembede argued that Africanism was based on the following 'cardinal principles':

(a) Africa is a black man's country.

(b) Africans are one.

(c) The leader of the Africans will come out of their own loins.

(d) Cooperation between Africans and other non-Europeans on common problems and issues may be highly desirable; but this must be between the African bloc and the non-European groups as units. 'Non-European unity is a fantastic dream which has no foundation in reality.'

(e) The divine destiny of the African people is national freedom.

(f) After national freedom comes socialism. 'Our immediate task, however, is not socialism, but national liberation; our motto: *freedom in our life-time.*'

In the same year the National Party came to power, the ANC Youth League issued a manifesto in which it re-affirmed the principles enunciated by the ANC in 1912 and committed itself to work for the removal of all racist laws and the admission of Africans to full citizenship. Africa had always been 'the black man's country', and while rejecting Marcus Garvey's slogan 'Africa for the Africans', the League foresaw Europeans and Africans sharing the fruits of the land only when Europeans had agreed to abandon domination, re-divide the land, and create a democracy of free peoples, in which racial oppression was outlawed.

From protest to defiance: 1949–1960

Programme of Action, 1949

Disenchanted by its own ineffectiveness, the ANC adopted a Programme of Action in 1949 — a milestone in Congress history. It came about as a response to the implementation of National Party policy, and as a result of new life injected by the ANC Youth League. The League had been founded for the dual purpose of working privately as a pressure group within the ANC and publicly to arouse political consciousness among Africans. Its leaders were extraordinarily able men, a decade younger than those who headed the ANC, and their life-experiences had made them cynical of the collaborationist stance of the ANC.

Prominent names included A. P. Mda (upon whom Lembede's mantle had fallen), Oliver Tambo, Walter Sisulu, Jordan Ngubane, Nelson Mandela, and Robert Sobukwe. Debates about more effective means of achieving liberation had been a feature of the ANC for some time. After the formation of the League two issues came sharply into focus, one concerning means and the other concerning the basic stance of the ANC. The Programme of Action was the outcome of pressure from the League to use more aggressive means and to develop mass appeal. The issue of basic stance would later be resolved when the PAC broke away in 1959 to promote a strongly Africanist position.

The Programme of Action accepted by the ANC marked a turning-point for the Congress. It proposed a council of action that would work for the boycott and abolition of all racially differentiated political institutions, especially the Natives' Representative Council. It suggested the employment of boycotts, strikes, non-violent civil disobedience, and non-cooperation as means to accomplish the aspirations of African nationalism. The Programme bore the imprint of Lembede and Mda in its exposition of black self-determination and in the absence of any direct reference to interracial cooperation; in fact it specifically rejected the concept of trusteeship or white leadership.

The Freedom Charter, 1955

The Programme of Action led to the ANC Defiance Campaign of 1952. Indeed, the whole period 1950–2 was crucial in ANC history. Walter Sisulu became general secretary of the Congress, and leaders of the Youth League gained key offices. The period saw a concerted effort to give flesh and blood to the Programme. At the same time the Nationalist government tightened its race policy: the Population Registration Act of 1950 aimed to give everyone a permanent racial classification, the Group Areas Act to define residential rights racially. The government also threatened the entire extra-parliamentary opposition with its Unlawful Organisations Bill, enacted in 1950 as the Suppression of Communism Act. Pressures to unite with other groups in opposition to government policy in terms of the Programme led to the appointment of a national council of action to plan 'a national stoppage of work for one day as a mark of protest against the reactionary policy of the Government'.

On 26 June 1952 the multiracial planning for the Defiance Campaign culminated in the largest non-violent resistance campaign ever seen in South Africa, the first mass campaign run jointly by Africans and Indians. The resistance won the recognition of the UNO and was responsible for focusing international attention on South Africa's internal policies. During the campaign some 8 000 blacks were imprisoned for defying apartheid laws, and ANC membership rose by tens of thousands. The campaign was a test of non-violent means. It failed to deflect the government from its policies or win the sympathy of the white electorate. But it did instil discipline and confidence in the ANC, and saw the rise to the presidency of the internationally esteemed Albert Luthuli in 1952.

After the relative failure of the Defiance Campaign, the ANC returned to its formal association with other organisations and other races in the struggle for liberation. Its energy and resources were further sapped by the countrywide arrests for treason in 1956 and by the Treason Trial which followed. The trial did not end until five years later, when all the accused were acquitted. The ANC joined the Congress Alliance, together with the left-wing white Congress of Democrats, the South African Indian Congress, the Coloured People's Organization, the South African Congress of Trade Unions, in a Congress of the People, which in 1955 adopted the Freedom Charter. This was officially endorsed by the ANC in 1956. The Charter is the more remarkable for its moderation when viewed against the implacable refusal of successive governments to accommodate African claims.

The Charter began with words that were to give offence to some

leaders of the Congress Youth League and to bring about the breakaway
of the Pan-Africanist Congress:

We, the People of South Africa, declare for all our country and the world to know:

that South Africa belongs to all who live in it, black and white, and that no
government can justly claim authority unless it is based on the will of all the people;

that our people have been robbed of their birthright to land, liberty and peace
by a form of government founded on injustice and inequality, that our country will
never be prosperous or free until all our people live in brotherhood, enjoying equal
rights and opportunities;

that only a democratic state, based on the will of all the people, can secure to all
their birthright without distinction of colour, race, sex or belief;

And therefore we, the People of South Africa, black and white together — equals,
countrymen and brothers — adopt this Freedom Charter. And we pledge ourselves
to strive together, sparing neither strength nor courage, until the democratic changes
here set out have been won.

The Charter affirmed its principles under the following headings:

The people shall govern.

All national groups shall have equal rights.

The people shall share the country's wealth.

The land shall be shared among those who work it.

All shall be equal before the law.

All shall enjoy equal human rights.

There shall be work and security.

The doors of learning and culture shall be opened.

There shall be houses, security and comfort.

There shall be peace and friendship.

Formation of the Pan-Africanist Congress

The group within the Congress Youth League of the ANC, which subsequently broke away to form the PAC, strongly opposed the opening
clause of the Freedom Charter. They argued that, by its proposal to
share the land with all who live in South Africa, the Charter conceded
in advance that it did not belong to Africans. Such a concession was
unthinkable to the Africanists within the League. For long they had
criticised the collaborationist policy of the ANC, and its willingness to
work with avowed communists. Following Lembede, they argued that
Africans needed an ideology to unite and motivate the masses, but that
ideology could not be multiracialism (the liberal alternative) or Marxism.
The only way to freedom lay in consolidating the African base, and this
required an exclusivist strategy in the short term. Non-Africans could
not be part of African nationalism or Africanism. Liberation from the
psychological shackles of domination could only be achieved by solidarity: this was the priority for Africans.

The Freedom Charter brought to a head a longstanding rift as to what basic stance the ANC should adopt. Once more, Lembede's cardinal principles of self-determination, psychological emancipation, and a black-ruled South Africa were asserted in opposition to the principles contained in the Charter. The latter principles were basically liberal ones with a strain of socialism, expressed in the proposal to nationalise certain industries. What the Africanists offered was an alternative value system and ideology. The breach could no longer be healed. In 1954 the Africanists issued occasional publications to represent the views of a Bureau of African Nationalism. In the same year the Orlando Youth League published a bulletin, *The Africanist*, under the editorship of Selby Ngendane. Among the authors who wrote of a 'pure' Africanism were A. P. Mda, T. T. Letlaka, Robert Sobukwe, and Potlake Leballo.

The Africanists drew on a long tradition of Pan-Africanism which existed in the United States, Europe, and Africa. But they did not simply import Pan-Africanism. Their most able theorists, Lembede, Mda and Sobukwe, gave a particular stamp to Africanism in South Africa. As far back as 1949 the ANC had criticised Africanists for being a 'black version of Afrikaner ideology'. The Freedom Charter opposed a racially based nationalism, which was the way they interpreted Africanism.

Fundamentally the difference between Africanists and the ANC can be seen in their conflicting answers to the question 'Who owns the land?' The ANC Charterists argued that it belongs to all, the Africanists that it belongs to the indigenous African people. As *The Africanist* put it:

The African people have an inalienable claim on every inch of the African soil. In the memory of humanity as a whole this continent has been the homeland of the Africans. . . . Their migration in their fatherland does not annul their claim to the uninhabited parts of Africa. . . . The non-Africans are guests of the Africans . . . [and] have to adjust themselves to the interests of Africa, their new home.

The PAC saw itself as the true custodian of Congress policy. Founding speeches ring with phrases reminiscent of Lembede's *Africanism*. Where he spoke of socialism, for example, the term now became 'Africanist socialist democracy', comparable it seems to the African socialism of independent states. But a liberal thread also ran through these speeches; for example, no guarantee of minority rights was envisaged in PAC policy, which was designed for individuals not groups. The outcome of this policy would be African majority rule.

The relationship between the ANC and the historic christian churches is well known. However, the PAC chose to identify itself with the independent churches by inviting to share in the inaugural convention Bishop Walter M. Dimba, head of the influential Federation of Bantu Churches in South Africa, and Rev. Nimrod Tantsi, a leader in the African

Methodist Episcopal Church. Indeed, calls were made at the inaugural for an African National Church, and Anglicans, Catholics and Lutherans were described as foreign. Elsewhere, at PAC meetings speakers sometimes invoked the sanction of African ancestors, or the 'gods of Africa'. The religious and cultural currents of traditional Africa ran strong in the PAC.

Non-violence abandoned, 1961

The PAC, with Robert Sobukwe as president, was confident it would achieve a membership of 100 000 by July 1959. It fell short of this target but was convinced that its pure nationalism and the 'natural nationalism' of the people would enable it to overtake the ANC. To achieve this, concrete results were needed. Only heroic leadership and a bold plan would convince.

In December 1959, the ANC decided to launch an anti-pass campaign on 31 March 1960. The PAC resolved to seize the initiative and launch a similar campaign before then. Sobukwe sent out final instructions to branches on 4 March, emphasising the need for strict non-violence. He later advised the Commissioner of Police that a 'sustained, disciplined, non-violent campaign' against the pass laws would be launched on 21 March, and PAC members would allow themselves to be arrested. The ANC declined to join, arguing that the people were not ready for such a campaign.

If the police at Sharpeville in Vereeniging had not fired into a crowd of demonstrators on 21 March 1960, the day might have marked yet another abortive African protest. The response to the PAC call had been negligible in Johannesburg, and no demonstrations were held in Durban, Port Elizabeth, or East London. From Langa, Philip Kgosana led a peaceful demonstration of 30 000 into Cape Town.

But at Sharpeville 67 people died and 186 were wounded. Albert Luthuli of the ANC called for a stay-at-home and day of mourning on 28 March 1960, which was to include the burning of passes. Large numbers responded. A state of emergency was declared, and the ANC and PAC were banned. Over 18 000 arrests were made, apart from those detained as political suspects. Sharpeville became the symbol of the tyranny of the rulers, as well as of the failure of non-violent attempts by blacks to achieve justice.

After Sharpeville some began to reassess the fifty-year-old tradition of non-violence in the ANC. Since its inception the ANC had been resolutely committed to non-violence, but in 1961 Nelson Mandela and others abandoned this policy.

There were, they argued, two alternatives — to submit or fight. Four forms of violence were examined: sabotage, guerrilla warfare, terrorism, and open revolution. Fears of open interracial civil war led to the deliberate limitation of violence to sabotage, and then with the proviso that, firstly, it should not injure or kill people, and, secondly, it should be directed at targets which would bring economic pressure on the white electorate to change. Thus was born *Umkonto we Sizwe* (Spear of the nation); and the first acts of sabotage were committed in 1961. The ANC's policy of non-violence was thus finally abandoned by men who felt that all channels of peaceful protest had been closed.

Poqo is a Xhosa word meaning 'independent' or 'standing alone'; it was also the vernacular equivalent of PAC, *UmAfrika Poqo* or 'Africans Alone'. As an organisation *Poqo* was an offshoot of the PAC, a spontaneous popular movement in the western Cape and Transkei, comprising groups who had only tenuous links with one another and with the leaders of PAC in South Africa and Maseru. These groups adopted terrorist tactics, and many whites and blacks feared a Mau Mau type movement in South Africa. *Poqo* was held responsible for the murder of coloured, African and white people during 1962–3. There is evidence that the movement was Africanist: for example, in quasi-religious oathings, during which *Poqo* members were assured of the help of the ancestors and protection from the bullets of the white man. By 1963 the police had succeeded in infiltrating *Poqo* and effectively stopped the movement with the arrest of some 3 246 alleged members.

Ideological emphases

Different ideological emphases can be identified in the history of African nationalism.

Charterists versus Africanists

The Freedom Charter was the result of the culmination of nearly fifty years of claims by blacks — Africans, coloureds and Indians. It is a mixture of classical liberalism and modern African socialism (as expressed especially in those articles relating to the redistribution of wealth, and ownership of land, resources and means of production). It envisaged a multiracial South Africa, shorn of apartheid.

The PAC regarded the Charter as a denial of Africanism, as expressed in theory by Lembede and in practice by the Ethiopian churches and independent African religious movements. But the aim of PAC policy was a future South Africa in which all are Africans regardless of their colour; hence its refusal to recognise minority groups in its scheme of things.

Liberals and communists

Many of the ANC's leaders were drawn from an educated, middle-class elite, greatly influenced by liberal ideals of the kind embodied in the Cape liberal tradition. Hence the antagonism evoked among the ANC leadership when expressions of Africanism were voiced by Lembede and others: they seemed to be 'black versions of Afrikaner nationalism'.

While the ANC was prepared to work formally with communists, a Marxist analysis of the South African predicament in terms of class gained little credibility among its members. The reasons are complex, including ANC loss of face because of communist policy changes as in the communist support of white workers in the 1922 general strike. The African worker did not have common cause with white workers; indeed, white workers had frequently sided with government against him. For both the ANC and PAC race, not class, lay at the root of the problem. ANC willingness to work with communists brought the charge from the PAC and Africanists that the ANC was communist-controlled. After the Suppression of Communism Act (1950) this charge was calculated to challenge the standing of the ANC in the eyes of whites and some blacks. The ANC made the countercharge that the PAC was promoting a sectional nationalism, 'doing the government's dirty work for them' — a telling blow at a movement pledged to oppose the government policy of self-determination.

After Sharpeville: 1960–1982

Organisationally, neither the ANC nor the PAC were well prepared for the new conditions of illegality imposed after Sharpeville, though on balance the ANC proved better able to adapt. As we have seen, both produced insurgent movements, *Umkonto we Sizwe* (ANC) and *Poqo* (PAC). Both faced the problems of setting up foreign missions, re-establishing internal activity, and holding the exile movements together without the guiding hand of Luthuli and Mandela (ANC) or Sobukwe (PAC).

The ANC

In anticipation of being outlawed, the ANC despatched its deputy vice-president, Oliver Tambo, to London in 1960. During 1960–3 foreign missions were established, funds raised, and a military training-programme organised. The Organisation of African Unity (OAU) took the ANC under its wing in 1963; Dar-es-Salaam became the ANC's centre of gravity and Tanzania its chief African supporter.

During the period 1963–9 *Umkonto* undertook a joint operation with ZAPU, aimed at infiltrating South Africa via Rhodesia (Zimbabwe), and giving its guerrillas operational experience with ZAPU forces in Rhodesia. By 1970 the debilitated ZAPU movement was in trouble and the ANC–ZAPU operation collapsed. There was internal dissension in *Umkonto*. A 'consultative conference' was held in Morogoro in 1969, which focused on organisational reforms and policy matters. A decision was taken to permit whites to join the external ANC, although they could not serve on the national executive. Policy decisions also included the adoption of a Revolutionary Programme, a document which essentially elaborated on various clauses of the Freedom Charter. For example, in the section 'The People Shall Govern' it was made clear that no political institutions serving racial minorities would be permitted in a liberated South Africa. Tom Lodge comments on the Revolutionary Programme that 'its specifications still remained compatible with the preservation of a form of welfare-state capitalism in South Africa', a point worth noting in the light of the accusation that the ANC was under the control of the South African Communist Party.

By 1975 the ANC had succeeded in making several incursions into South Africa, and there is evidence of internal support, including that of the largely white, anti-communist ANC faction, *Okhela*, with which the Afrikaner poet Breyten Breytenbach was associated.

International relationships were strengthened through the ANC's diplomatic efforts. These were not without controversy: witness the World Council of Churches' Programme to Combat Racism, the ANC's siding with the USSR in the Sino–Soviet dispute, and its support of Russia's invasion of Czechoslovakia in 1968. The ANC's main support in the West came from the Scandinavian countries and Holland.

In the period since the Soweto uprising of 1976 it appears that the ANC may have established itself as the political movement with the greatest popular support in the black townships in South Africa. (In mid-1978 South African security police estimated that some 4 000 refugees were undergoing ANC training while some 2 500 had been brought to trial for sabotage.) In 1982 at least 29 sabotage attacks, 2 assassinations, and an armed operation could be attributed to the ANC. South Africa's counter-insurgency strategy was to put pressure on neighbouring countries believed to host ANC members, and to direct attacks on ANC targets in these host countries. Meanwhile, there has been a growing tendency for African governments to accord the ANC 'sole legitimate representative' status.

A reaffirmation of the principles of the 1955 Freedom Charter occurred in 1983 with the founding of the non-racial United Democratic Front (UDF), in opposition to the Nationalist government's constitutional proposals and the so-called Koornhof Bills concerning the freedom of movement of black people in South Africa. The Charterist tradition in black politics is still very much alive, though it remains to be seen whether the UDF will become a major political force. There does not appear, however, to be any direct connection between the UDF and the ANC, although the ANC called for international and internal support for the UDF in 1983. For obvious reasons it is not possible to estimate the popular support enjoyed by the ANC in South Africa, although there is evidence that it is widespread.

The PAC

The PAC-in-exile, under the leadership of Potlake Leballo, perhaps had an even more torrid history than the ANC. Headquartered in Maseru, Leballo was designated acting-president by Robert Sobukwe in 1962. Offices were subsequently opened in a number of cities, including London, Accra, Cairo and Dar-es-Salaam, but representatives tended to operate independently of the Maseru base. An innovation in 1963 was the admission to membership of the former Liberal Party leader, Patrick Duncan.

Guerrillas were trained at the FNLA's camp in the Congo, the plan being that they would gain practical experience by joining forces with SWAPO and Mozambican forces in their fight against the Portuguese. But the venture was not totally successful because of the internal leadership strife and conditions in the camp in the Congo.

The PAC turned to China for financial support, not because it had changed its anti-communist position but because efforts to raise funds in the West were unsuccessful. This alliance with China placed the PAC in an ambiguous position, and was further cause for internal dissension.

After transferring its headquarters to Zambia, the PAC held a conference in which confidence was expressed in the PAC leadership. Stung by an OAU motion calling on it to 'justify its existence', the PAC embarked on a more active phase in 1967. Its attempted incursions into South Africa proved abortive. Various efforts were made to find routes into South Africa, but lack of internal cohesion and the politics of the frontline states made this difficult, and there was growing frustration among PAC guerrillas, who had spent long years in bush camps. By 1976 the PAC-in-exile was weak and poor, internal dissension and the failure of aid from China being the chief reasons.

Between 1975 and 1977 a group of ex-Robben Island prisoners actually established PAC committees in Johannesburg and East London, and drew young people to the PAC in the turmoil of the Soweto uprising. By 1978 PAC insurgents had returned from training in China, but the South African state security system proved too strong, and most were arrested.

The death of Robert Sobukwe in 1978 created a struggle over leadership. Leballo emerged as leader, but there was a breakaway in the form of the Azanian People's Revolutionary Party (APRP), and bitter fighting ensued between factions. In 1981 John Pokela was elected to leadership, having recently arrived in Dar-es-Salaam from a long prison term on Robben Island. He managed to unite the PAC and APRP, and the PAC gained official recognition by Zimbabwe. The future plans and prospects of the PAC are not known, nor is it possible to measure its internal support in South Africa.

The Africanist tradition in South African black politics surfaced again in 1983 when the National Forum (NF) was founded to oppose the Nationalist government's constitutional proposals. The NF clearly reflects an Africanist ideology but it has no known link with the PAC.

This chapter has outlined some of the dimensions of black nationalism and black dissent over seventy turbulent years of South African history. The ANC and PAC were founded to protest against the erosion of black civil and political rights. These movements have become increasingly radicalised as they have sought to express growing black dissatisfaction about the allocation of land, franchise rights, and the distribution of wealth in South Africa. Since 1961, when outlawed, they have been involved in a protracted guerrilla war against the white regime in South Africa. While the outcome of this war remains uncertain, what is certain is that the fundamental questions of land, franchise, and the distribution of wealth continue to be the unresolved issues for blacks in South Africa.

7 Black consciousness

The black struggle for human rights and civil liberties in South Africa has a long history, extending as far back as the nineteenth century. In the previous chapter we explored the history and ideas of black nationalism as expressed through the ANC and the PAC. This chapter deals with the history and ideas of the Black Consciousness Movement (BCM) which, rising like a phoenix out of the tumultuous events of the 1960s, saw its role as continuing the black struggle while at the same time making its own unique contribution.

The history of the BCM can be divided into two phases. The first phase concerns the development of black consciousness as a black liberation movement from its beginnings in 1967 until its major organisations were outlawed in October 1977. The second phase concerns internal and external developments after 1977: these include the creation of new institutional expressions of black consciousness in South Africa, and the shifts and changes that have taken place in its analysis of South Africa and its strategies for action.

Black consciousness, 1967–1977

Formative influences

The BCM filled the vacuum created by the banning in 1960 of the ANC and the PAC. Although its philosophy owes something to black political thought in the USA, it has its roots in South African history: its ideology, policy and strategy were designed to fit contemporary black experience in South Africa.

The ferment among black Americans in the sixties influenced the emergence of black consciousness as a social-political force in South Africa. In particular, the writings and activities of Stokely Carmichael, Rap Brown, George Jackson, Malcolm X, James Cone, and Albert Cleage attracted lively interest among early exponents of black consciousness in South Africa, and helped to fan the flames already burning there. But while leading figures in the Black Consciousness Movement drew on the

American experience, there were considerable differences between the two situations. Generally speaking, black Americans did not challenge the American social and political system as such. They demanded full integration, based on the already accepted principle of equality. As a minority they wanted to exercise, without any restrictions, their citizen rights as guaranteed by the US Constitution. In contrast, blacks in South Africa claimed they constitute the majority of the population and could no longer be denied full citizenship. Like their black American counterparts they are victims of racism. But unlike black Americans, blacks in South Africa argued that full citizenship involves a radical dismantling of the South African system because its constitution, laws, and economy favour the dominant white group. Blacks cannot appeal to an inherently non-discriminatory constitution to redress the injustices meted out to them.

There were other external influences on black consciousness in its formative period. Of importance were the writings of African leaders engaged in the struggle against colonialism, such as Julius Nyerere, Kenneth Kaunda, Leopold Senghor, Kwame Nkrumah, Amilcar Cabral, and Frantz Fanon. Nearer home the lessons of the protracted struggle for independence in Mozambique and Angola made a deep impression on black consciousness leaders. Another influence, though indirect, was the student revolt of the 1960s in Europe, Britain, and the USA. Further diverse influences, such as continental humanist philosophy, the writings of non-African Third World leaders like Fidel Castro and Mao Tse-tung, Paulo Freire's 'pedagogy of the oppressed', and Latin American liberation theology, all had a profound impact on the young black intellectuals who fashioned the philosophy of black consciousness.

The rise of black consciousness

The story of the founding in 1968 of the South African Students' Organisation (SASO) as a result of the revolt and secession of black student members from the National Union of South African Students (NUSAS) is well known. In essence it was young black intellectuals such as Steve Biko, Barney Pityana, and H. Nengwekhulu who led the breakaway. They regarded NUSAS as a forum for liberal rhetoric, which seldom led to meaningful action, while being divided into black and white camps. They felt the time had come for blacks to operate on their own. As a delegate to NUSAS congresses of 1966 and 1967, and to the newly formed University Christian Movement (UCM) in 1967 and 1968, Steve Biko became convinced that he was expressing a widespread feeling among black students that a black organisation be formed.

Black consciousness crystallised later, as attempts were made to name and describe the ideology that had fuelled the breakaway and promoted black solidarity.

SASO began encouraging blacks in areas other than student affairs to organise themselves independently of white-dominated liberal organisations. The procedure of 'infiltration' was later developed into a major policy, and blacks in all community organisations were challenged to 'go it alone'. Thus Black Community Programmes (BCP) were formed, aimed at coordinating black welfare projects. The Black Peoples' Convention (BPC) was started, initially in an attempt to unite at national level black voluntary associations, including the Association for the Education and Cultural Advancement of African People of South Africa (ASSECA), and the Interdenominational African Ministers' Association of South Africa (IDAMASA). The BPC became a political organisation, with Steve Biko as its first honorary president. Among high-school pupils the South African Students' Movement (SASM) was launched in 1967, independent of SASO. As black consciousness philosophy was clarified and elaborated, numerous other organisations came into being, including the Black Allied Workers' Union, the South African Black Social Workers' Association, the South African Black Travellers' Association, and the Black Women's Federation.

By 1977 there were a great number of institutional carriers of black consciousness, all actively engaged within their own spheres in promoting the cause of black liberation. However, increasingly punitive action by the government against leading figures in the movement — Biko was among the people banned — culminated in the banning of the important black consciousness organisations in October 1977, and the confiscation of their assets. Biko himself died in detention on 12 September 1977.

The basic philosophy of the BCM

The BCM has always held that its own existence would be irrelevant and unnecessary in a non-racial, non-exploitative society. But racism is institutionalised and blacks are politically oppressed and economically exploited in South Africa. In black consciousness thinking, the history of South Africa can be interpreted according to a dialectical process. From the thesis of white racism and the antithesis of black solidarity a synthesis will emerge: true humanity without regard to race or colour. In the past, it was argued, the ANC and the PAC had chosen the strategy of confrontation, first through moral persuasion, then non-violent extra-parliamentary campaigns, including boycotts, strikes and stay-at-homes, and finally armed insurgency. The BCM believed these strategies were premature and thus doomed to fail. Instead, black consciousness held that in order to play a positive role in the liberation struggle, blacks had to develop a sense of solidarity through the concept of group power, and in this way build a broad base from which to counter the divide-and-rule strategies of whites.

How would such solidarity be achieved? In the main by formulating a clear working philosophy of black consciousness. What was required was a 'black renaissance', a new definition of the problem and new ways of confronting it. These could only be achieved by reawakening black people in South Africa to their dignity as human beings, and by their recognising their own collective strength. SASO defined black consciousness as an attitude of mind, a way of life. It required blacks to reject all value systems that made them aliens in their own land. The black person needed to 'come to himself', and to be reminded of his 'complicity in the crime of allowing himself to be misused' by others (usually white) for their own purposes. Black consciousness advocates an awareness of and a pride in blackness — and thus the rejection of white stereotypes. As Biko declared:

What black consciousness seeks to do is to produce at the output–end of the process real black people, who do not regard themselves as appendages to white society. Some will charge that we are racist but these people are using exactly the values we reject. We do not have the power to subjugate anyone. Racism does not only imply exclusion of one race by another — it always presupposes that exclusion is for purposes of subjugation. Blacks have had enough experience as objects of racism not to wish to turn the tables.

Enabling people to 'walk tall' and with dignity calls for a psychological revolution in the black community. Three hundred years of racial and economic oppression have generated deeply ingrained stereotypes of a negative kind. No man can wage a meaningful war of liberation unless and until he has effectively eradicated his 'slave-mentality' and his feeling of inadequacy. This liberating process can only be achieved by blacks for blacks. Black consciousness takes the one symbol which historically has had a fundamentally negative meaning — the symbol black — and challenges the deeply rooted alienation which it entails with such slogans as 'Black is beautiful', 'Black man, you are on your own'.

Black consciousness seeks to liberate people not only from psychological alienation, but also from physical oppression. To this end blacks need to be made aware of the political, social and economic conditions of their oppression. What is required is clear-sighted analysis of the situation. Thereafter the total resources of the black community must be mobilised to achieve liberation.

In black consciousness thinking, liberation was conceived in holistic terms, and affected every aspect of black society. Black consciousness engaged in cultural activities such as music, drama, literature, the re-

interpretation of black history, and in general the rediscovery of black
people's cultural roots. It engaged in welfare work, programmes of self-
help and development by blacks for blacks, such as Black Community
Programmes. It launched a drive to enlist as many blacks as possible in
the political expression of its philosophy. It recognised the religious
quality of traditional and modern African culture and sought to express
its philosophy in Black Theology. It worked for the economic progress
of blacks through cooperatives, 'Buy Black' campaigns, and trade union
activity. It engaged educators, scholars, and students in reflection on
their tasks from the perspective of black consciousness in schools and
universities.

The means black consciousness chose to realise its objective was that
of 'conscientisation': blacks began exploring their situation in order to
raise their awareness of the dimensions of oppression in South African
society. In the process it was recognised that most blacks are peasants
or industrial workers. Legal and customary apartheid and the migrant
labour system make it virtually impossible for blacks to feel 'at home'
in the white urban industrial centres in South Africa. Black consciousness sought to articulate these feelings of alienation and, what is more
important, to direct these feelings and perceptions. Conscientisation is a
method forged in Latin America to enable largely illiterate adults to
'name' their world of oppression, to develop critical tools for analysis,
and to mobilise their resources with the aim of changing their life-world.
Education and training were thus used extensively by the BCM to instil
in people a sense of self-reliance, initiative, and solidarity. It sought to
examine critically white racism and capitalist exploitation, and the roots
of psychological servitude, which have emasculated blacks during years
of oppression.

Black communalism

The term black consciousness gave to its political and economic policies was black communalism. In their analysis black intellectuals saw a
close link between the politics of white domination and the economics
of capitalism. Taking as its model 'African family-ism' or African socialism, black consciousness developed a political and economic policy aimed
at modifying the worst elements of capitalism and fundamentally challenging apartheid in South Africa. In so doing it created an indigenous
model, which embraced what were accepted as established ideals in
western democracy.

From the beginning the BCM asserted that social and political change
in South Africa would mean little unless there was a corresponding
change in the economy of the country. Real change required a funda-

mental redistribution of wealth and resources in a land where these were skewed in favour of whites. A change in the colour of government as such might not necessarily affect the maldistribution of wealth. A fundamental restructuring of the economy would therefore require public intervention, which presupposes a change in political power.

In economic terms black communalism is said to be rooted in traditional African culture. The continent has always been characterised by 'an indigenous socialism': in this respect one can point to the absence of private land-ownership in Africa, the egalitarian nature of traditional society, and the network of reciprocal relations and obligations based on an extended kinship system. Black communalism as an economic policy was based on the principle of sharing, and emphasised the communal ownership of property and wealth. It attempted to adapt this principle to the conditions of modern South Africa with its highly industrialised and sophisticated economy. It advocated a balance between private and public ownership, and envisaged a much larger role for the state in planning and controlling economic development, but foresaw a measure of free enterprise and private ownership under strict state control.

There was a certain plasticity in the economic policy of black communalism. For this reason one looks in vain for a detailed economic policy, the closest being a thirty-point statement of policy published by the BPC in 1971. This document sought to avoid the dilemma of choosing between capitalism and 'scientific socialism'. In opting for a socialist solution as an 'authentic expression of black communalism', it proposed significant modifications to the South African economy by advocating state ownership of all land, state participation in industry and commerce, especially in mining and forestry, and an even larger role for the state in planning and control. It also proposed, inter alia, state supervision of workers' rights, and regular wage-reviews, agricultural cooperatives and state-assisted markets, minimum foreign investment in commerce and industry, and welfare for the aged and infirm.

This programme, it was hoped, would ensure a more equitable distribution of wealth and resources. But black communalism believed the final shape of economic policy would be determined by the outcome of bargaining between blacks and whites, who together would have to determine ultimately the economic policy of the country.

In ideal terms, the political goal of black communalism was an open society, based on universal adult suffrage irrespective of race, colour, religion or nationality. The practical consequence of this would be majority rule, in the sense of a predominantly but not exclusively black representation in Parliament. Black communalism favoured the term non-racialism rather than multiracialism, because it emphasised the rights of individuals rather than those of groups. It argued that universal adult suffrage in a modern democratic unitary state can work, despite gross discrepancies in education and wealth, provided adequate means of communication are built into the system so that the people can understand the issues for which their mandate is sought.

One can also detect an element of plasticity about the exact nature of its political policy. Whites and blacks would need to negotiate the terms of a political system, in which the legitimate aspirations of all parties can be met. In principle black communalism did not exclude whites from the political process, although it did reject outright any suggestion that blacks could exercise their political rights in independent homelands. Beyond this its political policy was open to bargaining; it is not clear, for example, whether a one-party or a multi-party democracy was envisaged.

The question of means

Black consciousness began from the premise that already there is real conflict of a violent nature between the interests of whites and blacks in South Africa. It is a society in which racism has long been institutionalised in the political and economic spheres. In order to break this log-jam two distinct phases were seen as necessary. Firstly, there was the stage of psychological liberation through the conscientisation of blacks. But even in the early days of the movement some members foresaw a second phase, which would involve the movement in the armed struggle already being waged by the ANC and the PAC.

Prior to 1977 the focus was directed on psychological emancipation. The BCM believed that the ANC and the PAC had entered into confrontation with government prematurely and without sufficient preparation. To avoid this error the BCM imposed on itself a period of relative withdrawal from direct confrontation in order to prepare the ground for future bargaining. In the short term this meant excluding even wellmeaning and sympathetic whites, because blacks needed to close ranks and develop a strong base of solidarity. But in the long term a just future for South Africa could only be assured if blacks and whites negotiate with each other from positions of strength. This process of bargaining was not something that would begin at some future date but was a process already at work in South Africa. Black consciousness looked to a time when it could authentically represent black aspirations, and bargain collectively from a position of strength. This process would take time, though no rigid timetable was envisaged. But the outcome was beyond doubt because black consciousness believed it had read the South

African situation aright, and eventually whites would have to accommo-date black aspirations.

It was recognised that choosing to work within the law would never-theless evoke conflict. Having cut his ties with Europe, the Afrikaner had nowhere to go: he regarded himself as an African. But he had set his face against power-sharing in a unitary state. Since this was the goal of black consciousness, escalation of conflict between blacks and whites was inevitable. Ultimately, however, the future South Africa would be comprised of whites and blacks. Whatever maintained goodwill and en-hanced the success of the bargaining process had therefore to be wel-comed. At the same time, internal and external pressures on the system had to be maintained.

In rejecting violence, Biko argued: 'Violence brings too many residues of hate into the reconstruction period. . . . If at all possible, we want the revolution to be peaceful and reconciliatory.' But he was all too aware that blacks were engaged in a struggle for power, and it would be met with force on an escalating scale — a view vindicated by history.

Biko was once asked for evidence to support the view that black consciousness was a force to be reckoned with. He replied, 'In one word: Soweto!' — referring to the countrywide urban unrest of 1976. He con-tinued:

The boldness, dedication, sense of purpose, and clarity of analysis of the situation — all these things are a direct result of black consciousness ideas among the young in Soweto and elsewhere. . . . The power of a movement lies in the fact that it can change the habits of people. . . .

The strength of the influence exerted by the black consciousness move-ment may also be gauged from the response of the government. At first, SASO and BPC were taken to represent black expressions of the govern-ment's separate development policy, and were tolerated and perhaps even encouraged. However, once it became clear that black consciousness was not purely a cultural movement and once the real possibility of pol-itical conflict was perceived, security raids and bannings began. Liberals, too, expressed the fear that black consciousness was anti-white, particu-larly because it defined itself in opposition to white liberal institutions and criticised some liberal precepts, especially the notion of multi-racialism.

Hostility towards the BCM mounted. On 19 October 1977 most known black consciousness organisations were outlawed by the South African government, and many of its leaders banned, detained or forced into exile.

Black consciousness after 1977

Transition

The outlawing of organisations within the BCM in 1977 raised questions about the future role of the movement in South Africa. 'Would black consciousness survive as an ideology after its leaders were banned, detained, jailed and exiled? And if it does survive, what form would it take and what would be the strength of its support?' (V. Soni) What new carriers of its philosophy would emerge? What would be the relationship of black consciousness with other internal political movements such as *Inkatha*, and externally with the ANC and the PAC? How would it relate to the workers' struggle and to the trade union movement?

The United States Study Commission on South Africa, *South Africa: Time Running Out?* (1981), identified several trends in the politics of black dissent post-1977. These included a greater acceptance of revolutionary violence and a growing interest in radical (Marxist) ideology. Other observers have noted that the liberation struggle has been increasingly defined in terms of class as well as race, and observed a decreasing use of racially exclusive rhetoric such as black consciousness, and growing use of phrases such as the non-racial democratic struggle, signifying a shift from race to class as the basic category of analysis.

The BCM since 1977 must be seen in the context of these changes. In the pre-1977 phase Marxists criticised the movement for its failure to understand the nature of capitalism and the class struggle in South Africa. SASO had, however, rejected all approaches which might blunt or confuse popular anger, arguing that its main task was to raise people's consciousness of their alienation as a result of racist oppression.

But, as Richard Turner observed, 'being black is not a political programme'. Black consciousness, Heribert Adam has argued, 'must equally face the fact that "self-love", "identity", "cultural assertion", are not sufficient to effect real change. The crucial question remains how this cultural revolution in the minds of the subordinates can be translated into political action.'

By 1981 the annual congress of the Azanian People's Organisation (AZAPO), itself a vehicle of black consciousness philosophy, was beginning to ask questions along these lines.

How to interpret black consciousness as an ideology for liberation is now the black consciousness dilemma. In the early days of black consciousness, it was more a matter of conscientizing blacks about their oppression. Now it is a question of how to galvanize blacks into a vehicle for liberation, for repossessing the land.

The answer to this self-imposed question, it turns out, was an attempt to transform black consciousness into class consciousness. And internally this meant shaping a concrete political strategy based on class interests, centred on the role of the worker.

An explicit analysis of the South African political economy began to emerge. Attention was given to the ways in which the generation of wealth and capital in South Africa is made possible by the collective effort of black workers. Black consciousness had thus far underestimated the role of the black worker. It was realised that black power in the market place, if properly organised, could exert enormous pressure on the capitalist system and thereby on the political system. By awakening black workers to their inherent power as a collectivity, black consciousness would cease to be just a pervasive philosophy concerning black dignity and the evils of apartheid; it would become a force to be reckoned with. But the shift towards an emphasis on the class struggle, it was held, should not negate the emphasis on racial conflict. The two are interlocked. 'It is economic and political exploitation that has reduced the black people into a class.'

At the same time, a greater degree of radicalisation also occurred in the external arm of the BCM. For example, the Black Consciousness Movement of Azania (BCMA) in exile released a statement asserting that 'black consciousness [is] a liberatory ideology' based on 'the principles of scientific socialism', and it recognised the role of 'the oppressed black worker as a major factor in the struggle for liberation and the creation of the democratic socialist state of Azania'.

New black consciousness movements

To fill the vacuum in black politics caused by the banning of the BCM movements, AZAPO was launched in May 1978 and announced itself as 'the main black political organization operating above board in South Africa today, and having taken black consciousness beyond the phase of black awareness into the class struggle'. The following week key members of AZAPO were detained. Only 16 months later were its constitution and policy officially adopted. A congress of the organisation was held and Curtis Nkondo was elected as first president.

In political terms, AZAPO envisages a future state, in which all persons shall have the right to property and participate freely in the political machinery of the country. As a strategy AZAPO nevertheless advocates exclusion of whites from its organisation and activities, since whites are 'part and parcel of the oppressive system'. There can be 'no meaningful integration between unequals'.

AZAPO is not without its critics. Some see its emphasis on identification with the workers as a mere way of counteracting the charge that it is elitist; while others, though basically agreeing with its policy, argue that it has not gone beyond the rhetoric of worker participation. Others still are critical of its emphasis on class, with its obvious Marxist associations, while it is also argued that this emphasis accurately reflects South African realities and does not necessarily reproduce a Marxist position. Clearly there is no consensus as to the 'correct' ideological interpretation of black consciousness.

Part of AZAPO strategy in recent times has been to launch the National Forum (NF), which it did in June 1983, as a response to proposed legislation affecting the freedom of movement of blacks in South Africa, as well as to the government's constitutional reforms. Some 800 people representing 170 organisations, including trade unions, met for two days to discuss issues of black opposition, against a background which included the launching earlier in 1983 of the United Democratic Front.

The NF adopted as its policy statement the Manifesto of the Azanian People, a socialist document based on four main principles: anti-racism and anti-imperialism; non-collaboration with the oppressor and his political instruments; independent working-class organisations; and opposition to all ruling-class parties. The manifesto opened with the statement:

Our struggle for national liberation is directed against the system of racial capitalism, which holds the people of Azania in bondage for the benefit of the small minority of white capitalists and their allies, the white workers and the reactionary sections of the black middle class. . . . Apartheid will be eradicated with the system of racial capitalism.

The manifesto ended with the demand for the 'establishment of a democratic, anti-racist worker republic in Azania, where the interests of the workers shall be paramount through worker control of the means of production, distribution and exchange'.

Can the NF and the UDF resolve their ideological differences, differences which first emerged nearly two decades ago when the PAC broke away from the ANC over the wording of the Freedom Charter? What is clear is that those who subscribe today to an Africanist philosophy within AZAPO and the NF are using an explicit class analysis, and identify the root problem in South Africa not as racialism but racial capitalism.

AZAPO's policy extends the black consciousness philosophy in two ways. Firstly, it recognises that some blacks collaborate with the system because it is in their class interests to do so. 'Black' therefore means 'oppressed', yet some blacks belong to the 'oppressor' class. Secondly, it insists on the importance of the trade union 'as an instrument that can bring about the redistribution of power'. Despite this assertion, AZAPO does not appear to have formal links with significant labour organisations, not even with the Council of Unions of South Africa (CUSA), the only significant black union grouping which has claimed black consciousness as its guiding philosophy.

Another organisation within the Black Consciousness Movement is the Azanian Students' Organisation (AZASO), founded in November 1979 in an attempt to forge a movement among students after the banning of SASO. The organisation is based on three principles. It seeks

(a) to promote the role of black students as a vanguard in the struggle for liberation;

(b) to affirm and clearly articulate their faith in the universality of students' rights and the dignity of black people;

(c) to maintain the supportive role of black students in the community.

AZASO recognised the need for blacks and whites to work together.

We [must] understand very clearly the difference between a democratic non-racial alliance and a liberal multi-racial jargon. . . . One of the future tasks is to draw more people into the democratic front, including whites who have come to accept the righteousness of our demands. (J. Phaahla, President of AZASO)

Collaborating closely with AZASO is the Congress of South African Students (COSAS), also founded in 1979. It stood in conscious opposition to those organisations which claim to be inspired by black consciousness. In 1982 Wantu Zenzile, COSAS president, stated:

the struggle knows no colour. The enemy is neither black nor white. This means the solution will never simply be a black government. . . . We must work together towards a free, democratic and non-racial South Africa.

AZASO and COSAS have shifted more radically than AZAPO, and cannot be regarded as black consciousness organisations. Psychological liberation of blacks by blacks, emphasis on the worker struggle, politicising of parents and adults in the black townships, and a willingness to work with whites in a democratic front — these are the hallmarks of the organisations committed to political radicalism in South Africa.

The question of means

Rhetoric alone will not change an oppressive situation. As early as 1973 young blacks began leaving South Africa for military training. Some black consciousness leaders saw quite clearly that the phase of psychological liberation, while necessary, was only a stepping-stone to active engagement in the armed struggle that was being waged against the South African state. Indeed, according to official South African sources, some 4 000 Africans left the Witwatersrand for military training in the two years after 1976, and a steady exodus continues and includes coloureds and Asians. The external leadership of the BCM has declared itself a movement of scientific socialism, committed to the 'armed struggle' for the 'liberation of Azania'.

In 1979 black consciousness groups in exile pooled their resources to form the Black Consciousness Movements of Azania (BCMA). It included the BPC, SASO, the National Youth Organisation (NYO), and SASM, the Black Allied Workers' Union (BAWU), and the Soweto Students' Representative Council (SSRC). This umbrella organisation regarded itself as an external wing of the Black Consciousness Movement in South Africa. One of its objectives was to prepare the way for a unification of all external liberation movements. Above all this would mean joining forces with the ANC and PAC.

By 1980, however, it became clear that unification would not work. Many exiles had become disillusioned with the BCMA and resigned to join the ANC. Of the issues in contention between the BCMA and the ANC, most serious were the ANC's policy of admitting non-blacks to its membership, and the ANC's Marxist leanings. Despite criticism, the ANC attracted BCMA members, perhaps because its policies were orientated towards action, and as a body was well organised. The exodus left the BCMA devoid of prominent black leadership. As one observer noted, 'Black consciousness was not designed for exile, and is breaking up.' Those who remain in the BCMA have, like the ANC and PAC, committed themselves to a protracted armed struggle against South Africa.

Some members of the BCMA have sought affiliation with the PAC, their positions being similar in some respects. The PAC has long criticised the ANC for admitting whites. The PAC espouses African socialism while the ANC is criticised for its communist links.

An assessment

From its inception as a liberation movement, born out of the black experience of oppressive apartheid and disillusionment with liberal multiracial opposition politics, black consciousness was a movement whose main concern was political. It saw itself as an heir to the heritage of black nationalism of the ANC and PAC. Its basic category of analysis was race, not in an ethnographic sense but in the sense that the oppressed group in South Africa was black. 'In the South African context, there are only two classes of people, the oppressor and the oppressed. The oppressed and exploited are disenfranchised, and can therefore not join hands with whites — no matter how sincere those whites may be.' Black consciousness was nationalist in the sense that it sought restitution of land and franchise to 'the people' from white 'colonisers' and the 'agents of colonial dispossessions'.

Gradually a significant shift has taken place in black consciousness, both externally and internally, at the level of analysis and strategy. At the analytical level black consciousness leaders are using sophisticated Marxist and neo-Marxist analyses of South Africa. In essence, they argue that the conditions of colonial or settler domination under which capitalism arose and continues to reproduce itself, have profoundly affected the formation of classes in South Africa. The development of capitalism was achieved by the systematic exclusion of blacks from the political process. This was effected by the denial of franchise and other human rights, such as freedom of movement, residence, and association. Blacks therefore have an interest in the removal of the political and economic structures of domination which whites wish to maintain.

Events since 1977 have forced the BCMA-in-exile into alliances with the ANC and the PAC, and resolute commitment to the armed struggle within South Africa. Internally black consciousness is expressed primarily through AZAPO and the National Forum, whose target is 'racial capitalism' and whose declared agency for change is the 'worker struggle'.

In sum black consciousness may be seen as an essential phase in the black liberation struggle, appealing primarily to black intellectuals, but its future shape and significance do not lend themselves readily to assessment.

On Black Theology

If NUSAS provided the immediate launching-pad for the founding of the first black consciousness organisation, SASO, some of the generative ideas of the movement sprang from membership of and contact with the University Christian Movement. Those ideas were expressed in a South African black liberation theology, namely Black Theology.

Black Theology regards itself as no more than a form of christian theology. Allan Boesak declares:

Black Theology is the theological reflection of Black Christians on the situation in which they live and on their struggle for liberation. Blacks ask: what does it mean to believe in Jesus Christ when one is black and living in a world controlled by white racists? And what if these racists call themselves Christians too?

Black Theology in South Africa sees itself as a liberation or political theology, not an African theology seeking to 'indigenise' Christianity in Africa. Desmond Tutu maintains:

Black theology is more thoroughly and explicitly political than African theology is. . . . It has an existential urgency which African theology has so far appeared to lack.

Black theology, then, is the explicit attempt by black christians to confront the conditions of political and economic exploitation endemic in South Africa: to use such biblical symbols as exodus and resurrection to conscientise blacks and motivate them to become engaged in the over-throw of the conditions of their oppression. As such some black theologians may make use of a class analysis of South Africa without necessarily espousing all the categories of a Marxist analysis of the human condition.

8 Black ethnic regrouping in South Africa

The reader will have noted that the chapters on African nationalism and black consciousness contained no reference to ethnicity, despite obvious cultural differences among the Bantu-speaking peoples of South Africa. This is because black nationalism and black consciousness recognise the dangers inherent in accentuating potentially divisive ethnic differences among blacks, and because both movements are implacably opposed to white attempts to use ethnicity as an organising principle in ruling the black majority.

The roots of racial and ethnic segregation run deep in South Africa. Successive white governments throughout South Africa's history have used race/ethnicity as a means to 'divide and rule' the black majority. But since 1948 the ruling Nationalist government has through its 'Bantustan' or 'homeland' policy extended this principle further than any other government.

The controversial issue which this chapter addresses is whether there exist in South Africa black 'ethnic-nationalisms' — ideological responses forged in reaction to white attempts to superimpose a racial/ethnic template upon the black population. In other words, has the policy of separate development generated a variety of 'ethnic-nationalisms'? Can one describe, for example, the policies of the ruling parties in Ciskei, Venda, Transkei or Bophuthatswana as ethnic-nationalisms? How is one to understand *Inkatha*'s political philosophy and its appeal to Zulu-speaking people in KwaZulu and elsewhere?

We can define an ethnic group as one characterised by relatively fixed and enduring qualities such as race, colour, religion, and language, in various admixtures. These qualities assume a life of their own, even in relatively open societies usually described as plural societies, where different ethnic groups maintain their respective identities while also identifying themselves with the larger society. But a group's ethnic identity can also be used to determine its access to wealth, power, and prestige. In such a case cultural pluralism is oppressive and can be fundamentally incompatible with democratic precepts.

From 'native reserves' to 'national states'

This section seeks to trace the major developments in government policies towards Africans, particularly as they concern black rights to land and franchise in South Africa. In this regard Hermann Giliomee, whose analysis we shall follow, identifies three distinct phases.

Interaction and separation

By the 1770s whites and blacks were mingling freely in the Zuurveld, between the Sundays and Fish rivers. For the following seventy years governments sought to implement a policy of separation by attempting to limit or prevent interaction so as to avoid friction.

No government succeeded, however, in curbing white expansion. By the end of the nineteenth century white farmers occupied most of the land surface of what is now South Africa and vast numbers of blacks had entered their service. The attempts to prevent intermingling had demonstrably failed. But in the eastern Cape, Natal (including Zululand), the Free State, and the northern and western Transvaal, a series of reserves or locations had been demarcated for exclusive African occupation. Over these areas tribal authority was exercised.

On the question of acculturation, there were two distinct approaches. The 'integrationist' approach is usually associated with Sir George Grey, who wanted 'gradually to win [African tribesmen] to civilization and Christianity, and thus to change by degrees our at present unconquered and apparently irreclaimable foes into friends'. Sir Theophilus Shepstone adopted a 'segregationist' approach, insisting that separate reserves be set aside, in which the authority of the chief and customary law were upheld, so that contact with whites would be minimised and Zulu culture left relatively uncontaminated. As David Welsh says, 'It is a myth that apartheid is the exclusive product of Afrikaner nationalism: its antecedents are to be found in Natal rather than in any other province.' Powerful Afrikaner voices in the late nineteenth century in fact argued that concentrating Africans in a reserve where the tribal system was preserved 'created a state within a state of a most pernicious kind' (President F. W. Reitz). General Smuts took the view, which finally prevailed, however, that 'the vast majority of the Native population — whether in locations or on farms — do not work at present' and that the system of reserves encouraged Africans to 'simply continue their old life of lazy barbarism'.

Segregation and separate development

The Land Act of 1913 set aside black reserves as 'scheduled areas' for black ownership and occupation, and provided for enlargement of the reserves. This provision has led some to see that Act as the beginning of a policy of separate 'homelands'. Scholars like Francis Wilson have argued cogently that the main concern of legislators was to provide labour for farms and mines.

The economic effect of the Act was to force blacks to sell their labour on white farms and to the mines, and to participate in the industrial process. The political effect was the emergence of what Edgar Brookes has called the ideology of possessory segregation. Political power and land-ownership went together.

Black claims to land and political rights in 'white' South Africa were diverted by the device of transferring some political functions to the reserves. By the 1920s official policy included as a formula the intention of granting a degree of self-government to these areas. But even so, Hertzog warned that the reserves 'would never become the independent states of which some Natives sometimes speak'.

In 1936 the Native Trust and Land Act was passed. It released more land to Africans, so that ultimately 15 million hectares (or 13 per cent of the land surface of South Africa) would fall under black occupation. It also abolished the right of individual Africans to purchase land in the reserves and introduced the Natal principle of trust tenure, which in effect prescribed communal grazing and one-man one-lot agriculture, thereby preventing 'the emergence of a new class of African "kulaks" or rich peasants' (Giliomee).

In 1955 the Tomlinson Commission proposed the abandonment of one-man one-lot in order to increase agricultural productivity in the reserves; in this way they could provide for the influx of blacks from white areas as a result of the application of apartheid policy. The government did not support this proposal, and in 1971 reaffirmed its policy of not permitting the acquisition of more than one farming-unit per individual, on the grounds that individual landholding on a large scale would undermine tribal authority.

During the Verwoerd era eight black ethnic units were granted separate 'homeland' status, with the prospect held out of their developing full independence. As Verwoerd explained, 'Here in South Africa there will be a white state, a big strong white nation' existing alongside 'various Bantu [sic] national units and areas (or states, if you like)'. The object of this grand design was the 'political and economic development of these homelands . . . as a *quid pro quo* for removing black political claims in white South Africa.'(Giliomee)

Observers believe the Bantustan policy had two major objectives. First, it sought to ensure white rule over 'white' South Africa. This not only entailed the abolition of black representation in Parliament; it also meant that blacks would have to accept citizenship of the homelands and exercise their political rights there. Second, it sought to provide an outlet for the political aspirations of blacks. Verwoerd argued that it would be wrong to 'retain control over what belongs to other people'. In this regard the homelands policy was designed to meet the 'ever-increasing desire for self-government which exists among non-whites'.

While political and administrative structures have been established in the homelands, thereby creating a measure of autonomy, it remains the case that all the homelands are greatly dependent on South Africa for economic development, defence and internal security: in effect they enjoy very little freedom of action.

Homeland autonomy deflects black political pressure away from 'white' South Africa. But the costs to the homelands are high; they include ongoing dependency on South Africa and a greatly strengthened conservative element in the homelands, focused on the chiefs. As one study observes, a consistent theme in the policy of separate development is the 'preservation and strengthening of the role of traditional rule in African societies', to the extent that the dominant role in homeland governments is played by chiefs whose status is ascribed and not based on election. Nancy Charton remarks, 'The chief then has emerged from the semi-obscurity of the colonial period to inherit the post-colonial kingdom. . . .'

A further goal of the policy was to deflect international pressure by granting a measure of autonomy to homelands and creating a community of cooperating homelands, while preserving the sovereignty and dominant position of the white South African state.

In the 1960s *verligte* Afrikaner nationalists began to urge the development of homeland policy in the direction of 'meaningful partition', which would involve granting 'separate freedoms' to white and black 'nations'. In the 1970s B. J. Vorster launched his outward policy of 'dialogue' with African leaders. It is no coincidence that this development impacted on internal policies. The homelands moved rapidly toward 'self-government' and by 1977 Transkei had become 'independent', and Bophuthatswana, Ciskei, Lebowa, Venda, Gazankulu, Qwaqwa and KwaZulu 'self-governing states'.

Yet it was internal political pressure that won the day. John Dugard noted that if South Africa had any hope of achieving international recognition for Transkei (the test case) it was imperative that Xhosa-speaking blacks living in urban areas in South Africa should not lose their South African citizenship with independence. However, by 1976 one of the main goals of the government's homeland policy was to eliminate as many blacks as possible from citizenship in South Africa. Speaking in the House of Assembly in 1978, Dr Connie Mulder expounded:

If our policy is taken to its logical conclusion as far as black people are concerned, there will be not one black man with South African citizenship. . . . Every black man in South Africa will eventually be accommodated in some independent new state in this honourable way and there will no longer be a moral obligation in this Parliament to accommodate these people politically.

From homelands to national states

In 1979 Prime Minister P. W. Botha announced his policy of a Constellation of States, a concept which had been present in government thinking for some time. Verwoerd, for example, had envisaged a South African commonwealth to which independent homelands would belong. This would comprise a grouping of independent states 'with mutual political interests', forming an economic 'common market'. P. W. Botha's Grand Constellation embraced some seven to ten states, including Zimbabwe, Botswana, Lesotho, Swaziland, and independent former homelands (now called national states). However, the vision was short-lived because none of the internationally recognised states, such as Botswana, would join the constellation. To have done so would have been to recognise the products of apartheid — the former homelands — as their equals in status.

When the 'Grand Constellation' failed, an 'inner constellation', later called a Confederation, was proposed. This would comprise South Africa and various homelands only. The policy also involved a new approach to the problem of economic development of the homelands. It was recognised that the Verwoerdian goal of economically viable homelands was impractical. As previous attempts at economic decentralisation had also failed, Botha announced a 'new regional economic strategy', based on 'economic cooperation transcending political borders' between South Africa and the homelands. Regions would be defined to meet the 'requirements for economic development', and 'balancing growth points' would be developed to offset the economic power of South Africa's metropolitan areas.

The political and constitutional aspects of the Confederation were left open. Botha urged business leaders in 1980: 'Let the constitutional debate continue. But let us cooperate now in combating poverty, unemployment, malnutrition and deprivation . . . [and raise] the standard of living and the quality of life of all sections of our diverse population.' A Development Bank was proposed as a means of achieving this.

Later it became clear that regional economic development would in no way diminish South African control or erode the political objectives of its homelands policy. By 1981 Botha had committed himself to the

principle that blacks in 'white' South Africa would have to exercise their
political rights in the homelands. 'He indeed insisted that there was not
a single black man in South Africa who is not in one way or another
connected to one or other national state' (Giliomee). Urban blacks in
South Africa would be linked through urban constituencies to the homelands and thereby to the Confederation. Regional economic development, it seems, does not in any way imply a form of regional political
integration in an evolving federal framework. On the contrary, the 'independence' of Transkei, Ciskei, Bophuthatswana and Venda has meant
that Xhosa, Tswana and Venda resident in 'white' South Africa have
been deprived of their South African citizenship. The political effect of
this has been to reduce substantially the number of people with claims
to political rights in the South African state. This process has been accompanied by a concerted effort to 'relocate' as many blacks as possible
from 'white' South Africa to the homelands.

In essence, then, the objectives of the homelands policy as outlined
by Verwoerd retain their currency. They involve safeguarding white
rule; providing some outlet for black political aspirations; and countering
world criticism. Of these, the first has been, and still is, paramount.
Frank Molteno has argued that the official homeland policy is a highly
rational attempt to ensure that no political rights are granted to Africans
within a common South Africa, since this would set in motion a process
whereby whites would lose their dominant position. The homelands
policy, in fact, represents a systematic attempt to 're-tribalize African
consciousness' in such a way that the resultant fragmentation into tribal
units would obstruct the emergence of an overriding African nationalism
in South Africa.

As a result there has been a shift in focus from race to nation in the
homelands, and a partnership between chieftainship and an emerging
black middle class has been created: their preoccupation is with 'nation-
building' rather than the struggle for equal rights in a non-racial democratic South Africa, which forms the traditional focus of African nationalism in South Africa.

Themes in ethnonationalism
Published speeches, party manifestos and press reports of the 1960s
and 1970s reveal certain themes emphasised by black political and cultural leaders in their response to South African government policy.

Nationalism
'I am a disciple of nationalism. I believe in Xhosa nationalism because
I was born to it. . . . My heritage commands me in the name of nation-

hood to sacrifice the best of my abilities to the advancement of my own nation in its own country, according to the terms of its own culture.' In this statement K. D. Matanzima of Transkei articulates the self-perception of many homeland leaders. For L. Sebe of Ciskei:

It is only in those days of conflict [in our history] that we were a real nation, bound together in one endeavour. . . . I feel that if I can again arouse in my people feelings similar to those which helped us withstand the armed might of Britain, then I will have achieved something in my life, and I can die happily. . . . I can one day stand before those great ancestors of mine, . . . and I can say to them 'Father, there is your nation.'

Pragmatism

The task of homeland leaders, as they see it, is to serve their people's best interests. To do so requires a pragmatic approach. According to L. Mangope of Bophuthatswana, 'the homelands are a reality with which we have to learn to live. . . . Of overriding relevance is the question whether we are happy with the various facets of this new reality.'

Pragmatic calculation is also involved in the decision to work within the homeland system. According to Matanzima, one can accept present conditions in South Africa, engage in revolution to change them, or 'try to achieve the same end without violence and bloodshed by working within the system'. Change should come about through negotiation and discussion because, as Sebe warned South Africa, 'my generation is the last generation of African men who will be prepared to sit down at a conference table and discuss our mutual future with you'. Working within the 'separate-development framework' is necessary, states Matanzima, because 'neither of the races inhabiting this country is prepared to sacrifice its own traditions, culture and national identity into a conglomerate blood mixture of an integrated society. Separate development is the answer. . . .' Indeed, he sums up a widespread feeling among homeland leaders: 'The policy of separate development, now the basis for the future development of all homelands, has demonstrated in no uncertain terms that if it is carried out to its logical conclusion, it will demonstrate to the world that black and white in South Africa can live together side by side, peacefully and respectfully.'

Collaboration with separate development

Acceptance of separate development is usually justified on two grounds. Some use separate institutions to undermine white domination (Bophuthatswana, KwaZulu); others to advance the cause of ethnic unity (Transkei, Ciskei, Venda).

Excerpts from K. D. Matanzima's *Independence My Way* indicate how independence is viewed by the dominant party in the Transkei. 'The black people of Africa can never be entirely free until the blacks of South Africa are free. Transkei's independence will be a material contribution to that cause.' Moreover, Transkei is 'doing nothing more than regaining sovereignty over its traditional territory'. It 'received its name in the 1880s which makes it older than the Union of South Africa, formed in 1910'. It existed as a state prior to apartheid and is thus not its creation. Indeed, 'Just as Jews everywhere gained a new stature with the coming into being of the Promised Land, Israel, so too we Transkeians have given all blacks in South Africa a new dignity by blazing the trail and founding a black Transkei.'

A similar national sentiment is to be found in speeches and writings of Ciskeian leaders. According to L. Sebe, in striving for independence, 'We as Ciskeians are not prepared to lose that which identifies us not only as Ciskeians, but in the broader context as South Africans.' Indeed, 'I know positively that the aspirations of my people are to achieve nation-hood for themselves as Ciskeians and citizenship for themselves as South Africans.'

Some homeland leaders see independence or self-determination as a strategy for undermining apartheid and racism in South Africa. Chief Mangope of Bophuthatswana has declared:

. . . our greater independence will put us on the road towards all those things which generations of our people have been . . . yearning and praying for. . . . At last we can demand that our human dignity be respected. . . . Let it be known that our main reason for choosing independence is that we utterly abhor racial discrimination.

Independence was chosen because the people of Bophuthatswana

desperately needed . . . a power base . . . to assert the principles that will forge the road into a meaningful future, not only for us as a nation, but for ourselves as inte-gral members of the southern African community. [It makes us] . . . a catalyst for accelerated change, so as to overcome . . . racialism on the sub-continent.

The role of the chiefs

All the homelands have unicameral legislatures in which appointed members, mostly chiefs or their representatives, play a dominant role. Moreover, all constitutions require that the chief minister be a chief. Traditional authority, which tends to be conservative, carries more weight in homeland politics than do parties and ideologies. It also tends to enjoy substantial support. With respect to urban Africans the situation is different: few show a desire to participate in homeland politics.

Chieftainship can be said to be at the heart of ethnic resurgence in the homelands. The manifestos of most political parties in the home-lands pledge support for preserving the tradition of chieftainship and tribal identity. The manifesto of the Transkei National Independence Party guarantees 'just and equal treatment to the various tribes living in the Transkei, and promises to foster a spirit of true Transkeian loyalty . . . bearing in mind the sanctity of its special customs and traditions for each tribe'. The Ciskei National Independence Party attempts to amalgamate traditional and modern political institutions. Its principle is 'the preservation of the institution of enlightened Chieftainship, which serves as a symbol of traditional leadership and a rallying point for tribal unity; and the operation of such chieftainship along modern democratic lines'.

Custom and ancestral land

Powers vested in traditional institutions cannot operate in a vacuum, and we must therefore consider the key question of land. The different ethnic groups each lay claim to an ancestral patrimony. The allocation of land in terms of the Land Acts of 1913 and 1936, which have been enforced by successive white governments, cuts across ancestral boundaries.

Just as the authority of the chief is invested with a sacred aura and embodies traditional values, so ancestral land is endowed with mystical power. It is believed, for example, that members of an ethnic group should be properly buried on their own ancestral land. For some, therefore, the establishment of homelands and the redrawing of boundaries are akin to return from exile from the uncertain existence of landlessness that characterises township life. Land, like chieftainship, binds members of an ethnic group into a firm collective unit. It sets them apart and evokes a spirit of national consciousness, be it Tswana, Xhosa or Zulu.

A dramatic example of the way ancestral land inspires nationalist feeling can be found in Ciskei. Ntabakandoda, a mountain in the Amatola range, has been made into a national symbol — 'the symbolic representation of the people because of their great historical association with the sagas and legends of the past'. To consolidate Ntabakandoda as a national symbol, the reburial took place there of Maqoma, an heroic nineteenth-century chief. In his eulogy Chief Sebe said: 'While Maqoma spent his life on the actual battlefield in mortal combat with the enemies of our beloved homeland — defiantly defending our national sovereignty — we today are fighting in a different way but this time with the same objective . . . constitutional advancements through democratic elections have taken the place of arms and spears.' Impressed by the Masada fortress, on a visit to Israel, where soldiers are 'transformed into defenders of the nation', Chief Sebe plans the construction of a sanctum on Ntabakandoda, which he hopes will 'inject the same spirit of nationalism in Ciskeians'. All Ciskeian chiefs who have died will be buried in the Heroes Acre there.

Perhaps the sentiment which best sums up the ethnic-nationalism as exists in the homelands is expressed in Chief Sebe's statement to the National Party caucus in 1979: 'All my people ask today, is what the Afrikaner asked fifty years ago — that is equality of opportunity, separate identity and respect.'

Inkatha: a special case

Thus far, there has been little discussion of KwaZulu. While KwaZulu occupies the same position as the other homelands, its leaders have totally rejected independence within the separate-development scheme. Further, while dealing with similar issues and problems, *Inkatha* provides the Zulu with an organised and self-conscious means of mobilisation for 'national' aims, whether these relate to the Zulu, or to all South Africans.

Inkatha ka Zulu was founded in 1928 by King Solomon kaDinuzulu as a cultural movement that would help preserve the Zulu heritage and offset estranging western cultural patterns. It was revived in 1975 as *Inkatha Yenkululeko Yesizwe*, the National Cultural Liberation Movement, by Mangosuthu Buthelezi. While the original *Inkatha* was committed solely to preserving the Zulu ethnic group as a cultural identity, the new body has extended its objectives to include black liberation within the wider context of South Africa. The main thrust is to thwart the aim of the Nationalist government to break up South Africa into black mini-states. But in order to achieve this, the *Inkatha* leadership has deemed it proper to mobilise on ethnic lines. The six million Zulu are held together by a sense of common origins, a common historical experience of conquests and defeats, common ties of loyalty to the same king, common traditions and customs. This strong collective identity is highlighted by the geographical boundaries imposed under the policy of separate development. Thus, while *Inkatha* was formed for specific, rational purposes, it banks on spontaneous ethnic attachments for its continued existence. We thus need to consider the extent to which *Inkatha* is a Zulu or a black nationalist movement, in practice and in self-perception.

The movement has had phenomenal appeal. As of 1979 it claimed to represent more than 250 000 paid-up members, with the support of several times that number of Zulu, as well as of other ethnic groups. Some 20 per cent of its membership were said to be non-Zulu. Chief Buthelezi has declared that the restricted membership with which *Inkatha* began was a strategy devised to block the imposition of so-called independence, by gaining control over the KwaZulu Legislative Assembly and so ensuring that 'independence cannot be forced on us . . . by Pretoria'. But while in 1979 membership was opened to all black people, its ethnic character still looms large. Its daily operations are limited to the advancement of the Zulu people in such areas as education, agriculture and community projects. However, through the South African Alliance, formed in March 1978 by the joining of forces between *Inkatha*, the (coloured) Labour Party and the (Indian) Reform Party, *Inkatha* has attempted to reach out to other groups. It is claimed that most of the influx of members comes from urban areas and that the Youth Brigade is the fastest-growing wing. Others argue that most of the membership is middle-aged, and the urban youth especially are highly critical of *Inkatha*. Clearly, it is difficult to evaluate the extent of support for *Inkatha*. We must therefore examine how *Inkatha* presents its aims, and what programmes and principles it has to offer.

On the occasion of the refounding of *Inkatha*, Chief Buthelezi declared:

[1975]

After a period of more than 5 years operating within the framework of separate development policy, we have decided to get out of the defensive and reactive roles. We have decided to mobilise ourselves by reviving our National Cultural Liberation movement.

Among the aims and objectives of the movement, as expressed in its constitution, are:

fostering the spirit of unity among the people of KwaZulu throughout South Africa, and between them and all their African brothers in southern Africa, and keeping alive and fostering the traditions of the people;

helping promote and encourage the development of the people of KwaZulu, spiritually, economically, educationally and politically;

establishing contact and liaising with other cultural groups in southern Africa with a view to the establishment of a common society;

promoting and supporting worthy indigenous customs and cultures;

cooperating locally and internationally with all progressive African and other nationalist movements and political parties which work for the complete eradication of all forms of colonialism, racialism, neocolonialism, imperialism and discrimination, and striving for the attainment of African unity.

Inkatha draws on a wide range of symbols and traditions in stating its objectives. Its vision is of a non-ethnic, democratic, unitary state (forged within a multiracial framework), and it is totally opposed to the independence of any part of South Africa.

I am not prepared to accept the so-called 'independence' of only regions of our country — Shaka's country is the whole of Natal. We have indicated that if it was given back to us, we would be prepared to accept <u>brown and white Zulus</u>, since we are not racists. We see the autonomy of such a state as <u>one federal multi-national state</u> of South Africa. This is <u>a compromise solution and an interim measure, before we can expect a one-man, one-vote situation which is ultimately inevitable</u>. *DATE ?*

Inkatha draws on *Ubuntu-Botho*, the philosophy of African humanism, which values the person, without regard to race, sex or antecedents. In an apartheid society, where blacks are continually degraded and denied their rights, *Inkatha* seeks 'to return to black people some of the dignity which was assailed and taken away since our conquest'. It is wrong to emphasise political problems to the exclusion 'of those other problems which keep us in a state of deprivation, about which we can do something even now to liberate ourselves'. Hence the strategy of liberation through culture. Each individual is urged towards self-help and self-reliance. This form of heroism in their daily lives will advance the people to a new nationhood free from the oppression of apartheid.

Chief Buthelezi is an advocate of <u>the politics of realism</u>. Organisation and discipline are two key values. 'Our sense of commitment must . . . earn ultimate victory through the hard grinding work of organising and disciplining a people's response. There is no substitute for constituency politics and disciplined approaches. We cannot allow outbursts of anger which lead to irresponsible behaviour.' *Inkatha* aims to build up grass-roots support, participating in 'constituency' or 'market-place' politics. It stands for non-violence and negotiating a common future for all the races of South Africa. Its approach is thus many-sided. 'The struggle for liberation is fought in our daily lives wherever we are. . . . We will fight the battle on the political front. We will fight it on the social front. We will fight it on the economic front.' *dates ?*

For *Inkatha*, this approach means fighting Pretoria in the constitutional area of separate development. *Inkatha* is strongly linked with the KwaZulu government. No person can be selected as a candidate for any parliamentary or local government election unless he is a member of the movement; the chief minister is also the president of *Inkatha*; and the members of the KwaZulu Legislative Assembly serve on the *Inkatha* National Council. Chief Buthelezi has often stated that *Inkatha* will prevent the KwaZulu Legislative Assembly from accepting 'independence' for KwaZulu, as *Inkatha* is a much truer reflection of the wishes of the people.

This is the major rationale for participating in 'homeland' politics. For Chief Buthelezi, politics is 'the art of the possible', and in the present situation, there are no options. <u>Moreover, for Chief Buthelezi</u> himself, there is no choice: he was born into Zulu royalty, and as such he cannot simply abandon his inheritance of chieftainship, nor can he forsake the Zulu people whom tradition has delivered unto him to lead, simply out of ideological puritanism. Involvement in the Legislative Assembly is considered as nothing more than involvement in local administration, and not a preparation for the eventual 'independence' of KwaZulu. Clearly, rejection of independence is the major basis for the claims of Chief Buthelezi and *Inkatha* for credibility and support.

Inkatha sees itself as the legitimate heir of the ANC, carrying its policy forward into the future. 'We owe it to the founding fathers of the ANC now banned, and to their successors, some deceased, some exiled and some incarcerated, to uphold the tradition of this titanic struggle for liberation.' Again, Chief Buthelezi has claimed: 'From jail I hear a message from Nelson Mandela and Walter Sisulu telling me to go on doing what I am doing on behalf of millions of black people. From my brothers in exile I get the same message.' However, *Inkatha*'s loyalties are rooted in the pre–1960 ANC, and in recent years there has been increased conflict and bitterness between the ANC-in-exile and *Inkatha*. Clearly, *Inkatha* is inspired most by the ideas of Dr A. B. Xuma, ANC president-general in the 1940s, who believed in non-violent mobilisation based on strict organisational discipline as the best strategy for success.

Contrary to those who see KwaZulu as a Zulu imperium or tribe, Chief Buthelezi stresses: 'We are a black national grouping or a cultural grouping within the South African nation.' This does not mean, however, that the Zulu are ashamed of their history and must apologise for being descendants of the Zulu kings. Their commitment to their ethnic identity is equated with their commitment to the rest of the South African people. 'National unity and models for development should be based on values extrapolated from our culture and adapted to our present-day needs and situation.' *Inkatha*'s economic policy is known as 'capitalism with *sisa* and *ubuntu*'. (*Sisa* is the Zulu custom of sharing with a less privileged neighbour.) The aim is 'to have a pinch of *ubuntu*, or African communalism, diluted into the free enterprise capitalist system'. We find in KwaZulu tripartite agreements between the KwaZulu Development Corporation (KDC), white entrepreneurs, and black citizens, in an attempt to implement these policies. As even after the time of liberation people will continue to live in the KwaZulu area, development is considered essential, and disinvestment by international companies can only cause greater harm and suffering.

One of *Inkatha*'s major weapons is the syllabus which it has introduced into all schools. This focuses on the development of the individual in the context of the family and then in the wider community. Self-realisation, self-help, and a keen sense of nationhood through knowledge of African culture and history are its cornerstones. The interdependence of the races in South Africa is stressed and the homelands policy is examined within the context of the future of South Africa. According to Oscar Dhlomo, 'We needed to create a reservoir of enthusiasts inspired with the aims and ideals of *Inkatha* and ensure it would be replenished from the bottom all the time.' *Inkatha* has a strong Women's Brigade, and a Youth Brigade which is taking on an increasingly paramilitary character (referred to, derogatorily, as 'Buthelezi's impis').

The lynchpin of the movement is Chief Buthelezi. 'The chief is a very valuable commodity to us — a man with great charisma and pull, from whom the people accept change requirements they wouldn't accept from anybody else.' According to his biographer, Buthelezi

remains a proud Zulu who sees himself first as a South African and then in terms of his ethnic background. Many see Chief Buthelezi, the hereditary Prime Minister and descendant of the Zulu royal family, as the modern-day Shaka who will unite the people and restore them to glory out of their suffering as peasants and workers in South Africa. Chief Buthelezi himself has an inescapable sense of his destiny. 'God help those who try to stop me from fulfilling my duty to the people.'

As already mentioned, there is increasing criticism of *Inkatha*, particularly by black radicals and the militant youth, who regard *Inkatha* as a 'Zulu broederbond', a sell-out, moderate organisation, and Buthelezi as a homeland leader and puppet of the government.

The central question, then, remains whether *Inkatha*'s ethnic base will carry the movement beyond white domination or whether it is destined to remain, because of the limitations imposed by its ethnic framework and official policy, a symbol of traditional opposition to white domination, without the real muscle to achieve meaningful change.

Conclusion

The political options of homeland leaders, whose parties are dominant because of ethnic resurgence, are severely circumscribed by the absence in South Africa of any opportunity for Africans to choose between a multiracial, unitary South Africa and separate development. The only real choice has been whether and to what extent they should participate in the separatist institutions created by the South African government.

Those who chose to participate and emerged as homeland leaders have followed one of two courses, and promoted ethnic-nationalist sentiments in the process. The US Study Commission, *South Africa: Time Running Out?*, summarises the courses of action in this way. Some leaders 'seek to use the separatist institutions to undermine white domination'. Others 'accept separation and use the new institutional framework to advance the cause of their own ethnic and regional unit. . . .'

Those who have accepted independence justify this step according to one or more of the following positions:

(a) The homeland was not the creation of South African policy but had existed as a state prior to apartheid (Transkei).

(b) Independence was necessary to prevent domination of a smaller African group by a larger one (Venda and Bophuthatswana).

(c) The choice was not between multiracialism and separation but between a racist status quo and the increased although flawed freedom resulting from independence.

Those who oppose independence argue that it:

(a) legitimates white rule in the common area;

(b) fragments African political opposition and thereby strengthens white rule;

(c) reinforces the rural–urban inequalities in South African society and deprives homeland populations of their birthright in a common South Africa;

(d) postpones peaceful change and genuine reform and makes these more difficult to achieve.

Public opinion surveys indicate that the majority of the African population would prefer a multiracial, ethnically plural, democratic South Africa. Urban Africans are most opposed to the homelands policy, while inhabitants of the homelands are more willing to accept a second-best separatist option in the absence of alternatives.

Homeland leaders who have pursued the option of becoming a self-governing state or chosen the path of independence have frequently generated national sentiment and ethnic pride to gain popular support for their policies. The themes of opposition to racialism, human dignity, pride in cultural identity, freedom, national development, land consolidation, support for traditional institutions such as chieftainship, and rights to nationhood, occur frequently in the speeches of leaders and the manifestos of their parties.

Criticisms of homeland leaders and their policies stress repressive and coercive policies carried out through security legislation in violation of civil liberties; economic corruption; oppression of trade unions and their leaders; conservatism among chiefs and headmen; a self-serving African petty bourgeoisie; perpetuation of the migratory labour system; and the dire economic plight of millions of Africans living in overcrowded conditions, with little hope of employment and the prospect of starvation an ever-present reality.

In these circumstances the question of whether or not there exists an ethnic-nationalism in the homelands may appear academic. So too is the question of whether the official policy is the cause or consequence of such ethnic-nationalism as may exist.

What is clear is that neither the melting-pot theory of ethnicity (ethnic identity ceases over time to be of significance) nor the cultural-pluralist theory (ethnicity can be an organising principle in politics) holds for South Africa. While ethnicity may be a significant factor in a person's or a group's identity, history tells us that it frequently takes on a reality of its own and becomes instead an instrument for subjugating those who affirm their cultural identity in ethnic terms. Lorraine Hansberry expressed this well in her play, *Les Blancs*. Against the background of an anticolonial war in a fictional African colony, Tshembe, an African revolutionary educated in Europe, and Charlie, a liberal white journalist from the United States, debate the limits of race as an explanation for colonial domination.

TSHEMBE Race — racism — is a device. No more. No less. It explains nothing at all.

CHARLIE Now what the hell is that supposed to mean?

TSHEMBE (*closing his eyes, wearily*) I said racism is a device that, of itself, explains nothing. It is simply a means. An invention to justify the rule of some men over others.

CHARLIE But I agree with you entirely! Race hasn't a thing to do with it actually.

TSHEMBE Ah — but it has!

CHARLIE (*throwing up his hands*) Oh, come on, Matoseh. Stop playing games!

TSHEMBE I am not playing games. (*He sighs and now, drawn out of himself at last, proceeds with the maximum precision and clarity he can muster.*) I am simply saying that a device is a device, but that it also has consequences: once invented it takes on a life, a reality of its own. So in one century, men invoke the device of religion to cloak their conquests. In another, race. Now, in both cases you and I may recognize the fraudulence of the device, but the fact remains that a man who has a sword run through him because he refuses to become a Moslem or a Christian — or who is shot in Zatembe or Mississippi because he is black — is suffering the utter *reality* of the device. And it is pointless to pretend that it doesn't exist — merely because it is a *lie*!

In the real world of South Africa the feelings of millions who take pride in being Xhosa, Zulu or Tswana may be better understood if for 'race' we read 'ethnicity' in Hansberry's script. Once invented and then secured it takes on a reality of its own and can be invoked as a cloak for conquest.

Part three
SOCIALISM AND SOUTHERN AFRICA

The contending ideologies described in Parts One and Two have arisen mainly within the context of race relations and capitalist development, and owe their shape and emphasis to the particular (some would say unique) development of South Africa. In Part Three we turn to the socialist critique, specifically of South African capitalism, and more generally of capitalist development policies in sub-Saharan Africa. This section includes a brief history of the Communist Party of South Africa, and a description of social democracy and democratic socialism. Other chapters discuss African socialist and Afro-Marxist development policies in black Africa. These chapters are basically descriptive and make no attempt to incorporate the theoretical foundations of Marxist socialism.

9 Socialism, Marxism and communism in South Africa

Socialism in its many forms has historically been imported into South Africa by white immigrants, mostly from Britain. European artisans formed craft unions in South Africa along similar lines to those in Europe. They accepted without difficulty that all the unskilled labour was performed by Africans and coloureds, receiving wages far below their own. These unions and their political expression, the South African Labour Party (formed in 1909), were for 'Europeans only'. Though the South African Labour Party was affiliated to the Socialist International, it was only nominally socialist.

The chief channel through which Marxist and Marxist–Leninist thinking has exerted influence in South Africa is the Communist Party of South Africa (CPSA). Founded in 1921 and outlawed in 1950, it was the first communist party to be established on the African continent, in the country which has the highest degree of industrialisation and the most developed working class in Africa.

Socialist beginnings

In 1915 a group of left-wing socialists broke away from the largely white Labour Party and formed the International Socialist League (ISL). Though mainly concerned with white workers it was especially through D. I. Jones and S. P. Bunting that socialist thought began to influence the African working class. In 1917 the ISL started the 'Industrial Workers of Africa', an organisation of unskilled labourers in Johannesburg, hoping that it would develop into a large trade union. But it soon faded out after the 'bucket strike' of 1918. When in February 1920 about 40 000 African mine workers came out on strike, the ISL appealed to the white workers in the name of the unity of the working-class movement not to break the strike. But the reality of personal privilege was stronger than socialist theory of worker solidarity.

Industrial and Commercial Workers' Union (ICU)

Founded in 1919 as a trade union of dock workers in Cape Town, the ICU developed into the general union for 'non-European' workers. It grew under the remarkable leadership of Clements Kadalie from an initial membership of 24 to 250 000 in 1928. From its beginning it was in contact with European Marxists. Members of the ISL assisted in drafting its preamble and constitution; this included several passages of Marxist analysis which Kadalie defended even after the expulsion of the communists from the ICU in 1926.

The foundation and beginning of the CPSA

In 1921 the International Socialist League, together with the Social Democratic Federation, the Durban Marxist Club, the Cape Communist Party, and the Jewish Socialist Society, formed the Communist Party of South Africa on the basis of the twenty-one points of the Communist International. Until 1924 the CPSA had little influence, except through the ICU, on African workers. Only gradually did it develop a non-racial class analysis of South Africa. After the departure of Jones for Russia in 1922, Bunting remained the only leader genuinely interested in African workers. The CPSA's main focus of concern lay in exerting influence over white workers in order to defeat the Smuts government. It supported the Hertzog–Labour pact, and in this way the communists helped the Nationalists to come to power in the election of 1924.

At the national conference held in Johannesburg in 1924, the breakthrough came for those in the party who wanted to concentrate on the African workers as the real proletariat. They defeated by a small majority those who wanted to apply again for affiliation with the Labour Party, an application which had been refused on three earlier occasions. The Young Communist League, the junior section of the party, was advised by the Young Communist International in Moscow to avoid segregation within the youth movement in South Africa and to combine with Africans in a common organisation. This in turn led to a rapid decline of white membership in the party. It took several years of diligent organisation, trade union efforts, and night-schools for Africans under the leadership of T. W. Thibedi to build up a predominantly black membership. Two of the Africans whom the CPSA won into its ranks were S. Silwana and T. Mbeki; together with young white communists, they started the first Witwatersrand branch of the ICU. In the beginning collaboration between the CPSA and ICU was very close, and membership often overlapped. The CPSA's newspaper, the *South African Worker*, exhorted people to join both the CPSA and the ICU.

But the change came quickly. The disproportionately influential left-wing group in the ICU, led by communists (four of whom sat on the executive of the ICU), attacked Kadalie and the right wing in the

ICU for their reformist policy. They wanted action, strikes, and boycotts. Apart from this militant stance they opposed the dictatorial attitudes of Kadalie and other leaders, and above all they severely criticised the ICU's financial dealings. The inevitable clash came to a head when at an executive meeting of the ICU in December 1926, the motion was carried that 'no officer of the ICU shall be a member of the CP'. This decision was confirmed in the subsequent annual meeting of the ICU, when all members of the ICU were forbidden to identify themselves in any way with the CPSA.

The CPSA and the ANC

Though the ICU continued to flourish for a short while, it started to disintegrate rapidly after 1928. The interests of the CPSA shifted increasingly to the ANC. The vice-president of the ANC, J. Gumede, after a visit to Russia in 1927, seemed to welcome the communists as allies. He introduced a stream of radical thinking into the Congress, thereby tempering its mostly liberal racial analysis and strategy. The CPSA had from its beginning developed a class analysis of South African society as the basis for unifying all races in a struggle against capitalism. By 1930 communist influence in the ANC had reached a climax. There was a strong cooperation with the ANC especially in the western Cape, where the Congress members supported the CPSA campaign to down tools and burn passes throughout South Africa on 16 December 1930.

1930 marked the peak in membership and influence of the CPSA. By 1928 they counted 1 750 members of whom about 1 600 were Africans. By 1930 they had grown to a membership of 3 000 and were affiliated to a trade union federation of 10 000 members. The intense work of the preceding years had paid off and they had established themselves firmly as a predominantly African movement. It had, under the leadership of Thibedi and Weinbren, formed the first proper African Trade Union whose headquarters was in the communists' offices at Fox Street, Johannesburg.

Many members of the CPSA had very little political knowledge. The Comintern, which developed an interest in the CPSA after 1928, were preoccupied with the purity of orthodox doctrine and suggested that the CPSA should remain a small and select body of trained revolutionaries working through a larger body in order to lead the masses.

Within the ANC opposition to communist influence and to the pro-Soviet and anti-religious crusades of Gumede mounted. At the ANC Congress in April 1930 a clash developed between the radical and the moderate wings of the ANC. Gumede defended the communists, identifying himself with their slogan of a 'Native Republic' and the League of

African Rights. Whereas he adopted a militant stance of struggle against imperialist capitalism, the moderate majority of Congress was in favour of a round-table conference of Europeans and Africans and adopted the resolution of observing 31 May as a day of prayer and protest. Gumede's defeat caused the CPSA to turn to the radical members of the ANC, mainly from the western Cape, who in November 1930 launched the Independent ANC with a manifesto which showed clear signs of the CPSA's influence.

In the 1930s the CPSA played a peripheral role in African politics. Deprived of its influence in the ANC and in the declining ICU, it became more and more subject to the often disconcerting orders from Moscow. In 1928 the Comintern decreed the adoption of the slogan of a 'Native Republic'. But as soon as the League of African Rights was successfully formed it was condemned by Comintern as reformist. From then on an increasing bolshevisation of the party took place. The new leaders, D. Wolton and L. Bach, followed a rigid Comintern line. They tried to re-structure the party as a select group of well-trained functionaries. This led to the 'liquidation of the right-wing danger' and the expulsion of some of its most experienced members, among them S. P. Bunting.

The dogmatic decrees from above cut the CPSA off increasingly from the main stream of the African resistance movements, and all for the purity of the party line, which opposed any attempts to collaborate in a common popular front. In a belated effort to have some say in the All-African Convention (AAC), formed in 1935 under the initiative of ex-pelled party members, the Seventh International suddenly allowed collaboration with popular fronts and national liberation movements. With party membership at a low point the CPSA slowly reconstructed its forces. After abandoning the slogan of a 'Native Republic', it returned to a non-racial class struggle and later to increasing support for the ANC. Some party members, like Moses Kotane, J. B. Marks and Edwin Mofutsanyana, were to play important roles in the ANC. This contributed to a strand of radicalism which was to emerge within the ANC in the Youth League.

The years of the war

The CPSA had initially, mainly under the leadership of Y. M. Dadoo (later the leader of the South African Indian Congress), opposed the participation of Africans in the war against Nazi Germany since Africans were not allowed to carry arms. But when in 1941 the German army invaded Russia, the CPSA, obedient to the dictates from Moscow, supported the government's war effort.

Trotskyism

The only left-wing groups opposing the war as imperialist were the Trotskyists, who fought international Stalinism and accused the CPSA of betraying Marxist–Leninist doctrine. Trotskyists were strong among European intellectuals, especially in the Cape, and later among coloured teachers and university students. One of the Trotskyists, Max Gordon, played an active part in organising African trade unions. Through the Workers' International League the Trotskyists controlled a number of African unions in the 1940s.

The Unity Movement of South Africa

The Unity Movement of South Africa, a direct descendant of the All-African Convention, was formed by African intellectuals under the leadership of Dr I. B. Tabata. It proclaimed itself a Marxist movement and had Trotskyist leanings. They realised that the sole hope of a revolutionary upsurge in South Africa lay with the black proletariat. In order to overthrow capitalism they wanted to equip the people for an armed struggle, but this never materialised. Tabata had to flee, and set up headquarters in Lusaka. For many years he was one of the most outspoken practitioners of Marxism in South Africa.

Work with trade unions

During the years of the war the CPSA was active, with varied success, in establishing African trade unions. 1931 and 1932 saw the first attempts by the communists to organise African mine workers. They were behind the formation of the African Mine Workers' Union in 1941 under their leading protagonist G. Radebe. In 1942 the first conference of the new Council of Non-European Trade Unions (CNETU) took place in Johannesburg. They elected as chairman Gana Makabeni who co-operated closely with the communists. In 1945 he was succeeded by the communist, Marks, secretary of the African Mine Workers' Union. By 1945 CNETU claimed to represent over 150 000 organised African workers. A series of strikes swept the country. The climax was reached in August 1946 when about 60 000 mine workers on the Rand came out on strike and demanded 10 shillings a day and better food. The strike was suppressed by the police. Some 52 persons, leading members of the African Mine Workers' Union and the CPSA, were charged with conspiracy and with promoting an illegal strike. The first charge was finally dropped. In November 1946 the whole national executive committee of the CPSA was tried on a charge of sedition in connection with the mine workers' strike. After trials lasting nine months the charge was withdrawn.

In 1947 the CPSA faced a major split in the African unions with the establishment of the anti-communist Council of African Trade Unions. But the mine workers' strike, and especially the advent of the Nationalist government in 1948, brought about a new phase of collaboration between the CPSA and the ANC through the radical wing in the ANC, namely the Congress Youth League.

The communists and the Congress Youth League

During the years of the war the ANC remained committed to a non-racial, politically and economically integrated South Africa, and continued to pursue a strategy of non-violence and passive resistance. In 1944 the Congress Youth League (CYL) was founded by a group of young Africans who saw the need for new forms of mass protest and mass action. Influenced by Pan-Africanism, the relatively small core of about 60 members developed a militant African nationalism based on a predominantly racial analysis of South African society. From the very beginning there was a small group around W. Nkomo that leant towards a Marxist analysis, but the majority in the CYL was suspicious of communist influence. They considered communism a dogmatic ideology controlled from abroad and foreign to African nationalist interests. They feared that the communists' class analysis would divert their attention from a self-asserting African nationalism challenging white domination, and that they would be used as a mere tool in the ultimate interests of Soviet-led international communism.

With the coming to power of Afrikaner nationalists in 1948 much changed. The common struggle against apartheid united the ANC via the CYL with the CPSA and the Indian Congress, now under the leadership of the communist, Yusuf Dadoo. Already in 1946 Kotane and Marks, both communists, as well as D. Tloome, a close sympathiser, had been elected to the national executive. In 1950 Marks became the president of the Transvaal Congress. Through numerous individual contacts, strengthened by the entrance of a group of young radicals from Fort Hare to the ranks of the CYL, Marxist thinking was absorbed by many African nationalists, who, despite their continuing differences with communism, began to use the terms of Marxist analysis. The Programme of Action presented by the CYL in 1948, and finally endorsed by Congress at the end of 1949, called for mass action through strikes, boycotts and civil disobedience, derived from the initiative of the left wing of the Congress.

The Suppression of Communism Act

The organisation of a 'Freedom Day' on May Day 1950, called for mass demonstrations in defence of 'full franchise rights and the abolition of all discriminatory legislation'. It was essentially a communist initiative, as official ANC support was withdrawn at the last moment. It presented the final opportunity the government needed to outlaw the communists.

The Suppression of Communism Act of 1950 was one of many statutes passed to entrench the power of the National Party. The definition of communism contained in this Act (variously amended) is so wide that it includes many more individuals and groups than the communists. The Minister of Justice is given discretionary power to ban individuals and organisations involved in any doctrine or scheme 'which aims at bringing about any political, industrial, social or economic change within the Union by the promotion of disturbances or disorder, by unlawful acts or omission, or by the threat of such acts and omissions, or by means which include the promotion of disturbances or disorder, or such acts or omissions or threats'. The CPSA dissolved itself just before the Act came into effect.

The CPSA after 1950

Since 1950 the CPSA has continued as an underground organisation, and has set itself up in exile. It is still very much under the control of Moscow, being constantly under orders from the Central Committee. The CPSA-in-exile continues its popular-front policy. It still supports all 'progressive forces' within the South African liberation movements. It opposes all 'ultra-left' attempts to by-pass 'historically necessary stages', as well as 'reformist' social democratic tendencies, which are only obstacles on the way towards revolution.

The influence of the CPSA on African nationalism has been and continues to be both stimulating and divisive. It contributes to a political awareness among the African masses of the national liberation struggle, and at the same time tries to tone down the racial features of African nationalism in favour of the spread of class consciousness, in preparing for the establishment of a socialist republic.

The party continues to support the ANC and the Indian Congress. These two bodies, together with the Congress of Democrats, formulated the Freedom Charter adopted by the Congress of the People at Kliptown in 1955. The attempt of the Nationalist government to link the ANC with the illegal CPSA in the famous Treason Trial of 1956–61 failed. All the persons accused were acquitted. The prosecution could not prove that the ANC had become a communist organisation intent on overthrowing the State by violence. But this judgment did not prevent the banning of the ANC and the PAC in 1960. Many of their leaders left the country. The executive of the ANC set up its headquarters at

Morogoro, Tanzania. The prominent South African communist, Joe Slovo, was elected into the leadership of the ANC, at the Morogoro Conference. To the degree which the liberation struggle is radicalised, the influence of radical ideology increases. This leads to the strengthening of the radical wing in the ANC and to a closer collaboration with the CPSA-in-exile.

Marxist influence in present-day South Africa

The Suppression of Communism Act and its application in the last thirty years have had a paralysing effect on any real critical dialogue in South Africa with Marxism in its many forms. Bannings and censorship have led to fear and ignorance on the one hand, and to an almost mystical attraction to Marxism on the other. Official pamphlets treat Marxism as an expression of the 'red danger' and attribute to agitators any disturbances to law and order. Marxism is stereotyped as Soviet communism, and, some would argue, even this in a distorted form. For those who want radical change of the present system Marxist literature has the taste of forbidden fruit. It is relatively difficult to gain access to the literature, hence the prevalence of handy oversimplified slogans.

The teaching of Marxism has been almost absent from the syllabi of South African high schools, colleges, seminaries, and universities. With a Mugabe-led Zimbabwe and Marxist–Leninist Angola and Mozambique on South Africa's doorsteps, and with a growing number of militant blacks adopting a more revolutionary stance, Marxism has again become one of the main ingredients of the South African ideological scene, in thought and in deed.

Besides its influence in the labour movement, there is an increasing radical trend in South African historiography. Radical writing of South African history, influenced by the intense neo-Marxist debate of the last forty years or so, otherwise so often forgotten or unnoticed in South Africa, has attempted to review South African history. These alternative histories are written from a different perspective to that of Afrikaner nationalism, and especially to the liberal version as epitomised in the *Oxford History of South Africa* (1969 and 1971). Put simply, liberals view the history of South Africa in terms of the two basic factors of culture and race (racial analysis). Radicals, like S. Trapido, M. Legassick, F. A. Johnstone, H. Wolpe and C. Bundy, view history from the angle of the needs of capitalism, its main need being cheap labour (an economic analysis). In contrast to the liberals who maintain that economic growth is an integrative and progressive force, radicals try to show that apartheid and segregation have arisen not in spite of but on account of capitalism, with the result that the present-day apartheid is not an outmoded relic but a highly sophisticated form of maintaining the economic privileges of the white minority.

Bram Fischer: the agony of choice

We include here a biographical sketch of one of the best-known members of the CPSA, Bram (Abram) Fischer. He symbolises the agonising choices of a white South African who has come to realise he can no longer justify the very society which has given him all he has, and risks ostracism by his own people in the process.

Born in 1908, the son of a judge president of the Orange Free State, and grandson of a prime minister of the Orange River Colony, Bram Fischer was brought up as an Afrikaner nationalist. He became, in 1929, the first nationalist 'prime minister' of a student parliament, and remained a nationalist until, with the rise of Nazism, he began to doubt that racial segregation could provide the solution to South Africa's problems. A Rhodes scholar at Oxford, he qualified as a barrister and practised in Johannesburg. He was later elected to the Bar Council whose chairman he was for some years.

Bram Fischer joined the Communist Party in his early thirties for two main reasons, as he told the court in Pretoria at his trial in 1966. The first was that the Communist Party rejected any colour bar and believed in the final brotherhood of man, in opposition to the glaring injustice and irrationality of racialism. The second reason was his growing awareness that members of the Communist Party were ready to sacrifice most in the struggle against discrimination. Even after the Suppression of Communism Act of 1950, he continued to be a member of the Communist Party in disobedience of the law, which, in his opinion, had become immoral since it required the citizen to participate in an organised system of oppression that deprived the majority of the people of the most elementary human rights. For him a higher duty compelled him to continue his work in the Communist Party. The application of the political theory of Marxism, the active liberation of the African people, and the eventual establishment of a socialist state—these Bram Fischer saw as the only means of overcoming the injustices of apartheid society and the only means of achieving equality without the otherwise inevitable violence, terror and war, which he opposed throughout his life.

As Queen's Counsel Fischer led the defence in various political trials, in particular the Treason Trial of 1956–61 and the Rivonia Trial in 1963–4. In September 1964 he was charged under the Suppression of Communism Act. Briefly released on bail to argue a case in London, he returned to South Africa and went underground. There he continued the struggle, as he explained to the court, out of loyalty to his (Afrikaner) people. Despite the risk entailed to his own life he felt there ought to be at least one Afrikaner who stood out in protest. He was chairman of the central committee of the CPSA, and its acting chairman. In November 1965 he was captured and brought to trial under the Sabotage Act and the Suppression of Communism Act. He was sentenced to life imprisonment, and died in May 1975.

Bram Fischer ended his statement to the court in Pretoria, on 28 March 1966, with the words of one of Afrikanerdom's great leaders, President Kruger, which aptly sum up for Bram Fischer his own life and hope, and that of many others in South Africa: '*Met vertrouwen leggen wij onze zaak open voor de geheele wereld. Het zij wij overwinnen, het zij wij sterven: de vrijheid zal in Afrika rijzen als de zon uit de morgenwolken.*' (With confidence we lay our case before the whole world. Whether we win or die, freedom will rise in Africa, like the sun from the morning clouds.)

In different historical circumstances Bram Fischer might have been one of South Africa's greatest sons. For some he remains that.

10 Socialism in Africa and problems of development

With the suppression, dissolution or banning of the South African Communist Party, the ANC, PAC, the Unity Movement of South Africa, and various black consciousness organisations, there are few public voices left that are advocates of socialism in South Africa. Yet one can safely say that the majority of blacks who support the broad aims of the liberation movements envisage some form of socialism as political-economic ideology for a future liberated South Africa.

The Freedom Charter of 1955 advocates government by the people and a basic redistribution of land and wealth. Policy statements of the ANC and black consciousness organisations (as, for example, the Manifesto of the Azanian People adopted by the National Forum in 1984) speak in broad terms about a new democratic socialist order. Many, among whom also an increasing number of committed christians, believe that, given the basic economic and political injustices of the present system, socialism is the only morally acceptable alternative framework within which a just solution for all South Africans can be found.

What concrete form would this socialism take? There seems to be a necessary vagueness about socialist views of the future. If it is a mark of genuine socialism that it is not to be imposed from the top but emerges from the struggle of the people for their liberation, then it is impossible to predict the concrete form socialism would take. To the degree to which one can learn from the success and failure of others, blacks in South Africa will look to the rest of Africa, and in particular to some of its neighbouring states, for alternative models of socialism.

In the first part of this chapter we shall explore the record of African socialism as implemented in the first wave of socialism in the sixties and seventies, before we turn to some countries that belong to the second wave of socialism, having gained their independence in the seventies and eighties, and which have opted for 'scientific socialism' or Marxism-Leninism. We shall also deal with the difficulties of building socialism in Africa, and conclude with a note on the role of Soviet Russia on the African continent.

The first wave of socialism in Africa

For most of Africa, colonialism and the struggle against colonialism have been powerful historical factors. Although the colonial period lasted for only 60–80 years, it dramatically changed the face of the African continent. African peoples lost their freedom and their traditional cultures; western education profoundly altered patterns of thought; subsistence economies were transformed into cash-crop farming; the colonial powers drew often arbitrary boundaries, and used the colonies as providers of cheap raw materials for the mother countries.

In their revolt against colonial powers the liberation movements were motivated not by Marxism but by nationalism in its various forms. First it was expressed in armed rural revolts in the years 1900–20, then through growing nationalism in the twenties and thirties, led by the black elites (mainly educated in the United States), who introduced the ideal of Pan-Africanism. Its weakness at this stage was that it was limited to an educated elite in a few urban centres. With the exception of Egypt, the third and final stage in the liberation struggle began after the Second World War, when nationalism spread to the masses, and organised itself in parties of opposition to the colonial powers.

The British were the first to relinquish colonial power. Ghana received independence in 1957 and by 1965 almost all of British Africa had become independent. Between 1959 and 1961 all the French colonies became independent, while remaining in a kind of French commonwealth under the firm control of France (except for Guinea).

In most cases independence was not a revolutionary change, it often only involved a change of rulers. The colonial masters left their machinery behind: the civil service, army and police force. Independent countries remained economically dependent on their former colonisers. The new rulers, under the constant threat of tribalism, faced enormous problems as they struggled to build their nations into united states. In order to differentiate themselves from the colonial past and their former masters these newly independent African states looked for a unifying ideology. At the Dakar Colloquium of December 1962, some outlines were formulated: African socialism began to emerge, in which 'nationalism, Pan-Africanism, and socialism are woven together to create an overall African ideology of modernization'.

National modernisation represented the attempt by a westernised elite to create modern states in the independent countries. It expressed itself in differing degrees of radicality, and a wide spectrum of policies ranging from a traditionalist conservatism to a radicalism which sees all traditional elements as obstacles in the way of modernity. Wide-scale education aimed at national unity, and repression of any opposition, are characteristics of these new states.

The key to modernisation is believed to lie in the rapid industrialisation of the country (Tanzania is the exception). In general, African states have chosen socialism as the most effective and rapid way to development. This socialism is not western or Marxist, but *African*, steering a course between the extremes of collectivisation on the one side and capitalism on the other. The choice of socialism has, besides economic motives, moral implications as well. African leaders react against the individualism, profit-seeking and ruthless competition of the free market as foreign to the basic values of African communalism.

While African leaders criticise the excessive collectivism of communism, its suppression of the individual, and its materialism and atheism, which are so alien to the 'African personality', certain aspects of Marxism appeal to them. They see their own struggle against their colonisers in terms of the class struggle. In general they accept Lenin's theory of 'imperialism as the highest form of capitalism' for it strengthens their awareness of having been exploited by capitalist colonial masters. They argue that they have been used by the so-called developed countries, and their own underdevelopment is the immediate result of this. This critique of imperialism, however, applies in the eyes of many of them not only to the capitalist West but also to the communist East. Africa looks for a middle way between the forces of 'anti-communism' and 'anti-imperialism', as Julius Nyerere puts it.

Though not a total Marxist himself, Kwame Nkrumah introduced many facets of Marxist thinking into Africa. In his theory of neo-colonialism he pointed out that the 'independent countries' were not really independent, since they continued to depend on the capitalist system by maintaining economic ties with their former colonial masters. Through what he called 'consciencism' he wanted to awaken Africa to a more radical socialist change. But the means he chose were not Marxist: in his exhortation 'seek ye first the political kingdom' he favoured the superstructure as the means of creating a new consciousness; a Marxist would see the emergence of a new social consciousness as dependent on a change in the superstructure of the forces and relations of production.

Nkrumah's theory of neo-colonialism as being the prime enemy is a development of Lenin's theory of imperialism. With the transformation in capitalism through the emergence of multinational corporations which have successfully penetrated the ostensibly independent African economies, the old model, in which colonial governments divided Africa into separate spheres of influence, has, however, reappeared in a new form. Only Tanzania and Algeria have made significant steps towards a self-reliant socialist economy, whereas many African states, despite a declared commitment to socialism, have created an emergent class of bourgeois bureaucrats which has advanced its own power. While a kind of growth is evident in some of these states, they have created policies enabling multinational corporations to dominate their national economies, and the majority of the people have suffered even further impoverishment.

Despite a certain sympathy in African socialism for some aspects of Marxism or Marxism–Leninism, the critique of many other aspects seems to prevail to the degree of moderation or radicalism adopted by individual leaders.

African socialism is above all a *nationalist* socialism; it claims to act on behalf and in the interests of the people as one nation. Therefore Marxist analysis which is based on the existence of classes and the resulting class struggle is rejected. Mboya, Senghor, Nyerere and even the more radical Sekou Touré of Guinea have denied the existence of conflicting classes. In building the nation they have tried to prevent the emergence of classes for the sake of unity, often remarking that class struggle is foreign to African communalism. Sekou Touré claimed that Africa is already a classless society. It is only under the influence of the more radical thought of Frantz Fanon and Amilcar Cabral that a recent scholar, I. G. Shivji, in his book *Class Struggles in Tanzania* (1976) concludes differently.

From the denial of class conflicts in African socialism follow some of its more important differences with Marxism. The role of the state is seen much more positively as representing the interests of all; there is little hint of its withering away, there is no need for the 'dictatorship of the proletariat'. The thinking on revolution among African leaders is again influenced more by Fanon and Cabral than by Marx and Lenin. It leans heavily on the theory of guerrilla struggle as developed by Mao Tse-tung and R. Debray, drawing on the experience gained in China and Cuba, and as practised by Eduardo Mondlane, Samora Machel, and the leaders of the Zimbabwean Patriotic Front.

African socialism is *humanist*. As such, it recognises with Marxism, the alienation of western man through capitalism, and tries to build an indigenous socialism on the traditional values of African communalism. Its chief spokesmen are Kenneth Kaunda, Julius Nyerere, and Leopold Senghor. African humanist socialism strongly opposes the materialism and atheism inherent in Marxism–Leninism. No opposition between its spiritual and religious values need exist, as Nyerere explained in an interview in November 1976:

TANU is in no way an atheist party. We reject atheism in principle, because we reject — as a matter of principle — the idea that we have a right to ask our members whether they believe in God or not. We do not believe that this is the business of a political party. We believe that communists are wrong in asking the question, 'Do you believe in God?', and rejecting you as a party member if you say 'yes'. We believe that metaphysics is not the business of a political party — and so TANU does not raise the question at all. . . . So we and the communists differ — I sometimes wonder if the Church realizes how much we and the communists do differ on this matter! In fact we differ fundamentally, absolutely. We claim they are wrong in this matter.

African socialism is a socialism planned by an elite for the people. The masses are to be 'conscientised' through large-scale propaganda and education to develop a new socialism imposed from above which, however, claims to correspond to the African roots of the people. Usually it takes the form of a single party system with strong military support under the leadership of a popular, charismatic leader. Parliamentary democracy is, in general, seen as incapable of providing the effective leadership which is needed to fulfil the gigantic task of modernisation and socialism in underdeveloped countries. Of course this makes these regimes very vulnerable to military coups. From 1965 onwards we have witnessed a wave of military coups in many states of Africa.

The ideological and the political struggles to achieve socialism are relatively easy compared with the mammoth task of implementing a socialist economic policy. In general most states have avoided large-scale nationalisations. Apart from state control over private business the more moderate governments favour investment by foreign private capital, while the more radical states prefer government loans and investments. Both the reformist and radical states agree on economic aid 'with no strings attached' from East or West — a position in harmony with their policy of non-alignment.

Non-alignment is a practical as well as an economic doctrine. Most African states have, after independence, adopted it in order not to rely exclusively on either of the two rival power blocs. They established political and economic relations with countries from both East and West, but they insisted on economic aid without reciprocal commitment from the recipient. This has led some African states to prefer multilateral aid (aid through joint bodies such as the World Bank or the International Monetary Fund) to unilateral aid from individual countries. In practice two groups soon emerged: the Casablanca group and the Monrovia group. The Casablanca group, comprising Ghana, Guinea, Mali, Algeria, Egypt and Morocco, was the more radical, and developed a militant stance with regard to the liberation of the rest of Africa from colonial rule, and leaned towards friendship with the eastern bloc. The Monrovia group includes Nigeria, Liberia, Ivory Coast and Sudan, and they lean towards the western bloc. The existence of these two groups threatened the unity and coherence of the Organisation of African Unity (OAU), which was created in 1963 to assert Africa's policy of 'positive neutrality'.

The OAU is a league of independent African states 'to coordinate and intensify their cooperation and efforts to achieve a better life for the peoples of Africa' and 'to work for the eradication of all forms of colonialism on the African continent'. A Committee for Liberation was set up to coordinate assistance to the freedom fighters in Angola, Mozambique, Zimbabwe, Namibia and South Africa. Its headquarters are in Tanzania. After the fall of the Portuguese colonies the strategy of the OAU was clear: the liberation of the remaining countries under colonial rule, first Zimbabwe and Namibia, then finally South Africa, if possible by peaceful means, otherwise by violence and war.

Economic and political non-alignment imposes strict limits on weak and poor nations such as the fifty or so African states. Most former French colonies are militarily and economically dependent on France, most former British colonies rely on Britain. The most important economic partner of almost all the African states is not the Soviet Union nor the USA, but the European Common Market (or the European Economic Community) (EEC). Despite warnings from Nkrumah that this would doom the economy of Africa to a state of perpetual subjection to Europe, eighteen of the French-speaking countries became associate members of the EEC in 1963, in the so-called Yaoundé Agreement (renewed in 1969), followed by the Lomé Agreement in 1975. In 1979 the Lomé Agreement was said to be

the most comprehensive trade and aid agreement of all times between two sets of regional states. The EEC is obliged to absorb some 15 billion dollars worth of imports from the African, Caribbean and Pacific states (the so-called ACP groups) per annum. In addition, per annum, the EEC, through the Lomé Convention, provides the ACP group of states with aid running at 850 million dollars. . . . The central point to be made is that the West, through the EEC, is heavily involved in a far-ranging relationship with almost every African state. As a composite package, Lomé far outweighs anything the 'other side' can offer the states of Africa, either bilaterally or multilaterally through its own economic grouping, Comecon.

In 1981 Lomé II came into effect, joining 57 countries, mainly from Africa, but also Caribbean and Pacific states, to the European Economic Community. When Lomé III was signed in December 1984 it linked 65 ACP countries to the EEC. While Lomé III presents some substantial modifications of Lomé I and II, and improves the terms of the inter-relationship between ACP and EEC members, there is no doubt that the actual implementation of the Lomé Agreement remains far behind original expectations that it might significantly alter a neo-colonialist pattern of relationship.

If it is true that Africa's first problem is economic, and not political, what meaning does African socialism have if the continent, despite its policy of non-alignment, is so strongly dependent on western capitalism? One does not have to be a Marxist to see the fundamental importance of the economic basis for the political and ideological superstructure of a society. Is socialism in most African states anything more than mere rhetoric?

It is interesting, in this regard, to look at a Soviet critique of African socialism by Potekhin:

What is 'African Socialism'? No single, complete theory of this concept exists. Each individual advocate of 'African Socialism' has his own ideas about it . . . but they are all united by a common desire, to abolish the exploitation of man by man. How can this great and noble aim be achieved? This is where the difference of views begins. . . . Scientific Socialism holds that the decisive condition for abolishing the exploitation of man by man is to abolish private ownership of the means of production and to socialize them. The advocates of 'African Socialism' overlook this cardinal question, and it therefore remains uncertain how they think the exploitation of man by man can be ended. Some of them even acknowledge the possibility of private capitalist enterprises existing under socialism. . . . Today millions of exploited people dream of socialism. But it is not enough to dream; one must know how to make the transition from existing society to socialism.

According to this estimate, most African states which embarked on the first wave of socialism have failed the crucial test of implementing truly socialist economic policies. They lacked the two basic organisational requirements of such a socialist transformation: a coherent revolutionary ideology and effective leadership at all levels. Thomas M. Callaghy maintains that in most countries in Africa we find a kind of African neo-mercantilism: centralising authoritarian bureaucratic states favouring political capitalism in a mixture of state-regulated capitalism and state enterprise in the parastatal sector:

the short-run future of most African states will probably be as weaker or stronger versions of neo-mercantilist states, achieving, at best, moderate rates of growth and development. Successful socialist transformation attempts may well be out of the question under current African conditions. It might be possible in the future for some African states to 'muddle through' to a radical socialist position.

The basic, underlying ideology is not Marxism in any form but nationalism, or better still, modernising nationalism. Modernising nationalists accept certain aspects of Marxist analysis but reject the more basic ones. In many ways African socialism is not socialism but populism. This is different from Marxism–Leninism in at least six ways: (1) While African populism (as exemplified especially in Nyerere's Tanzania and Cabral's Guinea-Bissau) rests on the authority of a charismatic leader, Marxism–Leninism rests on the party as the vanguard of the workers. (2) Populists emphasise the ethical dimension of leadership and development, Marxists subordinate ethical to sociological consideration. (3) Populists stress political mobilisation of the masses, Marxists stress social mobilisation. (4) While populists stress solidarity and unity of the people, Marxists place less importance on the racial and cultural aspects of colonialism. (6) Populists emphasise the national, Marxists the international dimension of the socialist revolution.

The Tanzanian case: problems of socialist development

Tanzania remains the only former British colony that developed according to the first wave of socialism, which is still explicitly dedicated, after two decades of independence, to building socialism. Tanzania, though faced with huge obstacles, is observed with great expectations by poor and disillusioned people from the Third World. This includes many blacks in South Africa, though the two countries seem so radically different. Perhaps for them Tanzania asks the right fundamental questions about authentic development, even if the answers are more difficult to provide.

Some basic principles of socialist development in Tanzania

Nyerere adopted the Swahili term *ujamaa*, meaning familyhood, to describe the form of African socialism that he envisaged for Tanzania. *Ujamaa* socialism tries to extend the communal 'attitude of the mind' characteristic of traditional family life (such as belief in the values of equality, democracy, sharing, self-reliance and the obligation to work) beyond the extended family to the country as a whole. As its basic principles, *ujamaa* socialism seeks to:

(a) nationalise all key industries and natural resources.

(b) concentrate on rural, not on urban industrial and commercial, development.

(c) limit dependence on foreign aid and expertise to the absolute minimum — build on local resources and foster the spirit of self-reliance.

(d) create an egalitarian society modelled on the principles of the African extended family; widen the sense of family loyalty progressively to include the whole nation, over the whole of Africa.

(e) involve every member of the community in the development process by education, by creating a sense of initiative and competence in decision-taking, by consultation and common agreement; eliminate the authoritarianism of political leaders, government institutions and experts, even if this means that development takes more time; decentralise decision-making processes and take care that the dictatorship of the central government is not replaced by local or regional dictatorships.

(f) develop people, not things or structures — African socialism is not meant to comprise only state control of the economy but an attitude and a style of life; create a sense of dignity, identity and common humanity; fight racism, tribalism and elitism — development depends on freedom as freedom depends on development.

(g) instil a spirit of public responsibility, discipline and hard work in the population as a whole — everybody must pull his or her weight.

(h) ensure that in all social processes the party (TANU) offers strong leadership. Both the government and the army are controlled by the party to avoid the abuse of power. The party must be based on the rank and file of the people. But party members and functionaries must be carefully selected, properly educated in party principles, and subjected to party discipline.

(i) exercise strong control over consumption. Luxury imports are not allowed. It is difficult to transfer money out of the country. Incomes above a certain amount are severely taxed. Houses that are not occupied by their owners are expropriated (with exceptions to avoid hardships). Political leaders, parliamentarians and government officials are expected to lead a modest style of life, not to waste money on luxuries, and to set a good example.

(j) provide education for every child. But children have to make their contribution. Older children teach younger ones in order to alleviate the shortage of teachers. Children are also expected to work with their own hands to contribute to the expenses of their schooling. Students are admitted to the university only after they have proved themselves in a practical profession and after the party has scrutinised their attitude of seriousness and responsibility towards society.

Difficulties of implementation

The Arusha Declaration of 1967 spelled out in practical terms the central features of *ujamaa* socialism. It contained three basic guidelines for practical implementation:

(1) *Nationalisation of the major means of production and exchange*. This plan was rapidly implemented. Banks were nationalised, as were major importing and wholesale companies. The government acquired majority shares in local affiliates of transnational firms, which, however, retained a strong position, since the government had to rely on them for capital, technology and expertise. As a result the parastatal sector grew rapidly, but so did a group of corporate managers with significant power, that was in danger of becoming a bureaucratic elite with vested interests apart from the mass of the people.

(2) *Adoption of a code of socialist conduct* by national and local leaders. Government and party personnel were prohibited from participating in private business. Leadership in Tanzania is in danger of easily becoming a leadership from the top, that treats people as objects to be educated and conscientised, and that is accountable not so much to the people themselves as to the government and the party.

(3) *Emphasis on agricultural development*, with the stress on self-reliance, in the sense that local resources would be used before foreign resources. As a basic prerequisite it was envisaged that all rural dwellers would be settled in villages. This was only the first step on the path to cooperative work and finally to cooperative production for the benefit of the community. Today more than 85 per cent of all Tanzanians live in villages. Cooperative work in community buildings such as schools or roads has been relatively successful. The productivity of communal production is still very low, and has encountered numerous difficulties. The movement in *ujamaa* villages was first achieved by persuasion, then increasingly by inducement, and finally by coercion.

There are many reasons for the limited success of communal production. Apart from a serious drought in the early seventies, peasants were slow to respond to such a new economic institution as production outside the family unit. Failure to develop tools at appropriate levels of technology and to keep basic consumer goods at a low price has meant that the quality of life in rural areas has not been sufficiently transformed. Nyerere had hoped that the creation of *ujamaa* villages would prevent marked economic differences from developing among peasants, yet such stratification did emerge, especially in the cash crop areas in Tanzania's coffee and cotton regions, and it continues to exist. Resistance to 'villagisation' came especially from a small group of relatively wealthy peasants. Where they joined the villages they often assumed leadership positions and used *ujamaa* in their own interests. Overall, the attempt to bridge the existing inequalities between poorer and richer farmers through cooperative production has so far largely failed. Often the costs of villagisation and administrative structures had to be paid out of the small profits the cooperatives were making; and the returns for the peasants were meagre and future participation was discouraged. Local leadership failed to a large extent to involve the rural people in formulating their own proposals and needs.

At present the Tanzanian economy is in great trouble. A large balance-of-payment deficit has arisen. Many planned projects have had to be stopped. The war in late 1978 to oust Idi Amin was a costly enterprise for the already weak Tanzanian economy, as is its continued support of liberation movements in southern Africa. Measures of austerity and a shortage of necessary items mark the country. Tanzania is increasingly dependent on foreign aid, some of which has political strings attached. The country is the largest single recipient of western aid in Africa. Does all this mean that *ujamaa* socialism in Tanzania has failed?

Critical assessment

The Tanzanian case can be assessed in three different ways.

The critique from the right. For those who support capitalism as the quickest and best method of development, Tanzania is a perfect example of the argument that the basic problem is socialism itself. Socialism kills initiative and does not take into account man's basically selfish nature. It lends itself to corruption and totalitarian methods. The introduction of socialism favours a top-heavy administrative machine, discourages valuable inflow of foreign capital, and drives away enterprising whites with the necessary skills and expertise.

The critique from the left. This critique has two sides. One affirms that *ujamaa* socialism is a valid means of socialist development but that its relative failure in Tanzania can be attributed to the restraints of the capitalist system from within and without the country. Transnational corporations and the International Monetary Fund have prevented a full socialisation of the basic means of production, and they continue to impose their conditions. The growth in the parastatal sector has favoured the emergence of a new bourgeoisie that seeks its own interests rather than the implementation of socialism. In 1978 the Tanzanian Parliament raised the salaries of top government officials and introduced severe measures against domestic criticism, especially from university students. The revenues from the export of cash crops like sisal, coffee, cotton, tobacco and cashew nuts either slumped or oscillated because of fluctuating prices on the world market and the introduction of synthetic substitutes for cotton and sisal. At the same time, about half of the country's earnings from exports are swallowed up in purchasing the necessary commodity of fuel.

The other side of the radical critique emerges from more orthodox Marxists, who see in African socialism a disguised form of international capitalism. They emphasise the existing class structures within Tanzanian society, the need for a peasant–worker alliance in the class struggle against the bureaucratic and financial bourgeoisie, and the need to form a strong vanguard party to introduce a truly scientific socialism. A strong working class is lacking and the country has not sufficiently developed an industrial sector to enable the transition to socialism to take place. All this raises the question whether it is at all possible to move to socialism from a basically traditionalist subsistence economy without modernisation and a certain degree of capitalist development.

A middle position would argue that the basic difficulties in the implementation of Tanzanian socialism lie in the traditional structures and values of the peasantry, who form the great majority of Tanzania's people. Under whatever system, capitalist or socialist, it requires a long time for subsistence peasants to make the move into a modern integrated society. Tanzania's problems in this regard are compounded, since it is one of the poorest countries in the world, by very limited mineral resources. It inherited from the British colonial masters an externally dependent economy and an educational system that favoured an urban elite and neglected or excluded the masses in the rural areas.

Perhaps a further disability is the fact that Tanzania gained independence peacefully, without a protracted national struggle that could have generated a set of values necessary for a socialist transformation.

African theorists have difficulty in proving that African traditional society embodied communal values that form a natural basis for the building of socialism. And perhaps one of the lessons of the Tanzanian example is the fact that the implementation of socialism in a largely traditionalist agrarian society is not possible without a certain amount of coercion, in order to overcome those cultural aspects that hinder socialist development.

Has socialism failed in Tanzania? It is too early to say. Some would say it has not really been tried. Yet Tanzania, more than any other African country that gained independence in the sixties and early seventies, has made decisive steps towards the transition to socialism. From a strongly disadvantaged starting-point Tanzania has continued to ask the right questions about the nature of development, about a technology which incorporates consideration towards people, about production that weighs equity against the goal of growth, about the nature of leadership with regard to the masses of the poor people, about mass participation and motivation for self-reliance. These questions are going to decide the future of our planet. The success or failure of Tanzania's struggle to build a socialist society that answers the needs of the great majority of her people, will continue to be an inspiring example for many in the Third World.

One thing seems certain: the implementation of socialism will take longer than expected, as Nyerere conceded in early 1977:

In 1956 I was asked how long it would take Tanganyika to become independent. I thought 10–12 years. We became independent 6 years later! In 1967 a group of youth who were marching in support of the Arusha Declaration asked me how long it would take Tanzania to become socialist, I thought 30 years. I was wrong again: I am now sure it will take us much longer!

The second wave of socialism in Africa

With the end of the sixties, and increasingly during the seventies, the ideological spectrum in Africa underwent a considerable shift. African socialism, espoused officially by the great majority of African states which had achieved independence during the sixties, was on the retreat. Because of the difficulties in implementing African socialism, and even failure, many critics, especially from the more orthodox Marxist camp, seemed to be proved right. African socialism was naïve and ambiguous, and in most cases not more than a facade hiding the clear interests of a new bureaucratic elite, and continuing colonial exploitation. In this context, there arose the demand for a more scientific socialism that would adhere more strictly to Marxist thought. Those countries that comprise the second wave of socialisms in Africa opted for scientific socialism or explicitly for Marxism–Leninism as the official state ideology.

A number of military regimes opted for Marxism–Leninism: Congo-Brazzaville (1969), Somalia (1970), Benin (1974), Madagascar (1975) and Ethiopia (1976). Similarly Mozambique (1977) and Angola (1977), which became independent from Portuguese colonial rule in the mid-seventies, opted explicitly for Marxism–Leninism. Zimbabwe, too, seems set to pursue a scientific socialist and Marxist–Leninist course in the long term.

Most of these scientific socialist or Afro-Marxist regimes share a common set of ideological features that distinguish them from the first-wave attempts: (1) the adoption of scientific socialism rather than some kind of African socialism; (2) the attempt to create effective Leninist vanguard parties in contrast to the single mass parties of the populist socialist regimes — these parties have supremacy over the state in defining its political choices and act as instruments of conscientisation and the embodiment of the masses of workers and peasants; (3) a greater readiness to use coercion, especially against internal opposition; (4) a stress on class analysis and the ongoing class struggle against bourgeois elements in society; (5) commitment to a non-capitalist path of development; (6) a flexible eclecticism in ideological interpretation of Marxist theory and practice; (7) a link with external socialist powers, which does not necessarily include Soviet Russia, and does not usually interfere with their official policy of non-alignment that allows them to receive aid from and to have trade links with both the western and the eastern blocs.

The questions arise: what is the gap between ideology and commitment, between theory and practice? How serious is the implementation of concrete policies in countries that embark on the transition to a socialist society? Let us glance at various Afro-Marxist countries, emphasising the two countries that have a particular importance for

South Africa: Mozambique and Zimbabwe.

In 1969 the new military regime of Congo-Brazzaville announced its adoption of Marxism–Leninism, to be followed in 1974 by another former French colony, Benin (Dahomey). Both countries remain heavily dependent on France and their economies differ little from those of states that reject Marxist doctrine. Somalia declared itself a socialist state in 1974 and in 1976 adopted scientific socialism as its programme. It has made serious attempts at a more egalitarian structure, but since the early nationalisations of key sectors of Italian colonial capital no significant socialist transformation in the economic sector has taken place. In 1977 a marriage of convenience between Somalia and the Soviet Union came to an end, because of the Soviet Union's support for Ethiopia in its war against Somalia. Somalia then made overtures to the USA, which in exchange for arms was given the former Soviet base at Berbera for the establishment of American military facilities. Somalia shows that Afro-Marxism can go together with a strong anti-Soviet position. Ethiopia, committed to Marxism–Leninism since 1976, has performed a remarkable land reform in the search for greater socio-economic equality. Despite twenty-year friendship treaties with both the USSR and East Germany, and despite the strong military contingent of Cuban soldiers and advisers, Ethiopia is fairly pragmatic and receives a considerable amount of aid from the West. Like Somalia, Ethiopia adheres to the Lomé Agreement.

After years of protracted struggle against Portuguese colonial rule, Angola achieved independence in 1975 and has clearly opted for Marxism–Leninism. But this Marxist option is eclectic: while official analysis of capitalism and imperialism is fairly orthodox the basic thrust is nationalist and informed by Third World themes, as articulated by Amilcar Cabral, Che Guevara, and Fidel Castro. Angola is still burdened with the cost of the continuing war against UNITA, backed by South Africa, and the costs of the presence of Cuban troops. It has struggled to restructure the economy after the sudden departure of the Portuguese, and bring production back to the 1973 level, in order to meet the basic needs of its population. At the same time a Marxist–Leninist vanguard party has been built to carry through the transition to socialism. It is too early to assess the effect of socialist measures in war-torn Angola.

Circumstances force the Angolans to be eclectic in their Marxist stance and adapt ideology to their needs. When 90 per cent of the Portuguese left the country after the collapse of the colonial regime, the state had no choice but to take over companies, farms and shops. While all the banks are nationalised, and exports and imports tightly controlled, transnational companies are allowed to continue, with increased shares held by the state. Angola acquired a majority of shares in Gulf Oil and in diamond-mining concerns, the revenues of which play a critical role in Angola's economic survival. Agriculture has not yet recovered and experiences great difficulties, especially on account of the breakdown of infrastructures through the crippling effects of UNITA's South African-backed war against the MPLA. A promising start has been made with cooperative farming. The government encourages cooperatives but avoids any compulsion. The independence of Namibia seems to be a necessary prerequisite for decisive steps towards socialist transformation, with the consequent departure of both South African and Cuban troops, and the ending of the civil war with the rival faction of UNITA.

From a socialist perspective, then, one could sum up Angola's venture as one that is firmly set on a socialist path and promises, if external circumstances permit and the present difficulties, largely due to persistent South African pressure and aggression, can be overcome, to become a creative example of an indigenous socialist experiment.

The example of Mozambique

The socialist experiment in Mozambique, rather than Angola, presented a kind of showcase for the viability, practicality and shape of socialism on the African continent in the immediate years after gaining independence from Portuguese colonial rule. With the growing criticisms of African socialism, and the difficulties encountered by Tanzania, interest shifted to Mozambique where conditions for an exemplary socialist experiment appeared to be present. It enjoyed a committed and united leadership, a clear ideological identity, a strong coherent party with a lot of credibility among the masses, and a country which, although it is still suffering from the aftermath of the liberation struggle in Mozambique itself and in neighbouring Zimbabwe, has relatively good agricultural and industrial potential. The signing of the Nkomati Accord with South Africa on 16 March 1984, preceded by the near collapse of the economy in early 1983, dealt a severe blow to optimism in the Mozambican socialist experiment.

While Tanzania achieved independence peacefully, Mozambique had to fight hard for it during long and difficult years, from 1964 to 1975. The fruits of this war and the credibility derived from it seemed to be Mozambique's greatest asset in building socialism. Some, however, would go so far as to say that the Portuguese colonial power collapsed too early for the transforming power of the struggle to have reached the more developed and richer southern parts of the country. While the basis for Frelimo's struggle lay in the 'liberated zones' of the north, the south was handed to them on a plate. The struggle generated a new solidarity between the party and the masses of peasants and workers ready to die for liberation from colonial rule. It broke down certain traditional values that are an obstacle, as evidenced in Tanzania, to the integration of the country into a nationwide political economy, and it brought leadership and people into close contact with each other. The leadership had to recognise the power and potential of ordinary people, and learned how to be accountable to them and how to involve them in the planning and decision-making involved in the construction of a more democratic and participatory socialist order.

Even during the war Frelimo began to build the outlines of a new society in the 'liberated zones' of the north. Peasants in the rural areas learnt about scientific socialism, exploitation and class struggle, as Machel likes to point out, not from books by Marx or Lenin but through their own experience of suffering and struggle. So-called 'dynamising groups' linked the party with the people. It was their task to conscientise the people, to help them articulate their own needs and to share in the decisions affecting their own lives and the direction the country takes, mainly through the election of local leaders. The members of the dynamising groups, not necessarily party members, are also elected for their leadership qualities. These groups played a vital role in the generation of a socialist consciousness, especially in the regions of the south relatively unaffected by the war. They encouraged cooperative work, the emancipation of women, and campaigned against corruption and sabotage among leaders and people. At the beginning of 1980 Frelimo itself launched a cleaning-up campaign, designed as part of the class struggle of the peasant–worker alliance against the petty bourgeoisie, to deal with corruption and inefficiency at all levels. Dozens of officials were sacked and the government was reshuffled. An egalitarian commitment is visible in the relatively low income levels of civil service salaries, and in the immense efforts being made to extend adult literacy, and to develop a simple but effective health service in the rural areas stressing preventive medicine. Cooperative villages are seen as the backbone of agricultural development. Yet, in general, villagisation so far has occurred only on a limited scale and without coercion.

In 1972 Frelimo was still largely nationalist and populist with regard to its ideological commitment, but the Marxist–Leninist ingredient has grown steadily. In 1977 the party opted for Marxism–Leninism as official ideology, and declared itself to be a Leninist-type revolutionary vanguard party intent on carrying through a 'people's democratic revolution' which would move towards the socialisation of the basic means of production. Basil Davidson says with regard to both the MPLA in Angola and Frelimo in Mozambique: 'These movements may be said to have been the first in Africa to have fully indigenized a Marxist analysis; and they were certainly bent on finding alternatives to the capitalist nation-state. But what their evolution really displayed was an African politics of mass participation in a mature phase.'

By 1978 the banks were fully nationalised. A huge state sector had been erected in vital areas like oil refining and coal mining. The government had to take over the enterprises abandoned by the Portuguese. In contrast to Tanzania, Mozambique has chosen the establishment of heavy industry as the pathway for socialist development, and the exploitation of its mineral resources. The voluntary formation of rural co-operatives is strongly encouraged in the communal villages built along the lines of the villages established in the liberated areas during the war. The estate farms abandoned by the Portuguese were converted into state farms, about 2 000 in number. The 1980s were ambitiously declared 'the decade of victory over underdevelopment'.

Mozambique inherited a difficult colonial legacy. Real development had only taken place in the three decades before independence, and had almost exclusively benefited the colonial community in the urban centres. The modern export sector such as harbour transport facilities and estates near Maputo and Beira were in the hands of transnational companies, operating mainly from their base in South Africa. Mozambique was integrated into the South African economic zone through projects like the giant Cabora Bassa Dam and South African management of the railways and port facilities. Before 1975 about 50 per cent of the foreign exchange earnings came through a gold premium paid by South Africa for the 100 000 Mozambican mine workers in South Africa.

After independence the government of Mozambique was faced with the enormous task of restructuring the country after the war, of integrating the thousands of workers who had emigrated to South Africa, and of recuperating from the disruption caused by the sudden departure of the vast majority of skilled whites. Mozambique's difficulties after 1975 were aggravated by its assistance to the liberation struggle in Zimbabwe, which, especially in the last years of the war, resulted in frequent raids deep into Mozambique by Rhodesian troops. Direct damage caused by Rhodesian military action was estimated at over $47 million. The application of UN sanctions against Rhodesia cost Mozambique a loss of about $450–550 million due mainly to the closure of the rail links between the two countries, with the port of Maputo being particularly affected. With the end of the war in Zimbabwe Mozambique's troubles have continued. The Mozambican Resistance Movement (MNR) — a movement of various elements which is sabotaging the present government of Machel and Frelimo's plans to establish a socialist society — poses a serious threat to the stability and survival of the new state.

The MNR has caused, and is still causing, immense damage. Thousands of Mozambicans have been killed and over a hundred thousand have lost their homes in the destruction of villages. The cost of MNR's undeclared war is colossal. But it was not only the external destabilisation through the MNR that led Machel into signing the Nkomati Accord with Pretoria. There were also a variety of internal developments that led to the near breakdown of the economy and the political structures of the state.

After the Third Congress in 1977, Frelimo built up a Marxist–Leninist-type vanguard party that pursued a technicist and statist economic policy. Heavy emphasis was placed on over-mechanisation, and cooperative and family agriculture was poorly managed by the state and starved of resources. Hopes of substantial investments from the USSR and other socialist countries have not materialised – a further indication that, unless scarce resources are at stake, Mozambique and other Afro-Marxist states do not rank highly on the priority list of those socialist countries.

The economy deteriorated so much that by the end of 1981 severe food shortages were experienced throughout the country. Authoritarian practices of state officials increased local resistance to the state, thus making it difficult to mobilise local resistance against the MNR. Coupled with this was the worst drought of the century, which brought the already ailing economy to a near collapse in early 1983.

Though the Fourth Congress tried to revitalise the party in its mobilisation against the MNR, this return to a Frelimo popular-base was counteracted by an increased centralisation of decision-making in a small secret group. Finally, Frelimo had no option but to sue for peace with Pretoria and to sign the Nkomati Accord.

Though in the official Mozambique media, the Nkomati Accord was hailed as a victory, it seems clear that the Republic of South Africa is the main beneficiary. Rather than a victory for socialism, the Nkomati Accord could appear as a victory for South Africa's aggressive policy of destabilisation, consisting of a coupling of military support for MNR, economic disruption for Mozambique and support for a policy of western capitalist investment.

Since the end of 1979 Machel has tried to attract western capital for development programmes. 'There is a place in our economic development effort for the participation of international firms and foreign capital. We are open to mutually advantageous cooperation with firms from other countries. We need technology. We need finance.' Does this mean an abandonment of a socialist pathway to development? Perhaps more accurately it shows the flexible, pragmatic attitude of Afro-Marxists, who adapt scientific socialism to the specific needs of their people regardless of doctrinaire purism. As some argue, sometimes one step back today allows two steps forward tomorrow.

The task ahead for Frelimo and the Mozambican government is formidable. The major question seems to be whether the MNR can be neutralised and the momentum towards a socialist economy and society regained and maintained, given the degree of Mozambican dependence on the world capitalist system and especially on the South African economy. Only the future will tell whether Mozambique's promising socialist experiment will be a success or a failure as experienced by the masses of ordinary people in Mozambique.

Zimbabwe: quo vadis?

On 18 April 1980, Zimbabwe became independent under Prime Minister Robert Mugabe, leader of the ZANU-PF (Zimbabwe African National Union–Patriotic Front) party which had won an absolute majority of the 100 seats of Parliament in the elections of February 1980. Zimbabwe has not adopted an official Marxist–Leninist policy like South Africa's other two neighbours, Angola and Mozambique, but this could just be a question of time. Mugabe considers himself a Marxist, and claims a Marxist–Leninist stance for ZANU, and though he is taking a pragmatic, gradualist approach in planned reforms, in a long-term perspective they can be characterised as socialist-oriented.

Historical flash-back

In 1953 the two British colonies of Northern and Southern Rhodesia were joined in the Federation of Rhodesia and Nyasaland. Rising opposition among Africans in the south against discriminatory land policies led to the formation in 1957 of the Southern Rhodesian African National Congress (SRANC) under the leadership of Joshua Nkomo, which was banned two years later. African opposition organised itself in the National Democratic Party (NDP), and opposed the constitution of 1961, which, in its qualified franchise regulation, excluded 96 per cent of the African population from political decision-making. The NDP was banned in 1961. So was the Zimbabwe African People's Union (ZAPU), led by Nkomo. After the Rev. Ndabaningi Sithole had broken away from ZAPU and formed the Zimbabwe African National Union (ZANU), fighting broke out between ZANU and the Nkomo-led People's Caretaker Council. Both were outlawed, and most of the leaders of the African nationalist movements were detained or placed in restriction camps. Robert Mugabe spent altogether eleven years in gaol for his part in black nationalist politics.

The silencing of the black nationalist opposition went hand in hand with the strengthening of the white right-wing Rhodesian Front, which won the elections in 1962. Under the leadership of Ian Smith it pressed for independence from Britain under white rule. Upon the refusal of the British government, Smith unilaterally declared independence on 11 November 1965. A programme of sanctions was applied and failed largely because two countries, vital to its success, refused to abide by the UN decision, namely South Africa and Portugal.

The following years saw the emergence of a new black nationalism in the African National Council led by Bishop Abel Muzorewa, and after 1972, increasing activity of the guerrilla alliance, the Patriotic Front (PF), under the leadership of Joshua Nkomo and Robert Mugabe. Though Smith had stated that he would not accept majority rule for Rhodesia 'in a thousand years', the Kissinger and Owen–Young initiatives forced him in September 1976 to agree to majority rule in Rhodesia within two years. Excluding the participation of the PF leaders, Smith entered into negotiations with three moderate black leaders, Muzorewa, Sithole and Senator Chief Chirau. Although Muzorewa's United African National Council (UANC) won 51 of the 100 seats in Parliament (of which 28 were reserved for whites) in the elections of early 1979, the new dispensation did not receive international recognition, and the guerrilla war increased in intensity.

Upon proposals from Tanzania's President Julius Nyerere, Mrs Thatcher's government, in the person of Lord Carrington, convened the rival parties around the conference table at Lancaster House, beginning on 10 September 1979, to draw up 'a genuine majority rule constitution'. The delegation from Zimbabwe/Rhodesia was led by Muzorewa and Smith, the Patriotic Front by Nkomo and Mugabe. After 103 days of tough negotiations an agreement was reached, and the ceasefire was signed in December.

The 20 white seats in parliament were all won by the Rhodesian Front. In the election for the 80 common-roll seats, Mugabe's ZANU-PF won 57, Nkomo's ZAPU-PF 20, and Bishop Muzorewa's UANC 3 seats.

The way into the future

Zimbabwe became an independent republic on 18 April 1980, with a parliamentary system based on the Westminster model. The constitution includes a bill of rights which enshrines freedom from deprivation of property. Special minority representation is entrenched in the constitution.

Mugabe's government strongly opposes the South African apartheid policy. It broke off diplomatic relations with South Africa and promised to support diplomatic and financial opposition to South Africa. Mugabe said he would retain trade links with the Republic as long as necessary. Within Zimbabwe the party has begun to restructure the country's health and educational system. In education a specific stress is laid on the pre-school and the gradual implementation of compulsory primary education, in order to enable more women to enter the labour market. Technical and vocational training suited to the needs of a developing country is also a priority.

It remains to be seen in what sense Mugabe and his government can be called Marxist. Apart from radical jargon in the media and the presence of some more radical members in his party, the economic policy is socialist-oriented only on a long-term basis. At present little has changed. A type of mixed economy, a state-controlled capitalism, is pursued. Foreign investment is encouraged in the heavily capitalised sectors of mining and manufacturing. By a programme of agricultural development in cash crop farming such as tobacco, cotton, and coffee, it is hoped to make Zimbabwe increasingly independent of foreign aid. The government continues the former policy of state control on the export and import of foreign exchange, and intends to prevent any individual or company from gaining too much power in the country. It remains to be seen how far the government goes in implementing a one-party state and, in the proposed labour legislation, in involving workers in the direct running of companies.

Robert Mugabe, brought up as a Roman Catholic, sees the church as a partner in the development of the country. He seems to represent a 'scientific socialism', which he sums up as a 'blend between Marxism and Christianity'. He does not accept the atheism and materialism of orthodox communism.

On 6 February 1982, Mugabe, in a major address to the Catholic Justice and Peace Commission, said:

ZANU has defined its stand of socialism as scientific socialism based on Marxist–Leninist principles. In other words, socialism is not a fortuitous process occurring at random but a systematic doctrine following a given pattern in the course of which serious contradictions are corrected and socialist or people-oriented goals are fulfilled. I am sure many members of our clergy are filled with revulsion at the thought that our brand of socialism is one based on Marxist–Leninist principles, for they cannot forget that Marx said of religion that it was the opium of the masses. Whatever his own religious views might have been, and he was free to express them, I wish to stand firm on the assertion that the morality of socialism in terms of its principles and objectives to free people is far higher than the morality of capitalism, if capitalism has any morality at all. As we have repeatedly held, ZANU does not see any contradiction between socialism and Christianity.

It is difficult to predict Zimbabwe's future. The new government embarking on its course of reconciliation has so far avoided any drastic change in the inherited capitalist economy. It has with relative success tackled the integration of the guerrillas into the regular army, but has faced increased disruption and violence by dissidents mainly in Matabeleland. The great question seems to be whether government and party officials will squander the credibility derived from the successful struggle, and develop into a bureaucratic elite. How serious is the commitment of the leadership to socialism? How far will it succeed in involving the rural people in building a self-reliant, egalitarian, and participatory socialist order? Will Zimbabwe be able to control successfully the restraints which an increasing dependence on foreign aid from the capitalist world and on investment by transnational companies has placed on the development of a socialism that is geared primarily to meet the needs of the masses of its people?

Possible consequences for South Africa

The Zimbabwean experience has, and will have, serious consequences for Namibia and South Africa. According to the plan of the OAU, increasing pressure will now be put on the liberation struggle for the independence of Namibia. This will leave South Africa as the last target of a combined African effort to establish black majority rule. Much will depend on how black majority rule in Zimbabwe will work out in the future. While admitting important differences between former Rhodesia and South Africa, there seem to be enough similarities to allow some cautious projections for the future — especially seen from a black perspective:

(1) A political system which is unacceptable to the majority of the people will be difficult to defend, on a long-term basis, by legislation and military power. A military solution cannot therefore replace a political one.

(2) People choose their own leaders once they are allowed a voice, and reject the proxies of colonial presence. Oppressed people identify with those who fight their oppressors.

(3) Black nationalism is not to be confused with communism. The fact that a group receives financial and military aid from the communist bloc does not make it communist. Legitimate grievances cannot be minimised by attributing unrest to agitators.

(4) It is a mistake to exaggerate the importance of ethnicity in the hope that different African 'minorities' would confront each other rather

than collectively confront their common oppressors. The victorious parties in Zimbabwe are non-racial and have committed themselves to establishing a non-racial society.

The role of Soviet Russia in Africa

A simplistic view might expect that Soviet Russia would support all those states on the African continent which, especially during the second wave of socialism, have declared themselves 'Marxist–Leninist' or 'scientific socialist', and back them financially and militarily. But this is not the case. Ideological affinity has been a source of tension as much as a source of unity between Afro-Marxist states and Soviet Russia. Since Afro-Marxist states have been very eclectic in their acceptance of Marxism–Leninism, and have adapted it to the specific needs of their countries, their theory and practice often differ considerably from the official 'scientific socialism' of the USSR. In order to give a brief overview of the relationships of Afro-Marxist states to the Soviet Union we shall first glance at the theory and practice of Russia's involvement in Africa before attempting a short assessment.

Marxist theory and the Third World

Marx's view was Europe-centred. He expected the socialist revolution to take place in the most advanced industrial western European countries. When these hopes dimmed attention turned to Russia and Asiatic countries, particularly India. The capitalist chain would break at its weakest link, the revolution in a predominantly agrarian feudalist country would be the fuse to ignite the socialist explosion in the advanced countries.

Recently, in an attempt to find backing for the fact that all the successful revolutions occurred, not as orthodox Marxism had predicted in the advanced industrial countries under the leadership of a united working class, but in undeveloped countries, mostly with the support of the peasants, one aspect of Marx's thought on historical materialism has been rediscovered. This has been the centre of an interesting debate on Marx's concept of the Asiatic mode of production, which allows for a multilinear view of history. Until recently a simplified Stalinist unilinear scheme of successive modes of production, which has its backing in the *Communist Manifesto*, has been regarded as the orthodox position. This unilinear scheme consisted of five stages which succeeded each other almost inevitably, each one presupposing its forerunner: from early communalism to slavery, to feudalism, to capitalism, and finally to socialism–communism. The sequence in the East was said to resemble that of the West, a fact that, for many leaders in Third World countries, was the sign that Marxism was a foreign Europe-centred ideology which had nothing, or little, to offer to non-European countries in Asia or Africa.

The only difference was that eastern feudalism was static, and capitalism, introduced from the West with technology, industrialisation and urbanisation, would provide the means of destroying the feudal, agrarian structure of Asia and lead to a successful proletarian revolution. This would result in socialism and communism — a classless, non-exploitative society in which people share as equals material wealth and decision-making.

This scheme led to the conviction that capitalism was an almost necessary step for a successful socialist revolution. Lenin said about Russia after 1917 that it suffered not so much from capitalism but from an insufficient development of capitalism. This ideological multi-linear scheme is one of the factors which explains why before the 1960s, Russia had very little interest in Africa, apart from highly industrialised South Africa which, with Algeria, had until recently the only organised communist party. Another reason for the lack of involvement of Soviet Russia in Africa has been the Stalinist doctrine of 'socialism in one country', which deprived Marxism of its drive for a world revolution. The Comintern used the communist parties in other countries as ambassadors for Soviet foreign policy. They had to obey the inconsistent and incoherent twists and turns decreed by the almighty Politburo in Moscow. Even African states influenced by Marxism have heavily criticised Soviet policy and taken drastic measures against communist subversion. Nasser was perfectly willing to use the Soviet Union for his own purposes when he wanted to reduce his dependence on the West for military and economic aid, but Egypt felt quite free to get rid of the Soviets and denounce their foreign ideology when the tide changed.

Since the sixties, partly as a result of the de-Stalinisation begun under Khrushchev, Soviet Russia began to show fresh interest in the Third World. A new interpretation of the Asiatic mode of production became ideologically important. It has been based mainly on Marx's *Grundrisse* and creatively developed by Russian and other Marxists. This opens the way for a less Eurocentric view of change in the direction of socialism. It allows for multilinear schemes of understanding history in the West and East, and for an African road to Marxist socialism.

By 1960, then, orthodox Marxists hailed the newly independent African states that adopted African socialism as national democracies led by 'revolutionary democrats' who, supported by socialist powers, would eventually lead their countries to socialism without passing through the capitalist stage. Disappointments with newly independent

African states led to Soviet Russia losing interest in Africa, until the rise, especially in the mid-seventies, of Afro-Marxist states. Soviet Russia supported the liberation movements in their struggle against colonialism. In the eyes of the Soviets a democratic revolution constitutes the first step in the transition to socialism. This had to be prepared for through the creation of vanguard Leninist parties.

The praxis of USSR involvement in Africa

We shall limit ourselves to the Soviet Union's involvement with the Afro-Marxist states of the seventies, and for this purpose we distinguish between political, military and economic levels.

Political involvement. Special treaties of friendship with the USSR have been signed by Egypt (1972), Somalia (1974), Mozambique (1977), Angola (1977), Ethiopia (1978) and Congo (1981). Egypt and Somalia have since abrogated their treaties.

Military involvement. The USSR has served as a major supplier of arms to most Afro-Marxist countries, but also to others, on commercial terms but under less restrictive conditions than other western countries and the USA have insisted on. In general, Afro-Marxist states have refused to allow the USSR to establish naval or air bases in their countries. African states have also, in general, kept to their non-alignment policies: delivery of arms is welcome, yet without strings attached. The USSR has supported militarily the MPLA in Angola, Somalia until 1977, Ethiopia from 1977, and the Patriotic Front in Zimbabwe (while Mugabe's ZANLA troops were supported, like Frelimo, mainly by China) and it continues to support the remaining liberation movements in Africa. The massive presence of Cuban troops in Angola and Ethiopia certainly serves the USSR's interests yet it would be too simplistic to see them only as Russia's 'proxies'. Cuba also pursues its own interests in Africa and has developed its own initiatives that do not always directly coincide with Russia's intentions. For example, the relationship between Angolans and Cubans goes back to the early 1960s.

Economic involvement. Here one can distinguish between economic aid and trade, and investment links. On both scores the Soviet Union is remarkably weak and parsimonious. In the period from 1954 to 1978 the People's Republic of China, for instance, gave economic aid to African countries in the form of grants and credits that amounted to double the size of the Russian equivalent. The outstanding example of Chinese aid has been the construction of the Tazara railway from Dar-es-Salaam to the Zambian copperbelt. Russian economic aid has proved a great disappointment to African states. There are also complaints about the quality and suitability of Soviet economic advisers; their Chinese or

Cuban counterparts are usually preferred in countries like Angola, Mozambique or Ethiopia. Apart from financial difficulties in the USSR, the low volume of economic aid also reflects the relatively low interest the USSR has in sub-Saharan Africa compared, for instance, with its concerns in the Middle East. There is a level of mistrust in the stability and seriousness of USSR ideological commitment even in the Afro-Marxist states.

Trade and investment links are relatively weak between African countries and the USSR, especially if compared with the countries of the European Common Market or the USA. In 1976 only three African states numbered the USSR among their top five trading partners: Egypt, Somalia, and Cameroon. For the rest of the African states the USSR remains a minor trading partner. There is a twofold reason for this perhaps striking fact: the USSR does not need most African minerals since they are rich in minerals, and they are not interested in importing luxury goods such as tea or coffee. On the other hand, African states do not have great interest in Soviet goods since they usually compare unfavourably with those supplied by western countries. An exception is the supply of armaments where the USSR imposes fewer restrictions than western countries.

The question arises: does the specific ideological commitment make any difference with regard to African countries' relationships with the USSR? In general, one can say that the ideological stance does make a difference, yet in a surprisingly flexible way. Other variables often exercise more influence than ideology. In general, African countries committed to either African socialism or scientific socialism in the form of Marxism–Leninism have been eclectic, pragmatic, and unpredictable. They have maintained a policy of non-alignment even when leaning more towards the Soviet Union or China.

It is not easy to assess comprehensively Soviet Russia's role in sub-Saharan Africa in the seventies, and its prospects in the eighties. Although there is some agreement among analysts on various key points there are also considerable disagreements.

Everybody agrees that the 1970s constituted a new era in interest shown by outside powers in general and the USSR in particular. The main reason for this lay in the increasing level of military conflict that began during the seventies, providing opportunities for outside intervention. The struggle against the Portuguese in Angola and Mozambique, the 1977–8 war between Somalia and Egypt, the guerrilla war in Zimbabwe, and the ongoing struggle along the borders of Namibia and Angola, presented the Soviets with the chance to establish themselves as champions of the liberation movements, thus weakening the Chinese competition.

It is difficult to establish a clear strategy on the part of the Soviets. Rather one sees haphazard and often ill-chosen *ad hoc* reactions to changing opportunities, and to the tactics of the USA, West European countries, China and Cuba. However, the result of Soviet involvements in the seventies has been to replace China as the most influential partner to the liberation movements and Afro-Marxist states. It has gained territorial support, and a strategically important foothold on the Horn of Africa, enabling it to wield influence on the continent.

There is disagreement, however, about the degree of priority the Soviet leadership attaches to sub-Saharan Africa. One can distinguish in this regard between a majority and a minority perspective. The majority perspective holds that sub-Saharan Africa rates relatively low on Russia's list of priorities, and that the Soviets are rather cautious about committing themselves militarily in Africa. This also reflects their basic mistrust about the reliability of the ideological commitment of the Afro-Marxist states. The minority perspective holds the opposite view that, due to sub-Saharan Africa's strategic value, it rates among the major concerns of Moscow. The minority view contends that due to a shift of the balance of power in its own interest, the USSR is increasingly prepared to capitalise on its enhanced chances and to pursue its expansionist objectives in southern Africa. In this strategy the Cuban troops serve as proxies and the Afro-Marxist states will increasingly serve as footholds for a 'communist siege' of the rest of southern Africa.

It is difficult to predict the future role of the Soviets in southern Africa. It depends on too many variables, ranging from the USSR's interests elsewhere, its finite resources, and changes in its domestic policy, to the moves of its rivals, the western powers and China, and to the attitudes of the African states themselves towards Soviet Russia. Perhaps it is best to agree with Albright's cautious conclusion that 'the Soviet role in Africa seems unlikely to diminish in the first half of the decade. If it alters at all, it will probably grow.'

Assessment of ideology and performance

We have surveyed the performance and implementation of socialism in its two main forms in sub-Saharan Africa — the populist type of African socialism, and scientific socialism, as represented especially by a small number of Afro-Marxist states. Other countries like Kenya or Nigeria have chosen the market-capitalist path to development. Thus sub-Saharan Africa seems to present the ideal terrain to test the relationship between ideological commitment and performance of these three routes to development in Third World countries.

This test, however, presents many difficulties. The availability of reliable data for various countries is difficult, and often extends over too short a period of time (as in the case of most Afro-Marxist countries). It is often impossible to decide whether the success or failure of certain developments is due to the ideological commitment as such, or to factors such as the nature of industrialisation itself, or to external circumstances like the after-effects of war on countries like Tanzania, Mozambique or Zimbabwe, or to the mismanagement by the respective leadership.

Crawford Young in his *Ideology and Development in Africa* (1982) uses six criteria — growth, equality, autonomy, human dignity, participation, and capacity expansion — to measure the relationship between ideology and performance in Africa. The three types of ideological commitment he considers are market-capitalism, populist African socialism and scientific socialist Afro-Marxism.

The first two criteria, growth and equality, are perhaps the two most important if they are seen in correlation with each other. One would expect African socialist and Afro-Marxist countries to perform better in terms of equality and market-capitalist countries to fare better in terms of growth. But this conclusion is not as neat as expected. Afro-Marxist states have in general not experienced rapid growth, but none is bankrupt either. Is this relatively slow growth due to the 'soft version' of scientific socialism adopted, or to socialist measures themselves, or to the specific circumstances? Market economies in Africa have, on the other hand, not experienced successively high growth rates. Afro-Marxist states and some African socialist states fare relatively well in terms of egalitarian commitment especially due to broad development in the education and health sectors, as well as to a greater bridging of income gaps between elite and masses, between town and country, or to successful land reforms. But even this conclusion is not universally applicable.

While both types of socialist-oriented economies aim at greater autonomy and self-reliance, it seems that no country in Africa has escaped a high degree of dependency on the world capitalist centre on which all three types have to operate. While one might expect that in terms of human dignity the liberal capitalist countries fare slightly better than their socialist counterparts, Young comes to the conclusion that the violation of human rights is attributable more to paranoid and insecure rulers than to ideological commitments.

Socialist countries often have a commitment to a broad participation of the masses, and market economies stress private initiative. In most countries, no matter what type, the great danger consists in the increasing control by bureaucratic elites or vanguard parties over the masses of the people. As shown above, in terms of participation the two countries of Tanzania and Mozambique are of special interest.

Regarding capacity expansion one can state that strong state intervention is found in all three types, and that the effectiveness of the state apparatus does not present a direct link with the ideological commitment.

Ultimately one is faced again with the question: does ideology matter at all? One can safely say that ideological commitment does influence the particular performance of a country. Ideology makes certain choices more likely, and presents a special vulnerability in specific areas. Yet, besides ideological commitment, there are other factors that influence performance, success and failure. Among these are climate; resources, especially mineral resources; world market prices for food and raw materials; and proximity to conflict zones. Each ideological framework also leaves a wide margin for the skill, competence, and rationality of the respective governments.

The comparative assessment of the three types of ideological commitment and paths to development in Africa remains inconclusive; it relativises the impact of ideological commitment and defers a more definitive evaluation to a later date. It seems that the 1980s could prove decisive for a more accurate and balanced assessment of the socialist experience especially with regard to Mozambique and Zimbabwe.

Towards regional development in southern Africa

For many countries in sub-Saharan Africa, and especially for those located in the southern parts of Africa, one of the major constraints in building some form of socialism adapted to the needs of the people is their dependence on the world capitalist market. They are dependent on the so-called First World, with its centres in the USA, western Europe, and Japan — a reality that conditions also the policies and affairs of countries in the so-called Second World under the leadership of Soviet Russia. The Republic of South Africa is used by the transnational countries as a peripheral centre and base from which to extend their markets into the rest of Africa and to exploit its resources and labour.

The Republic of South Africa has in its plans for a constellation of southern African states attempted to use its economic leverage to attain the political goal of stability and peace under the leadership of the South African government. Partly as a reply to the initiative of South Africa, nine southern African states, Angola, Botswana, Lesotho, Malawi, Mozambique, Swaziland, Tanzania, Zambia and Zimbabwe, held a meeting at Arusha in 1979. This was followed by a meeting in Lusaka the following year, to launch the Southern Africa Development Conference (SADCC). The following four development objectives were identified:

(1) the reduction of economic dependence, particularly, but not only, on the Republic of South Africa;

(2) the forging of links to create a genuine and equitable regional integration;

(3) the mobilisation of resources to promote the implementation of national, interstate, and regional policies;

(4) concerted action to secure international cooperation within the framework of the strategy for economic liberation.

The advantages of regional integration are immediately apparent for a region that comprises a total population of over 50 million, has good agricultural and mineral resources, and provides an extensive market. The Arusha Coordinating Conference proposed, as a first step, the creation of a Southern African Regional Transport and Communications Commission. Other commissions would coordinate the financial institutions and mechanisms, agriculture, energy, water and minerals, employment and skills, and trade patterns in the region.

The implementation of a regional industrial and agricultural strategy would require major changes in the inherited political and economic institutions. These it is argued were created to serve the needs of the colonial powers and of transnational corporations (with their platform in South Africa) rather than the needs of the African people. In which direction would these changes point? Everything suggests that in the long term the SADCC would pursue a more socialist pattern towards the restructuring of their political and economic institutions so as to favour regional collaboration. The Arusha Declaration of 1979 expressed its critique of a common market approach, that is basically designed to attract investments by transnational corporations and enhance rather than reduce uneven and externally dependent development:

The first main problem with common markets or customs unions is the growth of regional inequalities. . . . A basic requirement, therefore, for this degree of cooperation is political, that the participating states be prepared to forgo a degree of autonomy in decision-taking for the common good of all partner states, and that the political will exists on the part of the states who benefit most from the union to develop mechanisms to transfer part of their benefits to the not-so-fortunate countries.

It remains to be seen to what degree the participating states will be prepared for essential institutional changes to control the basic regional industries, the banking and financial institutions as well as foreign and international wholesale trading. As some of the major countries of the SADCC have already, at least in part, implemented similar changes in their own countries, there is a likelihood that it might succeed on a regional basis. This success would further strengthen the struggle to build socialism in sub-Saharan Africa. This zone could then, according to the hopes expressed in the Arusha Conference, include the mighty industrial complex of the Republic of South Africa. But this is at present a hope which is severely threatened by the strengthening of South Africa's plan for a constellation of states after the signing of a non-aggression accord with Angola and after the Nkomati Accord with Mozambique in 1984. There is a danger that the SADCC objectives could be used as just an instrument within the wider framework for implementing the constellation of southern African states policy.

The Arusha Conference was aware of the great difficulties ahead and that they were about to make only the first step on a long journey. They chose to preface their document 'First Steps Toward Economic Integration' with the Chinese proverb: 'Even the longest journey begins with the first step.'

11 Social democracy and democratic socialism

We have seen that there are two approaches to the problem of how the political economy should be organised, along the lines of either 'free enterprise' capitalism or Marxist–Leninist socialism. Both have their advantages which make them seem desirable and their disadvantages which make them quite unacceptable. To summarise them briefly:

(a) Free enterprise capitalism supposedly grants freedom. Individual and collective initiative and achievement are rewarded, the less efficient are punished or pushed out. Supply and demand automatically regulate the allocation of resources according to profitability and utility. A highly versatile, innovative, efficient and thus productive economy is the result. But the tiger let loose to develop his wildest instincts can also do most harm. In the free market it is not need which counts, but bargaining power. Bargaining power depends on control over institutionalised decision-making processes, resources, capital, expertise, labour and purchasing power. The market system invariably works not towards equilibrium, but to the greater benefit of the strong at the expense of the weak. While the entire population of a metropolitan country may benefit, it creates massive concentrations of power and wealth in the economic centres, and marginalisation and misery in the economic peripheries on a global scale.

(b) Marxist–Leninist socialism is committed to the abolition of the oppressive and exploitative concentration of power and wealth in the bourgeoisie and to the creation of the equality of a 'classless society' brought about by the 'dictatorship of the proletariat' — in fact the dictatorship of the leadership elite of the communist party. Practice has shown that while a totalitarian state is capable of enforcing a more egalitarian distribution of income, this may occur at the expense of liberty and productivity. State planning seems to be less efficient than the results produced by the free play of the market mechanism. The prescriptions of an incompetent and clumsy bureaucracy stifle initiative and versatility and devour resources while the concentration of power in the hands of a few is even more fearful than that in the free enterprise system.

Against this background the question arises as to whether it would not be possible to compute a system which retains the advantages of both systems and avoids their respective pitfalls. Since the positive aspects of the one are identical with the negative aspects of the other, this can only mean that some sort of compromise must be found in which the respective trade-offs are carefully balanced against each other.

Two such approaches have actually emerged over last couple of decades, social democracy and democratic socialism. Social democracy (also called welfare capitalism or a social market economy) is a capitalist, free-enterprise economy which has been modified considerably to incorporate egalitarian principles such as equality of opportunity, social securities and participation in decision-making. Democratic socialism is a Marxist, state-controlled economy which has been modified considerably towards entrepreneurial initiative and a free market.

Principles of social democracy

There are a number of variations of this system in western countries, the classic example being that of the Swedish economy. The following are some of the basic principles which are generally applied.

Parliamentary democracy. Social democrats believe that it is not only possible but also prudent to gain power through democratic means and then subject the existing capitalist system to progressive reforms, rather than to disrupt the economy by violent revolution and entrust a totalitarian regime with the task of constructing an entirely new system.

Free enterprise. The principle of free enterprise is retained to encourage private initiative and achievement. But the state has to lay down basic parameters within which the economy is allowed to operate. Examples of specific responsibilities of the state are peace and stability (military, police, legal system), education and training, social securities and health services, quality inspection, maintenance of economic growth and full employment, control of inflation, and a sound balance of payments. On the whole the guideline is: as much government as is necessary, as little government as possible.

Private ownership. The means of production remain in private hands but the state has to guard against undue concentrations of economic power. The ideal is to break up monopolistic conglomerates and ensure free competition. The state may take over key industries to protect essential infrastructural services from disruption (for example, the transport and communications network, power and water supplies). It may also acquire substantial shareholdings in private companies to gain experience of how the economy works and to influence the direction it takes.

Market mechanism. The free market remains the basic mechanism regulating the allocation of resources and the distribution of goods and services. However, the state may fix minimum wages for certain job categories. It may also regulate prices of essential commodities such as agricultural products, to cut out excessive price fluctuations or to aid disadvantaged sectors of the economy.

Equality of opportunity. Social democrats are moderately committed to egalitarian principles in that they are careful not to jeopardise economic achievement. Private initiative is encouraged but power advantages are neutralised as far as possible. Progressive taxation (which means the higher one's income, the higher the percentage of taxed income) and heavy death duties are meant to level out steep discrepancies in income and wealth. Positively, the weaker sections of the population are helped to become more competitive through such measures as regional equalisation policies, subsidies, free and equal education and training, consumer protection, state-run research or credit facilities.

Social securities. While competition is encouraged and achievement is rewarded, the less gifted or less fortunate are protected from dropping out completely and ending up in misery. Unemployment insurance, pension schemes and old-age homes, subsidised health services and medical schemes, life-insurance policies, and sub-economic housing are planned to try to ensure that nobody is left destitute.

Industrial peace. The freedom of contract is retained but trade unions are encouraged to counterbalance the power of employers' organisations. Channels of communication and negotiation between major interest groups as well as the legal instruments to settle industrial disputes are provided. To facilitate mutual understanding and to give those affected by decisions some say in the decision-making processes, workers or their unions are represented on the managerial bodies of the enterprises in which they are employed. In some cases workers or unions are encouraged to become shareholders in the enterprises concerned. Alternatively the state promotes the wide spread of capital ownership in the population.

Technological advance. Technological innovation is encouraged so that the national economy remains competitive in international markets. Workers are protected from losing their jobs through new techniques by extensive training programmes and the provision of alternative jobs.

It is often maintained that social democracy is an attempt to retain the efficiency, productivity and freedom of the capitalist mode of production while ensuring social security and greater equality in income distribution. To achieve increased competitiveness in world markets, however, social democrats have often abandoned extended welfare services or higher wages and encouraged the concentration of capital, fully realising that if more is produced, there is more to be shared.

Achievements of social democracy

Proponents of social democracy can look back on considerable achievements in the countries where it has been implemented, particularly in western Europe. Between the end of World War Two, when Europe was in tatters, and the early seventies these countries have witnessed a period of sustained growth, great technological innovations, rising standards of living for the entire population, increased equity and welfare, and a low rate of inflation. Industrial conflicts have been kept at a relatively moderate level and the previous trend towards violent revolution and radical solutions has been reversed. Where a close link between a social democratic government and a confederation of blue-collar trade unions existed, as in the Swedish example, workers have been persuaded to moderate their wage demands. Social democrats have ruled continuously for over forty years in Sweden, which suggests a high legitimacy of the party in the eyes of the less privileged majority. Its interests were seen to be taken care of. In West Germany a policy of regular productivity-related wage increases has led to considerable worker contentment and the emergence of mass purchasing power in the population. This again constituted a growing market for manufactured goods and made sustained growth of the economy possible without leading to high rates of inflation. In other words, social democrats were able to convince the population that all should cooperate to produce as much as possible, by any appropriate means, and then to distribute the proceeds as equitably as possible, while maintaining high productivity.

Problems of social democracy

While not ideal, social democracy certainly seems to combine the best features of both systems. Unfortunately the system is not without its problems. More especially, it has not been able to prevent a series of crisis-generating developments with which the modern world economy currently has to battle.

Stagflation. Since the early seventies the western world has witnessed a new phenomenon, the long-term combination of economic recession (stagnation) and rising prices (inflation), a phenomenon referred to as stagflation. Initially it was blamed on higher crude-oil prices imposed by the OPEC cartel. But other factors must be considered too.

In the first place the market no longer seems to operate according to textbook descriptions. The power of producers has become so great that they are able to fix prices and the power of trade unions is equally capable of insisting on wage demands — both at higher levels than a free market would have warranted. We have to add an automatically growing bureaucracy, and the so-called military–industrial complex, which, while it competes for an ever-increasing part of the budget, is not subject to the market and does not add proportionately to productivity. The pattern of high standards of living demonstrated in developed countries has affected the level of desired consumption in poorer areas, and the world population as a whole seems to be living beyond its means. At the same time consumption in western countries seems to be approaching some sort of saturation point, which is raised only artificially and strenuously to new levels by sophisticated salesmanship, while Third World countries have accumulated such enormous public debts that they are no longer able to absorb the surplus produced in the West. The result is that markets do not expand to the magnitude which a dynamic capitalist economy needs to remain healthy. Add to this the run-away development of technological innovations generating ever greater productive capacities without corresponding market demand — and one has all the ingredients for a long-term structural recession.

Power blocs. The concentration of capital in multinational corporations means that they can evade guidelines or restrictions imposed by national governments. On the other hand social democratic governments lose their legitimacy if they fall out with powerful trade unions within the country or the rank and file of lower classes in society. Under these circumstances economic discipline is hard to enforce.

Restriction to a world elite. So far social democracy has achieved greater equity and security only within nation states that belong to the world economic centre. Egalitarian principles and social securities demand a high level of economic output. Where poorer countries have been tempted to indulge in such policies the result has usually been rampant inflation, since one can only share out as much as has been produced. Moreover such a centre state will normally pursue its own interests in international markets at the expense of weaker competitors. Equity within a state does not imply justice between states — loving inner family circles can be ruthlessly selfish towards outsiders. The universal application of social democracy would presuppose a powerful world government, great sacrifices on the part of the rich and vastly increased output by the poor. This is not immediately foreseeable.

Technology. Social democracy has not been able to come to terms with the disruptive effects of technological innovations. On a national scale it may be able to rechannel redundant labour into sectors not yet affected by automation and computerisation. But this means that producers elsewhere on the globe have been thrown out of the market through the greater competitiveness of industrial products from the West. In other words, unemployment has been exported. More recently high and stubborn unemployment rates in the West suggest that the process has finally caught up with industrial countries as well.

Ethical foundations. A more radical stance would point out that social democracy does not challenge the cultural legitimation of greed as the prime motivational power in economic terms. It follows a half-hearted ethic of alleviating the harm being done without going to the roots of the problem.

The limits to growth. Social democracy has, like its more radical counterparts, continued with an economic policy based on growth. Whether unlimited and accelerating growth spread over the entire world population is possible on a limited planet has become more than questionable in recent years. Fiercer competition for the dwindling resources of the earth, particularly between the economic superpowers with their frightening arsenal of nuclear weapons, may plunge the globe into a holocaust if present trends continue.

In sum, while social democracy has gone a long way towards alleviating the more rampant consequences of capitalism within some industrialised countries, it has not been able to contain or redirect disconcerting developments in the global economic system. Since South Africa replicates the world situation in many ways this is an important observation for South Africans. The luxury of social democratic institutions among the privileged white elite to the detriment or exclusion of the black majority is an unacceptable proposition.

Principles of democratic socialism

Democratic socialism is less common than social democracy. There have been traces of it in many communist countries, notably in Czecho-slovakia during the short spell of the 'Prague spring' before the Russian invasion. The only prominent and enduring example is in Yugoslavia, which we shall discuss below.

One-party state. Democratic socialism emerged from a Marxist-Leninist structure. The control of the communist party over national affairs is retained in the democratic socialist system. However, leaders are committed to democratisation and the decentralisation of power. The ideal is participatory democracy — which means that those who are affected by decisions should be decision-makers. There is less repression and more freedom of expression, initiative, movement and organisation than in other Marxist–Leninist countries. The devolution of power into small local entities is, of course, also a way of retaining overall control in a society riddled with cultural, historical and regional divisions.

Worker self-management. This principle is implied by participatory democracy. It says that the employees of an enterprise have to do the actual running of the firm. In all non-agricultural firms employing more than five people, workers' councils are established. If there are more than thirty employers these become representative councils. Such councils are chosen and can be dismissed by the workers. The councils choose and can dismiss the managers of the enterprises. This type of participatory democracy is also practised in services such as hospitals, schools, courts, research institutions or cultural organisations.

State ownership. The socialist principle that capital is a social asset and should be owned by the state is retained. All enterprises above a certain size — thus excluding small workshops and family farms — belong to the state. Workers run them and benefit from them, but they do not own them. If a worker leaves a firm he has no transferable stake.

Free enterprise and the market system. The state lays down certain parameters within which all firms have to operate, and managers are controlled by the party, banks or local authorities. But within those limits there is a degree of freedom unusual for a Marxist state. Any person or group can start a new firm. The managers and their councils, who are accountable to their employees, find gaps in the market, determine what the firm should produce, and whether it should diversify. They obtain the raw materials and other resources, organise the productive process and establish marketing channels. They have to make profits or face the consequences of low productivity. They also distribute the proceeds after certain deductions. In short, democratic socialism has combined the market system not with private enterprise but with employee enterprise.

Socialist distribution. Firms have to make a profit. From this certain deductions are made for national concerns and the welfare of the community in which the firm operates. The remaining surplus is distributed by the worker committee among its employees — mainly according to their input, but need may be taken into consideration. The criteria for evaluating the contribution of each worker are laid down. There is, however, a guaranteed minimum income in proportion to the time spent at work. Distribution takes account of housing, recreation, creches and suchlike and is not simply the payment of wages. The basic principle is that work is regarded as a value and not just a resource to be paid a price determined by the market.

Achievements of democratic socialism

Yugoslavia is a developing country which was heavily devastated during World War Two. Its achievements must be seen in this light. Its growth rate averaged 5 per cent between 1960 and 1980 (RSA 2,3 per cent). Its gross domestic product per capita now equals that of the RSA, Brazil or similar semi-industrialised countries. There is, however, a much greater equality in incomes. The equalisation process between centre and periphery regions has continued to grow. There is more freedom and genuine consultation than in other Marxist states. The problems of cultural and regional diversity have been dealt with relatively successfully. On the one hand the system is built on the socialist creed, yet it seeks to avoid the inefficiencies of central planning and the stultifying effect of large-scale bureaucracy. On the other hand it takes advantage of the initiative and responsibility generated by free enterprise, risk-taking and competition without allowing the proceeds to go into the pockets of economic empire-builders who did not share in the generation of the wealth. The exclusion of the worker from the running of the productive process in which he is engaged and the alienation from the product he helps to produce are overcome to some appreciable extent. He is no longer just a labour unit or a cog in a machine, but a respected member of a team which cooperates for mutual benefit. A sense of belonging, dignity and indispensability and a motivation generated not only by the size of one's pay-packet but by participation in the enhancement of the wholeness of life have a chance to develop.

Problems of democratic socialism

One might gain the impression that democratic socialism, like social democracy, combines the best of two systems, though each having different components. But this system too has its difficulties.

Productivity. We have seen that the record for productivity is not as bad as capitalist doctrine would make us believe. Motivation can be generated in ways other than by private ownership. Yet there are a number of 'leakages' of productivity which have been observed. Worker-appointed managers may not always be the most competent to run a modern industrial firm. Alternatively they may be too lenient and gracious (so as to maintain their popularity) and allow apathy and inefficiency. Workers may be short-sighted and demand higher wages instead of allowing for the replacement of equipment and the accumulation of working capital. They may be tempted to 'milk' a firm which does not belong to them. Of course, in all these cases they are ultimately going to hurt themselves. With proper guidance and education such irrational behaviour may be overcome. Workers are bound to discover that it is in their own interest to appoint professional managers and to subject themselves to their discipline.

Inflation. Yugoslavia has been plagued by a fairly high rate of inflation (19,4 per cent between 1970 and 1980) if compared with fully industrialised countries. When one compares it with other semi-industrialised countries, notably in Latin America, the picture is less serious. Reasons for inflation may be found in the excessive distribution and price-fixing by monopolies (or the absence of effective local and international competition). The authorities encourage international competition to raise local efficiency, however, and one wonders whether these are growing pains which can be overcome.

Egalitarian principles compromised. Granting more freedom obviously leads to some compromise with egalitarian principles. Though Yugoslavian income distribution is more equal than that of most developing countries, notably South Africa, there is still a substantial hierarchy of income differentials. There are discrepancies between white- and blue-collar workers, between sectors of the economy, between firms and between geographical regions. Participation and equality within an enterprise do not automatically lead to an equitable distribution of wealth between such entities. In the same vein justice within a socialist country does not automatically lead to justice between countries competing with each other on an uncontrolled world market — a problem which we also addressed in the discussion of social democracy.

Authority. In spite of the ideals of grassroots democracy, authoritarianism may still emerge. Managers may use their committees as mere rubber stamps. Chosen representatives of workers may develop elitist attitudes. Participatory democracy is only feasible in small groups and decisions taken on higher levels are remote from the perceptions and influence of those affected by them. Another difficulty is the simultaneous presence of different types of authority: the communist party, the trade unions which are organs of the party but also channels of worker interests, and the workers' committees and their managers, which are supposed to be responsible to those selfsame workers.

Unemployment and technological advance. Marxists would deny that there could be unemployment in a truly socialist state. The unemployment rate in Yugoslavia is fairly high. Here too the competition between technological innovation and labour may play a role.

The limits to growth. Democratic socialism is no better than its capitalist and socialist counterparts in its failure to address the problems of economic growth in a world of limited resources and in not paying sufficient attention to the dangers of ecological destruction.

We have discussed two systems, one being a modification of capitalism, the other being a modification of socialism. Social democracy can best be understood as a system which has moved as far in the direction of egalitarianism as is feasible within a capitalist context, while democratic socialism has moved as far as possible in the direction of free enterprise within a socialist context. Social democracy has shown that it is possible to reach greater equity in a system made productive by private enterprise, simply by loosening the link between production and distribution. Democratic socialism has shown that free, risk-taking initiative can be allowed to develop in a system committed to the social ownership of the means of production, simply by separating ownership from control and usufruct.

In this way each has made an attempt to resolve the contradiction between economic achievement usually associated with free enterprise, and egalitarian principles usually associated with state intervention. They have also gone some way towards neutralising excessive concentrations of economic power and its abuse — whether by big business in capitalism or big government in socialism. The actual performance of both systems shows that they are not necessarily less capable of operating at viable economic levels than their more radical counterparts, while they greatly help to humanise modern economic processes.

We also saw, however, that both systems battle with problems generated by their own internal structures and have not addressed themselves sufficiently to overarching problems which they share with all existing systems, notably the problem of international equity and the limits to growth.

Between the two moderate systems there still exists a discontinuity but transitions and further compromises are conceivable. If in social democracy workers or their organisations acquire majority shareholdings in the companies by which they are employed — a policy pursued by the Swedish Confederation of Trade Unions — the transition to democratic socialism is being made. On the other hand worker-appointed managers may begin to act much like their shareholder-appointed counterparts in the West once the legal restrictions imposed by a socialist state are further relaxed. One can be certain, however, that there is no ideal combination which can be established for all times and situations. Trade-offs have to be weighed one against the other in a continuous process of assessment and adaptation, which is largely influenced by the power struggles between the interest groups concerned.

For South Africans the primary question is whether either system could be attained in a country which has neither a genuine *laissez-faire* tradition nor a consistent system of state planning, where neither free competition nor egalitarian aspirations determine practical policies, where the entire population is drawn neither into a process of grand economic achievement according to the great liberal dream nor into the spirit of mutual responsibility advocated by Marxism. It is possible to go from capitalism to social democracy or from Marxism–Leninism to democratic socialism. But if 'free enterprise' is reserved for a powerful elite and state planning is used as a tool to subdue the competitiveness of underprivileged groups we have a situation which resembles medieval feudalism. And feudalism boasts neither the structural presuppositions nor the mass mentality necessary to make either of the moderate systems work. So the distance South Africans would have to travel to be able to replicate either the Swedish or Yugoslavian model would seem to be long indeed.

But this is not to suggest that South Africa cannot move towards a more egalitarian system. All systems have evolved in time despite many development problems and as the outcome of many small steps in the desired direction in an evolutionary process. While we shall not reach an ideal system in this world, this should not prevent us from trying to move in the right direction: a direction which may be elucidated by our examination of a comparison between the Swedish and the Yugoslavian systems. Moreover, there is considerable evidence that important and large interest groups in South Africa, particularly amongst urban blacks, would be susceptible to movements committed to a combination of greater freedom and greater equity rather than to the more radical alternatives on either side of the spectrum.

Part four
BASIC IDEAS OF MARXISM AND SOCIALISM

Part Four departs in style and content from the rest of the book. While Part Three describes socialist and Afro-Marxist policies in some parts of Africa, our intention in Part Four is to explore the generative ideas that shape such policies. It is the most philosophical section of the book and seeks to describe in simplified form the basic analysis of Karl Marx, the key concepts of Marxism–Leninism, the essentials of anarchism, and recent developments of neo-Marxist theory in the West. It also describes a Third World version of Marxism–Leninism — the Maoist revolution in China.

There are two reasons why we believe there is an urgent need for such a description. Firstly, in contrast to developments in most parts of western Europe, the Americas, black Africa and Asia since the late sixties, in South Africa we have not been able to come to grips with socialist thought. The result is that the level of public debate among both opponents and proponents of socialism seldom rises above rhetoric and propaganda. Whether one supports or opposes the ideologies concerned, one nonetheless needs to know what the debate is about.

In the second place, it is of the essence of a democratic system that the public has access to diverse sources of information so as to enable it to base its choices on a knowledge of real alternatives and not of spectres. In a situation where ideologies are both the content and the target of propaganda, the attempt to offer authoritative and unbiased information is important for the very survival of democracy. It is self-evident that this attempt is not meant to indicate approval of the ideology which is being described. Readers are left to make up their own minds about the issues discussed in Part Four.

12 The Marxism of Marx

'A spectre is haunting South Africa, the spectre of communism.' This slight variation on a famous sentence expresses the feeling of many people in South Africa. South Africa is 'under siege', it is said; communist strategy is out to strangle and suffocate it; and world communism is behind every manifestation which seeks to oppose South Africa's policy of separate development. It is not surprising, then, that those who are opposed to the present regime often conclude that change can come only from communism.

Socialist presence in Africa

One third of the world lives under governments professing communism, and more than half live under regimes which claim to be socialist; but it is in Africa that communism, Marxism and socialism have made their greatest advances in recent years.

Marxism was introduced to Africa mainly by Nkrumah, though not strictly a Marxist himself. Following Nkrumah's Ghana, a number of African states have adopted Marxism or Marxism–Leninism in part or completely — Guinea, Congo-Brazzaville, Benin, Somalia, Ethiopia and, more recently, Angola, Mozambique and Zimbabwe.

With the independence of the former Portuguese colonies, Angola and Mozambique, in 1975, a new situation developed in Africa. Until 1974 there had existed only two organised communist parties in Africa, namely those in Algeria and South Africa (in exile). Before 1974 there was no Marxist power base in southern Africa. The Soviet Union relied on cooperation with revolutionary democratic governments to back up the liberation movements.

The MPLA in Angola and Frelimo in Mozambique have adopted Marxist–Leninist principles. Moreover the policy of the OAU is clear: after the liberation of Namibia/South West Africa all efforts are to be directed towards the liberation of South Africa/Azania from white domination, which would result one way or another in a socialist or Marxist–Leninist inspired form of black majority rule.

With the banning of the Communist Party, the African National Congress and Pan-Africanist Congress, there has been a progressive radicalisation of black opposition in South Africa. The Black Consciousness Movement has clearly shown a socialist orientation, especially in its economic policy; and with the increasing frustration of its aims and the banning of its leaders, it has been driven to a more radical position in its analysis and strategy. The chances cf a more pronounced Marxist and Marxist–Leninist tendency increase in proportion to the amount of pressure and oppression the South African government applies. For many, especially young blacks, socialism in one form or another represents the only viable alternative to the present oppressive political and economic system.

It is of the utmost urgency for all people in South Africa to face the challenge of socialism, Marxism and communism. The first requirement for doing this is to be familiar with and analyse these ideologies, which in some way will affect the future of South Africa. Before we can evaluate them in the light of the critique of other ideologies and discuss their relationship to Christianity, we must understand them in terms of their own history and in all their complexity and variety.

Socialism

Socialism was first used in England and France in the 1820s as a counter-concept to 'individualism', being born from the critique of liberalism and *laissez-faire* capitalism. Socialism has been defined (in *The New Penguin Political Dictionary*) as 'a political and economic theory, according to which the means of production, distribution and exchange should be owned and controlled by the people, everyone should be given equal opportunity to develop his talents, and the wealth of the community should be fairly distributed'. Common to all theories and movements of socialism is the commitment to a communal, cooperative society based on the equality of all people.

To bring about this socialist society, different strategies are suggested for different situations.

(1)   As regards the economy, one or more of:
— complete nationalisation/socialisation of the means of production;
— selective nationalisation of key industries, controlled private ownership of others;
— centralised state direction, with one overall plan of production and distribution;
— a market economy directed by socialist planners within a broad framework of guidelines.

(2)   As regards the society, one or more of:

— centralised direction by the government;
— as much decentralisation as possible, decisions being made by public boards, local governments, or self-governing producers' communities;
— workers' control;
— governmental planning boards.

(3)   As regards the distribution of what is produced in society:
— 'to each according to his work' (stage of socialism);
— 'to each according to his need' (stage of communism);
— adequate income for all, assuring a minimum level of housing, clothing and food, and free access to education, health and culture.

(4)   As regards government:
— equal political rights for all citizens;
— levelling of status differences, entirely, or with different degrees of decision-making powers.

Marxism

Marxism is that form of socialism which draws inspiration for its analysis and strategy from the thought of Karl Marx. All Marxists are socialists, but not all socialists are Marxists.

Communism

Communism is a movement and at the same time the goal of this movement. It is that form of socialism which works for the establishment of an international classless and stateless society beyond socialist communal states, by means of a revolution (violent or non-violent) which overthrows liberal capitalist society. All communists are socialists, but not all socialists are communists. Though Marx was a communist, not all Marxists are communists; not all communists are Marxists. And not all who claim to be, or are labelled, communists are communists.

SOCIALISM BEFORE MARX

Karl Marx is the central figure of socialism. One third of the world lives under political systems which claim direct inspiration from him, and no socialist movement can ignore his thought. On the other hand, Marx is himself part of a movement which forms our understanding of him, and which he shapes in a decisive way.

Historical origins

Socialist ideas are discernible in many cultures, especially in traditional societies. We find socialist ideals in Plato's *Republic*, in the communities of early christians as described in Acts 2 and 4, and in Thomas More's *Utopia*. But socialism in the strict sense has its roots in the social and economic transformations wrought in Europe by the Industrial Revolution.

Socialism is a response to the misery and degradation suffered by an urban proletariat under the conditions of early capitalism. Disrupted family and community life, low wages, social insecurity, long working-hours, and child labour characterised the lot of the early industrial workers. In contrast to the individualistic drive of the 'survival of the fittest' and an uncontrolled free market of capitalist society, socialism offered a vision of a community of producers, in which the working people would own and control the means of production. Socialism was the plea of oppressed workers for living conditions worthy of human beings.

The utopian socialists

Marx used the term utopian socialists for the early theorists of socialism: Henri de Saint-Simon (1760–1825), Charles Fourier (1772–1837) and Robert Owen (1771–1858). They were utopian idealists in the sense that they thought change could come about through peaceful reforms of the capitalist system. Such reform would start on the basis of small-scale experiments with the help of those in power, rather than through the concerted action of the oppressed.

Against the unbridled individualism of his time, Saint-Simon presented the future society as a gigantic cooperative workshop, where the rule of men over men would be replaced by a shared administration. Saint-Simon and his followers were among the first to proclaim that private property was no longer sacrosanct but that factories or warehouses, for example, should be owned communally.

Fourier envisaged model communities, the germ cells of the future society, consisting of 1 500 people each. They would not be ruled by experts, as Saint-Simon had thought, but would be bound together in love in a harmonious non-coercive order, guided spontaneously according to temperaments and inclinations.

Owen, known as a model employer and proprietor of a textile works in Scotland, denounced the principle of competition and proposed 'villages of unity and cooperation' where settlers, in addition to raising crops, would improve their bodies and their minds. Despairing of his fellow capitalists, Owen turned later to the emerging trade-union movement. He left a lasting imprint on the British socialist tradition.

Other early socialists included Louis-Auguste Blanqui, who was the first to call his radical socialist theory communist, and Louis Blanc, who advocated the establishment of national workshops with capital advanced by the government. These would be run by the workers themselves, who were to elect their own management.

Early social anarchists

Anarchism, as the word suggests, is the denial of authority, especially state authority. It is a condemnation of the present society, a concept of a future non-authoritarian libertarian society, and a social rebellion (violent or otherwise) to change the present society into the future one. The first to call himself an anarchist was Pierre-Joseph Proudhon (1809-65). He was the real inspiration for French socialism, and had a profound influence on Marx with whom he sat many a night in discussion.

Proudhon's book *What Is Property?* gave the celebrated answer (which was to become a catchword of the nineteenth century): 'Property is theft.' Proudhon was a pioneer libertarian thinker. He was what one could call a 'socialist individualist' who tried to elaborate a synthesis between communism, which destroys independence, and capitalism, in which private property destroys equality. But Proudhon did not create the anarchist movement. This was the work of one of the most spectacular figures of the nineteenth century, Michael Bakunin.

Michael Bakunin (1814-76), the great Russian libertarian activist and a restless, eccentric rebel, became the founder of the anarchist movement. He realised in the 1860s that the time was ripe for the discontented workers and peasants of the Latin countries to absorb anarchist ideas. This led him into the 'First International', or International Working Men's Association, held in 1864 in London. There he clashed with the authoritarian implications of Marxist socialism. The differences between the Marxist and anarchist conception were great: Marx was a centralist, Bakunin a federalist; Marx favoured nationalisation of the means of production, Bakunin control by the workers; while Marxists stood for the function of the state in the transition to communism through the 'dictatorship of the proletariat', Bakunin demanded the abolition of the state at the earliest possible moment. In 1872 Marx had Bakunin expelled from the International. Bakunin's influence declined and in 1876 he died, disappointed, a great and dramatic romantic revolutionary.

MARX BEFORE MARXISM

Marx without myth

'As for me, I am not a Marxist', Karl Marx is said to have remarked after the first volume of *Capital* had been published. One can only imagine what he would have said about the numerous interpretations of his work and the many different groups, movements and individuals claiming to be 'Marxist' that have arisen since his day.

Marx is seldom read and his work is often reduced to ill-digested slogans. The range and mass of his voluminous writings, covering such divergent disciplines as economics, philosophy, politics and social science, are partly responsible for this. There is also the difficulty of his philosophical thought and style, and the chaotic state in which he left his manuscripts. In fact, important aspects of his thought came to be known only in the 1930s, when his early writings were first published. (The seminal *Grundrisse* saw publication only in 1942.) English translations often followed much later. Moreover, the wealth of Marx's thought is lost when it becomes the bible of a mass movement; the open-endedness of his dialectic philosophy is ignored when it becomes the dogmatic ideology of a regime; the humanity of his personality is effaced when he becomes the idealised hero of communist world revolution or the bedevilled crusader of the 'red danger'.

Karl Marx (1818–83) was born into a comfortable middle-class Jewish family with a long rabbinic ancestry. He was a cosmopolitan, emigré intellectual, who lived in Berlin, Paris, Brussels and London. He could read most European languages and write in three; he was steeped in the classical humanities, read Aeschylus every year in the Greek original, and relaxed by reading Thucydides. He was a philosopher on a grand scale, who swiftly moved from romanticism to Hegelianism, to liberal idealism and finally to its radical critique. He was a polemical journalist with a biting wit, and a political activist with a quick and fertile mind. One of the last of the classical economists, he spent most of his thirty-four years in London in the British Museum engaged in meticulous research. He was a Victorian system-builder who believed in progress and rationality.

Marx never stormed the barricades or worked in a factory. He liked to take his family for Sunday picnics, and on Sunday evenings he met with his friends. He was a gentle father, who spent hours playing with his children and used his vivid imagination to invent stories for them. He used to say, 'children should educate their parents.' He was a loving husband; to his wife he dedicated two volumes of lyrical poetry, wasting, in his father's eyes, his first year of university at Bonn. He died in his armchair.

Influences on Marx

The thought of Karl Marx has three main sources: German idealist philosophy, French socialism, and English classical economics. These influences correspond roughly to the three main cities in which Marx lived: Berlin, Paris and London.

Marx and German idealist philosophy

From Hegel via Feuerbach to Marx. Hegel remained for Marx the great philosophical inspiration throughout his life. From him he learnt the *dialectic* style of philosophising. For Hegel and for Marx, all reality is a totality in process, which leads from an initial identity to its alienation from itself, and back from alienation to its progressive liberation, culminating in a final reconciliation. This final stage recapitulates the total wealth of all the previous phases of the process. For Hegel the driving force of this process is the *power of the negative*. This power engenders within each stage of the process its own opposition and thereby an awareness develops that this opposition is not external, but part of its own. In this way the process reaches a new stage of consciousness.

For Hegel *conscientisation*, or reaching new stages of consciousness, is a process of progressive freedom, of being one with itself in ever increasing awareness of its own riches. The subject of this process is the 'spirit', or the 'idea', which is the same as the totality of the historical world process in as far as it becomes conscious of itself. This 'world spirit' evolves, in an inevitable providential logic, from its deepest alienation in nature, through the basic forms of its subjective and objective stages, into the freedom of total self-consciousness.

There are three main incarnations of the absolute spirit; art, religion and philosophy (that is, Hegel's own philosophy). In the last, world spirit comes home to itself, into its full identity. It is now conscious of its identity with all the apparent non-identity, because it is now 'the identity of the identity and the non-identity'.

Through Feuerbach to a reversal of Hegel. For any philosopher after Hegel there were only two possibilities, since with Hegel the fulfilment and the end of philosophy had arrived: either he became an Hegelian or else he radically opposed Hegel's philosophy as did the Left-Hegelians, among them Marx, Feuerbach, Bauer, Stirner and Hess. Marx expressed his anti-Hegelian approach (which, while being in opposition to Hegel, was still dependent on him) when he remarked that he found Hegel standing on his head and put him back on his feet.

Feuerbach began the reversal of Hegel. He had replaced the 'idea' with 'nature'. What for Hegel was the deepest alienation of the spirit, namely nature, became for Feuerbach the real essence of man. Man is a natural being rather than a spiritual being. This reversal signifies a radical break with the basic Platonic tradition in western philosophy.

Marx went beyond Feuerbach in that he did not speak about an abstract essence of man, but about man in his concrete conditions, about natural man, social man, and economic man. For Marx the subject of history is man, who by active transformation of nature progressively creates himself in the totality of his objectifications in history. Man makes history. Though Marx never gave a systematic account in his work of the successive stages of the dialectic of history, one can identify perhaps five stages.

(1) *Primitive communism.* In the first stage, man lives in harmony with himself and with nature in the natural state of 'primitive communism'. He satisfies his needs through simple exchange with nature as collector and hunter. There is common ownership of natural resources, raw materials and tools.

(2) *Ancient slaveholder society.* As the population grows and its needs increase, man has to attack nature, plough the land, and fell trees, and so must leave his primitive natural paradise, because this new mode of production — agriculture — increasingly necessitates the division of labour. Classes now emerge: these are groups of people bound together by similar interests and by a similar relationship to the means of production. Ancient society consisted of those who owned the means of production and non-owners — the masters and the slaves: in other words, a two-class society.

(3) *Medieval feudalism.* As needs increase, new means of production develop (iron ploughs and looms) to satisfy them, and new classes arise: feudal lords, vassals, guild-masters, journeymen, apprentices, serfs. In short, we have entered medieval feudal society.

(4) *Bourgeois capitalism.* With the introduction of the manufacturing system, and especially the modern machine, industry begins a totally new epoch. Two main classes emerge: the bourgeoisie, the owners of the new means of production, and the working class. This is the phase of capitalism in which the alienation of the oppressed class reaches its deepest expression. Bourgeois capitalism is seen by Marx as a necessary phase in history.

(5) *Socialism–communism.* At the same time capitalism constitutes the possible turning-point, the moment of the great revolutionary leap forward when the proletariat, conscious of its revolutionary role as a united class, will take into its own hands the means of production. After a transitional socialist phase of the 'dictatorship of the proletariat', history reaches its final completion, the classless communist society where man will be finally reconciled with himself and with nature.

From theory to praxis. In the 1820s Hegel viewed the Prussian state as the highest incarnation of the objective spirit. But when in 1840 the Prussian government embraced the reactionary practice of royal absolutism, the young Left-Hegelians were forced to recognise that Hegel's political standpoint was conservative. They confronted non-rational reality with Hegel's own logic, which declared all of reality to be rational.

Hegelian philosophy was turned into a critique of philosophy and state. Speculative philosophy, grounded in the idea, became a philosophy of action and revolutionary praxis. Marx expressed this transformation in the celebrated eleventh thesis on Feuerbach: 'The philosophers have only interpreted the world differently; the point is to change it.'

French socialism and Engels

Marx's second main source of inspiration was French socialism. It was in Paris that he came into contact with the followers of Saint-Simon and Fourier, whom, together with Owen, Marx called utopian socialists. They had no thought of overturning society. Rather they believed they could, through enlightened legislation, create a centrally planned industrial society, by reforming the evils of the capitalist system. More important, it was in Paris that Marx began a lifelong friendship with Friedrich Engels, who had been working in his father's textile firm in Manchester. Engels introduced Marx to the actual workings of capitalism, and gave him concrete insight into the conditions of the English working class, about which Marx wrote so vividly in the first volume of *Capital*.

Marx was conscious of the social upheavals of the early Industrial Revolution, which had crowded labourers together in the desolate new industrial towns of England, and dehumanised country folk into slum dwellers and wage slaves. Marx tried not so much to complain, but to explain the economic machinery and the system. Why the long working hours of men, women and children, even under the age of twelve, the fall in wages, and the labour legislation? This explanatory process was what Marx termed scientific socialism, in opposition to utopian socialism.

English economists

The third main source of Marx's writings was the works of the classical English economists, Adam Smith, David Ricardo, Malthus and J. S. Mill. Their writings occupied him during the long years in London, where he wrote the main works of the last period of his life: *Outlines of the Critique of Political Economy*, or *Grundrisse*, and the material published in the three volumes of *Capital: a critical analysis of capitalist production*, with *Theories of Surplus Value*, which Marx intended to be a sort of fourth volume of *Capital*.

Adam Smith was the founder and the most influential member of the classical economic school. This school held that capitalism, as it emerged, was a self-regulating market system. If one left producers and consumers alone, in the liberal *laissez-faire* style, society as a whole would benefit.

The market system is upheld by two basic laws, which balance each other: every human being is motivated primarily by self-interest, to the ultimate benefit of society; and secondly, competition ensures that individuals are not exploited by others. Ricardo added what is known as the 'iron law of wages': workers get only enough wages to keep themselves and their children alive.

These 'natural laws' of economics, while legitimating the activities of the new capitalist class, required workers to accept their new conditions as part of a natural, fixed order of things. Marx, however, analysed the exploitative nature of the capitalist system. He sought to show that these laws were not natural but were created by man; their effect was to alienate him. The capitalist system could be and had to be changed. Marx's great achievement lay in bringing the science of economics once more within the bounds of a philosophy of man.

Marx's basic vision

In the following section, we attempt to collect into a coherent vision the various constitutive elements of Marx's thought. Certain aspects, to which we have already alluded from an historical perspective, will reappear more systematically.

The utopia of the 'whole man'

Ernst Bloch has described the work of Marx as consisting of ninetenths 'cold blue' scientific, social, and economic analysis, and onetenth 'warm red' utopian, revolutionary fire. This one-tenth makes Marx a passionate humanist, and permeates his entire work. Man is the beginning, the centre, and the goal of all history.

The whole man is often described by Marx as the 'universal individual'. Man is an individual, unique, free: these traits are never sacrificed to the collectivity. But man is also universal, a species being, a recapitulation of mankind and of all its potential wealth. He is a social being, he is with-others, and for-others, and from-others. He is an historical being, and he finds himself in all of history. He is an economic being, bound to the earth, and he sees in the total sum of economic production, only himself. Man is to come back home, conscious that the whole world and all of history belongs to him, that they are an extension of his body. The full realisation of this will occur in the communist society, which is the goal of all history. Individuality and freedom grow in proportion to man's universality. Only thus will man overcome the split between an isolated subject and external objects, the split between fact and value, cause and effect, nature and society.

Man is free and whole only when he knows that the object is waiting to be appropriated by him, to be the stuff of his own self-creation and realisation. Here lies the key to the philosophy of Marx. The basic unit of reality is not a thing but a relation. Marx's relational view of reality was a heritage from Hegel. It explains his adoption of dialectic as the fundamental approach to reality. The truth is the whole (Hegel). Only when I understand the singular reality within the context of the totality of its relations do I understand its truth. The focal centre is no longer the absolute spirit as for Hegel, but man as 'universal individual'.

Creative labour

Man's basic relationship is his relationship to nature. The basic activity of man is creative labour. This is in direct opposition to Hegel for whom, together with the entire tradition of the West since Plato, thought was the basic activity. Man, in this tradition, was seen as basically spiritual, with the precedence of spirituality over materiality, soul over body, heaven over earth. Here lies the root of what is often so thoroughly misunderstood. Marx's materialism is not necessarily anti-christian or atheistic, unless by christian one means Platonic and one forgets that Christianity is born out of Judaism.

Through creative labour man overcomes the apparent opposition between subject and object. The object becomes part of the subject and the subject appropriates the object. Man humanises nature and nature naturalises man to produce an historical world in which man is at home, is fully free, consciously at one with himself and the world.

Creative labour is man's 'metabolism with nature'; the product is man's 'extended body'. By exploring the latent richness of nature, man discovers the latent richness and potentialities within himself. It is in a communist society that man will experience the fullness of the creativity of labour, in the full satisfaction of human *needs*, and the full exploration and exploitation of human *powers*.

Alienation

The theory of alienation is the focal point of Marx's entire philosophy. It is the thread which strings together the various constitutive elements of the organic whole of his thought. For Marx man's condition in bourgeois capitalist society is one of alienation. That, as we shall see, takes different forms. Only a radical transformation of the whole of social life can de-alienate man and society. Only in a future communist society, stripped of the alienating features of capitalist society, will man no longer be alienated and really come into his own — though the precise nature of such a non-alienated condition is not clearly spelled out by Marx. All classes are alienated to the degree that they fall short of the communist ideal.

Alienated man is an 'abstraction'. He has lost the unique qualities of his species-nature which distinguish him as a human being. These are his relations to the product of his labour, to his activity, to his species and to other men. Alienated man is estranged: he is separated from essential parts of his being. He is mutilated, and the severed parts (relations) are undergoing their own transformation apart from man, to whom they belong. Alienation is the splintering of human nature into a number of misbegotten parts. Communism is its reunification. Communism is the complete return of man to himself as a social (that is, human) being — a return become conscious, and accomplished with the entire wealth of previous development. It is the positive transcending of all estrangement: the final coming home, the final healing of mutilated man.

Since capitalism is the exact opposite of communism, it is in capitalism that man experiences most deeply the alienation of his labour in the four basic relations of man.

(1) *Alienation from the product of his labour*. Man 'puts his life into the object' he produces in a capitalist society. Man is thereby estranged from his very life in the product, because he cannot use for his own needs that which he has produced. It enters into somebody else's control, becomes independent from him, and confronts him as an alien power. He cannot even recognise his products once they are alienated from him. Although he needs them for his consumption, he has no control over them, since they usually serve the greed of the capitalist. In so far as products are means of production, the roles are exchanged in the upside down world of capitalism. 'It is no longer the labourer that employs the means of production, but the means of production that employ the labourer.' Man becomes an appendage of the machine which he has produced.

(2) *Alienation from his productive activity*. Through increasing division of labour, man's activity becomes more and more limited and repetitive. Instead of developing man's creative powers it burns them up as if they were fuel, producing 'idiocy' and 'cretinism' in the workers. The worker feels at home only when he is not working, and not at home when he is working. He hates what ought to be his deepest fulfilment as a human being.

(3) *Alienation from his species*. For Marx the category 'species' denotes those potentialities which mark man off from other living creatures. Man is a conscious being, he is aware of what he is doing: he can choose, provide and plan. He can create things which are not of immediate practical need; he can create beautiful things. Under the estrangement of capitalism these advantages of human beings over animals turn out to be disadvantages. All these potentialities are frustrated since labour under capitalist conditions becomes a means of

staying alive. Man simply vegetates. This state is made worse since he is conscious of his species, of what he could be.

(4) *Alienation from his fellow men.* Man is a cooperative being. But in capitalist society one man produces for another man who controls the product. As the worker is alienated from his product, so is he alienated from the capitalist, for whom the product serves as an instrument of his power. Another expression of alienation is the relation between the different producers in society, which appears as the relation between their products on the market. The market dominates society and men themselves become things on the market — commodities. The capitalist himself is alienated because he is producing for profit rather than for use. His goal becomes the accumulation of capital, and he thus becomes the victim of a profit-oriented system which he himself has shaped. This alienation is expressed in the 'divine power of money' which is 'the alienated power of humanity'. Having prevails over being. Only those needs are met which can be met profitably, and new and often artificial needs are created in order to provide for profit.

Private property and the fetishism of commodities. Labour is man's species-nature, the collective creative activity of men. The division of labour destroyed the unity, and by introducing inequality between occupations created social inequality. The division of social production, necessitated through increasing population and production, leads to the creation of private property. For Marx this means chiefly the private ownership of the means of production, and it splits society into haves and have-nots, rulers and ruled, exploiters and exploited. Private property contradicts the social character of labour. This property has been wrested from the individuals who produced it. It becomes independent of the workers and is owned by others. The contradiction between the private ownership of the means of production and the social nature of production is the fundamental contradiction of the capitalist system.

To the degree that products are severed from their social relation to the producer, they become commodities on the market. They lead their own lives and exert power over men, concentrated, in a profit- and consumer-oriented society, in the power of money. Commodity is the *reification* of a social relation. It becomes a mysterious thing with all kinds of inherent objective qualities like a 'natural price'. It becomes a fetish. This fetishism of commodities is most clearly expressed in money itself for the capitalist, whose goal has become the accumulation of capital. Money has become an end in itself.

The materialist conception of history

'The materialist conception of history', as Marx liked to call it, was perhaps his most significant contribution. He never used the term 'historical materialism', let alone 'dialectical materialism', which is a creation of Engels and a perversion of Marx's thought in Stalinist textbooks. It is his analysis of history, his analysis of the conditions of alienation and oppression, as well as his strategy for radical change, which attract many to Marx, even though they are far from being Marxists.

Because Marx is often misread it is important to understand the sense in which he was a 'materialist'. He was not an empiricist or a positivist. He always scorned 'common sense', and warned against mechanical 'materialist' conceptions. Marx was not a materialist in the metaphysical sense either; he did not believe, as one reads in many books about him, that the world consists only of matter, that matter is eternal. Marx's materialism was a reaction against idealism, in particular against Hegel, who saw in history the process of the absolute spirit emerging from its deepest alienation in nature (matter as frozen spirit).

For Marx history is the liberation of alienated man. The changing economic basis of society, and the struggle between the classes to which it gives rise, are keys to the unfolding of history. The materialist conception of history means, simply, that man is not the product of material conditions, but that he creates himself in history on the basis of his material conditions.

The economic basis of society consists of the forces of production and the relations of production. *Forces of production* embrace all means available for the transformation of nature to produce material goods so as to satisfy man's needs. They consist of three elements: (1) the means of production: materials from natural resources and instruments of production; tools, machinery, factories and their equipment; (2) labour power: man's ability to work, without which all of industry would grind to a halt; (3) general labour: skills and experience of the workers, scientific and technical innovations accumulated over the past.

Relations of production are social relations between people. People with the same relationship to the forces of production form a class. In a capitalist system there are basically two such classes. The owners, or capitalists, are few in number and control the means of production. There are also the workers, or proletariat, the masses who have no control over the means of production.

Classes and class struggle. Marx nowhere offers a systematic analysis of what constitutes a class, or explains how many classes there are in a given society. In various places Marx seems to imply a variety of classes. He speaks of the peasants; of the lumpen proletariat, the poorest and most dispossessed, who live on the crumbs of society; or of those working in the service industries. What constitutes a class are similar relationships (as owners or non-owners) to the means of production, and corresponding economic conditions and interests. But for Marx another element was also important: consciousness of forming a class in antagonism towards another class (or classes). The proletariat, according to Marx, still had to become a class; it still had to realise its historical revolutionary role in bringing about the transformation to a classless society, where the means of production would be owned and controlled by all.

New classes emerge with the development of new means of production. The capitalist mode of production began when individuals, who had accumulated the first capital, established workshops where labourers worked for a wage for their employers. Mechanisation and factories enabled large-scale industry to develop, and with it came a new ruling class, the bourgeoisie, who replaced the feudal lords. At the same time a new class of wage slaves was created. This class was the proletariat who, owning nothing but their labour, possessed only the freedom to starve or to sell their labour to the capitalists. 'The history of all hitherto existing societies is the history of class struggle.' All history, at its core, is the history of ruling classes defending their economic and social privileges; it is a history of the struggle of the oppressed against the oppressors to gain control of the means of production.

Classes are the product of alienated labour. Men do not know themselves and others as social beings whose needs demand mutual cooperation. People know each other only as abstract objects of a class. Competition is the distinguishing factor of the struggle between the classes. Capitalists make individual fortunes on the buried hopes of the workers. Producers see themselves as ruthless competitors in business where the only criterion is success. Competition even reigns among workers at the factory gates – to get a job and win the favours of their employers.

The only alternative to this alienation as class-beings is the abolition of all classes. This will come about in the future 'classless society' of communism, when the division of labour and private property have been abolished.

To achieve this, the oppressed, who are the people interested in change, must overthrow the established order and liberate themselves and their oppressors at the same time. Commitment to the class struggle is not built on hatred but on insight into the economic conditions which enslave both oppressors and oppressed. Out of the sufferings and struggles of the oppressed – who progressively realise their power, their solidarity and their dignity – new values and a new humanity are born, which prepare the way for the new classless society.

Revolution and violence. A revolution is a radical change in the basic social economic structure. Revolutions are not made arbitrarily, they are born. The economic basis of a society must be ripe for a revolution. What constitutes the necessary condition for a revolution is the radical imbalance between the forces and the relations of production. New forces of production are constantly emerging, which give rise to new classes of owners. But the old ruling class does not want to let go of its privileges or the superstructure which legitimises these privileges. The new class will find itself more and more limited and frustrated, and will eventually seek to replace the old order. (When the manufacturing system progressively replaced the agriculturally based feudal system, a new class, the bourgeoisie owners of the new means of production, replaced the feudal lords.)

The relations of production tend to be static and immobile because they are sanctioned by laws and institutions controlled by those in power. These cannot but defend their own interests. Change can only come from below, from the conscientised masses of the proletariat. They recognise that power is already theirs since they are the real producers, and the decisive step to end the state of alienation lies in their control of the means of production.

The revolution is a political event and it involves a conscious class of oppressed people who want it and who make it. The necessity of the revolution is an historical necessity, not a causal necessity of rigid economic determinism. The revolution is not an automatic occurrence. Men make history and men make revolutions.

In general, Marx thought that capitalism was a necessary stage to be reached in order to establish a classless communist society. Only capitalism can engender a consciousness which is ready for a cooperative society based on equality. Only capitalism seems to be able to produce and accumulate the wealth which can then be commonly shared, owned and controlled. Communism is implicit in capitalism: many traits of the capitalist mode of production prepare the way for the birth of communism. Capitalism carries within itself the seeds of its own death and of the birth of communist society.

When would the revolution come? Marx was no prophet and he did not describe the future revolution in detail. In his more mature economic writings he foresaw a rather long period before capitalism would exhaust all its capacities.

Revolution, as understood by Marx, is not necessarily violent. He was scathing about those he called the 'alchemists of revolution', who provoked revolt whatever the socio-economic circumstances. Man can only 'shorten the birth pangs' of communism. Though Marx conceived of violence as a possible midwife of the revolution, he never approved of the use of revolutionary terror. He strongly denounced the terror of the Jacobins in the French Revolution. The more one had to impose the revolution by terror the more it showed its weakness and its failure. Besides, Marx thought that on a long-term basis no revolution could be successful if confined only to one country. Though he never founded a party he was convinced that a party and workers' organisation — not an army — were necessary to carry out a successful revolution. A radical change of the capitalist order required a new consciousness. Without this new social consciousness a revolution would only change the rider on the horse, not bring about a new relation between man and nature, and between man and his fellow man.

Ideology

Marx understood ideology as 'false consciousness'. It is false because it is unconscious of its real function, namely, to legitimise and sanction existing relationships of production. Ideology is a back-to-front picture of how things really are. *Religion* teaches that God creates man whereas man creates God in his own image; *ethics* makes people's actions appear dependent on absolute moral principles, whereas they actually reflect their class conditions and interests. In *politics* the state grants its citizens certain rights, whereas it is the people who grant the state its power. In *history* there is the belief that great men and ideas decide the course of events, whereas events and economic and social conditions shape ideas and determine historical importance. In *economics* people believe that capitalists serve the community by investing in the production of goods and jobs, whereas the community serves the capitalists by giving them the lion's share of what they produce. *Workers* believe that they are paid for their labour, whereas they are only paid a wage which does not reflect what their labour produced.

Ideology is half-truth presented as total truth. That ideology reflects reality is true, but it reflects an alienated reality and, as such, is a form of alienation in the realm of thought. Ideology is the result, and at the same time the premise, of this alienation. Religion is a reflection of man's alienation, and at the same time an instrument of alienation in the hands of the ruling class.

The dominant ideas in any period are the ideas of the ruling class. Morality, philosophy, religion, art, and literature usually serve the economic interests of those in power. The political set-up, the police, army, the laws of the country, and the educational system, are the reflection of the interests of the dominant class. They sanction and help maintain their privileges under the mask of law and order, of justice and obedience.

Not all the elements of the superstructure are to the same degree ideological. Some groups are relatively independent of the economic substructure, and can become critical of the status quo and initiate a new consciousness. But in the final analysis radical change cannot come from them, only from and with the alienated and oppressed masses.

Capitalism distinguishes itself from all other systems by a highly sophisticated mystification of its ideology. It takes a truly 'scientific' — that is, relational and dialectical — insight to penetrate the deceptive nature of such cherished concepts as wage labour, fair price, supply and demand, free enterprise, freedom, and democracy, to see what they really hide. The production of ideology is essential for the survival of capitalism.

The state. The main target of Marx's critique of bourgeois ideology was the state as the central institution of capitalist society. The state is opposed to the real interests of all members of society for it actually serves the interests of only a few. The state is at one and the same time the reflection of man's alienated essence and an instrument of class domination. The modern liberal democratic state best serves the interests of the bourgeoisie. It creates the illusion of belonging to a community, yet through its bureaucracy it becomes an alienated caste which monopolises the right of interpreting the interests of the state. With the abolition of classes the power of the state 'will disappear and governmental functions will be transformed into simple administrative functions'.

Religion. Hegel understood religion as one of the forms of the absolute spirit. According to Feuerbach religion was the exact opposite — man's highest abstraction from his real self, the projection of his unfulfilled wishes into an imaginary heaven. This is the way Marx regarded religion. It is the ideological embodiment of man's alienation, 'the expression of a real misery and at the same time its protest against it'. Religion expresses the hope for a better world, for a world of wholeness and justice, but it does nothing to achieve it. 'It is the sigh of the tormented creature, the heart of a heartless world.' It serves to legitimise the position of the dominating class over the oppressed. It is the 'opium of the people'; it lulls people into passivity and obedience, into accepting an unholy state of things as God's will. Institutionalised religion and also personal faith are thus obstacles to social progress. The churches allow the capitalists to make profits, and confine themselves to consoling the victims with an illusory heaven and teaching them to be charitable to their oppressors. Religion will vanish of its own accord when its *raison d'être*, man's alienation, is overcome. In the communist society there will be no need for religion. Man will be all in all.

Critique of capitalism

Marx's economics is embedded in his materialist conception of history, and can only be understood if once constantly bears in mind his relational view of reality. He borrowed most of his economic terminology from the classical economists, in particular Smith and Ricardo. Lassalle described Marx as 'Ricardo turned socialist', but there was a fundamental difference between the two. Marx did not take the capitalist mode of production for granted and simply explain its functioning. He wanted to 'lay bare the economic law' beneath the surface of capitalist phenomena, and expose it for what it was — the deepest form of man's alienation and therefore also the radical turning-point for overcoming it. Where alienation is deepest and affects the greatest majority of people, liberation is nearest.

The labour theory of value. Central to classical economics is the labour theory of value. According to this theory, the value of an object is measured by the amount of labour embodied in it. This notion fitted well into Marx's relational view of reality. A commodity is not just a physical object but embodies a social relationship: it is the product of human labour. It is this labour that gives *value* to an object. Natural wealth has potential value (iron-ore in the ground, the trees in a forest), but only through human labour do objects acquire value: the iron-ore has to be extracted, the oak tree cut down. The common content of all commodities, then, is the human labour that has produced them. Thus human labour is the only measure of value. One can conclude that the value of a commodity is determined by the amount of labour socially necessary to produce it.

Modern labour is complex. The amount of labour put into the production of the equipment necessary to make the object has to be added proportionately to the value of the object, as well as the amount of labour time necessary to train skilled workers and artisans. Given the immense complexity of modern labour it has become more and more difficult to estimate the value of a product by the amount of labour time embodied in it. This was first replaced by gold and silver as equivalents of all other commodities, and then by coins and bank notes: in short by money. Price is the monetary expression of the value of a commodity.

All commodities, according to Marx, have a dual aspect: they have a *use* value and an *exchange* value. The use value is the object's suitability for satisfying human needs (physical, cultural, leisure and pleasure). Exchange value is a quantitative relationship (one loaf of bread for 50 sheets of white paper), nowadays expressed by the price. All goods are either consumer goods if they can be consumed as they are, or capital goods if they are used to produce other objects.

Capitalism is characterised by the fact that the quantitative exchange value has priority over the qualitative use value. The capitalist produces in the first place not to satisfy human needs but to sell with profit on the market. Everything is reduced to being a commodity on the market. Even a man's labour power (that is, his ability to work) has to be sold if he wants to survive and feed his family. The capitalist can buy labour power on the market at the cheapest possible price according to 'supply and demand'. 'The worker sinks to the level of a commodity, and to a most miserable commodity.'

Capital and exploitation. In his analysis in *Capital*, Marx is mainly interested in one crucial question: where does *profit* come from? Or in more technical terms: what is the main source of *surplus value*? The gains of a business are its surplus over cost. Where does this surplus come from?

Let us consider the movement of exchange on a small-scale commodity production. The peasant sells his potatoes and buys bread with the proceeds:

$$\text{Commodity (C)} \longrightarrow \text{Money (M)} \longrightarrow \text{Commodity (C)}$$

The value of the commodity in the first stage is the same as in the last. But then a new agent appears on the stage, the man who has money (capital) and whose profession it is to exchange commodities. He does not sell in order to buy, but in order to resell. Then this would be the movement of exchange:

$$\text{M (money)} \longrightarrow \text{C (commodity)} \longrightarrow M^1$$

M^1 is the money at the end of the transaction. M^1 is greater than the initial M.

Where does this surplus $M^1 - M$ come from? It is the profit of the capitalist trader, obtained through the fact that the artisan weaver has handed over his cloth at less than its value to the trader. But then, at a certain stage, the capitalist trader becomes a capitalist manufacturer. He invests his money in buying machinery and equipment, which produces goods he can resell against money. The movement of exchange would look like this:

$$\text{M (money)} \longrightarrow \text{C (capital)} \longrightarrow M^1$$

Money creates more money ($M^1 - M = \text{surplus}$) by being invested as capital. Capital is money which generates more money. Where does this surplus come from? In the whole production the capitalist must have bought something of more value than it cost, as in the case of the capitalist trader. Since all the other inputs, apart from labour power, cannot

transfer any value onto the object, we come to the fundamental conclusion: surplus is unpaid labour. All value is created by labour, but all
surplus value is created by the exploitation of labour. Marx's main
presupposition is that owning capital is not a productive activity. The
capitalist only appropriates the products of the workers' labour because
he is in the position of owning the means of production.

The capitalist makes a profit because the wages he pays are less than
the value the worker creates. The capitalist lets the worker work longer
than is necessary to produce the value of his labour power. For example,
if the value of his labour power is about R5 a day (the amount of money
the worker needs to keep himself and his family alive) and he could produce this value in about four hours, and if he then works for another
four hours, he would produce R5 surplus for the capitalist. For four
hours he would in effect work for the capitalist for nothing. The rate of
surplus value is thus the rate of exploitation. It is measured as the ratio
of surplus to necessary labour time to produce the value of the worker's
wage or of his labour power, in our case 4/4 = 1 or 100 per cent. It is
necessary to distinguish, with Marx, constant capital (the capital which
does not change, like buildings, tools and equipment) and variable capital
(which undergoes change in the process of production, the capital going
into wages and salaries). Surplus value can come only from the variable
capital. The capitalist will try to maximise it by keeping wages as low as
possible, and extending the hours of the working day. These two factors
constitute the major issues in the great workers' struggle.

The capitalist breakdown. The theory of surplus value has far-reaching
consequences for the future of capitalism. Since only variable capital
determines the ratio of profit, Marx foresaw a decline in the rate of
profit for capitalists. Competition among producers would force them
to invest more in constant capital (machinery) in relation to money
paid out in wages. In order to compete, capitalists have to try to
cheapen their products by constant mechanisation in order to produce
the same amount with less labour. This results in accumulation of
capital. But accumulation of capital through mechanisation results in a
decline of profit for the capitalist, since only labour produces surplus.

For the workers this decline in the capitalist's profit, on account of
the higher degree of mechanisation, would show itself in the decline of
their standard of living. The high level of mechanisation would leave
many jobless and create what Marx called the 'Lazarus stratum of
society'. Given the presence of an 'industrial reserve army' of unemployed, capitalists would not need to raise wages beyond subsistence
level for too long.

All this would bring to the fore the central contradiction in capitalism.

Wages are low and, since the workers constitute the mass of consumers, effective demand lags behind production. Goods are produced
but cannot be sold because they cannot be bought. Overproduction
meets underconsumption. This disequilibrium between sale and purchase, Marx believed, would inevitably cause a grave economic crisis. It
could be the birth date of a new order, as Marx declared in the closing
words in volume 1 of *Capital*: 'Centralisation of the means of production
and socialisation of labour at last reach a point where they become incompatible with their capitalist integument. This integument is burst
asunder. The knell of capitalist property sounds. The expropriators are
expropriated.'

Marx realised that the inevitable collapse of the capitalist system could
be postponed by reducing the costs of raw materials. This could be
achieved through colonial expansion and extension of the capitalist
market to undeveloped countries. By providing cheap raw materials
countries become underdeveloped because they have to feed the 'developed' countries. But there are no long-term solutions. The degree to
which the workers became increasingly impoverished would heighten
their solidarity, and hasten their revolt as a class, conscious of its universal revolutionary role.

Post-revolutionary society

The socialist phase. Marx gave no blueprint for the future post-
revolutionary society. After a successful proletarian revolution there
would be a period of transition — the socialist phase — which Marx
occasionally referred to as the 'dictatorship of the proletariat'. 'Dictatorship' for Marx did not have the totalitarian ring it has for us: it was a
rule of a majority over a minority. In this socialist phase the state was
still a necessity. It would only wither away when the danger of counter-
revolution had passed. Class conflict would still occur because the
bourgeoisie would still exist, though stripped of its property and the
means of production.

Though the means of production in socialism would now be under
the control of the workers, there would still be various economic, political, and social problems. The economy would still be characterised by
scarcity, since certain sectors would not have been adequately developed
in the capitalist period. Certain goods would have to be rationed in order
to promote production. Everyone would be expected to contribute
according to his ability and rewarded according to the amount of work
he did. 'To each according to his work.' Many pre-revolutionary bourgeois
attitudes would still exist, and the distribution of wealth and goods
could not be completely egalitarian.

The communist society. Communism is the final stage of history, its completion: the 'solution to the riddle of history'. In this final classless society the free development of each is the condition for the free development of all. All will share ownership and labour. Everyone will contribute according to his *ability* but receive according to his *needs*. Man will no longer be alienated.

In a higher phase of communist society, after the enslaving subordination of the individual to the division of labour has vanished, after labour has become not only a means of life but life's prime want, after the productive forces have also increased with the all-round development of the individual, and all the springs of cooperative wealth flow more abundantly — only then can the narrow horizon of bourgeois right be crossed in its entirety and society inscribe on its banners: From each according to his ability, to each according to his need!

Some critical questions

Marx was a great thinker, in the sense that his thought is rounded. Everything hangs together in one organic whole. This is his strength and perhaps his weakness. One either gets inside the circle or remains outside. It is difficult to isolate one aspect from the whole.

One may perhaps ask, though:
— Is it true that man is the centre of history?
— What is man when set against the immensity of the galaxies?
— Is it true that creative labour is the basic dimension of man? Why not ecstasy, silence or sex?
— Is it true that man is fundamentally a 'social being'? Is he not a unique, spontaneous, fragile being, condemned to the useless passion of being himself?

Other questions may be asked, of a more operational nature:
— Does Marx's analysis work?
— Does his materialist conception of history provide basic elements to enable me to understand the society I live in?
— What happens if I apply his analysis? How does it make me act?
— Does it make me see what others cannot see?
— Does his analysis make me understand the basic laws of capitalism?
— Does the labour theory of value work?

There is a last type of question, which goes to the heart of Marx's world-view:
— How rational is history?
— How social can man become?
— How perfectible is our world?
— Is there hope for the victim?
— Is there hope for the martyr beyond being remembered by a few?

— Is there justification and justice for the poor masses, once crushed under the oppression of the powerful, now long dead?

— Is there hope for the dead?

— Is death normal?

— Is death not the deepest alienation?

To ask these questions is to have a greater need than Marx, to have a greater hope, and perhaps even to have greater stamina in the struggle for freedom.

13 Marxism-Leninism

Marxism–Leninism, often also called 'classical' or 'orthodox' Marxism, is that form of Marxism which carries most political weight in the contemporary world. It is the official ideology of Soviet Russia and its communist satellites. Without the successful October 1917 Revolution in Russia, Marx might have remained a relatively unknown and insignificant socialist author. Marxism–Leninism is one particular development of the ideas of Marx. The question whether it is a legitimate one, or whether it is a betrayal of some of the basic inspirations of Marx, divides orthodox Marxists from neo-Marxists.

Marx and the Marxisms after Marx

Marx did not elaborate an overall philosophical system. He did not present a total world-view. Unlike Hegel, who had to force the totality of reality and history into the all-embracing logic of the world spirit, Marx presented an analysis of capitalist society as the key to a strategy of radical social change. Underlying his analysis was a basic vision of man and history. But this vision was never developed into a fixed system of immutable dogmas. Marx's thought remained open-ended, unfinished. Many of his writings were occasioned by specific circumstances and were polemical in nature.

Character of writing

The fragmentary character of Marx's writings accounts for the many different interpretations of his thought. The official Soviet version is that Marxism is a total, scientific philosophical system that gives definitive answers to all fundamental questions. Others, however, see Marxism mainly as a method of social analysis. This view contrasts with the orthodox interpretation, which makes of Marx's historical materialism an economic determinism. The publication of some of the early writings in the 1930s (especially of the so-called Paris manuscripts of 1844) caused many to distinguish a young humanist Marx, strongly influenced by Hegel's philosophy, from the later scientific economic Marx of *Capital*.

For some, the young Marx, with his basic concept of alienation, was the real Marx, in opposition to all orthodox interpretations. It is the young humanist Marx who gives rise to the many neo-Marxist interpretations of his thought. Others reject the young Marx altogether and opt for the later 'scientific' Marx of *Capital*. For early revisionists Marxism represents mainly an ethical vision of a movement towards a more democratic and socialist society by means of a non-violent reform of existing structures. This can take different forms; for example, the ideological nature of science; technocratic reasoning which employs such terms as 'human engineering'; and it even encompasses a critique of 'scientific' Marxism.

Marx's 'missing links'

Marx developed a critical theory of society, and not an overall theory of reality. Marx's materialism is not an ontological but an historical materialism. Nor did he provide a cosmology, a logic, an epistemology, or a psychology. But what is missing above all in Marx is an ethical theory. It is not clear from his writings what role the individual plays in society. The basic idea of freedom is not developed. The rejection of bourgeois values implies certain ethics, yet what the criteria for good and evil are, remains an open question. What does it mean that praxis serves as the criterion of truth? Is Lenin right when he declares all actions morally good which are in the interests of the proletariat? Does this political utilitarianism follow from Marx's thought? Lenin's conclusion shows how, on account of its many missing links, Marx's thought is open to conflicting and co-existing Marxisms.

The debate on the labour theory of value

Nowadays one of the main areas of debate about Marx's relevance to changing conditions concerns his labour theory of value. Marx can be called the last of the classical economists, since he shared with Adam Smith and others the orthodox value theory: a 'labour theory of value'. However, the mainstream classical economists did not view their value theory as part of a wider theory of exploitation. Marx did. It is here that Marx's economics takes a revolutionary turn. For Marx a labour theory of value rests on the axiom that all economic value is produced by labour, and not by any other factors of production. The exploitative aspect of capitalism lies in the fact that labour power is just another commodity. Technological advance enables a worker to produce far above his and his family's subsistence needs. This excess or 'surplus value' is appropriated by the capitalist and constitutes his 'exploitation' of the worker.

This theory of value, it is said, cannot be reconciled with the supply-

and-demand value theory of modern western capitalism. The capitalist theory states that demand consists of the desires of the consumer plus his income, and supply is based on the marginal cost of production (that is, raw materials, wages, 'normal' profit, and other factors). At any given moment, when supply is fixed, a changing demand sets the price of goods.

The continuing attraction of Marxism

Marx's thought is embedded in the specific philosophical climate of nineteenth-century Germany, dominated as it was by German idealism. His theory of classes *is* dependent on the European situation. Some of his 'prophecies' have been refuted by historical experience. What, then, explains the continued appeal of Marx? There seem to be two main reasons for it. Firstly, if Marx is read at his deepest level of abstraction he provides a basic model of social analysis and of social change. By progressively introducing historical and cultural variables, the model can be adapted to any historical situation, and concrete strategy and tactics worked out. Secondly, Marxism provides a vision of hope for the oppressed masses. Victims without a future become the agents of their own destiny and protagonists of a universal redemptive mission. It is this messianic, utopian, quasi-religious ingredient which is the secret of Marxism's attractiveness.

Friedrich Engels (1820–1895)

One of the main reasons for the various interpretations within Marxism after Marx's death was the fact that it had two founders, Karl Marx and Friedrich Engels, and that the latter survived Marx by thirteen years. He became the authoritative interpreter of Marx's thought at a time when it was becoming the official doctrine of a political mass movement.

Engels first met Marx in 1842 at Cologne. He was Marx's closest collaborator and his lifelong friend, his 'alter ego'. It was a rare friendship. Engels supported Marx morally and financially for forty years, enabling the master to carry on with his research in the British Museum to write *Capital*. Engels introduced Marx to economics and familiarised him with the conditions of the working class in England, about which he had written a hard-hitting political tract (1845) that Marx appreciated greatly. Marx relied on Engels for scientific and military matters. Starting from a common philosophical conception, they wrote jointly *The Holy Family* (1845), *The German Ideology* (1846), and *The Communist Manifesto* (1848). Their collaboration was also close in *A Contribution to the Critique of Political Economy* (1859) and in the first volume of *Capital* (1867).

While Marx, after their first common phase of philosophical and political activity, turned to economics, Engels (especially from 1873) dedicated himself to the study of natural sciences and areas of philosophy hitherto neglected by both of them, such as logic, epistemology, ontology, and ethics, though without finding satisfactory answers. In 1878 Engels wrote, at Marx's request, his most influential work, the *Anti-Dühring*, refuting the revision of some basic ideas of Marx by the socialist author Dr Dühring. The book begins with an attack on Dr Dühring's 'bumptious pseudo-science' and ends with an outline of Marxist doctrine. For decades it was the classic account of Marx's thought. For the general public and the mass of workers, to whom Marx's philosophical and economic writings remained inaccessible, the *Anti-Dühring* provided the channel through which they were introduced to Marxism. Engels's main work, after Marx's death, was the editing and publication of volumes 2 and 3 of *Capital* (1885-94), a work which he completed only a few months before his death.

Engels kept Marx's archives and was the incontestable executor of Marx's intellectual heritage for generations of Marxists. How reliable is he? To what extent is Engels responsible for the stereotyped image of Marx, and the philosophically shallow slogans of professional Marxists? Engels was a quick and lucid writer, but we need to ask how much his vulgarisation of Marx contributed to the impoverishment of Marxist philosophy. The selections which Engels made of Marx's manuscripts present many problems of interpretation for those who want to know about the Marxism of Marx himself rather than Marxism through the eyes of Engels.

How much was Engels responsible for 'Marxism' as the cult of Karl Marx? Despite Marx's declared admiration for the intellectual talents of Engels, so much so that he could speak of himself as 'Engels's disciple', we must ask how much Marx identified with everything Engels said. Engels always considered Marx the real source of inspiration for all Marxists. 'Marx stood higher, saw further and took a wider and quicker view than all the rest of us. Marx was a genius: the rest of us were talented at best.' Engels had a quasi-religious attitude towards Marx. 'My destiny wants that I shall reap the honour and glory sown by one who was greater than I, Karl Marx.' It was Engels who adopted the terms 'Marxist' and 'Marxism', coined by his adversaries despite Marx's own categorical statement, 'All I know is that, as for me, I am not a Marxist.'

Friedrich Engels transformed the philosophy of Marx from a theory of social analysis and social change into a Marxist world-view. This transformation began with Engels's speech at Marx's graveside: 'Just as Darwin discovered the law of development of organic nature, so Marx discovered the law of development of human history.' Engels applied historical materialism to nature and created the pseudo-science of 'dialectical materialism'. This has become a cornerstone of Marxist–Leninist text-books all over the communist world. In Engels's hands Marx's dialectic of productive labour in history became the universal principle of all reality, not only in history but also of nature. Dialectic for Engels was 'the science of the general laws of motion and development of nature, human society and thought'. Through Engels, Marxism became a scientific, dogmatic, philosophical system.

Engels offers some beginnings of a materialist epistemology which defends the primacy of being over knowledge, thus rejecting Kant's transcendental approach. Knowledge is the reflection of material reality, objectively given through our senses. Through Lenin this naïve epistemological realism was to influence official Marxist–Leninist teaching. For Engels the relationship of knowledge to being (an epistemological question) is the same as the relationship between spirit and matter (a metaphysical question). Being equals matter, thought equals spirit. The primacy of being over knowledge and thought is the primacy of matter over spirit. This leads Engels to a materialist monism for which only material reality exists, and for which consciousness is the product of a material organ, the brain.

Dialectic conceives being (which equals material reality) as a process, in contrast with a metaphysical explanation of the world that does not have a dynamic but only a static conception of being. As Marx had shown the movement of history in historical materialism, Engels in his dialectical materialism wants to explain all of reality as a dynamic evolution of nature. He distinguishes this force from a 'mechanical materialism' which reduces all phenomena to an arrangement of material particles. In fact he recognises different ontological grades of being. Life, the purposeful organisation of chemical reactions, is a higher grade of being than inanimate reality. Human consciousness is something non-material, though dependent on matter. This means the dialectic has the difficult task of explaining how a higher being can evolve from an inferior being. Engels and Marxism–Leninism accept the law of causality. According to this, each being which does not have a reason for its existence in itself owes its existence to another being as its cause. He thus sees the cause of the evolutionary movement of nature in the contradiction or struggle of opposites. The movement originates from contradictions in nature.

Dialectical materialism explains all of reality in terms of the three laws of the dialectic. Their truth is verified through the results of the natural, positive sciences.

(1) The first of the three laws of the dialectic is the 'law of the transition from quantitative changes to qualitative changes'. This law is meant to explain the evolution of new and higher levels of being from inferior ones. Each evolutionary process has a double phase: an evolutionary phase during which an accumulation of accidental quantitative changes occurs; and a revolutionary phase during which, in the form of a qualitative leap, an essential change takes place. The proof of the validity of this law consists in a series of not always very fortunate or convincing examples. The classic one, used by Engels, is the process of heating water. After a gradual increase of temperature it reaches boiling point, when a sudden qualitative change occurs: water is transformed into vapour. A better, more modern example is the division of water (H_2O) into its constituent molecules, the result being two different substances, hydrogen and oxygen.

(2) The second law is the core of dialectical materialism: the 'law of the unity and the conflict of opposites'. It explains the source of movement not as something outside the movement but as within things and reality in movement. Lenin thought that mechanical theories of movement ultimately lead to an unmoved mover, which is the cause of movement in other beings. For Hegel the source of movement lies in the contradictions in things and events which are so intensified that a being has to move out of itself. Soviet philosophy, inspired by Engels and Lenin, illustrates this law by a variety of examples to show that the law is universally valid. Examples include: action and reaction in mechanics, positive and negative poles in physics, assimilation (life) and dissimilation (death) in biology, and a struggle of classes in society. Engels in the *Anti-Dühring* borrows a more convincing illustration from Hegel. Movement in itself is a contradiction in the sense that an object finds itself at one place and yet does not find itself there. Becoming is a contradiction between being and non-being.

(3) The third law, the 'negation of the negation', further determines the first law. Once a qualitative change has taken place, after an accumulation of quantitative changes, the new quality is the negation of the previous quality of the object. If this new quality is now subjected to a series of quantitative changes, until it is transformed at the critical point into a new quality, this third quality constitutes the negation of the second quality, which is itself a negation of the first. The first quality is affirmed, by the negation of the negation, on a qualitatively higher level, and preserved in all its richness. To illustrate this law, the seed of a plant is sometimes used. The negation of the seed when it dies means the life of a plant. If the plant dies, its seed is the negation of the negation. In Soviet ideology this is applied to the communist classless

society which returns, after a denial of all previous class societies, to primitive communism. Yet, like a spiral, the classless society is now on a qualitatively higher level, which integrates the richness of the previous stages.

Dialectical materialism, in its later Soviet version, conceives of matter as eternal in time and infinite in space. This thesis is important in regard to its denial of a transcendent Creator. If the world had a beginning there would necessarily develop the conception of a faith in a Creator. The eternity of the world is usually demonstrated by the physical law of the maintenance of energy. Despite all physical processes in which energy is transformed from one form into another, the actual sum of energy remains constant.

At various other points Engels introduces considerable and sometimes far-reaching changes into Marx's thought. The idea of human freedom, important though underdeveloped in Marx, becomes for Engels 'insight into necessity'. Here begins a deterministic view of history, which is seen as an inevitable process guided by 'natural' laws (as in nature). Man becomes a puppet in a predetermined movement of necessary progress. This results in a narrow economic determinism in orthodox Marxists like Kautsky.

Another important change introduced by Engels comes in his understanding of a mutual relationship between superstructure and economic basis. Engels goes beyond the Marxist view that ideas (of morality or religion for example) depend on the economic basis. He claims that these ideas have an effect on the substructure. Lenin and, later, Marxism–Leninism, developed this so that philosophy, art, and literature become tools in the propaganda struggle. Morality serves the political aims of the proletariat. Marx's relative indifference to religion was transformed into a militant atheism in Lenin and in later Soviet practice.

V. I. Lenin (1870–1924)

The third founding father of Marxism–Leninism was Vladimir Ilyich Ulyanov (who later changed his name to Vladimir Lenin). Lenin's most important achievement was the success of the October 1917 Revolution in Russia. This initiated a new epoch, not only in Russian history, but in world history and in the development of Marxism. Lenin always considered himself a faithful follower of Marx, yet his revision of Marx's thought was thorough-going. He adapted Marxism to the practical political requirements of the socialist revolution in Russia. Towards the end of the nineteenth century, Tsarist Russia was a backward, largely agrarian country with a tottering feudal structure. After the assassination of Tsar Alexander II, his son Alexander III vigorously opposed all revolutionary movements and built up a formidable police force. (In 1887 the Tsar's hangman executed Lenin's eldest brother. Lenin, then 17, was to have his revenge in the revolution of which he was the soul and inspiration.)

Among the opposition leaders of the Russian intelligentsia, many of whom were forced into exile in the West, two groups stood out. The *populists* hoped for a revolutionary solution which would bypass capitalism and reorganise Russia into a socialist society on the basis of the *mir*, or village collective. They saw the peasant commune as the germ of a future cooperative society that would immediately pass from a largely feudal agrarian order to a socialist state. A second group under the leadership of Plekhanov, known as the Emancipation of Labour, followed a wholly Marxist line, and rejected the thesis of the populists. In their view, only the working class, generated by an increasing capitalism, would be able to lead a successful socialist revolution.

Marx and Engels had expected the socialist revolution to occur simultaneously in the most advanced capitalist countries of the West, above all in England and Germany. But they did not exclude the possibility that the initial spark of revolution might be struck in an industrially backward country. A bourgeois revolution here would be the prelude to a proletarian revolution in economically more advanced countries. In the 1880s Marx and Engels turned their hopes mainly to Russia to become the vanguard of a socialist revolution in Europe.

The bourgeois-democratic revolution in Russia would be supported and transformed into a proletarian one by a much more strongly developed proletariat than in previous revolutions. This would then light the fuse for a proletarian revolution in the West.

In the beginning Lenin completely accepted these ideas. His *Two Tactics of Social Democracy in the Democratic Revolution* outlined the tactics of the Bolsheviks in contradiction to that proposed by the Mensheviks, who followed a more traditional Marxist line under the leadership of Plekhanov. The Mensheviks favoured a bourgeois revolution under the leadership of the bourgeoisie, relegating the proletariat to a party of opposition. Lenin foresaw that the bourgeoisie would work out a compromise with the Tsar, and in fact the revolution of 1905 was strangled by what we would call the fiction of a constitutional parliament.

As opposed to this, the Bolsheviks favoured a bourgeois-democratic revolution under the leadership of the proletariat, in close alliance with the masses of peasants. After a victorious bourgeois-democratic revolution, the working class, together with the semi-proletarian stratum of the rural population, would begin the struggle for socialist revolution in the West, which in turn would help the struggle for socialism in Russia. But the bourgeois revolution had to precede the socialist one in order to sweep away all feudal remnants and secure a rapid development of capitalism, for in Russia the working class suffered not so much from capitalism as from an insufficient development of capitalism.

While Marx was a revolutionary theorist, Lenin was a revolutionary activist. Lenin has been described as being 'occupied with the revolution twenty-four hours a day. . . . [He] has no thoughts except the thought of the revolution, and, even when he goes to sleep, dreams only of the revolution.' Lenin was a revolutionary volcano, the 'greatest engine-driver of revolution', as Trotsky called him. This explains the historical relevance of most of his writings. For Lenin, Marxism was essentially a philosophy of practice. Against deterministic and fatalistic views of history, he laid great stress on the will as an important factor, more so than did Marx himself. Lenin was often accused of being a voluntarist. In his important work, *What Is To Be Done?* (1902), he took to task the revisionists, who hoped to arrive at a socialist society by means of reform from within the framework of a bourgeois-democratic state and a parliamentary system. Believing in the automatic laws of economic and social development, they recommended that the Russian workers should confine themselves to the trade union aspect of the struggle. Lenin was convinced that the revolution would be the result only of a revolutionary struggle on the part of the workers in alliance with the peasantry. Trade unionism would lead only to immediate reforms for the workers and not to a spontaneous revolution of the masses.

For Lenin the revolution had to be made and planned. The vanguard of this revolution was for him the *party*, equipped with an advanced theory. This is perhaps the most important contribution of Lenin to Marxist theory, a point in which he decidedly differs from Marx and over which he clashed with the Mensheviks. Lenin wrote, 'Socialist consciousness cannot exist among the workers. This can only be introduced from without.' Though one can find in the *Communist Manifesto* a reference to the role of the communist party as the most advanced section of the working class and as the vanguard of the workers' movement, the central importance which Lenin attributed to a tightly knit party of professional revolutionaries is entirely new. Is this need to inject socialist consciousness into the working class not equivalent to a revolution from above? Trotsky accused Lenin of being the 'party disorganiser' and compared him to Robespierre. Plekhanov argued that Lenin had replaced the 'dictatorship *of* the proletariat' with a 'dictatorship *over* the proletariat'. In *One Step Forward, Two Steps Back* (1904) Lenin justified his views regarding the necessity and structure of the party. The authority of the party would, especially under Stalin, lead to disastrous consequences, and yet it was the secret of Lenin's success. He had great tactical sense, which adapted to the possibilities of the present, was not afraid of compromises, yet never lost sight of the final goal.

On the eve of the October Revolution Lenin wrote *The State and Revolution* (1917), in which he gave a concentrated exposition of Marx's view of the state. But on the whole he selected those passages which speak of the state as an organ of class rule and an instrument of the domination of one class over the other. Where Marx and Engels had allowed for the peaceful seizure of power in England, Holland, or France, Lenin emphasised the need for revolutionary violence to overthrow the capitalist state. After the capitalist state had been smashed, a new state, 'the dictatorship of the proletariat', would be established to break the resistance of the bourgeoisie and to avoid the possibility of counter-revolution. This did not prevent Lenin, in his article 'The Tasks of the Revolution', from seeing the possibility of a peaceful revolution if the majority of the soviets or councils could agree on a concrete programme and all power were transferred to them. On 7 November the Bolsheviks seized power in an almost bloodless insurrection. The state apparatus was not smashed, and, with the exception of the army and the police apparatus, the Bolsheviks inherited the old Tsarist bureaucracy.

In *The Immediate Tasks of the Soviet Government*, written in early 1918, Lenin analysed the issues facing the young Soviet state. It had been easy to expropriate the bourgeoisie. But to administer a backward country devastated by war, to ensure production and distribution of goods, and to create a new socialist consciousness, were quite other matters. In 1921 he launched the 'New Economic Policy' (Gorky called it the 'Old Economic Policy') which encouraged peasant private enterprise and private trade, and sought foreign help from capitalist countries. But above all, the transition to a socialist state was impossible without an 'iron hand' and dictatorship of the party. In his understanding of the 'dictatorship of the proletariat' Lenin went far beyond Marx and Engels. Dictatorship of the proletariat has two aspects in the post-revolutionary socialist phase: dictatorship against the defeated ex-bourgeoisie; and widening democracy for the working people until the state could finally wither away to a stateless communist society.

The relationship between the two proved to be full of contradictions. Dictatorship meant, for Lenin, dictatorial powers of individuals in the party. Its relationship to workers' control remained unsolved, and played a fateful role in the further development of the Soviet state. For Lenin dictatorship was 'state power based directly on violence' and on troops, and was unrestricted by any laws. The practical difficulty was how to guarantee that the *party* acted not only on behalf of the workers but under the control and with the collaboration of the workers. Lenin often warned of the danger of bureaucratism within the state apparatus and urged a greater participation for workers. With the raising of the country's cultural level Lenin hoped finally to overcome the dangers of bureaucracy. Lenin's objective of a state administered by the workers has yet to be realised. Within a short time the centralised party became the State, a repressive, authoritarian state. Dictatorship *of* the proletariat degenerated into dictatorship *over* the proletariat.

Besides providing a more voluntarist understanding of the revolution, and encompassing the importance of an elitist, militarily organised central party, Lenin made another important contribution to Marxist theory, adapting it to the more advanced conditions of capitalism at the beginning of the twentieth century. This is Lenin's theory of *imperialism as the highest stage of capitalism*, which he expounded in the book with this title in 1916. It is at the same time an attempt to explain why the revolution had not occurred as Marx had anticipated; why capitalism, rather than being near its inevitable collapse, seemed to be 'alive and well'. Already the revisionist Bernstein had tried to adapt Marx's theory to the fact that the increasing impoverishment of the workers and the crisis of capitalism had not occurred. In his *Evolutionary Socialism* (1899) he had only put into theory what the German Social Democratic Party was already practising. He substituted for the revolution the day-to-day struggle of the workers which would eventually lead, in a peaceful, evolutionary way, to a socialist society.

Lenin took another view. Through imperialism, capitalism had transferred its inner contradictions, which Marx had pointed out so clearly, to the global stage. Advanced capitalism develops into monopoly capitalism through a concentration of production. Credit banks turn into business banks and begin to dominate whole sections of industry. This leads to the formation of financial oligarchies which, through the system of large holdings of shares, control vast areas of the national economy, and through investments in other predominantly undeveloped countries divide the world among themselves. Colonies, as suppliers of cheap raw materials and as providers of investment opportunities, become indispensable for the capital-exporting monopolies. Hence the rush for the partition of the rest of the world among rival powers.

Capitalism can survive in what today we call the developed countries because the so-called underdeveloped countries help to solve the inner contradictions of the capitalist societies. The revolution is bought off for a time because, at the expense of the underdeveloped countries, the capitalists can raise the living standard of the workers and draw the upper level of the proletariat into the middle class.

Since the world has already been partitioned, a scramble starts for a repartitioning of the world. On account of the 'law of uneven developments' some countries with a strong economic potential lag behind and, through imperialist wars, try to make up the disadvantage. This has important consequences for a theory of revolution. On account of uneven development, Lenin foresaw that the socialist revolution would not necessarily be a simultaneous revolution involving the major industrialised countries. This opened the way for the justification of 'socialism in one country', which was to become so important under Stalin. It also showed the probability and necessity of national wars in the colonies and semi-colonies against the imperialist powers. When the chances of a socialist revolution in the West began to dwindle, Lenin turned to the East and began to attach more importance to the national revolutionary movements in Asia, particularly in India and China.

Though Lenin believed that the soviets were universally valid organs for insurrection and for seizing power, he was convinced that the revolution would have to take different forms in different countries. In 1922, in a report to the second Congress of the Communist International, Lenin distinguished between bourgeois-democratic movements and national revolutionary movements in undeveloped countries. In the latter, peasant soviets would have to be created since the proletariat in these countries was so little developed. Thus he anticipated elements of a revolutionary model which was to play such an important role in China and Vietnam.

Marx, in his brief allusions to the 'Asiatic mode of production', follows a very Eurocentric model. It presupposes that the precapitalist forms of society in Asia lack any dynamic development. Only the universalising force of western capitalism when it becomes world capitalism brings progress to the East. The East then follows a similar pattern to the West, when capitalism's own contradictions lead to socialism. Lenin seems to leave more room than Marx or Engels for different 'indigenous' ways to socialism.

In Russia, Lenin pleaded for the equality of all nations and for their self-determination as a means towards victory of the socialist revolution. He thought that the 'Bill on the equal rights of nationalities' should contain the granting of the franchise to Jews in Russia — a fact which seems to have been forgotten in Russia today.

Lenin was always convinced that the October Revolution would finally be victorious only when it embraced at least the most important advanced countries. He never gave up hope or his struggle for a world revolution.

In the beginning he thought it was close, later he anticipated a certain delay.

In 1919 the Third International (or Comintern) was founded to organise the world revolution. Adopting his own tactical model, Lenin wanted the Comintern to be a small, well-organised international body of professional revolutionaries to direct the world revolution so as to ensure that the movement in each country subjected its own interests to the general interests of the international revolution as a whole. At the second Congress in 1920 the formation of communist parties in all countries was urged. A twenty-one point programme was adopted which specified the conditions of admission. The communist parties were ordered to support all revolutionary movements and to fight all reformist and revisionist socialist movements. This was retracted the following year when everybody was ordered to work in a united front with the other socialists.

The Comintern, through its authoritarian changes of strategy from the top, soon lost importance and credibility. It became a loose structure of satellite organisations. The international revolution did not materialise, and Russia signed treaties with capitalist countries and participated in its 'war economy' in a basically capitalist international order.

The 'New Economic Policy' of 1921 was a retreat, and communism for a while was reduced to Lenin's famous formula: 'Communism equals soviets plus electricity'. The military battle had been won, but the economic battle still remained to be fought.

Lenin was a political revolutionary rather than a revolutionary philosopher. His two more philosophical works are *Materialism and Empiriocriticism* written in 1909 in Switzerland, and the posthumously published *Philosophical Notebooks* (1926). The latter is a collection of notes he took during the years of the First World War when he turned to intense philosophical studies, especially of Hegel, without using the interpretation of the young Marx.

Philosophy, like anything else, was for Lenin a function of revolutionary practice; it was never neutral with regard to political interests. Lenin reduced all philosophies to two opposing camps: idealism and materialism. There existed between these two no third way, such as positivism, which he rejected outright. All this contributed to an oversimplification in philosophy, and led to a dogmatic rigidity which was intensified by Stalin. Philosophy became a tool of propaganda and indoctrination.

On questions concerning the superstructure, Lenin displayed a crass utilitarianism which continued and intensified under Stalin and prevented the elaboration of a Marxist ethic. Morality stands only in the interests of the proletarian revolution. Everything which helps build the new communist society is moral.

Religion plays an important role in Lenin's philosophy. Brought up in an unbigoted religious atmosphere, Lenin lost his faith during adolescence and before he came into contact with Marxism. From then on he took atheism to be scientifically self-evident. He thought religious beliefs were an expression of the impotence of oppressed and poor people: 'Religion is opium for the people. Religion is a sort of spiritual booze, in which the slaves of capital drown their human image. . . .'

Religion and the churches were for Lenin 'a means of keeping the masses humble and submissive', an ideology and institution 'to keep the exploiters in power and the masses in a state of misery' (Kolakowski). This reflects his view of the Russian Orthodox Church, which was extremely otherworldly and almost completely identified with the Tsarist imperial regime.

Sensitive to Engels's warning about the folly of trying to abolish religion, Lenin adopted the tactic of toleration towards religion. The party from the outset upheld religious toleration, the right of the individual party member to profess faith or atheism, provided he was a genuine socialist. Atheism had no part in the party programme, but the party was committed to carrying on anti-religious propaganda. Whatever his tactical concessions, on political grounds, Lenin was a fierce opponent of religious belief. In his philosophical works he argued that religion in a humanist disguise was even more dangerous to socialism than the Orthodox Church because it deluded the unwary. He was prepared to compromise with believers on tactical grounds, but refused to admit any concessions to religious faith on the part of the party.

When the Soviet government came to power most churchmen were hostile to it. This, and the principles of Leninism, led to a church–state conflict. Church property was expropriated and the church was effectively deprived of all public functions. Persecution of the church and of believers varied in intensity, but not the principle that a socialist state must eradicate 'religious prejudices' and abolish the oppression of the working class which gives rise to religion.

With the contribution of Lenin to the work of Marx and Engels, Marxism–Leninism gains its classic form. Immediately after Lenin's death, Stalin defined Leninism as 'Marxism in the epoch of imperialism and proletarian revolutions'. Lenin's brand of Marxism was canonised. Lenin's statements, often taken out of context, became ready-made slogans and formulas for Marxist-Leninist textbooks. Lenin was a great revolutionary but he was a poor philosopher. Making Lenin the authoritative interpreter of Marxism led to the great poverty of Marxist-Leninist doctrine. The richness and the depth of Marx's vision and analysis were thereby lost.

Iosif Stalin (1879–1953)

With the elimination of Trotsky as a deviant on the left and of Bukharin and others as deviants on the right, Stalin established himself as the uncontested leader of the Soviet state after Lenin's death. The removal of Bukharin from the Politburo in 1929 marks the beginning of the era of Stalinism, the cult of his person, which ended only with his death in 1953. Stalin consolidated the Russian revolution. Through rapid industrialisation of the country and the collectivisation of agriculture, he created a totalitarian state machine, unparalleled in its control of all dimensions of life. He increased the power of the party, the bureaucracy, and the police. In the great purges of 1936–8 he executed as counter-revolutionaries over half of the 2 000 delegates who had attended the seventeenth Party Congress. Millions of kulaks, the more wealthy peasant farmers, became victims of the ruthless collectivisation of farming.

The most distinctive contribution of Stalinism is the doctrine of *socialism in one country*. Since the world revolution had not occurred, the proletariat in Russia, it was argued, had to build a socialist society in Russia first. In this way Russia would serve as a base for the building of socialism in other countries, and the final overthrow of imperialism. But this victory of socialism in Russia would not be complete as long as Russia was encircled by hostile powers. Hence the international proletariat had to subordinate its interests to the interests of Soviet Russia. Stalin emptied Marxism and Leninism of its revolutionary power and replaced it with a nationalistic socialism.

Rapid industrialisation according to five-year plans began in 1928, and the collectivisation of agriculture, which encountered enormous difficulties, brought about a further increase of state power and bureaucracy.

For Stalin socialism meant the replacement of private ownership of the means of production by state ownership or cooperative ownership under the direction of the state. The power structure of the state became a dictatorship over the proletariat. By means of the mighty Politburo and the congresses of the party, Stalin ruled supreme. He defended himself against the accusation of dictatorship by pointing out that the party was linked to the people by 'transmission belts' of bodies like the League of Communist Youth and trade unions.

Trotsky opposed the doctrine of socialism in one country, in *The Revolution Betrayed* (1936). The first duty of Russia, he believed, should be its commitment to the imminent world revolution. Otherwise the Russian revolution would never become a truly socialist and secure one. Backward and isolated as Russia was, there was also the constant danger of a bureaucratic power elite re-introducing private property and thus betraying the revolution. In 1927 Trotsky was excluded from the party and hounded into exile. He died after a fatal attack by a hired assassin on 21 August 1940.

Stalin, like Lenin, was no philosopher; yet he had a paralysing effect on Marxist–Leninist philosophy. Though he was acclaimed by philosophers of the Stalinist era, he wrote only a few pamphlets of philosophical relevance. Nevertheless these became the norm for what philosophy was to be taught and written in Soviet Russia and the communist world. He drew the worst conclusions from Engels and Lenin. 'Dialectical materialism is the *Weltanschauung* of the Marxist–Leninist party.' Indeed, Marxist philosophy, seen through the dialectical materialism of Engels and rigidly narrowed down by the 'Leninism' of Stalin's creation, became a normative ideology of power over people. Its function was to legitimise the policy of Stalinism. Stalin's *On Dialectical and Historical Materialism* (1939) exerted a true dictatorship over Soviet philosophy. In it he suppressed the 'law of the negation of the negation' because he saw in it the dangerous infiltration of something like Hegelian 'synthesis' into dialectical materialism. With regard to historical materialism, his insistence on the active role of the superstructure, especially of social theories and political institutions, is noteworthy. In these terms he justified the absolute rule of Marxist ideology and the communist party. The main task of philosophy became the faithful explanation and propagandisation of Stalin's writings. Philosophy became a dogmatic system of absolute truth, which had to be imposed from above.

Comintern and Cominform

The Comintern, conceived by Lenin as an international party to promote the world revolution, became under Stalin more and more a tool of Soviet foreign policy to safeguard its own interests. In 1924 the Congress abandoned its united front policy, and communist parties were ordered to regard social democratic parties, the friends of yesterday, as enemies. This had disastrous consequences for communist parties in most countries of Europe, especially in Germany and France. At the last Congress of the Comintern in 1935, the policy was retracted and new orders were given to form popular fronts with socialists, reformists, and liberals against fascism. It became all the more obvious that Stalinist Russia had sacrificed internationalism when it signed the pact of 1939 with Nazi Germany. The Comintern was quietly dissolved in 1943.

The Second World War marked an important step towards communist control in eastern Europe. The doctrine of socialism in one country became the doctrine of socialism in one zone. In a slice-by-slice movement ('salami tactics') Stalin strengthened the security of Russia by gaining control over adjacent countries in eastern Europe.

The Conference of Yalta in 1945 allotted to the victorious Soviet Union its own 'sphere of interest' for setting up governments friendly to its policy. Communist parties in various countries cooperated with national, socialist, and popular fronts and infiltrated high posts until they could take over with the help of Russian power. By one means or another, communist governments were set up in Poland, Hungary, Rumania, Czechoslovakia, Bulgaria, East Germany and Yugoslavia. Despite resistance to what amounted to a Russian take-over, these countries adopted a Soviet form of government, with all power vested in the party and its organs, which exercised control over all areas of life. In 1947 the Communist Information Bureau, or Cominform, was formed to integrate the economies of the eastern bloc and tie the communist satellite countries more closely to the Soviet Union. This was the beginning of the 'Cold War', the division of the world into hostile camps: the 'free' capitalist West and the communist East.

Communist revisionism

Communist revisionism began shortly after the death of Stalin in 1953. This is the process of de-Stalinisation and of a certain liberalisation of communism in Soviet Russia and its satellites in the 1950s and 1960s. It is associated with the name of Khrushchev, who gave the impetus to a wave of revisionism of Marxism–Leninism which even today has not ebbed.

Khrushchev's secret speech to the twentieth Congress of the Communist Party of the USSR in 1956 marked a new beginning. He catalogued Stalin's mistakes and crimes and attacked his 'cult of personality' and rule of terror. The internal changes were slight and yet significant: one-man leadership gave way to collective leadership, the powers of the police were reduced, a general decentralisation of power took place. Concessions were made to the peasants and more consumer goods appeared in the shops. The tight control on intellectuals was loosened, working conditions improved, and wages became more egalitarian than before. The Party Programme of 1961 announced that agencies of self-government would gradually replace state organs as steps on the way towards building communism in Russia.

Externally the doctrine of peaceful coexistence became the basis of a more pragmatic approach by Soviet Russia to the capitalist West. In an attempt to ease the tensions of the Cold War the existence of peaceful ways to socialism was affirmed, and a 'creative Marxism' was proclaimed which would adapt to the particular historical circumstances rather than follow slavishly the Russian model. Although Khrushchev's peaceful road to world communism was in the economic interests of Russia, it was considered by the Chinese a betrayal of the revolution.

Since Khrushchev's fall in 1964, Soviet Russia has taken a more cautious and conservative approach. Industrialisation is progressing, whereas collectivisation in agriculture does not seem to be a success. The question is: will further industrialisation mean a further 'western-isation' and leaning towards capitalism?

De-Stalinisation had a profound effect in the 1950s and 1960s on the European communist countries, which are in a different situation from Russia. For many, communist rule meant conquest by Russia, and nationalist feelings were strong. Although a socialist vision was accepted, Stalinism was strongly resented as was the imposition of the Russian model.

Opposition in these countries grew, especially among intellectuals, who were influenced by neo-Marxist ideas. Since the publication of Lukács's *History and Class Consciousness* (1923), and in the 1930s and 1940s of Marx's *Grundrisse* and of hitherto unknown writings of the young Marx, a new philosophical ferment entered the rigid party philosophy. Many rediscovered the moral and humanist elements in Marx's philosophy and turned against the party bureaucrats. Generally speaking, the revisionists, while always presupposing the context of truly socialist society, demanded greater democracy and participation by the workers, the acceptance of a variety of roads to socialism, less forced collectivisation from above, and greater economic decentralisation.

In East Germany there were strikes, and a popular uprising in June 1953 was put down by Soviet military intervention. Mainly as a result of Ulbricht's Stalinism, opposition was wiped out, and East Germany is still one of the most faithful pro-Soviet satellites.

In Poland nationalist anti-Russian feelings supported Gomulka in his attempt to find a specifically Polish road to socialism, from 1945 to his fall in 1971. In Adam Schaff and Leszek Kolakowski, Polish Marxism has produced two innovative Marxist thinkers. Though they are by no means representative of the party line, they show the creative ferment in Polish Marxism. One of the features of Poland's resistance to Russian imposition is the strong presence of a tightly knit Catholic Church. After 1956 a certain liberalisation took place, though this was halted by the imposition of martial law in 1981. In 1969 the party adopted plans for a new economic system, which foresaw more decentralisation and planning 'from the bottom upward'. Under its new leader Edward Gierek, a pragmatist who favoured decentralised management and incentive pay, Poland continued on its road to a more functional form of communism.

In Hungary there was a determined attempt to oppose the imposition of a communist state after the war. The government of Imre Nagy announced the abolition of the one-party state and withdrew from the Warsaw pact. The 'Hungarian Way' to socialism was strangled after a bitter fight as a result of the intervention of Soviet tanks in 1956. Janos Kadar, however, under strict party control and in loyalty to Soviet Russia, quietly introduced far-reaching economic reforms (known as 'goulash communism'), moving gradually away from a command economy to a more decentralised one with some western characteristics.

Tito's Yugoslavia was the first government to challenge the leadership of Russia over the communist bloc. It accused the system in Soviet Russia under Stalin of degenerating into a bureaucracy controlling an imperialist state, and of having become a state-capitalist despotism. Backed by the fact that the revolution in Yugoslavia had been the only indigenous one in all of eastern Europe, Tito steadily pursued Yugoslavia's own path to socialism — called Titoism. Factories, instead of being state property, were given to workers' collectives, and operated under market conditions regulated by the state. Tito encouraged grassroots participation through communes and workers' councils in an attempt to diminish the role of the state. With the end of Stalinism a period of reconciliation with Soviet Russia began, and the measures of liberalisation were toned down.

Yugoslavia is certainly the most liberal regime in the communist bloc, with what amounts to a market-system economy. Yet a man like Milovan Djilas had to go to prison for suggesting a multi-party system and the abolition of the political monopoly of the Yugoslav Communist Party. This proposal was pursued by men like Togliatti in Italy with his conception of polycentralism, which is the basis of 'Eurocommunism'.

The country which has gone farthest on the road to what has been called 'socialism with a human face' is Czechoslovakia. The revisionist movement is linked to the name Alexander Dubček, who attempted to replace the bureaucratic system of power with democratic socialism. For the economic sector this meant the introduction of a market mechanism into a decentralised socialist economy. Politically it meant a democratisation of the party and turning the parliament into the supreme legislative body rather than making it subject to party control.

Civic rights were to be restored, censorship was abolished, freedom of speech and of the press were reintroduced. The party was democratised through measures like secret voting, rotation of offices, and control of party bureaucrats by elected party organs. The 'Prague Spring' lasted only long enough to give the world a glimpse of what a 'humanistic socialism' could look like. The experiment was cut short in August 1968 by the intervention of Soviet tanks. The reformist leaders were arrested and removed, censorship and totalitarian ways returned. The new government became once again subservient to Russian dictates.

Eurocommunism

The concept 'Eurocommunism' is very recent (1975). Its reality goes back to what was called 'reform communism' in the 1950s and 1960s. Eurocommunism distinguishes itself from national communism by the fact that it not only seeks independence from Soviet leadership but also looks for a freer and more democratic form of society. It is a movement within communism which involves some European communist parties in the West, especially in Italy, France and Spain, and also in Japan and Australia. These parties have great autonomy in relation to each other, yet have some common traits which could be summarised in the following points:

(1) All communist parties are autonomous and have equal rights within the communist movement. Moscow is not the all-determining centre of world communism. Unity in diversity replaces the uniformity of communist world conferences like Comintern or Cominform which establish a general line of strategy and ideology that all have to follow. Eurocommunists seek dialogue with all progressive forces, including progressive christian forces, especially in the predominantly Catholic countries.

(2) Eurocommunists favour a democratic path to socialism, which relies on the support of the majority of the population. They reject the Soviet conception of a violent revolution and the establishment of the dictatorship of the proletariat. They accept the parliamentary system and the plurality of parties.

They differ from the social democrats in striving not only for the abolition of some major evils of capitalist society, but also for a radical structural transformation of society. These structural changes aim especially at the gradual nationalisation of the institutions of monopoly capitalism, private banks and insurance companies. These institutions are to be administered by democratically elected organs, with major participation by the workers. Small and middle private firms will not be directly affected. The private holdings of farmers are to remain but large estates and land speculation are to be abolished. Structural reforms are suggested in many areas, including those of education, mass media, and science.

(3) Eurocommunists favour a broad basis of cooperation between various progressive forces, without claiming the prerogative of being in a leading position. The various parties in the alliance are partners on the basis of tolerance, dialogue, and mutual autonomy. In this process Marxism–Leninism is no longer absolute and class analysis is modified.

(4) Eurocommunists reject the Soviet form of Marxism–Leninism as the uniform world-view, and its rigid dogmatic explanation of all reality. They speak of scientific socialism rather than of Marxism–Leninism. This allows for an open Marxism which permits a great variety of Marxist, neo-Marxist, and other socialist perspectives in free discussion with each other. It also lays the foundation for a new relationship with religion in general and with Christianity in particular. The commitment to scientific socialism does not entail a confession of atheism and materialism. Militant atheism is replaced by dialogue. The partners in this dialogue vary according to circumstances. In Italy, France and Spain the dialogue tends to be with Catholics, in Japan with Buddhists, in Australia and Sweden with the Protestant churches.

(5) Eurocommunists have a critical attitude towards Soviet Russia and to the eastern communist bloc. While acknowledging the importance of the October Revolution and the achievement of Russia, they do not accept the Soviet Russian system as an obligatory model that other countries must follow. They strongly criticise the remnants of Stalinism in the Soviet Union, the exaggerated centralisation and bureaucratisation in economics and politics, the underdeveloped sense of socialist justice and democracy. They opposed the Soviet intervention in Czechoslovakia and subsequent repressive measures there and in Poland.

(6) Eurocommunists have a pluralistic-democratic model of socialism. The centralist, bureaucratic, and dictatorial system in Soviet Russia is not even appropriate to its own stage of advanced development; it is certainly not adequate for advanced industrialised countries with a parliamentary democratic tradition. Most Eurocommunist parties favour free elections within a parliamentary framework which guarantees the basic rights of all citizens. There is no uniform state ideology but a plurality of party programmes.

(7) Eurocommunism does not accept the Leninist party structure which is known as 'democratic centralism' because it amounts to a bureaucratic centralism. The communist party is open also to members who do not accept the ideology of Marxism–Leninism. Free discussion, even in public, of diverging opinions within the party is encouraged; a

system of rotation guarantees a regular change in party functions.

(8) Eurocommunist parties pursue their own foreign policy, which does not have to be aligned with the one favoured by the Soviet Union. They do not consider themselves as an extension of Russia or of the Warsaw pact. They do not join the Soviet condemnation of the People's Republic of China. The communist parties of Italy and Spain support the Common Market. In general, Eurocommunists try to overcome the splintering of Europe into hostile blocs. They oppose Russian hegemony over the eastern European states.

The three largest and most important Eurocommunist parties in Europe are those in Italy, France and Spain.

The Italian Communist Party is the strongest communist mass party outside the Soviet communist bloc. Under its leader Palmiro Togliatti it has, since the twentieth Congress of the Communist Party, continuously developed its own Italian way to socialism: peaceful, parliamentary, multi-party, and democratic. Togliatti asserted the idea of different roads to socialism in his doctrine of polycentralism, which rejected the idea of a central direction of the communist world movement by Moscow. The 'historical compromise' of an alliance with all progressive forces has recently led to participation in the government coalition, together with the strongest Italian political party, the Christian Democrats.

The Communist Party in France is the second strongest communist party in western Europe. Until 1967 it pursued a strong, pro-Soviet Russian course and followed all the twists and turns decreed by Moscow. But critical voices within the party became louder, particularly the voice of Garaudy, since 1956 a member of the French communist politburo and in charge of the Marxist Research Centre. He demanded the revision of bureaucratic centralism and argued for more democracy within the party. In his book, *From Anathema to Dialogue* (1964), he made a strong plea for dialogue with christians. In the conferences of the *Paulusgesellschaft* (1965–7), he proposed a pluralistic socialist model and pleaded for an 'open Marxism'. After 36 years of party membership he was condemned as a revisionist in 1970 and excluded from the party. In 1970 the communists united in a popular front with the socialists and elaborated a common programme advocating, at the same time, solidarity with the Soviet Union. This brought the French Communist Party into line with the Italian model. The general secretary Marchais expressed this new trend in his book *The Democratic Challenge* (1973), in which he declared himself in favour of a pluralistic mode of society. The new orientation is less advanced, however, in France than in the communist parties of Italy or Spain.

A critique of Marxism-Leninism

Undoubtedly the two most powerful symbols and embodiments of Marxism-Leninism today are Russia and China. Both countries have made massive strides on the basis of Marxist-Leninist policies. The USSR developed from a backward agrarian country into an industrialised superpower within a half-century. China emerged from misery, against all odds, in only a quarter-century. The Russians and Chinese now enjoy a moderate but rising standard of living. There is no unemployment and economic needs of education and science receive great attention. Luxury spending is curtailed and social discrepancies are levelled out. Although there is a new privileged class, in China (at least) the income gap is smaller than anywhere else in the world.

The question is whether the price exacted in human terms for these achievements has not been too high. Even using Marxist criteria the answer appears to be affirmative. From a western perspective there are also serious flaws in Marxism-Leninism.

The totalitarian philosophy. Engels rather than Marx laid the foundations for an inflexible, doctrinaire system of historical-dialectical materialism as an infallible key to all truth. Human observations and interpretations are forced into a speculative strait-jacket, in which matter is the sole principle of existence and dialectics the sole principle of all processes. Lenin elevated this philosophy to a dogma, binding for every communist. Even in the sciences and arts no deviations are tolerated. The analytical and creative faculties of man are imprisoned in a world of make-believe, constantly upheld by fierce propaganda, censorship, isolation and the manipulation of the dialectical principle to cover contradictions within the system and between the system and reality. Soviet citizens are denied the right to look and think and decide for themselves. The campaign against all religions is well known.

Concentration of power. We criticised capitalism for allowing a concentration of economic power in the hands of a few. In communist countries it is worse. The real question is not who owns the capital (private individuals or the state) but who is in effective control of capital. In the West the power of capitalists is limited by trade unions, on whose cooperation they depend. Economic power is not in the same hands as political power. So there is a balance of power. Politicians are subject to democratic procedures and can be thrown out of office if they abuse their positions. There is an independent judiciary. There are no such controls in communist countries. All power — whether economic, political, military, or ideological — is concentrated in the same hands and can be manipulated at will. Trade unions are instruments of the authorities. Voters have to vote in public for the prescribed candidates of the communist party, and the outcome is always more than 99 per cent of the votes for the party. But even these 'representatives' have no real power. They only endorse the policies laid before them by acclamation. Often their consultation is not sought for years on end.

Ideological justification. Ideological principles serve to justify these practices. According to Marxism, history inevitably moves from capitalism to socialism and finally to the ideal stage of communism. Those who obstruct this inevitable process prove that they have a false (bourgeois) consciousness. They need to be guided and re-educated. The obstinate have to be forced to accept, or be eliminated. Contrary to Marx, Lenin shrewdly recognised that the workers themselves cannot be trusted to develop the right consciousness. He built up a disciplined combat-force to carry out the revolution, and a disciplined communist party (comprising in the USSR only about 5 per cent of the population) was entrusted with the task of leading the people to socialism after the revolution. But the rank and file of the party receive detailed instructions from the top, which they have to follow slavishly. So in fact it is only the leaders at the top who have the right consciousness and know what is good for the rest of mankind. Nevertheless communists claim to practise true democracy: the 'masses' are the proletariat, the interests of the proletariat are perfectly represented by its leaders. So the leaders speak and act in the true interests of the people, even if the people are unaware of that. Whoever disagrees simply proves that he has not yet developed the right consciousness to see what is good for himself and for mankind. He needs more intensive re-education. Marx's dictatorship of the proletariat has turned into the dictatorship of an elite under Marxism-Leninism.

Soviet imperialism. On the basis of Soviet imperialism whole nations are held in subjugation. Less than half of the Soviet population is composed of Russians. Ethnic groups which had opted out of the Russian Empire after the 1917 Revolution were forced back into the fold. Millions died and millions were deported to Siberia. Other communist parties all over the world were kept under strict control from Moscow because the Soviet Union was to be the pioneer and model of the communist world revolution. Only recently have some of them liberated themselves from that grip (most notably Yugoslavia and China). After World War Two had left eastern Europe under the control of the USSR, every attempt in these countries to shake off the yoke was crushed by the Soviet army, even if it was led by communists. A revolt against Soviet domination is by definition a 'retrogressive' step-back to capitalism. A revolt in any other country is by definition 'progressive' because it brings the goals of a communist take-over (and thus the ultimate goal of the classless society) nearer, even if the revolutionaries are inspired by other motives.

The development crisis. Communists do not seem to be particularly interested in the socio-economic development of poor but non-communist countries, unless they can reap some political benefits from them. Ultimately all non-communist governments are meant to collapse and it is precisely a situation of socio-economic deterioration which makes a nation ripe for a communist take-over. Communism so far has failed to conquer any of the well-developed, democratic countries. Against this background, the ruthless propaganda in international bodies becomes quite plausible. China ardently denies, for instance, that the Third World is facing an overpopulation crisis and maintains that all misery is due to capitalist exploitation – while at the same time applying birth control measures at home. The new futurological insights that our planet cannot bear the consequences of the uninhibited growth both of population and of industrial production very much longer are discredited as a clever device of the capitalists to keep the Third World poor. Communists continue to promise their own populations and the world at large that under communism everybody will enjoy unlimited prosperity despite indications that it is physically impossible to reach that goal on our limited earth. Instead of opposing the hedonistic and materialistic values of capitalism and showing ways out of the ecological dilemma, communism is competing with capitalism to bring us nearer to catastrophe.

The utopian goal as a palliative. The suffering inflicted upon their people by communist leaders is interpreted as a necessary stage in the historical dialectic. The hardships are nothing but the result of bourgeois obstructions and left-overs of the capitalist system, which need to be crushed with severity if the goal of the classless society is to be reached. Communists do not hesitate to sacrifice the present generation for the sake of the future. But the future is conceived of in such unrealistic terms that it is hard to believe it will ever materialise. The ruthlessness and cruelty of communist leaders do not seem to suggest that the communist re-education programme succeeds in its attempts to recreate man as a selfless social being. And one needs to believe in the dialectic to be convinced that tyranny can bring about liberty and social justice. The communist promises may very well turn out to be a giant deception with all suffering having been in vain!

Communism and anti-communism as ideologies. Karl Marx taught us that ideology is a means to cover up political and economic interests, and to justify the superior position and amoral action of a privileged elite. This definition seems to apply very well to the Marxist–Leninist leadership, which entrenched itself (or seeks to entrench itself) in a position of unlimited economic, political, military and ideological power. True communists may be sincere enough to sacrifice their lives for their convictions, and the truth of many of their contentions cannot be denied. But ideologies always contain some germ of truth.

All this applies equally to anti-communism in non-communist countries. Communists hold no monopoly of brutality and viciousness. Similar goals and means were promulgated in the name of Christianity long before communism was born. Aggressive capitalist expansion has exacted high costs. It should not be forgotten that the two world wars originated in the West. The threat of communism is often used as an excuse for the application of oppressive policies, the true aim of which is the maintenance of the privileges and powers of a ruling elite. But what is wrong in Russia — arbitrary detention, suppression of truth, mass removals of people, denial of civic rights — cannot be right in South Africa. Before one points a finger, one should put one's own house in order.

14 Anarchism

Libertarian socialists

For many the word 'anarchism' is associated with terrorism, nihilism, violence, and social disorder. Anarchists are thought to be ruthless criminals with a destructive urge, whose favourite occupation involves planting bombs and assassinating prominent personalities. Though violence has been defended by a number of anarchists and has been part of certain strains of anarchist political practice, not all anarchists have advocated it (Tolstoy, for example).

Anarchism, once used as a denigrating label by political rivals during the French Revolution, was first willingly claimed as a title by Pierre-Joseph Proudhon (1809-65). He inspired much of French socialism and had an important influence on Marx, with whom he was later to disagree. Proudhon used the word (which in its original Greek form simply means 'without a ruler') to designate a new and non-authoritarian order of society, with laws that are not imposed from above but emerge freely from below. He was what one could call a social individualist, who tried to elaborate a synthesis between communism (which destroys independence) and capitalism (in which private property destroys equality). He found this synthesis in the anarchist order of a federation of producers' communities — the 'mutualists' — where equality and justice coexist with independence and the recognition of individual merits.

Anarchism is thus the confluence of the two great currents of socialism and liberalism. As anti-capitalist socialism it opposes the exploitation of man by man, as libertarian socialism it opposes the dominion of man over man. Anarchism is the libertarian wing of socialism, in opposition to the authoritarian socialism represented by some followers of Marx. Anarchists are socialists who aim at the replacement of the authoritarian state by some form of non-governmental cooperation between free individuals. 'Every anarchist is a socialist, but every socialist is not necessarily an anarchist.'

Anarchists and Marxists

Though there is a great variety of trends within anarchism, from the mutualism of Proudhon and anarcho-syndicalism to the pacifist anarchism of Tolstoy, anarchists are all socialists who oppose the system of private property and wage labour. It should be stressed at this point that not all libertarianism, or libertarian socialism for that matter, is identical with anarchism. The New Right Libertarians, for example, are strong defenders of private property, and many libertarian socialists prefer to identify themselves as Marxists. Anarchists differ about the organisation of the future cooperative society and about the means of transition from the present authoritarian society to a future libertarian one. But they are united in rejecting a positive function for the state in the future socialist society. This brought them into conflict both with the representatives of social democracy, for whom the state was a fetish in anarchist eyes, and with authoritarian strands of Marxist socialism.

Authoritarian socialists called for a 'revolution from above' and saw a need for the continued existence of the state after the revolution. The conflict between anarchists and Marxists centred on the role of the state in the transitional period from the socialism of the dictatorship of the proletariat to the final classless society of communism. Marxists called for a conquest of the state, anarchists for the immediate abolition of the state, even at the risk of temporary chaos. For anarchists the interim dictatorship of the proletariat would not lead, as Marxists surmised, to a gradual withering away of the state, but to 'the reconstruction of the state, its privileges, its inequalities and all its oppressions'.

The conflict between anarchists and Marxists reached its climax during the period of the International, when Marx and Michael Bakunin (1814–76) clashed frequently. Bakunin was a great Russian libertarian activist and a restless rebel, who may be called the real founder of anarchism as a movement of historical importance. The first battle was fought at the Basel Congress of the International in September 1869. In Marx's absence, Bakunin dominated the conference with his impressive personality and defeated the plans of the Marxists. Marx had his revenge at the Hague Conference of 1872, where he succeeded in having Bakunin expelled from the International. Bakunin accused Marx of being the 'dictator of the International', and he likened his worship of the state and centralised authority to the Bismarckian urge to dominate. He reminded Marx of his own words from the programme of the International: 'The emancipation of the workers must be the task of the workers themselves.'

Most anarchists agree that the differences between Marx and Bakunin were great. Marx was an authoritarian, Bakunin a libertarian. Marx was a centralist, Bakunin a federalist. Marx advocated political action for the workers and planned to conquer the state; Bakunin opposed political action and sought to destroy the state. Marx stood for what we now call nationalisation of the means of production; Bakunin stood for workers' control. Bakunin expressed his criticism of 'scientific socialism' and communism in words that could be called prophetic: 'I detest communism because it is the negation of liberty and I cannot conceive anything human without liberty. I am not a communist because communism concentrates all the powers of society and absorbs them into the state, because it leads inevitably to the centralisation of property in the hands of the state, while I want to see the state abolished. I want the complete elimination of the authoritarian principle of state tutelage.' Either the state must be destroyed or one must 'reconcile oneself to the vilest and most dangerous lie of our century: Red Bureaucracy'. 'All political power inevitably creates a privileged position for those who exercise it. . . . Having taken over the Revolution, mastered it, and harnessed it, those in power are obliged to create the bureaucratic and repressive apparatus which is indispensable for any authority.' 'Take the most radical of all the Russians or give him dictatorial powers . . . and before the year is out he will be worse than the Czar himself.'

The main features of anarchism

Even leaving aside the contribution of Godwin and Stirner—great libertarian thinkers outside the anarchist movement, anarchism is as rich and varied as the divergent personalities of the Frenchman, Proudhon, an individualist social philosopher with a love for paradox; the eccentric rebel and romantic revolutionary, Michael Bakunin; another Russian exile, the aristocrat Peter Kropotkin (1842-1921), who made anarchism 'respectable' by his secular saintliness, invincible optimism and flair for science; and the audacious and often puerile Italian, Errico Malatesta (1853-1932), with his lucid and intransigent polemics.

But 'in spite of the variety and richness of anarchist thinking, in spite of contradictions and doctrinal disputes which were often centred on false problems, anarchism presents a fairly homogeneous body of ideas'. Following D. Guérin, we have listed some of the major features of anarchist thought and conviction.

A visceral revolt against authority

An anarchist is a man in permanent revolt against established society and its guardians, against the rulers, the masters, the rich, academicians, parliamentarians and priests. Sympathetic to non-comformists, outlaws and the lumpen proletariat, anarchists are driven by 'the impulse to liberty, the passion for equality, the holy instinct of revolt' against 'all the tormentors, all the oppressors, and all the exploiters of humanity—priests, monarchs, statesmen, soldiers, public and private financiers, officials of all sorts, policemen, gendarmes, jailers and executioners, monopolists, economists, politicians of all shades, down to the smallest vendor of sweetmeats' (Bakunin). Anarchist revolt is directed against the Church and the State, the two leading institutions of 'man's enslavement'. Inverting Voltaire's famous dictum, Bakunin concludes that if God really exists, it would be necessary to abolish Him! 'God being everything, the real world and men are nothing. God being truth, justice, goodness, beauty, power and life, man is falsehood, inequity, evil, ugliness, impotence and death. God being master, man is the slave.'

A passion for the freedom of the individual

For an anarchist the freedom of the unique individual is the origin and end of all social organisation. Social organisation must be based on voluntary association. But this does not lead to an egoistic and isolationist understanding of the individual. The freer a person the more he is able to enter into community with others. Man's natural desire to be free must be protected from any coercion, from any imposition of authority from outside. If crimes are committed they are to be regarded as disease; punishment takes the form of treatment, not of vengeance. 'The eternal aspiration to be unique will not be suffocated by levelling down. Individualism, personal taste, and originality will have adequate scope to express themselves.'

A reliance on the spontaneity of the masses

'The anarchist social revolution . . . arises spontaneously in the hearts of the people, destroying all that hinders the generous upsurge of the life of the people in order thereafter to create new forms of free social life, which will arise from the very depths of the soul of the people' (Bakunin). This reliance on the spontaneity of the masses made anarchists oppose any revolution organised from above by a party elite which exploits its intellectual superiority to usurp the role of the masses and paralyse their initiative. Leaders have to be catalysts of the people's natural instinct and midwives to their self-liberation. Here it should be noted that not all proponents of spontaneity as the proper form of revolutionary action are anarchists; Rosa Luxemburg is an example. Anarchists have often placed more hope in the peasants than in the proletariat as leaders of the revolution. The peasants are close to the earth and nature, with a long tradition of communalism behind them. It is among peasants that anarchist ideas have had most success, such as the poor peasants of Andalusia and the Ukraine.

A commitment to self-management and federalism

Against the statist conception, represented for example by the *Communist Manifesto*, which foresaw all the means of production centralised in the hands of an all-embracing state, anarchist economic organisation relies on free associations of workers and voluntary cooperatives of peasant communes in a regional, national and ultimately international federation. Peasants and workers must manage their own affairs, choose their own leaders, engineers and architects. Producers' cooperatives should own the means of production and share in the profits. They should compete with one another and yet be related to each other in the need for centralised planning, not from the top down, but from the bottom up. The ideal of libertarian socialism, to be pursued with all the compromises the situation imposes, is that of direct democracy from below, expressing itself economically in communes managing their own affairs. A federation of communes would administer the public services. A federation of federations would resolve all the problems which arise from the need to combine liberty with authority. It is interesting to observe that recent eastern European Marxist economists have put forward very similar ideas.

Anarchist revolutionary praxis

Through their decisive participation in the First International under the leadership of Bakunin, anarchism exerted an influence on the mass movement of workers. But soon after Bakunin's death anarchists found themselves in a minority since reformist social democrats had won over the majority of the workers to their side. The anarchists cut themselves off from the working class, many turned in on themselves, organised themselves into small clandestine groups, and turned to 'propaganda by the deed' through acts of direct violence.

After reaching a dead-end in 1890, they turned their attention once more to the working class, and began to influence workers through trade unions. They instilled in workers a more radical revolutionary consciousness and led them beyond the struggle for better working-conditions towards a conception of themselves as associations of producers, which could transform capitalist society into an anarcho-communist one.

The Russian Revolution provided a new platform for anarchist influence in the twentieth century. Though small in number, the anarchists played a very active part in the Russian Revolution. But the soviets and factory councils, which resembled too closely the anarchist idea of a federation of autonomous producers, were gradually replaced by the central economic planning of an authoritarian state bureaucracy.

The small nuclei of anarchists in Russia were quickly 'liquidated'.

Only in liberated Ukraine, under the inspiration of the peasant, Nestor Makhno, were the principles of libertarian communism and self-management put into practice on a regional scale, with great success. Peasants were organised in communes or free-work soviets, and these again were federated into districts and regions. The land was owned and tilled communally, and profits were shared on a basis of equality. Only the military power of the Bolsheviks was able finally to destroy this inspiring experiment of the Makhnovtchina.

Besides Italy and France, Spain became the country in which anarchism gained greatest momentum until World War Two. The struggle of the left against the fascist forces of Franco during the Spanish Civil War had all the characteristics of a people's revolution libertarians had conceived. Self-management was successfully implemented on a large scale by agricultural communes, and revolutionary workers' committees managed their factories, after many of the owners had left the country, without any interference by the state and sometimes even without managerial help. The war and the final crushing of the Spanish Republic ended the Spanish anarcho-socialist experiment, which Emma Goldman in 1938 hailed as 'the greatest achievement of any revolutionary period'.

Anarchism as a structured movement does not play an important contemporary role in any country, with the exception perhaps of Italy. It has also, interestingly, been almost completely absent from the South African political scene. None of the resistance movements or groups seem to have been decisively influenced by the historical sources of the anarchist movement.

Anarchism: a secular apocalypse?

'Let us put our trust in the eternal spirit, which destroys and annihilates only because it is the unsearchable and eternally creative source of all life. The passion for destruction is also a creative passion' (Bakunin). 'We are not in the least afraid of ruins. We are going to inherit the earth. There is no slightest doubt about that. The bourgeoisie may blast and ruin its own world before it leaves the stage of history. We carry a new world, here in our hearts. That world is growing this minute' (B. Durruti).

Critique

One major criticism of anarchism is that the model of social organisation which it proposes is unrealisable in the context of modern industrial society. It can be argued that the imperatives of organisation in industrial societies require centralised and highly bureaucratic forms of social and political control, which anarchists reject.

Marxists would consider as the main weakness of anarchism its lack of rigorous historical analysis and a well-developed socio-economic theory. Some would argue that its utopian character is also a major short-coming.

The liberal criticism would be levelled mainly against the anarchist rejection of private property.

Many would criticise anarchism on account of its association with 'propaganda by the deed' (violence), though this is not a necessary ingredient of anarchist thought and praxis.

There has been extensive debate in philosophy and the social sciences about the phenomenon of ideology. In chapter seventeen we attempt to distil the essence of that debate and provide a synthesis to assist readers who are interested in more than description of contending ideologies in South Africa. The descriptive part of this book was not written from any one of the approaches to ideology discussed here. But these approaches may assist readers in forming their opinions about the specific ideologies we have described. Given the initial impetus for this book from the South African Council of Churches, and the fact that the majority of South Africans claim some religious affiliation, chapter eighteen provides two specific theological perspectives from which the relationship between faith and ideology can be approached. Both move from an analysis of the structural inequalities of wealth and power in South Africa to a way of approaching the ideologies rooted in these structures. These perspectives are, in the nature of the case, incomplete. Since the problems inherent in the relationship between religious faith and ideology are not different in kind from the relationship between secular positions such as humanism and ideology, this exercise may be of interest to a wider readership.

15 Trends in modern European Marxist theory

In understanding many of the developments discussed in this chapter, two important historical phenomena must be borne in mind: fascism and Stalinism. It was the horrors of fascism and the Second World War that, in different ways, shaped the work of key figures of the Frankfurt School, such as Adorno, Horkheimer and Marcuse. Adorno's contribution, in *The Authoritarian Personality*, was an attempt to establish what factors contributed towards forming personalities susceptible to the manipulation of authoritarian political regimes. Likewise, it was experience in the French resistance that helped Sartre move away from the radical individualism of his earlier work. More generally, it was the phenomenon of fascism that led many Marxists to start thinking in more sophisticated ways about the nature of capitalist society. Experience of fascism made it impossible simply to assume any longer that no significant difference existed between the various kinds of political systems in capitalist society. Fascism was, after all, a very different phenomenon from liberalism or social democracy. In addition, the changing nature of capitalism caused Marxists to reforge many of their theoretical tools.

The other major historical development of the time, Stalinism, also forced anti-authoritarians, both on the left and on the right, to contemplate the dangers of repressive political systems. Moreover, it had the very special function for Marxists of making them reassess the whole socialist project. Their concern became one of trying to understand the preconditions for, and more specific arrangements of, a humane socialist society.

Important in this respect, too, was the growth of modern technology and the implications this had for the human condition — whether in terms of its impact on the factory floor or on systems of social control. It was in response to this that theorists of the Frankfurt School such as Marcuse and Habermas elaborated some of their more important writings.

Finally, of great significance was the very framework of dialogue and debate within which modern Marxist theory evolved. This was a framework formed by numerous influences, such as new developments in psychology, linguistics, and philosophy. Writing in twentieth-century Europe, one could not ignore the impact of psychoanalysis, the work of the Vienna Circle, or structuralist linguistics à la Saussure. If Marxism as a theoretical enterprise was to survive, let alone flourish, it would have to come to terms with these developments.

Some important trends

Contemporary research in sociology, political science, and economics increasingly reflects various kinds and degrees of indebtedness to an intellectual tradition that very broadly can be called Marxist or Marxian.

The task of establishing the nature and history of this tradition is considerably more difficult than the adjectives Marxist and Marxian might lead one to suspect. One of the reasons for this is that most of the more important thinkers who would be willing to identify themselves as part of the tradition have drawn heavily on intellectual sources other than Marx. Kant, Hegel, Freud, Wittgenstein and Weber all find a place, somewhere or other, in the works associated with this tradition. A second reason is that the various currents that comprise the tradition (especially in the broad sense in which we are referring to it) may be distinguished by very different ways of interpreting Marx's writings. Indeed, the conflict that has arisen over the question of interpretation sometimes makes it very difficult to speak of a tradition at all. Finally, there is the very large problem of the relationship between philosophy and theory on the one hand and political practice on the other. In this area, too, it is often very hard, if not impossible, to establish consensus within the tradition.

What, then, allows us to speak of a tradition at all, and in terms of which criteria do we define this tradition? Two criteria have been used here to establish whether or not a writer belongs to the tradition. Firstly, he should acknowledge belonging to the tradition, and secondly, his works should reflect some sort of indebtedness to Marx's views and a willingness to develop some of them further. In this way we include thinkers who, for example, do not hold to the view that the proletariat still constitutes the motor whereby the transformation to socialism will be effected.

As for those particular currents that will be discussed in this chapter, two further criteria have been used. The first is that the thinkers or movements referred to are generally considered important, either because of the bearing that their work has on social and political theory or because they raise important issues of a philosophical nature. The second is that their work should have relevance, in a more or less direct way, for the analysis of modern societies.

Marxist humanism

Marxist humanism is a very large category indeed. It includes thinkers such as Georg Lukács, Lucien Goldmann, Erich Fromm, Herbert Marcuse and Jürgen Habermas (although he will be discussed separately under the heading of existential Marxism). It could also include someone like Sartre, and empirical Marxists such as Eric Hobsbawm, Christopher Hill or E. P. Thompson (whom we shall discuss under the heading Marxist empiricism).

The most important figures in this broad category include, in addition to those mentioned above, various members of the Frankfurt School, such as Theodor Adorno and Max Horkheimer, and members of the more recent Budapest School, such as Agnes Heller. Various radical groups generally characterised by, among other things, a hostility to the currently fashionable structuralist Marxism can be regarded as being part of this stream. Among these one could count the Telos groups in the United States and Canada, the editors of the journal, *New German Critique*, and important contemporary writers ranging from the Hungarian emigré István Mészáros to the American Trent Schroyer.

What are the main themes, concerns and intellectual characteristics of this tradition?

First and foremost, what distinguishes the members of this tradition is their concern with the nature of consciousness and with the notion of human beings as historical actors — as agents who, even though they may not be able to make history entirely as they choose, are nevertheless the creators of social, political and economic institutions. Thus it is no accident that Lukács's most famous work is entitled *History and Class Consciousness*. This concern with consciousness and human agency distinguishes Marxist humanists quite sharply from the structuralist tradition, and is closely linked with the incorporation of Hegelian and, in many cases, Freudian ideas into their social theories. This means, too, that in their relationship to Marx, the humanists have tended to take the early Marx as seriously as (if not, in some cases, more seriously than) the later Marx. Thus, the exegetical concerns of Marxist humanists have tended to lie with such themes as the relationship of Marx to Hegel (Marcuse), alienation (Mészáros) and the relationship of man to nature (Schmidt). In their works on modern social and political issues they have in turn been concerned with alienation as a problem in advanced capitalist (and for that matter in advanced state socialist) societies, and the way in which technology and technical rationality have come to serve the cause of human oppression (Marcuse, Habermas).

Another central concern of this group has been the question of human emancipation. This has generally not been regarded as simple and unproblematic. Many writers within the tradition have discarded the idea that freedom is to be secured through the revolution of the proletariat (Habermas is perhaps the most interesting example), although they all share the view that real freedom is only possible within the context of some kind of socialist society. Almost all, however, are careful not to regard the countries of eastern Europe as in any way paradigmatic socialist states.

In so far as human oppression is seen as a complex issue, these writers have avoided focusing on economic exploitation alone as the main form of domination. They have concentrated (many would argue excessively) on the way the cultural realm serves the dominant ideology through the function of literature, the visual arts and music. In the course of this particular pursuit some truly great works in aesthetics have been written: for example, Lukács's writings on the novel, Adorno on music, and Arnold Hauser on the visual arts. More recently, Jürgen Habermas has focused on the role of language as an instrument of domination.

It is, perhaps, in order here to point out that the concern with domination is linked very closely to the question of the nature of consciousness. This has led, in the course of the development of Marxist humanism, to an interest in how, at the subjective level of the individual, the insights of psychoanalysis can provide a key for explaining how domination functions intra-psychically. The result of this interest was that bold and intellectually challenging attempts have been made to fuse the thought of Marx with that of Freud. The most famous are probably those found in the work of Erich Fromm and Herbert Marcuse. Of course, not all those working within this broadly humanist tradition have found themselves attracted to Freud. Agnes Heller (a Hungarian exiled in Australia) has recently argued very strongly against assimilating psychoanalysis to Marxian social theory on the grounds that it allows one to avoid the claim that human beings are responsible for their actions. Similarly, Sartre was unable for a long time to take Freud seriously.

Although it is primarily in the field of aesthetics that the Marxist humanists acquired their greatest fame, they also contributed (and this is especially so for those associated with the Frankfurt School) to the analysis of politics and economics. Especially interesting in this regard were members of the Frankfurt group, such as Franz Neumann, Otto Kirschheimer, Friedrich Pollock and, though more of an outsider, Karl Wittfogel, who wrote the highly controversial book, *Oriental Despotism*. More recently, the impact of Max Weber's thought on the nature of legal and bureaucratic rationality has been articulated by Herbert Marcuse, Jürgen Habermas and Trent Schroyer. Though they differ in emphasis and the nature of the theses that they argue, they hold in common the view that scientific and technological reason need not necessarily liberate man either from the grip of nature or from social and political domination, and that, contrary to the nineteenth-century belief in science and technology as a means of liberation (a view Marx held), they also serve to make more sophisticated the instruments of repression.

One of the most recent developments within this tradition has been the growing concern with the crisis of advanced capitalism. This theme has been most fully developed by thinkers such as Habermas and Schroyer, who have rescued Marx's notion of crisis but have argued that crisis cannot be understood as purely, or even primarily, an economic phenomenon. Crisis in advanced capitalism has, they argue, to be understood at the political and socio-cultural as well as at the economic level, and for Habermas crisis takes on its most significant form in the crisis of legitimation. Here, again, the importance of the level of consciousness becomes apparent, in that to speak of a crisis in respect of the legitimacy of a system one is necessarily talking about something which manifests itself as a problem at the level of consciousness.

Another important point to make about this particular tradition is that it does not hold the view that history is automatic. For this reason, the value of critique and the call on people to act responsibly with regard to the future are important aspects of this current of thought.

Existential Marxism

Although there are a number of thinkers whom one could place in the category of existential Marxism we shall here only refer to its most illustrious member, Jean-Paul Sartre. Sartre's position, as he defined it in his pre-Second World War writings and in *Being and Nothingness*, was one of radical individualism. During an extraordinarily complex process of intellectual development he moved slowly from this position to one that contrived to embrace aspects of his earlier existentialist thought with ideas of an essentially Marxian character. This is not the place in which to trace the development in detail (it has been very ably done by Mark Poster) but we need to spell out in very broad terms what this change involved.

In the *Critique of Dialectical Reason* human beings are no longer conceived as acting purely on their own. In special historical circumstances they are brought together as a group-in-fusion, where they act in pursuit of common interests. This situation is very different from the normal one, which Sartre characterises as that of serialisation. When serialised, people act in such a way that they are not really conscious of the fact that they share a situation in common with others who are oppressed and exploited and that they could act collectively to try to alleviate their position. Sartre's 'fused groups' (his most famous example is of those storming the Bastille) do not, however, guarantee that they will remain fused. There is always the difficulty of resisting a return to a serialised position, once a particular project has been completed. Nevertheless, two important points emerge. Firstly, the question of responsibility for action becomes one with a social as well as an individual point of reference. Secondly, Sartre provides here a rather useful set of categories for the analysis of processes of social and political change, of conflict and revolt. In terms of his social theory Sartre, like the humanists, posits individuals and groups as social and historical actors who make their own history. Again, however, they do not make it entirely as they choose. Sartre's actors are constantly confronting what he terms the practico-inert, that is, the institutions and structures that constitute the unintended consequences of their actions.

In illustrating his point Sartre used an example which has become famous. Chinese peasants each cut down trees for various purposes, such as building dwellings or making fires. This, of course, satisfies their immediate interests but the end result unfortunately is that they set in motion a process of deforestation. The problem is that each, in realising what he perceives as his immediate interest, acts against the interests of the peasantry as a collectivity. This example characterises very nicely Sartre's view of history as a process of totalisation without a totaliser.

Sartre also contributed in a very important way to aesthetics. His studies of Baudelaire, Genet and Flaubert are masterpieces in their own right and, in that order, reflect his movement from existentialism to an existential Marxism. For our purposes it is Sartre's social and political theory that is important.

Sartre's social theory has been used fruitfully in recent South African studies. An interesting use of Sartrean categories to illuminate the nature of the Durban strikes in 1973 may be found in a study published by the Institute of Industrial Education. Sartrean insights have also been used to explore the dynamics of these strikes, using the categories of fused group and seriality, in a very sophisticated study by Foszia Fisher.

Structuralist Marxism

The best-known members of structural Marxism are probably Louis Althusser and, among political scientists and sociologists, Nicos Poulantzas. Central to the structuralist position is the assertion that the proper object of investigation is the system of structures which characterises a particular society, and not the consciousness of individuals or groups. This particular perspective has been characterised as involving the 'de-centering' of man.

The structuralist approach was developed primarily in France and originated in the work of the linguist Saussure. Saussure studied *la langue*, not *la parole*, that is, not the spoken word but the system of signs. Thus, as opposed to Sartre, for example, who viewed language in the old-fashioned way as a tool for the expression of ideas, the structuralist perspective denies the significance of the human being as a subject or intentional actor.

The structuralist position was developed further by the anthropologist Claude Lévi-Strauss, in debate with Sartre. His concern lay not with history but with timeless structures, such as kinship systems.

The French structuralists constitute a large and heterogeneous group including Michel Foucault, Jacques Lacan and Louis Althusser.

Althusser's position is structuralist specifically in so far as he claimed that he was concerned with the science of society, and that 'humanism' (against which he waged a fierce polemical battle) is essentially ideological in character. In terms of his relation to Marx, he declared that Marx was really a structuralist before his time and that there was an epistemological break in his writings, which separated the pre-scientific from the scientific Marx. Thus the earlier works such as the 1844 manuscripts involved a concern with man and not with the structures of the capitalist system. It was only in his later work (which Althusser, over time, located later and later in Marx's corpus), where he focused on the mode of production, that Marx became truly scientific.

One of the problems with Althusser's structuralist reading of Marx is that, in so far as his concern is with structures not subjects, he cannot hold that there is a fundamental link between theory and praxis. What is also ruled out on account of his 'scientism' is the possibility of grounding the claim for socialism on a critique of capitalism, and of realising socialism through conscious revolutionary action. In Althusser's view, men are merely the bearers of roles. They do no more than serve as supports for structures. This has the effect, for Althusser and his followers, of focusing historical inquiry on structures and what they reveal. This, his critics charge, is detrimental to an understanding of the past that encompasses its flow, its changes and its complexity.

Thus the concerns of the humanist Marxists, with alienation, freedom, consciousness, and the role of those charged with the task of revolutionising society, are largely absent from Althusser's thought.

Althusser's ideas were developed with specific regard to the analysis of contemporary social formations by the late Nicos Poulantzas, who wrote on the relationship between political power and social classes, and the structure of fascism. Poulantzas's special concern with these 'exceptional' political forms associated with capitalism has made his work particularly influential among a number of scholars studying the nature of South African society (as in the study, *Capital, State and White Labour in South Africa*, by Robert Davies).

Empirical Marxism

Empirical Marxism is an awkward category, in that those whom we have identified as belonging to it could also have been included under the heading of Marxist humanism. One reason why we have chosen to list them separately is that they are almost all British and that their concerns have been primarily empirical rather than theoretical, at times in fact reflecting strong hostility to the theoretical enterprise. Another reason is that in considerable measure, their greatest impact has been in the field of history. Most important among these are the historians Christopher Hill, E. P. Thompson and Eric Hobsbawm, the political scientists Ralph Miliband and Leo Panitch, and sociologists such as John Westergaard.

A number of them, though not primarily theoreticians, have been engaged in fierce controversy with the structuralists. This is particularly true of Miliband and Thompson, who respectively have engaged Poulantzas and the structuralist movement more generally.

The main contribution of this group has been to re-establish, in a very sophisticated form, the validity of a number of Marxian categories and insights in historical, sociological and political analysis. Thus Thompson revolutionised not only our knowledge of nineteenth-century England but the whole issue of social class formation. Similarly, Miliband's study *The State in Capitalist Society* has become a *locus classicus* in the study of the modern state.

Postscript: Ernst Bloch

We include here a postscript on Ernst Bloch (1885–1977) because he has greatly influenced the European 'theology of hope', initially developed by Jürgen Moltmann, and Latin American liberation theology. His significance lies in his recovery of the tradition of utopian dissent in western social thought: this is of great importance for liberation theology, political theology and black theology in southern Africa.

Bloch considers himself a Marxist philosopher. The conclusion of the third volume of his magnum opus, *Principle of Hope*, is a chapter called 'Karl Marx and humanism, matter of hope'. Lukács invented the term utopian messianism for Bloch's work, which was then used to disqualify him as a Marxist. When in 1949 Bloch returned from America to settle in the German Democratic Republic he soon became an uncomfortable comrade. The publication of the third volume of *Principle of Hope* was withheld on account of its 'religious eschatologism', and in 1957 he was charged by students in a mock-trial for teaching a 'revisionist version of Marxism'. After the construction of the Berlin Wall he remained in the Federal Republic, where he accepted a professorship at Tübingen.

Bloch belongs to the neo-Marxists who sought to liberate Marxism from its Leninist and Stalinist dogmatism. Together with Lukács and Korsch, Brecht and Weill, and above all Benjamin, Bloch represents a form of humanist socialism which he called the warm stream in Marxism developed in opposition to the 'brown messianism' of Nazi fascism. Bloch has dedicated relatively little time to the analysis of present conditions of political economy. He explored rather the warm stream of messianic revolutionary thought back to its roots in the prophetic tradition of Judaism and Christianity and its history in the West, and forward to a future which goes beyond the goal of a classless society.

Marx protested not only against economic exploitation but also against oppressed human dignity. Bloch integrated the tradition of natural law and human rights, usually associated with the liberal tradition, into Marxism. 'The social utopias pictured conditions in which people are no longer burdened and oppressed; natural law projects conditions in which people are no longer humiliated and degraded.'

The final goal of history is not only negative freedom from everything which alienates and oppresses man. Positively it is what Bloch calls the 'human emancipation of man' that finds its fulfilment in a radical subjective natural law: 'from each according to his abilities, to each according to his needs.' The objective counterpart to this is solidarity. The state will have withered away with its laws and punishments, and man will enter the perfect kingdom of the 'naturalisation of man and the humanisation of nature'.

Bloch's main idea in his *Natural Law and Human Dignity* centres on Rosa Luxemburg's often quoted saying, 'No democracy without socialism, no socialism without democracy'. Bloch adds, 'This is the formula of mutual relationship that will decide over the future.' There is no human happiness without freedom from economic needs, yet there is also no freedom without respect for the dignity of man. Socialism with a human face is equally critical of the economic exploitation in capitalism as of the violation of human rights and the degradation of man in any form of totalitarian Marxism.

Bloch sees also a role for a church in the future society as a powerful guide of conscience free from the powers that be, a voice that is concerned with the direction of the economy, and keeps alive man's hopes and dreams beyond the achievements of the classless society. Bloch's greatest impact, however, has been on christian theologians. He has helped them to rediscover the Jewish roots and the liberation potential of the message of the kingdom as preached, lived, anticipated and guaranteed by the life and resurrection of Jesus of Nazareth. They have learned how to put messianic hope at the centre of a christian faith that refuses to function as opium of and for the people in the interests of those in power.

For a christian, Bloch has sacrificed messianic hope to a Marxism that is not open to the possibility of a revolutionary God who raises the dead, 'pulls down the mighty from their thrones, and lifts up the oppressed'. It is up to christians to demonstrate that their messianic hope does not alienate them from the struggle for a kingdom of justice and solidarity on earth. It is up to them to verify in their practice the hope that this kingdom on earth is pregnant with a future yet unseen and unheard of. 'It has not appeared yet what we shall be' (1 John 3: 3).

16 Maoism in China

Chinese culture and the Chinese polity date back to the third millenium B.C. The Chinese are the most populous nation in the world and comprise about a fifth of mankind. In size, their land surface is, after the USSR and Canada, the largest in the world. China is today on its way to becoming a third superpower; what happens in China will determine the future of Asia and profoundly influence the rest of mankind. Maoism, which forged the new China, is an extremely powerful revolutionary movement, with definite religious overtones, and has competed not only with western capitalism but also with Russian Marxism–Leninism. China poses as spokesman for the Third World against the superpowers and is a symbol for development in the Third World. It has also been the source of inspiration, training and funds for Robert Mugabe's guerrilla forces in Zimbabwe, and the PAC in South Africa. All this underlines the importance of a closer study of Maoism, the ideology of the Chinese revolution. We shall look at the Maoist takeover in the context of historical developments, sketch the main characteristics of the movement, and conclude with developments since the death of Mao in 1976.

Before Mao Tse-tung

From the time of the Han dynasty, which ruled China from 206 B.C. to A.D. 220, until the end of the Manchu dynasty, which was deposed in 1911, the socio-political order of China was based on the ethical code of Confucius (551–479 B.C.). China was governed by an intellectual and moral elite, whose position was based, at least in theory, not on heredity but on virtue. The four cardinal virtues of Confucianism were humaneness, obedience to parents, loyalty and justice. The elite was to rule by example rather than force. While Confucianism was the social ideology of the gentry, the peasant population observed traditional ancestor worship and other rituals amalgamated with the religion of the elite. On the social level there was a petrified patriarchal order. Some 4 per cent of the population owned over half the agricultural land, which they let to landless peasants. The peasants had to pay up to 80 per cent of the proceeds of their labour to the landlords. A serious population explosion (1730: 180 m people, 1950: 550 m, 1980: 800 m) progressively worsened the economic situation of the poor majority. Over the centuries various revolts indicated that the system was in an ever-worsening state of crisis. The Taiping revolt (1850–64), the most terrible of all, which was inspired by christian sectarian ideals, tried to bring about a redistribution of land and other social reforms. By the time it was crushed about 30 million people had lost their lives.

The inherent crisis was exacerbated by the impact of western expansion during the nineteenth century. Western trade introduced the beginnings of capitalism to China. The agricultural subsistence economy and traditional trades started to crumble. The illegal opium trade conducted by Westerners demoralised vast sections of the population. When the Chinese government tried to put an end to the smuggling, in 1839 Britain responded with a show of force. That was the beginning of a series of armed interventions in which the Chinese lost wars against Britain, France and Japan. Britain, France, Germany, Russia and Japan forced the Chinese government to open her ports to free trade, to agree to the rights of foreigners to establish factories and settlements not subject to the Chinese authorities, to keep troops on Chinese soil, to allow foreign ships to sail in Chinese waters and to accept missionaries. These so-called 'unequal treaties', imposed through force of arms, profoundly humiliated the pride of the Chinese who had always considered themselves to be the centre of the universe while surrounding nations were considered mere barbarians and could, at best, be granted certain privileges after having paid their tribute to the emperor, the 'Son of Heaven'. By the turn of the century foreign imperialism became more aggressive. China was forced to yield large tracts of land and the whole country was divided into 'interest spheres' of the imperial powers. The population was disillusioned with the powerlessness of their government. During the Boxer Rebellion in 1900 many foreigners, missionaries and Chinese christians were killed. Christian mission work had too obviously been partner to imperialism. After the revolt had been crushed, the foreigners exacted further demands.

The weakness of the Chinese was due not only to obsolete technology and weaponry but also to the tottering social system. It took some time before it was realised that it was not enough to take over western technology and arms. Japan, which had modernised itself according to western patterns, proved to be immensely superior and threatened to take control of the vast country. Under the leadership of Dr Sun Yat-sen a young generation of reformers, called the *Kuomintang* (National People's Party), deposed the Manchu dynasty in 1911 and proclaimed a republic in the following year. Sun Yat-sen was a man of vision and he tried to rebuild China on the basis of three principles: national sovereignty, democracy and social justice (including the redistribution of land). But the new republic was weakened by civil wars, in which regional military rulers attempted to gain autonomy, by the predominance of the interests of the elite, and by the constant threat of Japanese imperialism. Increasingly, young people realised that the solution to the national misery would be to eradicate the Confucian traditions and rebuild the society on western patterns. A strong inflow of western ideas also brought the influence of Marxism into the country. In 1921 two professors founded the Communist Party of China.

Sun Yat-sen died in 1925. Under his successor, Chiang Kai-shek, the *Kuomintang* became the most formidable political force in China. Still weak, the communists tried at first to cooperate with this party. Once Chiang Kai-shek had succeeded in conquering dissident areas and uniting China, he turned against the communists. The latter gave up their revolutionary struggle in the cities and moved into the rural hinterland. There they developed a new strategy: by establishing bases among the peasants instead of among workers in the cities, and developing a well-trained army which would gradually encircle the cities, they prepared themselves for a long armed struggle. In 1931 they managed to establish a 'soviet republic' in the province of Kiangsi, where they deposed the rural lords, introducing agrarian reforms, and reorganising the educational system. Because Chiang Kai-shek was a christian and anti-communist, he enlisted a great deal of support from western countries, especially the USA. But owing to corruption in its ranks and by failing to introduce necessary reforms, the *Kuomintang* was unable to inspire a disheartened population and its popularity began to dwindle.

In 1915 Japan had taken advantage of the war in Europe, and sought to impose her notorious 'Twenty-one Points', which would have turned much of China into a Japanese colony. The Treaty of Versailles gave a tract of Chinese land taken from Germany to Japan — to the utter dismay of the Chinese. In 1931 the Japanese invaded China and established a flourishing commercial and industrial colony in Manchuria. Chiang Kai-shek seemed to be more frightened of the communists than of the Japanese, and drove the communists out of their stronghold. On their legendary 'long march' in 1934 through eleven provinces, the communists covered a distance of 12 500 km, their numbers dwindling from about 100 000 to some 8 000. In the process the remnant became the core of a well-disciplined, highly motivated, thoroughly educated party or army, whose ideas and example affected all the regions through which they passed. During this period Mao Tse-tung became the chairman and undisputed leader of the party, maintaining this post until his death.

In the far north, in the region of Shensi, the communists again succeeded in establishing a stronghold with the centre at Yenan. They cooperated with other groups in the administration of the surrounding territories according to the three-thirds principle (one-third communists, one-third *Kuomintang*, one-third unaffiliated). Careful as they were to introduce only mild reforms, they compared very favourably with the *Kuomintang*. They gained ground rapidly. After the Japanese were defeated by the Americans, the Chinese civil war broke out in real earnest. The *Kuomintang* was defeated and supporters fled to the island of Taiwan. On 1 October 1949 the communists under the leadership of chairman Mao proclaimed the People's Republic of China.

Characteristics of the Chinese revolution

The peculiar character of the Chinese revolution is derived from three influences: Chinese cultural tradition, Russian Marxism–Leninism and the history of the Marxist movement in China itself. Traditional Chinese culture based on Confucianism was the object of a vicious and destructive attack by the Maoists. The hierarchical structure between elite and underdog, old and young, man and woman, was forced to make way for equality. The traditional orientation towards the past was relinquished in favour of an ardent dedication to the future. The conservative value of harmony between opposites was replaced by an attempt to eradicate the 'three great contradictions', namely, between head and hand, between urban and rural, and between workers and peasants. Confucianism limited the role of the state to a minimum, Maoism introduced the total politicisation of the remotest village in all spheres of life. The aloofness of the traditional educational elite was transformed into the principle of learning by doing and fighting.

Nevertheless the spirit of Chinese mentality was not destroyed completely: Maoism emphasised morality as much as Confucianism did; it believed in education rather than administration, in reformation rather than 'liquidation' of enemies. The aim was still one of realising perfect man in a perfect society. There remained the old Chinese feeling of superiority and isolation. Marxism had also become more 'religious' under Mao than was the case in other Marxist countries. In short, Maoism was peculiarly Asian and Chinese in its basic character.

Marxism–Leninism of the Soviet kind provided the foundation for Maoism. Between 1953 and 1957 the Chinese communists relied heavily on the Russian example, aid and expertise. From Lenin Mao inherited the concept of the party as the prime instrument of revolution; tactics such as cooperation with other parties as far as that is in the interests of the revolution; the expectation of a period of socialism before communism; and the emphasis on the collective not the individual. From Stalin he inherited a militarist cast of language; the idea that it is not the level of economic development but the level of social contradictions that makes a country ripe for revolution; and the theory that after revolution the class struggle is intensified because the really dangerous enemies then pose as Marxists.

The differences between Maoism and Marxism–Leninism are also significant. Maoism emphasises the participation of the masses. Other tenets mark the distinction. Revolution should not be imposed from the top but it should grow from the grassroots level. There must be a dialectical balance between the leadership of the party and the initiative and wisdom of the ordinary people. The revolution should not start in the cities but in the rural areas, not with workers but with the peasants. Maoism is suspicious of the urban elite: they were to be called 'down to the villages, up into the mountains' to learn the truth from the hardworking peasants. Instead of urbanisation, Maoism tried to industrialise the villages. Of particular importance is the Maoist belief that man can be re-educated: the bourgeoisie should be 'brain-washed'. Conviction is more important than external force, communication is more important than administration and legislation. In Russia it would have been impossible to destroy the party machinery for the sake of the revolution, as happened in China during the Cultural Revolution. Mao also did not believe in communism in one country, as Stalin did, but pursued a universalist approach.

Some of these differences can be attributed to the personal qualities of Mao Tse-tung's leadership; some to the early experience of the movement when the communists succeeded in building bases amongst the peasants; some to the experiences gained during the long march; some to the fact that China was far more underdeveloped economically than Russia at the time of the revolution and that it is severely handicapped in terms of its climate, agricultural land and resource base. It also has masses of impoverished people but no capital and little expertise.

The clash with the USSR may also have played a role. The Chinese could not forget the 'unequal treaties', whereby they had lost vast areas of land to Tsarist Russia, which were never returned. The Russians on their part were wary of the emerging superpower on their eastern boundaries and jealous of their own leadership position in the communist world. The Russians did not support the military offensive against Taiwan and sided against China in the border conflict with India in 1959-62. By 1960 they withdrew all economic aid, equipment and technicians from China — a severe blow to the latter. In 1963-4, when the de-Stalinisation campaign got under way in the USSR, severe ideological conflicts emerged, in which the Maoists accused the Russians of betraying the Marxist revolution and of harbouring imperialist motives. From then on China considered the USA and the USSR to be accomplices in their ambition to gain world domination. The Russians in turn tried to isolate China politically and militarily. Paradoxically the Chinese are now tending towards Europe and the USA to counterbalance the Russian threat.

Against this background some of the distinctive characteristics of the Chinese approach can be sketched.

Mao Tse-tung was the great theorist and practical master of guerrilla tactics. In using these means a great, sophisticated and well-organised army can ultimately be defeated by relatively small, poorly equipped but highly disciplined and dedicated groups. The guerrilla strategy has since been applied in many contexts. In Vietnam it proved to be successful even against the most powerful army in the world.

The adoption of guerrilla tactics is only symptomatic of a general approach; that is, the strength of the nation and the point of departure for social reconstruction lie not in the elite but in the masses, not in the highly developed cities and centres but in the poor and backward periphery, not in the sophisticated experts but in the practical wisdom of the simple peasant and worker. The city is to be conquered from a rural base, agricultural development is to provide the basis of economic growth, industries are to serve the rural masses, trained experts must dirty their hands, peasants are not to flock to the glittering lights of the towns but townspeople are to move down to the villages and up to the hills.

What this means is that practice is more important than theory. Indeed, insight comes from action. Prospective students are first sent to join peasants and workers in performing manual labour: they are allowed to study only if recommended by local party organs. Trained experts have to work with their hands at regular intervals to learn the realities of life from the masses. Party functionaries (cadres) spend a third of their time in administration, a third in supervision, a third in manual work. On the other hand, workers and peasants are periodically allowed to sit on the decision-making bodies.

Everything in the country must serve the masses. No elitist attitudes are allowed to develop. Instead of building highly sophisticated hospitals which serve only the rich, China has sent thousands of 'barefoot doctors' into the villages to fight malnutrition, lack of hygiene, and elementary diseases. Similarly, industries must serve the requirements of agriculture. The production, importation and consumption of luxuries are forbidden. There is a strong emphasis on small-scale, labour-intensive industry in the villages. Large-scale, capital-intensive industries are not neglected, but China wants to 'walk on two legs'. It has discovered that its greatest asset is its vast population, not capital or expertise.

For this reason decision-taking is decentralised. The society is organised from the grassroots level upward. Every small local group is responsible for taking its own decisions and solving its own problems. Self-reliance is a basic virtue. No accumulation of centralised power, privilege or initiative is permitted. Technocracy and bureaucracy are regarded as extreme dangers for society.

This implies that the party machine is not considered infallible. Nor is it immune from attack. During the Cultural Revolution the young people (Red Guards) destroyed the entire party organisation so as to eradicate an unwieldy bureaucracy and accumulated privilege. The youths had to learn the meaning of revolution by practising revolution against their own communist superiors. No new elitist class is allowed to emerge, thereby ensuring perpetual revolution.

All the same, the Chinese nation is in the tightest possible grip of the top party leadership. As in all communist countries, the party is in sole control of affairs. About 28 million people or 3,3 per cent of the population belong to the party. The party should hold a congress every five years but it is not called regularly. Theoretically the central committee of the party elects members of the politburo: in fact it only ratifies the nominations. Actual power lies in the hands of the very small permanent committee of the politburo under the leadership of the chairman. All the lower party organs are nothing more than highly disciplined lines of communication which reach into the remotest village and into all possible spheres of life. This network of communication is incredibly efficient. Directives from the political leadership reach the entire 800 million population almost simultaneously so that the vast Chinese nation can be mobilised by the leaders for any small or large mass campaign. It is a near-perfect dictatorship.

Such a manipulation of hundreds of millions of people can only work if the minds of the people are controlled. The control starts with an extraordinary emphasis on the comprehensive education and re-education of all sections of the population from the kindergarten upwards. The main aim is not to achieve a desirable level of sophistication but to instil the socialist moral motivation as defined by the Maoist ideology. Mao was convinced that human will-power and the proper organisation of the masses can achieve anything conceivable in the world: 'There is only unproductive thought, there are no unproductive regions!' This also means that morale is kept high by constant success stories of examples and models which can be copied, while news of disasters and failures is suppressed.

But the totalitarian methods go far deeper than mere education and information. Mao introduced mass utilisation of psychological manipulation methods reminiscent of Jesuit exercises. Each person is prompted by the small primary group, of which he is a member, to practise public self-accusation and self-purification. There is unceasing public debate and in this way ideology is made to penetrate every sphere of life. People who display the 'wrong consciousness' are subjected to psychological 'brain-washing' techniques. The population as a whole is pushed on in a rhythm of intensification and relaxation of the ideological struggle. Near-isolation from the outside world diminishes foreign examples, reference groups, and 'bourgeois' aspirations. In their stead the Chinese have the overwhelming symbolic figure of Mao, who is omnipresent in millions of pictures and in the constant recital of a selection of his works. The Chinese *Little Red Book*, containing ideological concepts and practical advice, is read communally and daily in periods of meditation. Maoism is a secular religion imposed on the minds of hundreds of millions of people through psychological methods. But this also means that primary group control — recognised by western sociologists as a powerful motivational force — replaces material incentives very effectively in the creation of a high work morale.

Chinese leadership utilises manipulative techniques to organise regular mass campaigns. They started with land reform, whereby the last remnants of traditional land-ownership were wiped out. There then followed the movement by which the *Kuomintang* was dismantled and the bourgeoisie (industrialists and traders) were 'liquidated'. In 1954 the 'anti-party clique' led by Kao Kang, which inclined towards the Soviet Union, was driven out of the party hierarchy. In 1956 when the de-Stalinisation campaign gained ground in the USSR, the Chinese leadership proclaimed the mass movement, 'Let a hundred flowers blossom!': people were encouraged to come out with their criticisms of the system and participate in improving it. The reaction against the regime was so fierce, however, that a new campaign was launched against the right-wing deviants, in which the most outspoken critics were eliminated. There followed the 'three red banners' campaign in which people's communes were established as the basis of Chinese society. The 'great leap forward' was also launched with the ideal of overtaking Britain economically before 1972. Great successes were followed by the 'three bitter years' of disappointment. When Liu Shao-chi and his followers set up an alternative programme, Mao's party found themselves in a minority in the central committee. This prompted Mao to launch the Cultural Revolution in which the Red Guards liquidated the stronghold of his opponents in the Communist Party. The party machine was largely smashed and replaced by revolutionary committees, on which the cadres, the military and representatives of the people served. By 1970 party organs were again established and the revolutionary committees were degraded into transmission agencies. Thus mass campaigns constantly cleanse and rejuvenate the nation along the lines laid down by the leadership.

The Chinese revolution is, as we have seen, characterised by the extraordinary attention given to the masses, the uneducated, the simple. An attempt was made to eliminate income discrepancies as far as possible, but this has not been entirely successful. Theoretically the rule is that lowest and highest incomes should not exceed a ratio of 1:3 but this rule only materialised on the lowest levels. Higher up the differential may be 1:7 or more, and at the top there are additional privileges such as holiday resorts, better housing, and official cars. There is also a difference between the agricultural and the industrial sector. But two great achievements must be recognised: firstly, it is claimed that the income gap is lower than anywhere else in the world, and secondly, there are no destitute people. Compared with the misery in China before the revolution and with the misery in Asian countries like India or Bangladesh, this achievement is remarkable. Of course, nobody in China is wealthy by international standards.

China after Mao Tse-tung

Mao Tse-tung died in 1976, aged 82. In the final reckoning Mao must go down as one of history's great achievers: he devised a peasant-centred revolutionary strategy which enabled China's Communist Party to seize power from bases in the country and against Marx's prescriptions; he directed the transformation of China from a feudal society, torn by war and bled by corruption, into a unified totalitarian state where nobody starves. But the costs of the Maoist era have also been enormous. And the question on everybody's lips after his death was: After Mao, what?

Given his failure to name a successor the People's Republic of China went through a period of turmoil after his death. For a period the 'Gang of Four' ruled with its radical ideology. That has now passed and China's new leaders have announced a pragmatic and massive programme of rapid modernisation in agriculture, industry, defence, and science and technology — what the Chinese call the 'four modernisations'. Foreign trade especially with Japan, the USA, Australia and Canada is growing. Western multinationals are involved in Chinese extractive industries (mining offshore oil), mineral processing and communications, as well as agriculture. Chinese students are studying at western universities and China has opened its doors to foreign scholars. Diplomatic initiatives on the part of the People's Republic and western and eastern bloc countries are keeping pace with these economic and intellectual activities. Chinese workers are being given material incentives to produce, and peasants are being promised better terms for their produce as an incentive to productivity.

The modernisation programme violates two core themes of the Chinese revolution — equality and national independence. There is evidence of conflict within the politburo over the pace and content of change. The Party will have to manage this change as well as reformulate policy. In this sense the modernisation phase will not be without conflict and difficulty. In the 1980s Chinese leaders appear to be united on the programme of modernisation but ideologically divided on how to handle the ghost of Mao Tse-tung. Their self-appointed task is to implement an awesomely ambitious plan to modernise the People's Republic by the end of the century, while maintaining a tolerable unity in the reformulation of ideology which must accompany that process. Tensions in the political system will require that 'modernisers' move cautiously, that the wounds of the Cultural Revolution (1966–76) are healed, and that a way can be found for communism and free enterprise to be accommodated in the same political economy. A tall order for so vast a nation, and one fraught with the dangers of backlash from those who, in the short run, will benefit least from the process.

Maoism in China was perhaps the greatest and most far-reaching experiment in political, economic and social engineering the world has ever seen. A fifth of mankind directly depends on its success or failure. It presents an enormous challenge to all other systems, whether capitalist, socialist or fascist. While certain aspects are frightening, especially the totalitarian procedures, much can be learnt. Mao showed that it is possible to make people work and develop initiative without material incentives; that it is possible to build an economic system not on the market mechanism and the marginal productivity of labour, but on the practice of giving work to all, even if it does not 'pay' (which still makes economic sense since everybody is doing something useful); that primary group control can replace other motivational forces; that morality can become a decisive power in economics; that the development of the mind and the will of people is more important than the development of sophisticated machines; that the greatest handicap of poor countries — overpopulation — can become their greatest asset; that the formation of elites can be effectively counteracted; that small communities can take the place of centralised bureaucracies as the basis of the social system.

The great question is whether such lessons can be learnt without taking over the Chinese approach as a whole. Is it a package-deal? Is it possible to reap the benefits without having to face the costs as well? Is it the highest form of humanisation or the highest form of dehumanisation — or, paradoxically, both?

Part five
IDEOLOGY AND THEOLOGY

There has been extensive debate in philosophy and the social sciences about the phenomenon of ideology. In chapter seventeen we attempt to distil the essence of that debate and provide a synthesis to assist readers who are interested in more than description of contending ideologies in South Africa. The descriptive part of this book was not written from any one of the approaches to ideology discussed here. But these approaches may assist readers in forming their opinions about the specific ideologies we have described. Given the initial impetus for this book from the South African Council of Churches, and the fact that the majority of South Africans claim some religious affiliation, chapter eighteen provides two specific theological perspectives from which the relationship between faith and ideology can be approached. Both move from an analysis of the structural inequalities of wealth and power in South Africa to a way of approaching the ideologies rooted in these structures. These perspectives are, in the nature of the case, incomplete. Since the problems inherent in the relationship between religious faith and ideology are not different in kind from the relationship between secular positions such as humanism and ideology, this exercise may be of interest to a wider readership.

17 On ideology

The Bedouins of the desert are said to have a hundred names for a camel. Ideology, in the crowded desert of contemporary political and social disputes, seems to be an animal with a hundred names, none of which captures adequately the elusive reality signified by the term.

For many the word evokes the devils of communism, Marxism and socialism. For others ideology is a form of false consciousness embodied in capitalism, Afrikaner nationalism and racialism. Those who accuse others of being ideological often presume that they themselves are free from ideology, while those who use it in a more neutral sense believe it refers to a world-view. Christianity is for some an alternative ideology; for others Christianity as truth is not ideological. So the use of the term ideology is itself the centre of ideological controversy.

Ideology has been used from its beginning in both positive and negative ways. When the word was first coined at the time of the French Revolution, ideology or the science of ideas was intended to provide a true foundation for all other sciences. When the ideologists fell from Napoleon's grace he dismissed them, ridiculing them as ideologues; and thus ideology became a term of abuse.

THE MAIN CONTEXTS OF THE TERM IDEOLOGY

'The meaning of a term is its usage in ordinary language.' Following this dictum we can identify different meanings of the term ideology by distinguishing between three contexts within which the term is used.

Critical positivist context

The most neutral concept of ideology is found in the school of thought which believes in the possibility and desirability of a 'value-free' science. We can call this a pre-critical positivist stance. According to this view, all individuals, groups and sections of society have a particular set of assumptions, certain patterns of thought, specific value-systems and norms. Such mind-sets are unavoidable. The task is not to judge but to analyse

their basic fabric, their derivation from and their impact on social processes. In colloquial language, the term ideology is used widely in this
purely descriptive sense. Critics have pointed out that even this apparently neutral stance is, in fact, not neutral but profoundly ideological.
It takes the ideological and social status quo for granted, without questioning critically its validity in terms of more basic human values.

For critical rationalists like Karl Popper (and from a different perspective, Althusser), ideology is opposed to science. Science, proceeding
from faith in reason, investigates facts that can be empirically verified
and objectively stated without subjective and political interests; whereas
ideology originates from faith in the meaning of history apart from the
decisions of human beings (which alone can confer meaning on facts).
Ideology in this sense stands for whatever is irrational, subjective, and
non-scientific. What is founded on metaphysical or theological speculation is usually in the service of specific, often totalitarian, political and
economic interests that destroy the 'open society'.

Critics of critical rationalism, like Jürgen Habermas, have tried to show
the underlying political and economic bases of positivism as the cult of
science. Positivism in its reverence for facts is an ideology that generally
plays into the hands of those in power. Can anyone be free from ideology?

Marxist and neo-Marxist contexts

By far the most important context for the discussion of the term
ideology in the contemporary debate is Marxism. Through Marx and
Engels the concept of ideology has itself become the focus of an ideological battle. Marx's use of ideology is neither consistent nor systematic, so that out of the shifts and variations within the texts of Marx
and Engels different interpretations have developed in the Marxist camp.

Marx

In general, Marx's notion of ideology refers to the conditioning of
ideas (in morality, religion, philosophy, art, literature) by the material
base or the economic substructure. The exact nature of this influence
is spelled out variously in different texts. In the early *German Ideology*,
ideology is a simple inversion of Hegel's idealist conception of ideas, a
mere reflection of the economic base. 'It is not consciousness which
determines being . . . social being determines consciousness.'

The production of knowledge lies in the hands of those who wield
economic and political power. 'The ideas of the ruling class are, in every
epoch, the ruling ideas. . . . The ruling ideas are nothing more than the
ideal expression of the dominant material relationships.' Therefore,

'ideology is a false consciousness of social and economic realities, a collective illusion shared by the members of a given social class.' Ideology is the distorted comprehension of the real relationship that exists between the body of ideas prevalent in a specific social formation and its economic base (that is, the productive forces that are controlled by the ruling class). It serves as a persuasive device to justify and legitimise the particular economic arrangement from which the ruling class derives its privileges. This is false consciousness for a specific group in society. Those who produce ideas in the name of the ruling class present these ideas as benefiting the whole community (whereas they benefit only a few); as as being just and claiming that a proportionate share is attributed to everybody according to his status in society or level of education (whereas status and access to different levels of education are unjustly structured); or as willed by God.

This false consciousness is mostly unconscious, uncritically accepted as the truth, as right and just, not only by the ruling class but also by the dominated classes. It thus forms the cohesive driving force that binds together the different economic, political and legal levels of society into a unified system. In capitalist societies, for example, the 'laws' of the competitive market are regarded as neutral and immutable, and private property is considered an inviolable human right, which justifies the subsistence-level wages that are paid to workers.

Marx did not want to affirm that a person's class origin and class interests necessarily determine his or her ideology. A class perspective can be transcended by a true consciousness. True consciousness is possible in a class that really represents the interests of all. This class is the proletariat, once it has become aware of its universal mission of liberating both the oppressed and the oppressors, and once it has demystified the 'iron laws' and 'natural rights' of liberal capitalism and shown them to be instruments for exploiting the majority in the interests of the few.

Engels

After Marx's death Engels sought to guard against too mechanistic an understanding of ideology as a mere passive reflection of the economic base. In a letter to Borgius in 1894, Engels wrote: 'The political, legal, philosophical, religious, literary, artistic, etc., development is based on the economic development. But they also react to one another and to the economic base. It is not that the economic conditions are the only active cause and everything else nothing but passive effect. There is a reciprocal conditioning, but always on the basis of the economic necessities that are decisive *in the last instance*.'

Lenin and Soviet ideology

Lenin moved away from a vulgar materialism, and stressed the relative independence of ideology and its conscious use by the ruling class as an instrument of domination. Religion is not only 'opium of the people' but also 'opium for the people', consciously administered in order to sanctify unholy things. But what is an instrument of domination can also become an instrument of liberation in the hands of the proletariat, which for the first time in history truly represents the interests of all mankind.

Thus, in the Soviet view the ideological battle against capitalism forms an important feature of the struggle for a communist society in the transitional period of socialism. The ideas expressed by propaganda and spread to the masses through political, scientific, moral, and aesthetic education play an important role in Soviet society in its efforts to create the new man free from all remnants of capitalist ideology. But the question remains whether Soviet ideology really represents the interests of the proletariat as the vanguard of a new society of justice and sharing, or merely the interests of a new party elite dominating the workers.

Lukács

The seminal work of Georg Lukács, *History and Class Consciousness* (1923), develops most clearly the notion of ideology as false consciousness, by returning to Hegel and the early Marx. An ideology is false because it is partial, incapable of grasping the total meaning of society and history. Lukács preferred the term world-view to ideology, and tried especially in his literary criticism to relate particular world-views to class outlooks. He contrasted the false consciousness of world-views with the true consciousness of the proletariat, which transcends all particular class standpoints. Through winning power the proletariat will not only abolish all ideology (together with all classes) but also the need for it. A non-Marxist would argue, however, that this view is utopian.

Gramsci and Althusser

Unlike Lukács, Gramsci and Althusser regard ideology as necessary in any society. 'Man is an ideological animal' (Althusser). Both authors (who exert considerable influence on radical analysis of South Africa) look upon ideology as more than a system of ideas that simply reflects the economic conditions of a society. Ideology is embodied in such social institutions as the school, church, family and political party. In these institutions people are socialised into an organic system of behaviour and belief. For Gramsci, ideology is not an illusion but a lived relation, which has a material existence of its own. So what counts is not the truth or falsity of an ideology but its function and efficiency in binding classes together in positions of domination (hegemony) and subordination. The truth of an ideology resides in its power of political mobilisation.

This concept allows one to analyse the role of ideology in its material forms in a given country at a given historical moment. It also enables one to study the organic interplay between the economic base and the ideological superstructure, and to recognise the relative independence of the state from that economic base.

Althusser (and his disciple Poulantzas) represent a structuralist appropriation of Gramsci's work. Althusser distinguishes between ideology and science. While ideology treats individuals as subjects, thereby expressing their relationship with their real conditions of existence in an imaginary form, science investigates subjectless structures. For Althusser, historical materialism is the science of ideology; it investigates the function of the dominant ideology in 'cementing and unifying' a social formation under the hegemony of a particular class alliance. Althusser rejects a mechanistic determination of the superstructure by the economic base. The superstructure, which consists of political, legal, and ideological levels, has a relative autonomy. While it is determined in the last instance by the economic base, it 'over determines' the latter in turn. In each social formation, therefore, the economic base is ultimately determinant, yet it does not have to be dominant.

The economic base (the forces and relations of production) is reproduced on the political and ideological levels by means of material force (the state) and moral power (ideologies). Althusser makes an important distinction between the repressive state apparatus (police, army, courts), that works primarily by force and secondarily by ideology, and the ideological state apparatuses (public and private schools, churches, family, legal institutions, political parties, trade unions, media, and cultural institutions in the fields of literature, the arts and sports) that work primarily by persuasion (ideology) and secondarily by force and repression. For Althusser ideology is closely linked to the problem of state power and class domination: 'No class can hold state power over a long period without at the same time exercising its hegemony over and in the ideological state apparatuses.'

Habermas

In their critique of ideology the members of the critical school of Frankfurt — Adorno, Horkheimer, Marcuse, and more recently Habermas — maintain the Marxist distinction between ideology and truth, even if for them this difference does not coincide (as it does for Althusser and the critical rationalists) with the difference between ideology and science.

For Horkheimer the error of ideology consists in its denying its link with socio-economic processes and the legitimation of existing power structures. Truth becomes ideology as soon as it is used as an instrument for legitimising domination by one class over others.

Jürgen Habermas, an influential contemporary neo-Marxist, has given special attention to the relationship between truth and ideology. Is there such a thing as truth which is free from legitimating interests? How is this truth known if it does exist?

Habermas's analysis distinguishes three different forms of science, each with their corresponding 'cognitive interests'.

(1) Firstly, there are the empirical-analytic sciences (physical or natural sciences). These are guided by technical cognitive interests since they are concerned with technical control and technological exploitation of the natural world. Habermas believes he has uncovered the ideology inherent in these so-called objective or positive sciences. In essence the logic of the natural sciences, when carried over to the realm of human endeavour, leads to activities like 'human engineering'; the view that problems in society can be resolved by technocratic means. Man becomes the slave of his machines and systems and feels a sense of alienation and loss of control over his destiny. In this respect Habermas builds on the work of Herbert Marcuse, who criticises the repressive logic of domination that marks the technological rationality of the natural sciences (technocracy).

(2) For the historical hermeneutic sciences (the human sciences), Habermas postulates specific practical cognitive interests that underlie attempts to understand and interpret historical and social phenomena. These practical interests are rooted in the social and historical situation of the interpreter and form the 'pre-understanding' that shapes the understanding of texts and events.

(3) Habermas contends that only the critically oriented sciences (especially the critical social sciences) are able to differentiate between true and ideologically distorted language, for they have no other interest but a critical cognitive interest. This emancipatory interest is free from technical and practical cognitive interests since it aims at truth for the sake of truth. The critical power of self-reflection strives for a consensus of truth in a dialogue that is free from domination. Thus the social sciences, involved in this unconstrained process of reflection and communication, become the possible agents of a true critique of ideology. Yet while they promote the movement towards a society of autonomy and responsibility, they seem to presuppose the conditions of such a society, needed for their very existence and functioning.

Is it realistic, however, to hope for an ideology-free critique of ideology?

Ideology in the context of sociology of knowledge

The third main context within which the term ideology is used is the sociology of knowledge. In contrast to the positivist and Marxist views, sociology of knowledge in general regards ideologies as inevitably linked to the uniquely human 'social construction of reality'. In this view ideologies, rather than being judged, are *described* in terms of their origin and function within society. They have become objects of a detached, value-free academic study.

Weber and Mannheim

Although sociology of knowledge acquired the standing of an academic discipline around 1920, Max Weber had tried before that time to establish the possibility of an objective, value-free social science through the disengagement of the intellectual from political causes. In his most famous work, *The Protestant Ethic and the Spirit of Capitalism*, Weber constructed the 'ideal types' of capitalism and Protestantism (in its Calvinist form) and demonstrated an 'elective affinity' between Puritan ideas and the accumulation of capital necessary for the development of modern capitalism. His study provided an alternative to the crude Marxian reductionism which held that the superstructure was determined by the economic base. Weber's analysis pointed to what modern Marxists call the 'relative autonomy' of the superstructure (ideas and institutions) and the economic material base. In this sense he contributed to an analysis of ideology by showing how an ideological formation emerges.

Karl Mannheim shared with Weber the concern to establish a sociology of knowledge. At its centre he located the study of ideology as a neutral, value-free science.

Mannheim distinguished between three different concepts of ideology: a particular ideology, that constitutes only a part of an opponent's thought; a total ideology that determines the whole of an opponent's thought; and a general ideology, characteristic of anyone's thought. The first two forms can easily be freed from ideology by showing that they express only specific historical perspectives. Any 'total' ideology, originating from a quasi-metaphysical search in man for absolutes, merely freezes reality, which is thoroughly historical. On the level of the general concept of ideology, the question then arises: if human thought is inevitably ideological, that is, expressing specific perspectives and interests, how can one escape the dead-end of relativism? If all perspectives are equally valid, are they not then equally invalid? At this point Mannheim introduced his 'relational' view of reality to counter a relativist one. A relational view of reality and ideology understands how the proper perspective is related to reality. Mannheim overcame the relativism of historicism, for example, by showing its own historical conditions. The fact that an ideology expresses certain class interests does not mean it is necessarily false. The relatively classless middle-stratum of intellectuals seemed to him to hold out most promise of achieving an unbiased understanding of the ideologies present in a particular society. They see the truth of the historical conditions informing the various ideologies; they command a perspective that transcends that of particular or total ideologies.

Are intellectuals, however, really so unattached that a sociology of knowledge can be developed as a value-free science, independent of the economic formations within which it operates?

Schutz, Luckmann and Berger

Alfred Schutz represents a phenomenological variant of the sociology of knowledge. Husserl, the father of phenomenology, was a philosopher of human consciousness, who wanted to learn how to see clearly and describe accurately what we see before we attempt scientific explanations. From this perspective Schutz and others view social reality as constructions of human consciousness in interaction — as 'objectivated consciousness'. The phenomenologist is interested in 'things themselves'. In a sociological context this means describing and interpreting the network of meanings which constitute the social world. In so doing, this approach seeks to discover underlying meanings of 'things themselves', including ideologies, rather than judging them as irrational (as critical positivists might) or as false consciousness (as Marxists might).

The phenomenological perspective is held to be the only free and unbiased scientific approach to the totality of phenomena, for it comes to grips with the genesis and essence of what they truly are — phenomena of consciousness. However, Habermas, for one, contends that phenomenology is also subject to the pitfall of the positive sciences, since it shares a similar concept of science and a similar set of practical interests.

Thomas Luckmann and Peter Berger in *The Social Construction of Reality* extend Schutz's line of thought. They see social reality as a construction of thought in its three movements of externalisation, objectivation, and internalisation. Thus, social reality is primarily a symbolic universe, with the various ideologies representing different interpretations of it. That these interpretations are then espoused by different groups to legitimise their interests is of secondary importance, and often simply determined by historical chance.

The question the Marxist asks of the phenomenological description is whether it comes to grips with the real function of ideologies in society. Sociology of knowledge in general seems to accept uncritically the existing social reality, which is then made the object of value-free academic research. In the background the 'free-floating' intellectual, who rises above the conflicting ideologies, operates without realising sufficiently that he is in fact already committed to one or other economic and political ideology. In fact Berger himself does not have the choice, for example, of operating within either a capitalist or a socialist framework, as he seems to presuppose in his book *Pyramids of Sacrifice*. He does as it happens operate within capitalist structures and his books themselves, it could be argued, perhaps veil the fact that they are in the interests of American capitalist society, precisely because they lend credibility to the view that one can settle for an ethically balanced middle-ground between capitalism and socialism.

What ultimately counts is a hard-nosed critical analysis of our own ideological assumptions. We must then decide whether we can assume moral responsibility for them. If not, we ought to become involved in transforming society and changing our own mental and structural commitment.

SYNTHESIS

In order to synthesise the different meanings of ideology as used within different contexts, we suggest four different levels at which the term can be understood. We start from the most general meaning as implied in the sociology of knowledge, and move increasingly to more restricted meanings.

Ideology as world-view: level of epistemology

Ideology is understood at this most general level as an organic system of ideas (usually centred on a basic value) that interprets reality from one specific perspective. Nationalism, for example, interprets the world from the vantage point of the nation. The identity of the nation creates symbols, which generate solidarity and enable people to understand their being-in-the-world. Such an understanding of ideology is neutral and universal. Every thinking human being has his own ideology or ideologies that constitute his symbolic universe. I am a christian, buddhist, or atheist, a nationalist, anarchist or fascist, a capitalist or socialist, or a combination of these — a christian nationalist capitalist, existentialist Marxian socialist, or a conservative African traditionalist.

Ideology as an action-related system of ideas and institutions: level of politics and economics

On this level we call ideologies only those world-views that have a specific political and economic outlook. Ideology is understood here as an action-related system of ideas and institutions, intended to change or defend an existing socio-economic order. We can distinguish between political ideologies (like nationalism, Marxism, anarchism, liberalism, fascism, racialism) and economic ideologies (like feudalism, capitalism, socialism). These ideologies present a specific analysis of the present social order, relate it to a future ideal, and outline a strategy to achieve the desired state, whether by maintaining the present order, or by reforming it, or by replacing it with a new order.

This second level is still universal. Everybody is involved, whether consciously or unconsciously, in a particular political and economic ideology. Some would say non-involvement is a political option, which favours parties in power. We are born into a specific political or economic ideology before we can consciously confirm or correct it. We grow up with it and take it for granted, because our ideology reflects, as a general rule, our class origin and position in society. In South Africa you are likely to be a liberal if you have grown up in a middle-class English environment, a black nationalist if you are an educated African, or an Afrikaner nationalist if you are Afrikaans-speaking.

Our class, origin, and position in society express the vested interest we have in maintaining or changing the present status quo. It is quite 'natural' for the black elite in South Africa to be committed to black consciousness and opposed to racialism because discriminatory laws prevent their enjoying a better life in accordance with their educational standards. It is quite 'natural' for white blue-collar workers to be nationalists because open competition with blacks would threaten their jobs and relatively high salaries. This does not mean, however, that our class position and interests necessarily determine our ideological commitment. Moral, religious, and psychological reasons and motivations can induce people to opt for a different society.

One can distinguish between ideologies of the dominant classes and ideologies of the dominated classes. In South Africa the most important political ideologies of the dominant classes are racialism, Afrikaner nationalism, liberalism, and the ideology of the national security state. Ethnic nationalism is propagated by the South African government and accepted by the 'homeland' elites because they perceive collaboration to be in their own interests. The dominant economic ideology in South Africa is capitalism. The prevalent political ideologies of the dominated classes in South Africa are black nationalism in its various expressions, black consciousness, and Marxism. It could be argued that the most important economic ideology of the dominated classes is one or other form of socialism.

As Gramsci and Althusser have pointed out, ideologies are not simply systems of ideas. They are embodied in social institutions like political parties, schools, churches, the army, and the media. The more powerful ideological apparatuses are of course in the hands of the groups in power, who control the army, the police, the press and the educational and legal machinery.

Ideology as false consciousness: level of sociology

This level presents the specifically Marxian understanding of ideology. As such it is more restricted and applies only to certain ideologies as understood on the previous two levels. Ideologies as false consciousness distort the truth, consciously or unconsciously; they are a deformed and inverted reflection of what is real. They conceal behind a mask of objectivity and moral acceptability the actual economic, political and social interests of a specific group. Afrikaner nationalism, for example, expressed at a certain period the genuine aspirations for justice and freedom of an oppressed group against the domination of British imperialism. When today it speaks of the self-determination of black people in their independent homelands, it veils the real interests of Afrikaner nationalism — to entrench white minority rule. If the government's 'total stategy' is justified by the 'total onslaught of a godless Communism' against a South Africa represented as bulwark of christian civilisation, it cloaks the fact that the ruling groups in South Africa are preparing for a total defence against the increasing resistance of blacks within the country.

Ideologies in the sense of false consciousness are found within dominant groups. They arise out of the desire of a group to justify before itself and before others its privileges, political power, social prestige, and financial benefits. Ideology as a mechanism of self-justification can create the collective illusion of legitimacy and acceptability; ideally this illusion is also shared by a considerable part of the dominated groups, thereby ensuring the cohesion and credibility of the dominant parties.

False consciousness can also be inherent in the ideologies of the dominated groups, in so far as they pretend to struggle for the interests and the liberation of all, but in fact only seek power for themselves. True consciousness, in this framework, is an ideology that really represents the interests of justice and liberation for the total community.

'Total ideology': level of religion

Certain ideologies can become total ideologies and assume a totalitarian character. These ideologies present an all-embracing answer to man's ultimate questions. They become like a religion, setting absolute value on a finite reality such as nation, culture, security or revolution, and are prepared to sacrifice any moral consideration on the altar of a man-made god. Hitler's nationalist socialism, fascism, many national-security-state ideologies, certain dogmatic forms of Marxism–Leninism, were and are total ideologies. Whereas the Marxism of Marx constitutes above all an analysis of capitalism and a strategy to overcome it, Soviet ideology has made of it a total ideology. It has become another religion, the total answer to man's deepest questions.

Total ideology is false to the degree to which it makes part of reality the total reality. It encloses the world, the real totality, in a narrow prison. To present the partial truth as the whole truth, it uses massive coercion and repression at all levels, physical, psychological, mental. It needs dogmatic formulas, infallible teachers, censorship, bannings, and torture. Defenders of a total ideology often present characteristics which are associated with irrationalism, emotionalism, fanaticism, scape-goating and rationalising. It compels consent by a reign of terror to make up for what it lacks in real support by the people.

When ideology (in the first and second sense) becomes a total ideology it degenerates from a symbol into an idol. A symbol discloses the world, an idol veils it. A symbol points beyond itself towards a greater reality whereas an idol, knowing only its own little truth, suffocates in its own prison. A symbol liberates and an idol oppresses. A symbol invites participation and stimulates creativity, an idol needs absolute domination and remains poor, for it excludes the totality of the richness of truth.

In the body of this book we have attempted to describe various ideological positions held with conviction by different sectors of complex South African society. We have not attempted to judge these ideological positions from some explicitly held 'objective' vantage-point, though we have indicated how a particular ideology is viewed by those who do not share it. The reader is invited to use one or other level of analysis outlined in our synthesis, or to draw his, or her, own conclusions.

18 Theology and ideology

Ideology and social structure in South Africa

In general theologians tend to underestimate the power which social structures and processes exercise over thought patterns and attitudes. Society is normally structured more or less according to the following model: there is a centre where potency factors concentrate political power, economic resources, social status and influence, educational standards, scientific and technological development. And there is the periphery where people are relatively powerless or impotent in relation to these factors. As a parallel, think of the difference between the centre of Johannesburg and a remote village in the Kalahari.

This structure of society leads to a very important difference in the dynamics of human relationships. A relationship between equals in terms of power is seen to be horizontal. The further you go to the periphery the more horizontal relationships become. The Venda and the Tsonga, for instance, are more or less equal in their common impotence. In contrast, a relationship between a dominant and a dependent partner is vertical. Relationships tend to become more vertical as you approach the centre. The English and the Afrikaner have been competing for centre power for decades. The relation between a centre group such as the English and a periphery group such as the Xhosa is, of course, vertical by definition.

So the social structure determines the objective character of a relationship in terms of power. And the objective character of a relationship determines your subjective attitudes towards the other person or group. In a vertical relationship, for instance, the elite tends to be either dominating or condescending. And if it condescends it expects the gratitude of the underprivileged, who, in turn, tend to be either submissive or rebellious. Neither of these attitudes should be considered normal. We expect mutual respect and maturity in both partners. Yet they are, strictly speaking, only possible in horizontal relationships.

The structural character of relationships also determines our perception and interpretation of social reality. If one takes racial discrimination as an example, it is apparent that the majority of whites believe in the merits of some sort of racial segregation, while the majority of blacks deeply resent it.

Racial segregation seems to divide the population in a horizontal fashion. That is the rationale behind the slogan 'separate but equal'. This slogan overlooks the centre–periphery structure of society. A horizontal division in fact produces a vertical ceiling: whites are above and blacks below the barrier. Being in an elitist position, it is in the interest of whites to close the door underneath themselves — both to keep challengers to their position at bay and to keep weaker members of their own group from dropping out. Racial segregation constitutes, for them, a platform for further advance.

Blacks wish to advance as well, but, being below the line, they bump their heads against the ceiling of racial segregation. So segregation is against their vital interests — whether political, economic or social. It is interesting to note that the Afrikaners, when discriminated against by the British, put up a violent fight, whereas they are now firm supporters of discrimination. It is easier to see the necessity for barriers underneath one rather than above.

The fact that black and brown Dutch Reformed Churches — similar observations could be made concerning other churches — strive for institutional unity while their white counterparts reject it, is not the result of a difference in ecclesiology. Black and brown theologians learnt their theology, after all, from their white counterparts! Rather, it is a reflection of the difference between their vital political, economic, social and psychological interests. Even language and culture are not as decisive as commonly assumed. The Afrikaner does not discriminate against the culturally and religiously different Jew, yet he discriminates against the coloured person who is of his own cultural and religious stock. The roots of these inconsistencies are not of a theological but of a socio-political nature and we conceal rather than reveal the problem when we theologise too much about them.

Ideologies legitimate social structures

What need concern us in this chapter is not the theological problem of social structures and processes as such, but rather the problem of what happens within our (collective) minds. Reflection of those social structures and processes on the level of our consciousness is called ideology.

People do not always act according to norms and values but also according to their vital interests. And there is a tension between the two. Norms and values are founded in a system of meaning, an overriding conviction, a religion of some sort — a spiritual control in essence. If a group pursues its own vital interests at the expense of the vital interests of other groups, and if the system of values and norms valid in that society prohibits that pursuit in principle, then this pursuit must be legitimised before the forum of the meaning-giving entity, such as God. The simple reason for this necessity is that no man and no group can permanently endure their right of existence — their right to be what they are and to do what they do — being questioned fundamentally.

Legitimation may take place in three ways. Either you interpret the meaning-giving entity (say the christian concept of God) in such a way that it legitimises your position. If you are in an elitist position you can say, for instance, that God elected your group to carry out a historic mission. He furnished you with the necessary power and leadership and placed you above the other groups as their guardian. You will find biblical texts to underpin your view, especially from the Old Testament. Or to put it simply: God in his unfathomable discretion decided that racial discrimination is acceptable in terms of his historic purposes.

Alternatively you can interpret social reality in such a way that it seems to fit the demands of the meaning-giving entity. You can deny, for instance, that current policies imply racial discrimination. Both *baasskap* and apartheid are alleged to be dead. Each ethnic group or 'nation' is given an equal opportunity to develop its potential, each in its own sphere. The whites have no political rights in Venda and the Venda have no political rights in white South Africa — what is wrong with that? Social reality is twisted to such an extent that it seems to be acceptable to the overriding norm-giving entity. Note that the sophistry in this case lies in treating vertical relationships as if they were horizontal!

There are a variety of ways in which this twisting of reality takes place. One is selective perception. You see things you want to see and you are blind to those you do not want to see. This natural tendency is often exploited by white propagandists. Thus whites would see, through media representation, impressive achievements in the black states created by their government, but blacks would tend to see increasing misery and hopelessness.

Another means of distorting reality is found in bias. Reality is interpreted in a way that seems to confirm the validity of your interests. When looking at the causes of poverty, for instance, poor people say that the rich should share more, while the rich say that the poor should work harder and have fewer children. That explains why in this country in general blacks opt for socialism, whites for capitalism. We subconsciously select elements from the given evidence and discard the rest.

The third way in which vital interests can be legitimised, in the face of contradictory values and norms, is to declare certain areas of life to be autonomous and thus not subject to the scrutiny of the central meaning-giving entity. Lutherans widely use their idea of 'two kingdoms' to that end. Another example could be found in business, where a different set of ethics has to be applied: turning the other cheek to your competitor ensures bankruptcy. In the same vein one hears the opinion that politics should not be preached from the pulpit — unless, of course, you preach in line with the prevalent political stance. Or the accepted view might maintain that the given spiritual unity of the church should not be confused with actually trying to live out that unity in daily life where it just does not apply.

There is a further characteristic of collective self-justification. Ideology is always community-based. It is difficult for an individual to justify an untenable position in opposition to all others. Collective reassurance is important. If I notice that what I do is done by many others around me, I am persuaded that I am doing the normal, which then conveniently becomes the normative for me. I do not need to justify myself because the group with which I identify does the justification for me. And because the primary group (those closest to me) is psychologically stronger than the secondary group (the others outside, with whom I also have to relate), I will be able to hold my own, against the whole world if need be, as long as I am in line with the group which I have identified myself with.

Of course, the group has to do the justification now. It builds up a system of perceptions and interpretations congenial to its interests. To protect this system from outside challenges, it creates a spiritual wall separating the 'we' from the 'they', the ingroup–outgroup phenomenon. It isolates itself as far as possible from others. Because those outside do not conform to group norms they are not acceptable within the group. Their views and actions are considered to be morally inferior. Their intentions are placed under doubt. Information coming from outside is screened or reinterpreted. Outsiders are stereotyped as communist, liberal, Afrikaner. The blame for what goes wrong is projected on those outside, the scape-goat phenomenon. Thus, for whites the greatest problem in South African politics tends to be the threat of Russian imperialism and communist agitation. It is unlikely that this is also the greatest political problem for blacks in South Africa!

Underlying these phenomena, however, is the necessity to justify yourself against any challenge to your right to be what you are and to do what you do, a necessity to legitimise your structural position — or, in the case of an underdog ideology, to justify your attempt to alter your position. Revolution is a terrifying prospect for those in power, while it is an heroic achievement for those below.

It seems as if disagreements among christians in modern times are largely due not to differences in theological conviction but to differences in ideology. These are, in their turn, rooted in the relation between vital interests and structural positions. If that is the case, we have to change our theological thinking about our common witness to the world very drastically. We have to find a way of dealing theologically both with social structures and with ideologies. In what follows we shall reproduce the perspectives of two theologies which have grappled with the relationship between theology and ideology in the context of the structural realities of South African society. Model One provides a Word-of-God theology for South Africa, while Model Two expresses a liberation theology.

Model One: a Word-of-God theology

The point of departure is the 'Word of God'. The Word of God is God's self-communication with man. Note that it is not identical with the bible, although the bible is its prime witness. For the christian the essential core of the message contained in the Word of God is God's creative and redemptive love in Christ. Love is a dynamic power, it always seeks its object — in this case man. That is why the Word of God entered human history. We call that incarnation. But that also means that it becomes a dynamic historical power which is called 'tradition' in theology. The only form in which human beings have the Word of God is in this living tradition.

The missionary dynamic of the Word

This tradition is not a fixed body of dogma which is handed from generation to generation, but develops its own historical dynamic. The driving force behind this outgoing, missionary dynamic is, again, the creative and redemptive love of God, which seeks its object. Propelled by this love the Word of God reaches ever new phases of history, ever new cultural contexts, ever new human situations and conditions. It enters them, penetrates them, makes itself relevant in them, incarnates itself in them. This implies that the tradition branches out into ever new subtraditions. The greater the discrepancies between the people it reaches, the further the subtraditions of the Word move away from each other. Thus the essential cause of the diversity of the church is the missionary dynamic of God's Word itself as it encounters the vast variety of human situations and conditions.

Diversity is not necessarily the same as disunity. On the contrary, the very concept of unity only makes sense where there is diversity. One could go further and say that not even the tensions existing within the

Body of Christ are a sign of disunity. On the contrary, tensions are a sign of life. A body without tensions is a corpse.

Disunity is caused by diversity or syncretism. And syncretism is unavoidable. When the Word enters a human situation it incarnates itself in the patterns of perception and interpretation prevalent in that situation, thereby becoming relevant to that situation. By doing so it inevitably gets mixed up with the hopes and the fears, the religious convictions and ethical rules, the vital interests and their ideological justifications in that situation. And that is just another way of saying that each of the new subtraditions is bound to be syncretistic in one way or another.

The Word may simply be incorporated into an existing ideology and greatly reinforce it. Alternatively it may displace the ideology but take over its function of justifying the vital interests of the group in question. The underdog may, for instance, be eager to identify with Israel in its struggle for liberation from Egypt. When his fortunes turn and he finds himself in a dominant position he may still want to identify with Israel — but now in its conquest of Canaan, in the subjugation of the former owners of the land, in its cultic separation from those unworthy of acceptance. In short, the Word itself becomes ideological.

Time also leaves its mark. In syncretistic forms the preached Word becomes dogmatised and the lived Word becomes institutionalised in a variety of ways as it continues its journey through time and space. Subtraditions may stagnate completely. If we remember that the Word does not enter into syncretism only with ideologies but also with religions, philosophies, world-views and the like, we have all the ingredients for a church splintered into an increasing number of antagonistic sections.

The ecumenical dynamic of the Word

The very power of God's creative and redemptive love can resurrect the Word of God, but not without agony and birth pains. When this does happen people discover that the love which motivates them leads them first and foremost to their heretical brothers and sisters. Divine love is unconditional. It accepts the unacceptable. And so, together with a centrifugal or missionary dynamic, the Word develops a centripetal or ecumenical dynamic. People deeply touched by God's love cannot want to be separate. Reconciled with God they are, of necessity, reconciled with each other on the basis of God's suffering acceptance. And so they congregate.

The result is an impossible community. Each member is not just a private person. He is also a representative of some group and thus an element in the social structure. He is black or white, rich or poor, employer or employee, security police or detainee; so the tensions and agonies of society are reproduced in the christian community. They are even heightened in this community because the contact is more immediate. In northern Namibia, for instance, there are christians who fight against supposed Russian imperialism in the name of God on one side of the border. And there are other christians who fight against fascist oppression and exploitation in the name of the same God on the other side of the border. And both may be quite sincere in their christian convictions.

In such situations of social conflict, in strikes, boycotts, riots or even less dramatic clashes, the real problems surface. This implies that if we want to be sincere we have to develop an ecclesiology not of harmony but of confrontation; otherwise we will continue to hide the cancer instead of excising it. An ecclesiology of confrontation could contain the following pointers. In the first place the Word of God horizontalises vertical relationships. It reminds both the elite and the underdog that they brought nothing into this world when they were born, and will take nothing out when they die — whether it be political power, economic resources, social status, technical knowhow or whatever. Moreover, both are sinners, having lost their right of existence before God, both are granted a share in Christ's new life as sons and daughters of God — the highest status possible for any human being. Thus on the level of consciousness (not yet on the level of social structure) they become equal. They are able to communicate from man to man on the same level without being either condescending or submissive.

This is the prerequisite for the second step, mutual exposure of each other's specific sins. Ideology is a blinding mechanism. We do not easily discover the ideology of our own group. Nor is it very likely that a member of our group, who shares its vital interests and ideological justifications, will effectively and ruthlessly reveal our shortcomings. By so doing he would cut too deeply into his own flesh. Just as much as the Word of God has to come from outside our hearts lest it be corrupted by our heart's desires, it must also come from outside our own group interests and group ideology. It must be an external Word. Our natural enemics will perceive our sin, in this case ideological bias, most distinctly and will be most eager to expose it as ruthlessly as possible. And so it is in confrontation that the sin-exposing function of the Word becomes most effective.

For the christian, this is the law of God. But the law does not redeem, it only exposes sins. If the community attempts to operate on the basis of demands posed by one to be fulfilled by the other, the ecumenical fellowship may be destroyed. The law can only perform its cleansing and screening function under the umbrella of the gospel. The gospel is the good news of God's unconditional acceptance of the unacceptable (justification by grace, not by human achievement). Acceptance of the unacceptable implies that the accepting person suffers a partner who is not able to fulfil his norms. This is the suffering of Christ in which we are called to participate. To accept a member of your own group is relatively easy. By loving him, you confirm your own right of existence. Even tax collectors love their friends, said Jesus. But if one accepts the unacceptable, if one loves one's group enemy, this is no longer 'cheap grace', because there are costs involved.

Thus the sin of our disunity does not lie in our differences, not even in the tensions between us, but in our refusal to expose ourselves to this highly uncomfortable, challenging and transforming encounter with our enemy brother, the refusal to suffer him as Christ has suffered us, the refusal to forgive the unforgivable, to accept the unacceptable. Christians who isolate themselves from ecumenical intercourse place themselves outside the realm of Christ's redemptive love. They get stuck on the level of the law where acceptance is conditional. There you have to satisfy certain criteria of acceptability. Setting up conditions of fellowship — whether dogmatic, ethical or cultural — denies the essence of the christian gospel, namely the self-giving, unconditional suffering love of God in Christ.

While christian fellowship has no preconditions it certainly has consequences. Christ does not suffer for us to confirm us in our sin but to overcome our sin. The overall effect of an honest ecumenical confrontation is that religious and ideological syncretisms begin to be filtered out. The perception of the Word of God held by each partner is radically challenged by that of his respective counterpart. That forces them to go back to the sources together and agonise about the meaning of the Word. The result will not be a 'pure' form of the Word but rather a revitalisation of the creative and redemptive power of God's love in Christ. And this will, in turn, lead not to an homogeneous form of the Word — that would only endanger its contextual relevance — but to new incarnations and resultant confrontations. It is an ongoing struggle heading for eschatological fulfilment. But, on the way, and time and again, it produces tentative situations in which different forms of the Word do not exclude each other but complement, reinforce and enrich each other. These are the occasions when joy is the reward of painful struggle.

The effects of ecumenical encounter

Confrontation not only challenges the perceptions and interpretations of the Word but also the perceptions and interpretations of social reality of each partner. The dialectical nature of human reality is discovered beneath the conflicting evidence. A common analysis of the situation, which takes due account of both, or all, points of view in their proper relation to each other, is possible. It may be a painful process but where it happens the prerequisite for a joint strategy to investigate structures is being reached. Structures can be changed only by collective effort. In such a strategy each partner may have his particular socially conditioned role to play, but with the roles of the partners no longer opposing, but complementing each other.

This presupposes that what happens in the ecumenical fellowship is carried into society. However, every participant is a structural element, a representative of a social group; going back into his own social context begins the painful process of confrontation all over again. Having discovered his brother in his enemy he will no longer be able to condone the blanket condemnation of the enemy group by his own group. Having discovered the shortcomings of his own group he will no longer be able to condone the ideological self-justifications he finds at home. He might be castigated — challengers and innovators are always marginals. It may well be that massive group pressure will be exerted to make him conform, but in this conflict he is the 'leaven in the dough'.

Seen in this light, ecumenical encounter is a profoundly subversive exercise. It may be more dangerous to a ruling ideology than communist or fascist propaganda. We should sympathise with those who become anxious when christians seriously begin to talk to each other; if you knock down the spiritual legitimation of a social structure the effects may be substantial.

The theological problem of structural change lies outside the scope of this model. It should be mentioned, however, that ecumenical conscientisation will lead to frustration and subsequent hopelessness if the structural problem is not tackled with the same amount of seriousness as the ideological one. Ideology and social structure mutually reinforce each other and need to be tackled together. Again, structural change needs to begin in the church. In this relatively foolproof area experimentation can be conducted and experience gathered which will be of utmost significance when it comes to effecting structural changes in society.

The often-advanced argument that what is possible in the church is impossible in the world because the world lacks regeneration by faith, is invalid. The church is not a redeemed community removed from the depravity of this world. It is nothing but another part of this unredeemed world. But it is that part of the world in which the Word of God has begun its redemptive work and which it uses to reach the rest of the world. That people become willing to suffer each other and look after the vital interests of their fellowmen rather than those of their own is as unlikely within the church as outside it. Yet the Word of God is quite capable of performing this miracle within the church and, through the church, in the world as well. We should beware of pious fatalism — particularly when it proves to be congenial to our vital interests.

Model Two: a theology of liberation

The following framework for dealing with the relationship between faith and ideology is situated within the broad tradition of 'liberation theology'. Its central justification is not the power of God's Word but the liberating power of a commitment to God's kingdom of the poor. Rather than focusing on a Pauline understanding of the gospel as justification of the sinner by faith alone, in the classical tradition of the Reformers, it goes back to the core of the synoptic gospels — to Jesus of Nazareth, the Messiah of the poor.

Liberation theology originally developed within the Latin American context of flagrant social injustice. It now increasingly emerges in different social contexts in the form of radical versions of black theology, feminist theology, political theology and Third World theologies.

A new method

Liberation theology above all encompasses a new method. Its agents are not learned theologians, but communities of poor and oppressed people struggling for survival, for recognition of their rights, for participation in decision-making, and for a new egalitarian society. Its point of departure is not the bible (as within the Protestant tradition), or dogma and doctrine (the Catholic version), or the individual experience of being baptised in the Spirit (the Pentacostal variant). It begins with a commitment to the cause of the poor, the deprived and oppressed. Liberation theology is born out of an option *for* the poor which inserts itself into an option *of* the poor for their own liberation, a liberation which is at the same time the liberation of all in a just and equitable new society.

In the relationship between faith and ideology, liberation theology does not regard the main problem as the conflict between rival ideologies and an ecumenical dialogue that helps to de-ideologise the respective attempts at self-justification. It emphasises the truly ecumenical commitment to changing those unjust structures between centre and periphery, nationally and world-wide, that give rise to legitimating ideologies. It is based on an insight into the power of socio-economic

confrontation between rival ideologies unless this is rooted in the effective challenge to the powers of oppression from the side of the poor and
oppressed.

For liberation theology the most fundamental de-ideologising power
lies in the struggle of the poor and oppressed for their own liberation. It
is convinced that certain eyes will be opened and certain hearts will be
changed only when the unjust structures that are the root cause of the
self-legitimating ideologies are removed. For these are the ideologies of
classes that are interested in maintaining the unjust status quo. The 'impossible fellowship' of the christian community will exist as long as the
gulf between rich and poor, between those in power and those who are
oppressed, has not been abolished or significantly reduced.

The Word of God — opium of the people?

Liberation theology points out the danger of a Word-of-God approach
that identifies the living Word of God with written words of the bible.
The bible then becomes a collection of sacred texts which contain the
answers to all possible situations. In extreme cases this approach leads
to a 'positivism of revelation', and a fundamentalism, which forgets
that the Word of God as documented in the bible is the embodiment of
God's deeds within a specific historical-cultural context. The text of the
bible does not give timeless prescriptive answers. The text should be
interpreted as a specific answer to a specific situation within a specific
context. Only then can it serve as a paradigm for understanding what
God is saying to us in our specific historical situation.

Liberation theology proceeds from the conviction that God still speaks
to us in our history, in the events that shape our lives, and in the struggles
of different classes of society. The bible and, in submission to this primary witness of God's Word, the traditions and basic teachings of the
churches serve in varying degrees as a mirror and model in order to
discern God's Word for us today as incarnate in history.

A deified Word-of-God perception that encapsulates God's living
Word in sacred texts is readily used and usable for legitimating purposes
in the hands of those in power, and often fails to respond to the living
God who still wishes to lead his people out of bondage into freedom. A
theology of a deified and hypostasised Word of God is oriented towards
conserving the past and degenerates into ideology. God's liberating Word
turns into an alienating 'opium of the people' and 'for the people'.

Between truth and ideology

Is there a criterion that helps us to discern between a liberating and
an alienating Word of God, between truth and ideology? In liberation

theology the basic criterion would be to establish whether the matter under consideration — be it a bible text, sermon, statement, legislation, economic policy, new political dispensation — is beneficial to the poor. Whatever is in the interests of the poor and oppressed is part of a true consciousness; whatever is in the interests of those in power at the expense of the poor and oppressed, because it maintains or widens the gulf between rich and poor, is ideology. Only the poor and oppressed can have a true consciousness; and whatever is not in accordance with a vision from their perspective, is bound to be, or to become, false consciousness, and thereby ideology.

Is this approach not too simplistic? Does it not deify, or at least romanticise, in a typically liberal and condescending way, the poor and oppressed? The assertion that a true consciousness is possible only from the perspective of the poor and oppressed is not a reflection on their moral quality; poor people are as fallible, as weak, as imperfect, as any others. It is the structural position of the poor and oppressed that is privileged and the justification for this can be established from a variety of viewpoints.

The poor and oppressed have the deepest knowledge of their situation, for the deepest knowledge is that of suffering. It goes deeper than purely intellectual perception. Only the poor, out of their suffering, know in their hearts, minds, and emotions what injustice, poverty, and oppression mean. Only they know what they need and what are the real solutions to end their suffering. Their knowledge is based on experience which does, however, need to be articulated.

The perspective of the poor and oppressed is the most universal, and the most inclusive. A study of perception shows that what we term 'reality' is related to our perception. All of 'reality' is relational and the result of modes of interpretation. To render an account of the truth, therefore, entails rendering a critical account of the totality of one's perspectives (class origin, position and interests, psychological conditioning from early childhood, motivation, experiences, ignorance...). The more a perspective is able to integrate the totality of all possible points of view within a given situation, the greater is its approximation to the truth.

The perspective of the dominant and auxiliary classes is essentially limited when compared with that of the poor and oppressed majority, for their perspective excludes that of the poor and oppressed while that of the poor and oppressed encompasses theirs as well. The structural position of the oppressors as defenders of civilised values, as agents of reform, benefactors, representatives of the people, 'instruments of God', is obvious only to the oppressed. The dehumanising position of the oppressor is clear to them; they can truly show a compassion that is not condescending. The poor and oppressed can see how the oppressors are victims of the structures of oppression which they themselves have created; only they can realise that they have to liberate their oppressors by not allowing them to continue to be oppressive.

Only the poor and oppressed can love universally, only they can truly love the rich and powerful as themselves. Only the love of the poor and oppressed is all-inclusive, whereas the love of the oppressor is exclusive. Only the poor can love unconditionally and thus implement the great christian commandment. The oppressors can love the poor as themselves only if they want them to be as themselves, have the same rights and opportunities as themselves in a society of justice and sharing which no longer structurally discriminates. An oppressor can love the oppressed only if he or she adopts, to the degree in which this is possible, the perspective of the poor, and commits himself or herself to a fundamental change of those structures that keep the poor and oppressed deprived and powerless.

The ideological captivity of the poor

The 'true consciousness' of the poor does not occur automatically, but is often the result of a struggle, of a long learning process, of a conversion. More often than not they have internalised the dominant ideology with the result that they consider their condition of oppression as the expression of God's will, as inescapable fate, or as an unfortunate accident of history.

They consider themselves inferior, or incapable, worthless and punished by the gods or ancestors. They find themselves imprisoned in a 'culture of silence' which prevents them from articulating their experience, analysing the root causes of their position, and, finding hope in a sense of solidarity and mission, knowing that they are the agents of a new society and the liberation of all.

Some have adopted the same values as their oppressors and have only one desire, to climb the social ladder and enjoy the privileges of the rich and powerful. They are prepared, if the occasion arises, and the bait is attractive enough, to abandon the rest of the oppressed and to have their share of wealth and power at the expense of their brothers and sisters.

Thus the poor often need a conversion as well and need to be liberated from the imprisonment of false, alienating values in order to explore the true potential which lies within themselves and in their situation. This raises the much debated issue of whether there is need for a small conscientised elite to inject a revolutionary consciousness into the masses of the poor and oppressed. If so, would this elite be accountable to the people and should it take its direction from them? Would this elite decide what the people need, and the direction history should be taking? Liberation theology usually favours more populist approaches that exert a style of leadership which is enabling rather than imposing, which is problem-posing rather than indoctrinating.

The bible of the poor

Liberation theology justifies the privileged position of the poor and oppressed by showing that in its fundamental traditions the bible originates from the struggles of the poor for their liberation. It can, therefore, best be understood by the poor.

The existence of Israel as God's chosen people is due to God's liberating intervention recorded in Exodus. In leading a group of slaves out of their bondage in Egypt into freedom God revealed himself as a God who sides with the poor and oppressed against those who perpetrate such oppression. Recent scholarship has explored how these liberated slaves built an egalitarian society in the promised land of Canaan in a federation of the twelve tribes and shared the available land equally among the families and clans.

But once Israel had opted for the institution of kingship the principle of parity and equality gave way to emerging inequalities between poor and rich in a centralised monarchy with a landed aristocracy and big landowners. But despite the social critique of the great prophets of the eighth century B. C., Isaiah, Micah and Amos, and despite the legislation of the jubilee year (Leviticus 25), which attempted to redress the emerging inequalities, social injustice continued to arouse the anger and indignation of the prophets who unquestionably took the side of the poor and oppressed.

It is among the groups of the 'poor of Yahweh' who after the exile were marginalised and deprived of any hope of being able to change their condition that the apocalyptic hope of a new world arose, which would be brought about by God's intervention on their behalf through the 'Messiah of the poor'.

The Messiah of the poor

Jesus situated himself within this tradition when he proclaimed and inaugurated the coming kingdom of God. He called the poor blessed for they would inherit this kingdom. Jesus identified with the poor and outcasts of his time, and only the poor identified with him and his hope of God's imminent reversal of the existing order. They had nothing to lose and everything to gain from God's promise as manifest in the message and person of Jesus of Nazareth.

The message of the kingdom presented a radical challenge to the rich and the powerful to make a choice between money and power or the new society of God's coming world where there would be no rich or poor. God's coming kingdom of justice, peace, sharing and solidarity in the imminent future became a new life in the present for the circle of disciples around Jesus, and the early Jesus movement. It was an anticipation and approximation of the classless society of the kingdom, in which everything would be shared, and everybody would receive according to their needs.

But Jesus' message of the kingdom was rejected and he had to die on the cross as an outcast and a criminal instead of seeing the new world breaking through. He suffered the same fate as the prophets who preceded him. They too had opted for God's poor. He became the victim of the religious and political establishment, which was threatened to its very core by the revolutionary message of the kingdom of God who 'pulls the powerful from their thrones and exalts the poor'.

Jesus' death, however, was not the end of the vision of the kingdom of the poor. By raising him from the dead, God in a definitive way took sides against the powers of death and oppression and vindicated the life and message of Jesus as the liberator of the poor. By empowering them with his spirit, Jesus calls followers to continue his vision. He summons them to side with the poor and oppressed and commit themselves to the cause of their liberation as an expression of their hopes in God's future.

The church and ideology

The church as a social institution is not a supernatural entity but is incarnate in a manifold way in the structures of society; as such she cannot claim a neutral stance with regard to various political and economic ideologies. The church as institution usually reproduces in her own structures the socio-economic patterns of the society in which she lives. She was feudalist in the Middle Ages. In a capitalist society she will, in her acquisition and distribution of money, in her investment policies, most likely follow capitalist patterns. In countries on the way to socialism she will, perhaps reluctantly, have to accommodate herself to socialist structures. In her decision-making procedure she will be either democratic or authoritarian, allow workers to have a decisive weight or not. In her statements or pastoral letters she will have a conservative, or liberal, or radical analysis and strategy in the interests of specific groups in society. It is therefore not a question whether the church should be ideologically committed or not – for she patently is – but whether the church can take a 'gospel responsibility' with regard to its present ideological commitments? The church has to take sides, she always has done so, even when she has chosen to remain silent.

The church on the side of the poor and oppressed

The scriptures of the Old and New Testaments are witness to the fact that God is a God of the poor and oppressed. Jesus' proclamation of the kingdom was 'good news to the poor'. The church, therefore, in ministering God's love and forgiveness to all has to make a preferential option for the poor and oppressed if she wants to follow in her Master's footsteps. Through her commitment to the poor and to their struggle for dignity, freedom and justice, the church is being reborn in the freshness of the gospel and is being freed from her compromise with the powers that be. The less the institutional church is structurally committed, in other words, the poorer the church is, the more free will she be to announce the justice and peace of the kingdom and to denounce those structures and ideologies that keep the poor oppressed. The poorer the church is the more mobile she will be to set fresh signs of a new order that reflects more concretely the final order of the total liberation, sharing, solidarity and forgiveness in God's kingdom; for she will have less to lose. For her people to remain as God's pilgrims on the march to the promised land ahead, the church will have to travel light, and only a poor church will be a church of the poor and for the poor.

Church-centred ideology

The church is not the kingdom, it is only its symbol, a sign that points towards the kingdom and an instrument that makes its values present. A church-centred ideology is the most dangerous ideology that can befall the church: it becomes the centre instead of God's kingdom, concerned about self-preservation, privileges and power rather than about the poor, the marginalised, the suffering people. Then the church degenerates from being a symbol into becoming an idol. She identifies with the kingdom and plays the power game in competition with the powers that be, becoming dogmatic, rigid, legalistic, intolerant and triumphalist. Diplomacy replaces prophecy. She confronts the state only when her power and privileges are threatened, she denounces the violation of human rights only when the right of religious freedom is denied. She is no longer the voice of the voiceless and the defence of the defenceless. She knows only her own voice and her own defence. She has ceased being salt of the earth, light of the world, and hope of the poor.

Christian faith and ideology

Having examined the theological approaches provided by the two models we return to the relationship between faith and ideology. In doing this we consider the four levels of meaning of the term ideology as outlined in chapter seventeen.

Christianity as world-view

In the first sense of the word Christianity can be considered phenomenologically as an ideology. It looks at the totality of the world from the perspective of the revelation of God in the life, death and resurrection of Jesus of Nazareth. Christianity shares with other religious world-views, as distinct from philosophical or political world-views, the claim to a totality of meaning of reality, even beyond the limit of death. It claims for itself a truth that transcends history, reaching towards an absolute reality, God and his kingdom, that, though it cannot be empirically verified within history, can be verified by the witness of those who believe that God's kingdom is humankind's absolute future.

Christianity and political/economic ideologies

On this level Christianity is not one ideology alongside others. Christianity does not necessarily identify with any specific political or economic ideology. In an absolute sense there are no christian politics, or economics, or civilisations, though the church in her long history has often succumbed to the temptation of a christian integralism that does not allow for a genuine autonomy of the secular sphere. Neither the bible nor Christ teach us how to run an economy or how to organise a state.

There is a constant temptation for the christian faith to degenerate into a political and economic ideology. This happens whenever the transcendent future that is peculiar to the christian faith is not kept open. The kingdom of God, though not independent of human efforts, is ultimately a gift of God in a future beyond this history. The freedom, peace and justice of this kingdom can never be fully realised within history, they can only be anticipated and approximated. The hope for this kingdom therefore relativises any value and any ideology centred on this value, cuts it down to human size and prevents it from becoming an absolute that can demand any sacrifice.

· The expectation of God's kingdom therefore determines a christian's attitudes towards ideologies in a double way: on the one hand, it makes him critical of any absolutising ideologies that use their power to dominate and oppress the poor, and, on the other hand, it makes him engage with, collaborate with, and commit himself to those ideologies which at a given time and place incorporate more fully the values of God's kingdom and the hopes of the poor. This requires constant spiritual discernment and practical judgment.

Christians will have to confront all ideologies that do not respect the dignity of the human person, created in the image of God and destined to be an heir to God's kingdom, that is; endowed with intellect and free will, from which flow certain universal, inviolable and inalienable human rights. They will have to be equally critical of ideologies that exalt individual interests to the detriment of the common good, as of those that sacrifice too easily the freedom and rights of individuals to the demands of an egalitarian society.

Christianity and false consciousness

Christians have a prophetic task of unmasking and demystifying those ideologies that conceal behind a moral and scientific façade a basic policy of domination and repression. Christians have to be especially alert where Christianity itself and christian symbols are used as window-dressing for morally unjustifiable policies and laws. In the name of the gospel of Jesus of Nazareth and his message of the kingdom, christians have to protest when their faith is used to put a halo around unholy things, and when their faith becomes 'opium of the people', that lulls them into a passive acceptance of injustice and useless suffering.

Christianity and total ideology

Total ideology is a 'false God' and has to be confronted by christians in the name of the true God who alone is absolute and who alone can demand absolute obedience. For a christian only God and the kingdom are ultimate realities, all others are penultimate, and cannot be taken with ultimate seriousness. Therefore one must 'obey God more than men', and the last weapon of the christian in the face of a totalitarian ideology remains the serenity that knows the power and the glory of God.

Bibliography

Within each of the chapters listed in the bibliography, the editors have asterisked those works which they consider especially important, and which they recommend to readers who wish to pursue a particular topic further.

Chapter 1: Capitalism: an introductory history and assessment

Bottomore, T. 1985. *Theories of Modern Capitalism*. London: Allen & Unwin

* Hunt, E. K. and H. J. Sherman. 1981. *Economics: An introduction to traditional and radical views*, 4th ed. New York: Harper & Row

Kubálková, V. and A. A. Cruikshank. 1981. *International Inequality: Competing approaches*. London: Croom Helm

* Lindblom, C. E. 1977. *Politics and Markets: The world's political economic systems*. New York: Basic Books

Novak, M. 1982. *The Spirit of Democratic Capitalism*. New York: Simon & Schuster

Smith, A. 1982. *The Wealth of Nations*, ed. A. S. Skinner. Harmondsworth: Penguin

Chapter 2: The growth of a capitalist economy in South Africa

Beinart, W. 1982. *The Political Economy of Pondoland 1860-1930*. Cambridge: Cambridge University Press

Bonner, P. 1978. The decline and fall of the I.C.U.: a case of self-destruction? In *Essays in Southern African Labour History*, ed. E. Webster. Johannesburg: Ravan

Bundy, C. 1977. The Transkei peasantry, c. 1890-1914. In *The Roots of Rural Poverty in Central and Southern Africa*, ed. R. H. Palmer and N. Parsons. London: Heinemann

Bundy, C. 1979. *The Rise and Fall of the South African Peasantry*. London: Heinemann

Davies, R. H. 1979. *Capital, State and White Labour in South Africa, 1900-1960*. Brighton: Harvester

* Greenberg, S. 1980. *Race and State in Capitalist Development: South Africa in comparative perspective*. Johannesburg: Ravan

Johnstone, F. A. 1976. *Class, Race and Gold: A study of class relations and racial discrimination in South Africa*. London: Routledge & Kegan Paul

Legassick, M. 1977. Gold, agriculture, and secondary industry, 1885-1970. In *The Roots of Rural Poverty in Central and Southern Africa*, ed. R. H. Palmer and N. Parsons. London: Heinemann

Nattrass, J. 1981. *The South African Economy: Its growth and change*. Cape Town: Oxford University Press

Palmer. R. H. and N. Parsons (eds). 1977. *The Roots of Rural Poverty in Central and Southern Africa*. London: Heinemann

Van Onselen, C. 1982. *Studies in the Social and Economic History of the Witwatersrand, 1886-1914*. 2 vols. Johannesburg: Ravan

Webster, E. (ed.). 1978. *Essays in Southern African Labour History*. Johannesburg: Ravan

Yudelman, D. 1984. *The Emergence of Modern South Africa: State, capital and the incorporation of organized labour on the South African gold fields, 1902-1938*. Cape Town: David Philip

Chapter 3: Ideological critiques of South African capitalism
Adam, H. 1972. *Modernizing Racial Domination: The dynamics of South African politics.* Berkeley: University of California Press
* Adam, H. and H. Giliomee, 1979. *The Rise and Crisis of Afrikaner Power.* Cape Town: David Philip
Berger, P. 1974. *Pyramids of Sacrifice: Political ethics and social change.* New York: Basic Books
Johnson, R. W. 1977. *How Long Will South Africa Survive?* Johannesburg: Macmillan
Razis, V. V. 1980. *Swords or Ploughshares? South Africa and Political Change: An introduction.* Johannesburg: Ravan
Seidman, A. and N. S. Makgetla. 1980. *Outposts of Monopoly Capitalism: Southern Africa in the changing global economy.* London: Zed
South African Research Service. 1983. *South African Review: Same foundations, new façades?* Johannesburg: Ravan
South African Research Service. 1984. *South African Review II.* Johannesburg: Ravan
Wassenaar, A. D. 1977. *Assault on Private Enterprise: The freeway to communism.* Cape Town: Tafelberg

Chapter 4: Liberalism in South Africa
De Crespigny, A. and J. Cronin (eds). 1975. *Ideologies and Politics.* Cape Town and London: Oxford University Press
Degenaar, J. 1978. *Afrikaner Nationalism.* Cape Town: Centre for Intergroup Studies, University of Cape Town
De Villiers, A. (ed.). 1976. *English-speaking South Africans Today.* Cape Town: Oxford University Press
Driver, C. J. 1980. *Patrick Duncan: South African and Pan-African.* London: Heinemann
Godsell, R. M. 1985. 'Liberal ethics in South Africa since 1948: power principle and responsive action.' M. A. thesis, University of Cape Town
Hinchliff, P. 1968. *The Church in South Africa.* London: S.P.C.K.
Hoernlé, R. F. A. 1939. *South African Native Policy and the Liberal Spirit.* Cape Town: University of Cape Town
* Marquard, L. 1965. *Liberalism in South Africa.* Johannesburg: South African Institute of Race Relations
Niebuhr, R. and P. E. Sigmund. 1969. *The Democratic Experience: Past and prospects.* New York: Praeger
Rawls, J. 1972. *A Theory of Justice.* London: Oxford University Press
Rich, P. B. 1984. *White Power and the Liberal Conscience: Racial segregation and South African liberalism.* Johannesburg: Ravan
Robertson, J. 1971. *Liberalism in South Africa, 1948–1963.* Oxford: Clarendon
* Slabbert, F. van Zyl and D. Welsh. 1979. *South Africa's Options: Strategies for sharing power.* Cape Town: David Philip
SPRO-CAS Political Commission. 1973. *South Africa's Political Alternatives.* Johannesburg: SPRO-CAS
Walshe, P. 1970. *The Rise of African Nationalism in South Africa: The African National Congress, 1912–1952.* London: Hurst
Welsh, D. 1971. *The Roots of Segregation: Native policy in colonial Natal, 1845–1910.* Cape Town: Oxford University Press
Wilson, F. and D. Perrot (eds). 1973. *Outlook on a Century: South Africa 1870–1970.* Lovedale: Lovedale Press and Johannesburg: SPRO-CAS

Chapter 5: Afrikaner nationalism as ideology
* Adam, H. 1972. *Modernizing Racial Domination: The dynamics of South African politics.* Berkeley: University of California Press
* Adam, H. and H. Giliomee. 1979. *The Rise and Crisis of Afrikaner Power.* Cape Town: David Philip
Bosch, D. 1985. The fragmentation of Afrikanerdom and the Afrikaner churches. In *Resistance and Hope*, ed. C. Villa-Vicencio and J. W. de Gruchy. Cape Town: David Philip

Degenaar, J. 1978. *Afrikaner Nationalism*. Cape Town: Centre for Intergroup Studies, University of Cape Town
De Klerk, W. A. 1976. *The Puritans in Africa: A history of Afrikanerdom*. Harmondsworth: Penguin
Du Toit, A. and H. Giliomee. 1983. *Afrikaner Political Thought: Analysis and documents. Volume One: 1780-1850*. Cape Town: David Philip
Du Toit, A. 1983. No chosen people. *American Historical Review*, 88, 920-52
Elphick, R. and H. Giliomee (eds). 1979. *The Shaping of South African Society, 1652-1820*. Cape Town: Longman
Hexham, I. 1981. *The Irony of Apartheid*. New York: Edwin Mellan
Moodie, T. D. 1975. *The Rise of Afrikanerdom: Power, apartheid and the Afrikaner civil religion*. Berkeley: University of California Press
O'Meara, D. 1983. *Volkskapitalisme: Class, capital and ideology in the development of Afrikaner nationalism, 1934-1948*. Johannesburg: Ravan
Seidman, A. and N. 1978. *South Africa and U. S. Multinational Corporations*. Westport: Lawrence Hill
Slabbert, F. van Zyl. 1975. Afrikaner nationalism, white politics and political change in South Africa. In *Change in Contemporary South Africa*, ed. L. Thompson and J. Butler. Berkeley: University of California Press
Treurnicht, A. P. 1975. *Credo van 'n Afrikaner*. Cape Town: Tafelberg
Van Jaarsveld, F. A. 1964. *The Afrikaner's Interpretation of South African History*. Cape Town: Simondium
Villa-Vicencio, C. 1985. Theology in the service of the state. In *Resistance and Hope*, ed. C. Villa-Vicencio and J. W. de Gruchy. Cape Town: David Philip

Chapter 6: African nationalism in South Africa
Adam, H. (ed.). 1971. *South Africa: Sociological perspectives*. London: Oxford University Press
Gerhart, G. M. 1978. *Black Power in South Africa: The evolution of an ideology*. Berkeley: University of California Press
* Karis, T. G. and G. M. Carter (eds). 1972-1977. *From Protest to Challenge: A documentary history of African politics in South Africa 1882-1964*. 4 vols. Stanford, California: Hoover Institution Press
* Lodge, T. 1983. *Black Politics in South Africa since 1945*. Johannesburg: Ravan
Nolutshungu, S. C. 1983. *Changing South Africa: Political considerations*. Cape Town: David Philip
Odendaal, A. 1983. *Vukani Bantu! The beginnings of black protest politics in South Africa to 1912*. Cape Town: David Philip
* Walshe, P. 1970. *The Rise of African Nationalism in South Africa: The African National Congress, 1912-1952*. London: Hurst

Chapter 7: Black consciousness
* Biko, S. 1978. *I Write What I Like*, ed. A. Stubbs. London: Bowerdean
Boesak, Λ. 1977. *Farewell to Innocence: A social-ethical study of black theology and black power*. Johannesburg: Ravan
* Gerhart, G. M. 1978. *Black Power in South Africa: The evolution of an ideology*. Berkeley: University of California Press
Johnson, R. W. 1977. *How Long Will South Africa Survive?* Johannesburg: Macmillan
* Kane-Berman, J. 1978. *Soweto: Black revolt, white reaction*. Johannesburg: Ravan
Lodge, T. 1983. *Black Politics in South Africa since 1945*. Johannesburg: Ravan
Motlhabi, M. B. G. 1984. *The Theory and Practice of Black Resistance to Apartheid: A social-ethical analysis*. Johannesburg: Skotaville
* Nolutshungu, S. C. 1983. *Changing South Africa: Political considerations*. Cape Town: David Philip
Study Commission on United States Policy Toward Southern Africa. 1981. *South Africa: Time Running Out?* Berkeley: University of California Press
Tutu, D. 1984. *Hope and Suffering: Sermons and speeches*, comp. M. Mutloatse. Johannesburg: Skotaville

Chapter 8: Black ethnic regrouping in South Africa

Butler, J., R. I. Rotberg and J. Adams. 1977. *The Black Homelands of South Africa: The political and economic development of Bophuthatswana and KwaZulu.* Berkeley: University of California Press

Charton, N. 1980. *Ciskei: Economics and politics of dependence in a South African homeland.* London: Croom Helm

* Giliomee, H. 1985. The changing political functions of the homelands. In *Up Against the Fences*, ed. H. Giliomee and L. Schlemmer. Cape Town: David Philip

Kruss, G. 1980. 'An examination of Inkatha Yenkululeko — the National Cultural Liberation Movement.' B. A. (Hons) thesis, University of Cape Town

Matanzima, K. D. 1976. *Independence My Way.* Pretoria: Foreign Affairs Association

Molteno, F. 1977. The historical significance of the Bantustan strategy. *Social Dynamics*, 3, 15–33

Sebe, L. L. 1980. *Challenges.* Cape Town: Via Afrika

Study Commission on United States Policy Toward Southern Africa. 1981. *South Africa: Time Running Out?* Berkeley: University of California Press

Temkin, B. 1976. *Gatsha Buthelezi, Zulu Statesman: A biography.* Cape Town: Purnell

Union of South Africa. 1955. *Report of the Commission for the Socio-economic Development of the Bantu Areas within the Union of South Africa* [Tomlinson Commission]. Pretoria: Government Printer

* Van der Merwe, H. W. *et al.* (eds). 1978. *African Perspectives on South Africa.* Cape Town: David Philip

Chapter 9: Socialism, Marxism and communism in South Africa

Davies, R., D. O'Meara and S. Dlamini. 1984. *The Struggle for South Africa: A reference guide to movements, organizations and institutions.* 2 vols. London: Zed

Roux, E. and W. 1970. *Rebel Pity: The life of Eddie Roux.* London: Rex Collings

* Simons, H. J. and R. 1969. *Class and Colour in South Africa, 1850–1950.* Harmondsworth: Penguin

Wright, H. M. 1977. *The Burden of the Present: Liberal–radical controversy over southern African history.* Cape Town: David Philip

Chapter 10: Socialism in Africa and problems of development

Albright, D. E. (ed.). 1980. *Africa and International Communism.* London: Macmillan

Arrighi, G. and J. S. Saul. 1973. *Essays on the Political Economy of Africa.* New York: Monthly Review Press

Astrow, A. 1983. *Zimbabwe: A revolution that lost its way?* London: Zed

Babu, B. R. M. 1981. *African Socialism or Socialist Africa?* London: Zed

Cabral, A. 1980. *Unity and Struggle.* London: Heinemann

Davidson, B., J. Slovo and A. R. Wilkinson. 1976. *Southern Africa: The new politics of revolution.* Harmondsworth: Penguin

Fanon, F. 1976. *The Wretched of the Earth.* Harmondsworth: Penguin

* Freund, W. M. 1984. *The Making of Contemporary Africa: The development of African society since 1800.* London: Macmillan

Hanlon, J. 1984. *Mozambique: The revolution under fire.* London: Zed

Lappé, F. M. and A. Beccar-Varela. 1980. *Mozambique and Tanzania: Asking the big questions.* San Francisco: Institute for Food and Development Policy

Palmberg, M. (ed.). 1983. *The Struggle for Africa.* London: Zed

* Rosberg, C. G. and T. M. Callaghy. 1979. *Socialism in Sub-Saharan Africa: A new assessment.* Berkeley: University of California Press

Seidman, A. and N. Makgetla. 1980. *Outposts of Monopoly Capitalism: Southern Africa in the changing global economy.* London: Zed

Shivji, I. G. 1976. *Class Struggles in Tanzania.* London: Heinemann

Staniland, M. 1985. *What is Political Economy? A study of social theory and underdevelopment.* New Haven: Yale University Press

* Young, C. 1982. *Ideology and Development in Africa.* New Haven: Yale University Press

Chapter 11: Social democracy and democratic socialism
De Kadt, R. 1979. Does social democracy constitute a realisable political alternative in South Africa? In *Ideologies of Change in South Africa and the Power of the Gospel*, ed. K. Nürnberger. Durban: Lutheran Publishing House
Derfler, L. 1973. *Socialism since Marx: A century of the European Left*. London: Macmillan
* Geiger, T. 1979. *Welfare and Efficiency: Their interactions in Western Europe and implications for international economic relations*. London: Macmillan
Turner, R. 1980. *The Eye of the Needle: Toward participatory democracy in South Africa*. Johannesburg: Ravan

Chapter 12: The Marxism of Marx
Avineri, S. 1968. *The Social and Political Thought of Karl Marx*. London: Cambridge University Press
Fischer, E. and F. Marek (eds). 1972. *The Essential Marx*. New York: Continuum Books
McLellan, D. 1976. *Karl Marx: His life and thought*. St Albans: Paladin
McLellan, D. 1977. *Karl Marx: Selected writings*. London: Oxford University Press
* McLellan, D. 1975. *Marx*. London: Fontana
McLellan, D. 1979. *Marxism after Marx: An introduction*. London: Macmillan
McLellan, D. 1980. *The Thought of Karl Marx: An introduction*. London: Macmillan
Mandel, E. 1982. *Introduction to Marxism*. London: Pluto
Matthews, B. 1983. *Marx: A hundred years on*. London: Lawrence & Wishart
* Ollman, B. 1976. *Alienation: Marx's conception of man in capitalist society*. London: Cambridge University Press
Pennock, J. R. and J. W. Chapman (eds). 1983. *Marxism*. New York: New York University Press
Singer, P. 1980. *Marx*. Oxford: Oxford University Press

Chapter 13: Marxism–Leninism
Anderson, P. 1976. *Considerations on Western Marxism*. London: New Left Books
* Bottomore, T. (ed.). 1983. *A Dictionary of Marxist Thought*. Cambridge, Mass.: Harvard University Press
Cliff, T. 1975–1978. *Lenin*. 3 vols. London: Pluto
Garaudy, R. 1967. *From Anathema to Dialogue: The challenge of Marxist–Christian cooperation*. London: Collins
Harding, N. 1977–1981. *Lenin's Political Thought*. London: Macmillan
* Kolakowski, L. 1978. *Main Currents of Marxism: Its rise, growth and dissolution*, trans. P. S. Falla. 3 vols. Oxford: Clarendon
* Lichtheim, G. 1975. *A Short History of Socialism*. London: Fontana
Lukács, G. 1971. *History and Class Consciousness: Studies in Marxist dialectics*, trans. R. Livingstone. London: Merlin
Schaff, A. 1976. *History and Truth*. Oxford: Pergamon
Schaff, A. 1981. *Alienation as a Social Phenomenon*. Oxford: Pergamon

Chapter 14: Anarchism
* Guérin, D. 1970. *Anarchism: From theory to practice*, trans. M. Klopper. New York: Monthly Review Press
Joll, J. 1979. *The Anarchists*. London: Methuen
Woodcock, G. 1962. *Anarchism: The history of libertarian ideas and movements*. Harmondsworth: Penguin

Chapter 15: Trends in modern European Marxist theory
Adorno, T. W. *et al.* 1969. *The Authoritarian Personality*. New York: W. W. Norton
Althusser, L. and E. Balibar. 1970. *Reading Capital*, trans. B. Brewster. London: New Left Books
Anderson, P. 1980. *Arguments Within English Marxism*. London: Verso
* Anderson, P. 1976. *Considerations on Western Marxism*. London: New Left Books
Anderson, P. 1983. *In the Tracks of Historical Materialism*. London: Verso

Bloch, E. 1976. *Das Prinzip Hoffnung*. Frankfurt: Suhrkamp
Boggs, C. 1976. *Gramsci's Marxism*. London: Pluto
Callinicos, A. 1976. *Althusser's Marxism*. London: Pluto
Davies, R. H. 1979. *Capital, State and White Labour in South Africa, 1900–1960*. Brighton: Harvester
Fisher, F. 1974. Class consciousness among colonised workers in South Africa. Paper presented to Workshop on the Social and Economic History of Southern Africa, Oxford, 1974
Fromm, E. 1956. *The Sane Society*. London: Routledge & Kegan Paul
Giddens, A. 1977. *Studies in Social and Political Theory*. London: Hutchinson
Goldmann, L. 1964. *The Hidden God*. London: Routledge & Kegan Paul
Habermas, J. 1971. *Toward a Rational Society*, trans. J. Shapiro. London: Heinemann
Habermas, J. 1976. *Legitimation Crisis*, trans. T. McCarthy. London: Heinemann
Habermas, J. 1979. *Communication and the Evolution of Society*. London: Heinemann
Hauser, A. 1962. *The Social History of Art*. 4 vols. London: Routledge & Kegan Paul
Institute of Industrial Education. 1973. *The Durban Strikes*. Durban: I.I.E.
* Jay, M. 1973. *The Dialectical Imagination*. London: Heinemann
Lacan, J. 1968. *The Language of the Self*, trans. A. Wilden. Baltimore: Johns Hopkins
Joll, J. 1977. *Gramsci*. London: Fontana
Lichtheim, G. 1971. *From Marx to Hegel*. New York: Continuum Books
Lukács, G. 1962. *The Historical Novel*, trans. H. and S. Mitchell. London: Merlin
Lukács, G. 1971. *History and Class Consciousness*, trans. R. Livingstone. London: Merlin
Marcuse, H. 1966. *Eros and Civilization: A philosophical inquiry into Freud*. Boston: Beacon
Marcuse, H. 1964. *One Dimensional Man: Studies in the ideology of advanced industrial society*. London: Routledge & Kegan Paul
Mészáros, I. 1970. *Marx's Theory of Alienation*. London: Merlin
Miliband, R. 1969. *The State in Capitalist Society*. London: Weidenfeld & Nicolson
Panitch, L. 1976. *Social Democracy and Industrial Militancy*. New York: Cambridge University Press
Parkinson, G. H. R. (ed.). 1977. *Georg Lukács: The man, his work and his ideas*. London: Routledge & Kegan Paul
Poster, M. 1975. *Existential Marxism in postwar France: From Sartre to Althusser*. Princeton: Princeton University Press
Sartre, J. P. 1956. *Being and Nothingness*, trans. H. E. Barnes. New York: Philosophical Library
Sartre, J. P. 1976–1978. *The Critique of Dialectical Reason*, trans. A. Sheridan-Smith. 2 vols. London: New Left Books
Schroyer, T. 1973. *The Critique of Domination: The origins and development of critical theory*. New York: George Braziller
Thompson, E. P. 1968. *The Making of the English Working Class*. Harmondsworth: Penguin
Wittfogel, K. 1957. *Oriental Despotism: A comparative study of total power*. New Haven: Yale University Press

Chapter 16: Maoism in China
Fitzgerald, C. P. 1976. *Mao Tse-tung and China*. London: Hodder & Stoughton
* Schram, S. R. (ed.). 1974. *Mao Tse-tung Unrehearsed: Talks and letters, 1956–71*, trans. J. Chinnery and Tieyun. Harmondsworth: Penguin
Schram, S. R. 1969. *The Political Thought of Mao Tse-tung*. New York: Praeger
Wilson, D. (ed.). 1977. *Mao Tse-tung in the Scales of History*. Cambridge: Cambridge University Press

Chapter 17: On ideology
* Berger, P. L. 1974. *Pyramids of Sacrifice: Political ethics and social change*. New York: Basic Books
Berger, P. L. and T. Luckmann. 1967. *The Social Construction of Reality*. London: Allen Lane

Habermas, J. 1972. *Knowledge and Human Interests*, trans. J. Shapiro. London: Heinemann
Laclau, E. 1977. *Politics and Ideology in Marxist Theory: Capitalism, fascism, populism*. London: New Left Books
* Larrain, J. 1979. *The Concept of Ideology*. London: Hutchinson
Larrain, J. 1983. *Marxism and Ideology*. London: Macmillan
Lukács, G. 1971. *History and Class Consciousness*, trans. R. Livingstone. London: Merlin
Mannheim, K. 1936. *Ideology and Utopia: An introduction to the sociology of knowledge*. London: Routledge & Kegan Paul
Schutz, A. 1972. *The Phenomenology of the Social World*, trans. G. Walsh and F. Lehnert. London: Heinemann
Weber, M. 1976. *The Protestant Ethic and the Spirit of Capitalism*, trans. T. Parsons. London: Allen & Unwin

Chapter 18: Theology and ideology

* Gutierrez, G. 1974. *A Theology of Liberation*, trans. C. Inda and J. Eagleson. London: S.C.M.
Lash, N. 1981. *A Matter of Hope: A theologian's reflections on the thought of Karl Marx*. London: Darton, Longman & Todd
Miguez Bonino, J. 1975. *Doing Theology in a Revolutionary Situation*. Philadelphia: Fortress
Miguez Bonino, J. 1983. *Toward a Christian Political Ethics*. Philadelphia: Fortress
Moltmann, J. 1974. *The Crucified God*, trans. R. A. Wilson and J. Bowden. London: S.C.M.
* Moltmann, J. 1967. *A Theology of Hope*, trans. J. W. Leitch. London: S.C.M.
Nürnberger, K. 1984. *Power, Beliefs and Equity: Economic potency structures in South Africa and their interaction with patterns of conviction in the light of a Christian ethic*. Pretoria: Human Sciences Research Council
Segundo, J. L. 1984. *Faith and Ideologies*, trans. J. Drury. Maryknoll: Orbis
Segundo, J. L. 1975. *The Liberation of Theology*. Maryknoll: Orbis
Therborn, G. 1980. *The Ideology of Power and the Power of Ideology*. London: Verso
Thielicke, H. 1979. *Theological ethics*, vol 2: *Politics*. Grand Rapids, Mich.: Eerdmans
Wogaman, J. P. 1977. *Christians and the Great Economic Debate*. London: S.C.M.

Index